COUNT CAGLIOSTRO

In this colourful and engaging account of the roguish life of Count Cagliostro, Constantin Photiadès offers the reader a meticulously researched biography of an extraordinary historical figure. Donning such varied personas as magician, alchemist, colonel, swindler, mythical priest and founder of Egyptian masonry, Cagliostro is a delightfully enigmatic character. Photiadès details the Count's life from its humble beginnings in Palermo to his adventures in Europe and finally his demise in a remote fortress.

COUNT CAGLIOSTRO.

COUNT CAGLIOSTRO

AN AUTHENTIC STORY OF A MYSTERIOUS LIFE

CONSTANTIN PHOTIADÈS

Routledge
Taylor & Francis Group
LONDON AND NEW YORK

First published in 2005 by
Kegan Paul International

This edition first published in 2011 by
Routledge
2 Park Square, Milton Park, Abingdon, Oxfordshire OX14 4RN
Simultaneously published in the USA and Canada
by Routledge
711 Third Avenue, New York, NY 10017

First issued in paperback 2014

Routledge is an imprint of the Taylor & Francis Group, an informa business

British Library Cataloguing in Publication Data
A catalogue record for this book is available from the British Library

ISBN 978-0-710-30982-2 (hbk)
ISBN 978-1-138-86779-6 (pbk)

Publisher's Note

The publisher has gone to great lengths to ensure the quality of this reprint but points out that some imperfections in the original copies may be apparent. The publisher has made every effort to contact original copyright holders and would welcome correspondence from those they have been unable to trace.

PREFACE

THE eighteenth century, the age of reason, common sense and enlightenment, was not without its mysteries; and perhaps the most baffling of them all, to the biographer, is the life of Cagliostro. It is, indeed, frequently dismissed as the life of a charlatan, but those who believe that that description all too often conceals only ignorance and prejudice would wish to probe beneath the scornful epithet and get at the facts. On the contrary, there are others who readily assume that anyone who has dabbled in the occult, who has suffered persecution and inspired the blind devotion and loyalty of innumerable followers must be invested with the majesty, the sacredness and the inscrutability of a semi-divine personage. In their eyes, any attitude save that of admiration and uncritical wonder stands condemned as a wilful rejection of the credentials of a superhuman being. If they were to examine dispassionately all the circumstances of Cagliostro's life, his inexplicable perversity, his petty deceits, his dissolute if not criminal youth, as well as his magnanimity, his unselfishness and the innocence which at times brought upon him unmerited suffering, they might perhaps be induced to hold to their faith a little less credulously. It is such an impartial statement of verified fact as is needed for these purposes that M. Photiadès offers the reader.

He does not, however, dispel the mystery—the mystery of a personality that could both evoke sublime reverence and stoop to incredible folly; it remains. Simply, the author has endeavoured to present the material upon which alone a sound judgment can be formed. And it may truly be said that none of his predecessors has discharged the task more admirably. No one has surpassed him in the thoroughness of his research. Hardly a single conceivable source of authentic information has escaped his zealous attention. Private letters long buried in half a dozen different municipal archives, police records, and documents in the Vatican library—all have been ransacked to provide the substance of a book for which we may claim that it contains, at least in as far as the facts are concerned, the last word on a much debated subject. Whether Cagliostro was an unscrupulous adventurer or a Messenger who vainly tried to convey ineffable truths to an unheeding world, it is for the reader to decide.

Historically accurate as the book is, it is not a tedious and pedantic recital of facts. It is an imaginative re-creation of one of the most astonishing careers of modern Europe—a career which enthralled Goethe and provoked a vigorous diatribe from Carlyle. It is, besides, a brilliant contribution to the literature of the picaresque, and combines the fascination of a " thriller " with the charm of a romance, a series of romances. Interwoven with it is not only a picture of various aspects of eighteenth century Europe, but a graphic account of the activities of the Masonic and other secret societies which have hitherto remained an obscure if remarkable feature of the age. And through it all, with a masterly array of minute though essential detail, M. Photiadès traces his hero's life from its beginnings in the slums of Palermo, to its apogee in the courts and country houses of Europe, down to its tragic end in a remote fortress in the Apennines.

K. S. Shelvankar
Translator

CONTENTS

LIST OF ILLUSTRATIONS

COUNT CAGLIOSTRO

I

CAGLIOSTRO'S BIOGRAPHER

IF Rovereto, the essentially Italian town in the Venetian Tridentine, found itself in the possession of the Hapsburgs in September 1788, it was in consequence of having, once upon a time, torn into shreds and made a bonfire of the standards on which the lion of St. Mark was picked out in gold against a background of dark purple, the colour of clotted blood. Thereupon, fearing reprisals on the part of the most Serene Republic, it had had the folly to throw itself into the arms of the Emperor Maximilian.

During the three centuries of Austrian rule, the rebellious city had, indeed, escaped the horrors of war. Invading armies had passed her by. But her historians ignored that period in silent indignation.

Her material prosperity, however, made her an object of envy among the poorer people of the peninsula.

"How happy are our brothers in Rovereto"—the peasants and artisans would plaintively sigh. "*They* may prune their vineyards in safety, and raise their silkworms, and prosper by their toil. But we others, we have to pass our lives in fear for our fields and cottages."

On Sundays and holidays, leaving the *piazzetta*, where the startled birds wheeled petulantly round, the young people of Rovereto would clamber up, laughing and playing, to the old feudal castle, whose turrets overlooked the wide plain. From that fortress, laid out like barracks, one had a bird's-eye view of the town, from end to end, with its red and ochre coloured villas, its steep precipitous streets, and the cloisters where Franciscans and Camaldules piously knelt behind their rude screens. The slender campaniles of San Marco and Santa Maria del Carmine towered over the foliage. And at sight of such a stately landscape, the eyes of even the most indifferent spectators would brighten with tears of admiration and filial affection.

Rovereto stood on the left bank of the *Adige*, some distance from the stream. Its buildings rose tier upon tier on the slope of a hill, on the summit of which stood the castle, while down below in the valley flowed the *Adige*, its waters cool and icy as the springs from which they were fed. Vine and olive, mulberry and elm trees, surrounded it with their green foliage. A fierce mountain torrent, the *Leno*, which divided the town, rushed towards the *Adige* with a loud roar. But Rovereto heard it without anxiety. Lying in the Lagarina valley, an orchard murmurous with the sound of bees and birds, the lovely little city dreamed away at the foot of the Alps.

. . . .

This earthly paradise was not, however, in the backwoods. In the eighteenth century, a passionate interest was taken there in European affairs. Situated as it was on the shortest route between Germany and Italy, Rovereto would be awakened every morning to the sound of cracking whips and the din of horns and bells. Far from complaining about it, her burghers would joyfully run to their windows, in their night-dresses, and leisurely watch the cavalcade.

What an endless variety of vehicles ! Ecclesiastical litters, red or violet, according to the rank of the occupant, drawn by ceremonial mules, harnessed with straps of curious workmanship, their heads decked with black ostrich feathers, went by at a funereal pace. Monstrous German coaches, with their leviathan bodies, their masses of leather, their roofs loaded with luggage, their wide steps and platforms and folding-stools, rudely jostled the landaus and the phaetons and the barouches. If, perchance, a cabriolet bumped into a military carriage, a stream of oaths and invectives would be let loose to the great delight of the idlers. Public curiosity was directed also to the mail coaches, and the livery coaches, and much more still, to the small vehicles where couples shut themselves in so willingly for their amorous exchanges. If there was nothing more interesting, it fixed itself on the vans and the stage-coaches.

This traffic gave an extraordinary life to Rovereto. The very heart of Europe seemed to throb there. What an excitement there would be when relations grew strained between two or more Powers ! News-sheets in hand, the wiseacres would rush to the cafés where clematis and honeysuckle were fondly intertwined with each other. Learned arguments would presently begin at one table after another, under the leafy bowers, where, among the bird-cages, hung metal balls of blue and green and red. The foolish twitter of canaries and chaffinches mingled with the most erudite expositions, and the gathering would disperse at dusk. If His Majesty the Emperor, or King Joseph II ever saw them eloquently discoursing thus in their bowers, they would surely have appointed them as members of their own Councils.

Oddly enough, these politicians had quite other interests as well. They honoured the Muses. Virgil and Horace were their gods. Petrarch and Dante appealed to their imagination as strongly as Machiavelli. The cult of Latin and Italian literature had its most fervent devotees among them. And as for music, they enjoyed it so much that they would have sacrificed the most important business to a concert.

The visit of the youthful Mozart in December 1769 was a great treat to them. They did not merely welcome him as a virtuoso; they fêted him as though he were a little angel-musician strayed from his celestial company. After a performance at the residence of the Baron Todeschi, the child promised to try the next day the newly restored organ at San Marco. But when he and his father arrived, at the appointed hour, at the main gateway, the crowd was so thick that they found it impossible to reach the platform with its gilded woodwork. Two local champions had to be summoned, and the giants, with their merciless fists, slowly made a path for the father and son.

Seventeen years later, on the 11th September, 1786, Goethe passed through Rovereto on his tour. The nobility and the intellectuals would surely have been happy to welcome the author of the *Sufferings of Werther*, the intimate friend of the Duke of Saxe-Weimer. But Goethe travelled incognito. At that period he was less anxious to meet people than to discover an atmosphere and a climate where he could meditate. His first impressions of Italy, however, were gained at Rovereto : the chirping of crickets at even-fall, the old bramble-covered walls where the raisins ripened, and the melodious language, vibrating around him, charmed him.

For him, as for Mozart, the inhabitants of Rovereto would have gladly rung their bells and hung out their flags, for they were admirers of intellectual achievement. Their vineyards and their silkworms gave them less pride than the local academy, the *Accademia degli Agiati*. As a matter of fact, this institution, though of recent origin, had roused the envy of the most venerable societies in the Italian peninsula.

. . . .

The *Accademia degli Agiati* was really the creation of two wealthy individuals, Joseph Valeriano Vannetti and his wife, the noble Lady Bianca-Laura de Saibanti, who had founded it in 1753 and had since then liberally subsidised it at need.

These excellent people were such great lovers of literature that when their son, Clementino, was born on the 14th November, 1754, they had both prayed that he might become a second Pico della Mirandola in intellect and erudition.

Divine providence had granted their wish. Under the tutorship of the Abbé Gattardo Festi, the young Clementino made incredibly rapid progress. He was always in advance of his years. When they heard him speak Latin, about the age of eleven, with the elegance of a cardinal, they did not know which to admire more, his intelligence or his industry or his graceful manners. With these endowments, and the fear of God, he would preach to the faithful. What a crowd he would draw to the church! What a display of fervent devotion!... The whole town praised him, and his parents thanked God for him.

Like so many of his companions, the prodigy did not have to choose between a clerical and a military career. The wealth of his parents and their intense zeal for literature left him free to follow his taste. He began by nourishing his mind on the classics. And later, when he was obliged to lay before the public the first-fruits of his study, he was the only one to be surprised at the applause he evoked. Since then several academies had considered it proper to co-opt him to membership, a young author whom the severest of critics set by the side of the brilliant luminaries of the Renaissance. One after the other, they conferred on him their diplomas. But, devoted son and irreproachable citizen that he was, his supreme joy was, at twenty years of age, to be made the permanent secretary of the *Accademia degli Agiati.*

Even the Austrian authorities, who venomously criticised every crudeness and inelegance, showed an exceptional tenderness for Clementino. When, in 1782, Pope Pius VI passed through Rovereto on his way to Vienna, Clementino was presented to him. A scholar with a fresh complexion and youthful and dimpled cheeks being a rare find, the Holy Father smilingly gave him his blessings. He did not wait until he got to Rome to make himself acquainted with the young man's works, of which the *Accademia* had offered him a copy, gorgeously bound with the arms of the Braschi: he had them read to him in the carriage, en route. Later, Vannetti had reason to congratulate himself on this encounter, for the kindness of the Sovereign Pontiff was to stand him in good stead in a situation which might have had serious consequences.

Solitary and meditative in this world of poets and sages, whose laurels exhaled a bitter perfume, the young scholar refused to take a wife. Flirtatious young ladies and intriguing mothers vainly tried one artifice after another. Clementino explained his position frankly: a man like him could not, at the same time, serve his wife and the Muses. Besides, he considered a theological or historical discussion sufficient relaxation for an academician who was devoted to his duties. And when he had leisure, he amused himself by writing lively and playful letters, in which his correspondents admiringly recognised the dialectical eloquence of Cicero and the graceful irony of Pliny the Younger.

. . . .

On the evening of the 25th September, 1788, Vannetti was writing to one of his closest friends, the Abbé Joseph Pederzani at Verona, reproaching him for not coming to see him at Rovereto. . . .

The clocks struck seven. Suddenly, with a grating of wheels, a heavy carriage pulled up in the square, almost at his door. . . . To judge by the noise, they must be unharnessing the horses. As he was in the mood for writing, it did not occur to the academician to interrupt his letter even for a second. But at length, surprised by the increasing commotion outside, he laid aside his pen and began to fold the letter.

A lady and gentleman in travelling clothes were standing by the carriage from which they had just descended. The man, of medium figure and a vigorous corpulence, attracted all eyes by his cocked hat, which was lavishly decorated with feathers and gold lace. With the vehement gesticulation of a southerner, he was giving orders to a big fellow in green livery who seemed to be his servant.

In the already darkening twilight, his companion's face was scarcely visible. Besides, a large straw hat more than half concealed her. A grey veil encircled its wide brim. Motionless, in an attitude of tired resignation, or perhaps indifference, she listened to the conversation between the two men. The strange gentleman suddenly turned towards her with an imperious gesture, and she began to move like an automaton. All three entered the inn in the square, which was supposed to be the best in the town.

Clementino Vannetti could not repress an impulse of curiosity. Much later, going back over the incident, he asked himself if it was not, perhaps, an obscure premonition. He sent a servant to find out the names of the strangers, and the answer brought to him filled him with astonishment. It was the Count Alexander de Cagliostro and the Countess Serafina, his wife, accompanied by a servant, who were being shown to their rooms. And like a madman, the innkeeper was dancing and skipping in front of his saucepans, thanking the angels who had caused such famous names to be inscribed on his register.

In a few seconds the tremendous news had spread through the town. It was quickly carried through the countryside. Passing by Isera, it surprised the tanners of Marco and Sacco at their evening meal, then went farther to awaken the proud Lizzara of which the ruined walls gloried in once having given shelter to the fugitive Dante. . . .

. . . .

Because of their love and admiration for him, his best friends would often upbraid Clementino Vannetti. Why, they asked, did he treat his reputation so lightly? Another man in his place, instead of frittering away his best years at home, would travel and visit the various Italian academies of which he was member. And the *Occulti* in Rome, the *Inestricati* in Bologna, the *Olimpica* of Vicenza, the *Filammonica* of Verona, and the *Accademia del Scienza e Belle Lettere* of Mantua, would receive him with such honours that his fame as a man of letters would increase and spread.

Touched by their concern in him, Clementino thanked them. But though he admitted they were right, he would shake his head with a dubious air. He preferred, he would say, a front seat in his village to a back seat in Rome. As a matter of fact, Clementino was attached by every fibre of his being to that little spot of earth, that quiet city of the *Adige* and the Alps, so utterly his own by a perfect reciprocity of loving confidence that it seemed to belong to him like a fief to its lord. Where else could he meet with the same respect and devotion as was accorded to him in Rovereto ? From his infancy he had been idolised by the town. And the conviction that that privilege would be his until the very end, had given him, since he was twenty, peace and security of mind.

For twenty years ! But on this September evening a tremor of anxiety ran like fire through his nerves. Some sinister foreboding oppressed him. There was a murmur, there were muffled sounds in the air which disturbed him profoundly. Never had the people of Rovereto behaved in this fashion. What madness had suddenly seized them ? And why, God in Heaven, why ?

The Chevalier did not go on with his letter. It was finished some days later, and the Abbé Pederzani received it at Venice at the end of the week.

The next morning, September 25th, 1788, the servants found to their dismay that their good master had not been in bed. Pillows, sheets, blankets, quilts, all lay just as they had been made. The fruit, too, was untouched, and the Bologna sausage and the Parma ham, which used to be kept in a sideboard for him every evening since the day he had complained of hunger during his nocturnal study and meditation. A flagon of Marsala, which he scarcely ever touched, saying that a sound head had no need of anything but fresh water, was empty by a third. And the kitchen-maid, for whom a folding bed had been put in a garret above the library, had heard the Chevalier rapidly pacing about for hours like a man tormented by some cruel perplexity. What was amiss ?

. . . .

In his boundless love for Rovereto, it had never occurred to Vannetti that his beloved town might ever be untrue to him. Such confidence, no doubt, would have been perfectly justified in ordinary circumstances. But let a great man of dazzling fame, someone with whom a provincial academician, even though he were permanent secretary, could scarcely compare himself, drop from the sky like a meteor, and what would happen to such devotion ? It would cease ; the mystical tie would dissolve. Vannetti would be relegated to second place, perhaps even forgotten.

So such was to be his fate ! To a clear-sighted person like Vannetti, there could be no doubt of his impending disgrace. But he was not bitter in his disillusionment. No railing against his fellow townsmen ; not the slightest censure of their ingratitude. He only despised himself heartily for being unable to stand comparison with his formidable rival.

He even deemed himself unworthy of the esteem of the cultured—so mediocre his literary achievements now seemed to him. For the first time, the parent was ashamed of his offspring. He saw something trivial in his productions. What, after all, did they amount to? A commentary on Plautus and Terence, which the *Agiati* declared to be illuminating. He had rushed to the defence of the illustrious Tiraboschi when he was engaged in a miserable dispute over Martial. He had published an Italian translation of Pliny the Younger, a masterpiece of accuracy and elegance. To him a delicate rhymester of the seventeenth century owed his resuscitation. He had written some introductory notes to the posthumous writings of his masters, the Abbés Tartarotti and Grasser. . . . But what was the use of prolonging such a dull and uninteresting list?

In the blessed days of the Renaissance, an Angelo Politan, a Marsilo Ficinus, a Peter Bembo could march abreast with the divine Leonardo, with Raphael and Michael Angelo. But the world now scoffed at humanists. To those colossal geniuses, those giants of erudition, Muratori and Tiraboschi, it scarcely offered a wreath. . . .

Vannetti occupied a very enviable place in the ranks of the poets. There were some who even went so far as to prefer his free verse, his *versi sciolti*, to his prose. Ippolito Pindemonte, that master of measured language, had not been sparing in his praise of Vannetti's rhymed epistles. Besides, the Chevalier had a good precedent to follow: his late father, Joseph-Valeriano, had successfully cultivated a fugitive talent in poetry, and an echo of his fluty rustic notes persisted in some handsome little books, from which Donna Bianca-Laura, in her widowhood, would frequently ask to be read. Age had not diminished her interest in literature, and it fell to Vannetti to re-read the *Ninfa del Leno*, a mock-heroic impromptu on the flooded *Adige*, or perhaps the *Barbalogia*, a fantastic burlesque on beards. But while the good lady, sitting in an easy chair, smilingly listened to the reading, her son would scarcely be able to repress his tears. Those lifeless rhymes would fill him with acute despondency. Poor sheaves without fragrance, drier than the flowers in the herbarium! *His* poems, too, would soon be like these. Skilful versifier though he was, he lacked the supreme gift, the gift par excellence of lyricism. A sonnet in which he had satirised the Germans of the Tyrol had had some success. What was the good! Among his colleagues of the *Accademia degli Agiati*, more than one thought himself capable of doing as much. Thus Signor Gianviglio had dished up some pretty epigrams in the guise of a sonnet, but nobody thought of looking upon him as a child of Apollo. His friend, Ippolito Pindemonte, he was a real poet. At the proper moment, he would lift his head against his rivals, and assert his title successfully. . . .

History, perhaps, offered to Vannetti a less dubious chance of fame? Who could tell? He had often reflected over the inexhaustible interest aroused by the *Lives of the Philosophers* of Diogenes

Laertius. That dull compiler, without a trace of talent though he was, had yet more readers than Herodotus or Tacitus. What an extraordinary reversal of rank and fame! The secretary did not consider it over-ambitious to aim at similar success. As he had already celebrated the principal humanists, he would start forthwith on a *Life of Cicero*. But first, to deal with such a vast subject adequately, to write a biography of such importance, he would have assiduously to collect an enormous amount of material.

Clementino was now at about the middle of his career. In September 1788 the youthful prodigy of Rovereto was approaching his thirty-fourth year. In a few months from now, he would have joined the ranks of the dull, shrivelled, cloistered pedants, ageless and sexless, whom nature excludes alike from her relaxations and her pleasures. Was it for this, then, that he had refused to get married, laboured and meditated in the solitude of libraries? Alas! how could one deceive others, when one has such a poor opinion of oneself? . . .

All that night, the night of the 24th September, Vannetti was tormented by these agonising reflections. He clasped his head in his hands. Now he took a sip of Marsala to pull himself together, and now, closing his eyes, he tried to collect his thoughts.

But at length, overcome by fatigue, he had a dream. . . .

In a hall of extraordinary height and spaciousness—a convent refectory or a hospital ward—sick men of all sorts, mingled with a ragged crowd, were pressing around a figure of imposing presence.

They were all appealing, all holding their hands out to him. And he, with his fixed gaze, serene as a god, looked at them one by one. Then, contracting his eyebrows as for some intense effort, he plunged within himself like a diver into the sea. In a moment he had emerged from his meditation. He then left the hall with his servant, and returning soon after with some pills, tablets and pots of unguents, bags and some bottles of elixir, he distributed them among the patients. To each one he said something which was passed from mouth to mouth, amidst deafening chatter; then they all went back to their homes, reassured, certain that they would be cured if they followed the instructions of the ministering angel.

When he spoke to his patients, the messenger from Heaven seemed to be of more than human stature. What mattered it that he was short in the leg, or even that he had a fat belly? His eloquent face was transfigured by enthusiasm. His features were modelled upon a sublime pattern. Nothing seemed to escape those flaming eyes; they pierced to the depths of the soul. In the presence of certain visitors, he divined at once the trepidation, the pained recoil of their shame. Then, out of kindness, he would go into the smallest details of their diet, and give them some money with which to buy wine, soup and chicken, so that his drugs might be the more effective, and always with so much tact that his benevolence never seemed like charity.

And how they praised him!

"For months he puts up sick men and admits them to his table. . . ."

"And without accepting payment in return. . . ."

"Oh, no, he never takes any remuneration. . . ."

"When he is compelled to accept some gift, he replies by giving one more splendid still. . . ."

"Last Sunday, when it was pouring with rain, he was wearing an embroidered cloak, and did not expect to go out. But someone came to call him to the bedside of an old beggar, who was dying of fever. And he at once went out into the deluge, as fast as he could, without even taking the trouble to ask for his top-coat. . . ."

Through the haze of his dream, Vannetti heard these remarks without much surprise. The man in question was truly a messenger of providence. Physician of the body as of the spirit, he seemed to bear on his outstretched hands the entire burden of human misery. While the vast hall resounded with thanksgiving, while his patients, his protégés, wild with gratitude and love, prostrated themselves at his feet, clasping his knees like petitioners in old tragedies, the mysterious philanthropist could scarcely control his tears. They gushed out in spite of him. Throwing back his head, so as to display his fine majestic countenance, his nostrils quivering, he would gaze towards Heaven like a priest in ecstasy.

Clementino saw, at the same time, thanks to the curious simultaneities of dream, a lady seated in a little boudoir adjoining the hall of audience. She had a modest appearance, and was dressed simply. But a group of distinguished ladies deferentially surrounded her, sewing and knitting, as at some charity gathering where garments are made for the poor. Suddenly the connecting door flew open, and the thaumaturge entered, with the supremely inspired face of a hierophant, and his eyes shining with a sacred fire: the spirit of well-doing. And once more Vannetti contemplated, with an indefinable mixture of admiration and uneasiness, the powerful physiognomy which it was impossible to forget when one had once seen it. . . .

How could he fail to recognise it? For a dozen years painters and sculptors had been striving to reproduce it. In 1786 Francesco Bartellozzi had made a sketch of it from life in London. Excellently engraved by R. S. Marcuard, the portrait was later sold in all the print shops with the following legend:

Here's the astonishing man whose sublime gift
Daily cheats death of its greed,
And who is inspired by no motive other than
The welfare of mankind.

Elsewhere, Clementino could read this curiously enigmatic motto:

Pour savoir ce qu'il est, il faudrait etre lui-meme.

Surely this was the healer with the infallible remedies, who had performed miracle after miracle among the Russians, the Poles and the Germans ; the man who had been crowned with glory in Strasbourg, Bordeaux, Lyon and Paris ; the same seigneur and the same lady who had, since the previous evening, been staying at the Rovereto inn.

Abruptly the scene changed. Without any transition, and still under the sway of the capricious dream-world, Clementino was watching some extraordinary and alarming happenings. . . .

Early in the morning, a dozen policemen broke into a peaceful house. Arresting its chief occupant, they examined in his presence all his furniture, chests, cupboards, desks and caskets. Indefatigable, they put their ears close to the walls to catch any suspicious sounds; they tested the panelling and the boards of the parquet floor, and probed the cushions and mattresses with long needles. Then, grabbing their captive by the collar, as though he were a miserable criminal, they marched him out to a hackney cab. . . .

The horses finally pulled up before an enormous gateway bristling with spikes and protected by iron chains. The drawbridges were down ; the portcullises up ; bolts and padlocks rattled ominously. The keys grated in the century-old locks. The soldiers threw their bayonets into the sentry-boxes. The feet of the sentries echoed on the flagstones of the courtyard ; they occasionally called out to each other from one sentry-box to another. The vaults and ceilings of the building echoed mournfully. They walked through a maze of galleries and passages, down a stone staircase, and at length the procession entered a dungeon gloomy as a tomb.

The poor man was left absolutely alone in the depths of that prison. The next day, he was so dejected that an officer was detailed to divert no less than to watch him. The days and the hours seemed to run into one another and congeal into unbroken monotony. Time, like a frozen river, stood still. The seasons succeeded one another, autumn after summer, spring after winter, and then, but only then, the first gleams of hope stole through the bars. One day in May, the prisoner was summoned before his judges, and there, before an august tribunal, the calumnies against him were disproved, and the darkness melted away. And from that city, until then crushed by the fear of despotism, there broke out a great shout of joy. Men breathed again. Thousands of citizens wished to form an escort for the innocent man, to draw his carriage through the streets. For never had a victim of arbitrary government seemed to the French more interesting, more worthy of love, than the Count de Cagliostro on his release from the Bastille. . . .

. . . .

The sound of these rejoicings awoke Vannetti. It was broad day. One could hear the coming and going of the servants, for Donna Bianca-Laura, harassed by insomnia, woke them early. Clementino Vannetti could recognise his mother's deep, masculine voice. Outside, the country carts filled with melons, figs and raisins of every variety, were gathering in the market-place. The merchants put up their straw umbrellas ; chattering, they laid out their goods, and the fat bitter apples were crowded together with the aubergines and the pepper plants. In front of the postmaster's stall, there were already several carriages waiting for fresh horses. . . .

Pensively, Vannetti cast his eyes over the book-covered walls.

After a moment his gaze rested, and he went to look for a fat fifteenth-century folio, dog's-eared and gaping, bound in yellowish parchment, on whose cover was the title in faded gilt letters : *Iamblichus de Mysteriis Aegyptorum, Chaldaeorum, Assyriorum.*

The illustrious Marsilio Ficinus had added to the Latin translation of Iamblichus copious extracts from Porphyry, from Proclus, from Synesius and Psellus, so as to form an almost complete encyclopædia of the Neo-Platonic teachings. Thanks to this collection, Vannetti was able to peep furtively into that mysterious and shadowy sphere which hems in on all sides the paltry knowledge of which we are so proud. His feeble steps had ventured on to the edge of the sanctuary. Half-way to God, with a beating heart, he had dared to steep his lips in the sovereign elixir, the drink of the strong. And a few drops had sufficed to replace obscurity with light. His spirit, which was judicious but of moderate scope, owed incalculable extensions to those visions, swift and dazzling as lightning. He had a longing for the mysterious, a respect for influences which transcend our faculties.

His study of the Neo-Platonists was such a private and intimate thing that he did not breathe a word of it to Donna Bianca-Laura for fear of displeasing her. What was the use of making the old lady uneasy ? For himself, his conscience was at rest. Sincerely attached to Catholic teachings though he was, he was too well-versed in the early history of Christianity not to be aware what strong temptations, in this respect, the most venerated among the Church Fathers had experienced.

Quite close to him, in a region dominated by the priests, an ecclesiastic of high piety had had the courage to challenge the monster of superstition. At a time when the masses still firmly believed in magic, when, before the gates of Rovereto, the executioner slowly roasted innocent peasants who were suspected of sorcery, one of the intellectual luminaries of the town, the Abbé Tartarotti, convinced that his religious character singularly qualified him to enlighten his brethren, had not been afraid to make a protest. "There are no sorcerers," he cried at the top of his voice. "The Witches' Sabbath is only a fable, an old woman's tale." And since then, a quarto volume printed in Rovereto in 1749, *Des Assemblées nocturnes des sorcieres, avec deux dissertations sur l'art magique* had justly carried the Abbé's fame far beyond the frontiers of Trentino. . . . Who knows ? A similar reward might accrue to Chevalier Clementino Vannetti himself in a few months. . . .

. . . .

For he was contemplating a history more instructive than a *Life of Cicero*, more gripping than any account of witchcraft; a story of which the success was assured, since even romantic fiction was not so sensational. Here Fortune had scattered violent and pathetic contrasts in lavish abundance. To the public, the career of the Count de Cagliostro, whose origins were lost in obscurity, appeared as a melodrama, in which palaces and country houses suddenly alternated with the Bastille, and apotheoses with abnormal degradation. Nothing could be more utterly opposed to Clementino Vannetti's own respectable life, where everything was open and plain. The two men were as poles apart. Between the magician and the scholar there was no link, no common measure. Besides, in point of splendour and variety, the Chevalier sustained the comparison so badly that his defeat seemed to be certain, unless there was some timely and helpful intervention.

And just at that moment, the guardian Muses flew to his aid. They did not mean to forsake the polished rhymester who had worshipped them so devotedly since childhood. And Clio, the first among them, smilingly showed him how he could defend himself. . . . All gifts and attainments, were they not indeed united in history like floods in the sea? Is not History the guardian of that enormous and eternal chasm which engulfs all men, regardless of their fame? Since the last word belongs to History, since she alone definitively keeps a register of the dead, writes and effaces their epitaphs, all that was required to gain the advantage over Cagliostro was to become his historian. Thus Clementino Vannetti, deprived of his halo though he was, had only to sit at his desk to regain his supremacy. The gods had sent him, in the person of his rival, an unhoped-for subject.

Scarcely had Vannetti emerged from his dream than this idea took shape. The interest of the narrative, its form, its divisions, and a few characteristic details, Vannetti thought he already saw perfectly clearly in his mind.

In love with his future work, impatient to put it before the world, he paced about for hours in the throes of inspiration. Now he would go to his desk and jot down a fugitive idea; now he would rush to the window. And there, upright, with his forehead against the pane, he would gaze interminably at the village inn, where the Count and the Countess de Cagliostro were staying.

His mind was made up. Abandoning Cicero, he gave himself with all his energy to the Count de Cagliostro. To rummage among a formidable mass of documents, to collate gazettes, pamphlets, tracts and news-sheets; to plunge, head foremost, into the enormous amount of evidence that had been accumulating for the last ten years round a semi-legendary figure—this necessity, truly alarming to one who lacked endurance, did not make Vannetti recoil. To the secretary of the *Accademia degli Agiati*, it was, in fact, but child's play. . . .

II

THE DISCIPLE'S REVERIE

ABOUT the middle of October 1788, when the vine trees in Rovereto were still green, heavy fogs were rolling on the banks of the Rhine. A thoughtful and affectionate woman of Basle, like Gertrude Sarasin, would not be the one to let her husband leave for the country without first wrapping him warmly in a thick overcoat.

Between the autumnal equinox and the winter solstice, the mists usually curled up toward the sunless sky. Jacques Sarasin, curled up in a corner of the carriage, groaned at having to travel blind. Now and then the haze would lift for a moment, and he could see through the gaps a bit of pasture-land shivering under the willows. . . .

As the dilapidated state of the Chinese pavilion made a visit indispensable, it was necessary to get there before the autumn. And Jacques Sarasin did not spare himself reproaches. . . . What a contrast to the busy comings and goings of 1782, when his old friends Messrs. Bischoff and Ritter had offered him a small site in their French garden at Richen to build a pavilion according to Cagliostro's plans ! Leaving his wife at Strasbourg, where she was at the time taking a treatment under that modern Æsculapius, M. Sarasin appeared unexpectedly on the scene. He pressed the workmen hard, scolded them, urged them to ever more diligence. He would not even wait for the foundations to be dug, so anxious had he been to finish the building soon. But, for all his zeal, bad weather had held up the work.

In the spring of 1783, it had been necessary to go to Strasbourg for instructions about the smallest details. The Count de Cagliostro kept him waiting. His reply was usually sent through M. Ramond de Carbonnieres, Cardinal de Rohan's young and brilliant secretary, or good M. Straub, the director of the royal factory for the manufacture of swords, bayonets, etc., at Strasbourg. Sometimes, also, the Count borrowed the services of M. Le Barbier de Tinan, war commissioner at Strasbourg. It was thus, indirectly, through the intermediation of his followers, that he forbade M. Sarasin to make even the smallest alterations in the arrangement of the windows. The little bells at the four corners of the roof might be gilded, but only the lower parts of the clappers. As for the arms of the weather-vane, they must have on them, in gold letters, the initials of the four cardinal directions. And M. Sarasin had to obey. . . .

As soon as the paint had dried, M. de Cagliostro came in person to see that everything was as he wanted it. He and M. Sarasin were closeted together for a long while in the hunting-room, but nothing was ever heard about that conference. Then, returning the keys of the pavilion to the gardener who was in charge, the two entered their carriage. And never again were they to be seen together at the kiosk.

The same summer, M. Ramond de Carbonnieres had a fancy to stay in Riehen with a gentleman who was also attached to the Cardinal de Rohan's suite, the Baron Frederic de Planta. MM. Ritter and Bischoff eagerly offered the hermits the use of the main building, which stood close to the entrance gates. And during the ten months of their residence there, Jacques Sarasin visited them frequently. But the doors of the pavilion remained shut. In February 1785 its furniture was taken away, and M. Sarasin appeared to have lost all interest in it.

The fact of the matter was, this rich silk merchant, whose factories in Basle employed a large number of workmen and agents, could not, as he pretended, have his eye on everything. Not only did he himself select all the designs, from the smallest to the large floral patterns, but he watched carefully over the state of his looms and tested with his own hands the softness and the texture of his fabrics. Letters came to him from the ends of the earth, and he would go through them all himself. Jacques Sarasin had been early initiated into the silk industry. While studying cocoon culture at Bergamo, he had established business relations among the producers of the Trentino, of which his cash-boxes now showed the results.

Jacques Sarasin—" M. Sarasin the Younger "—as the citizens of Basle called him, to distinguish him from Lucas, his elder brother, had the generosity of heart that ennobles wealth. He and his brother occupied on the Rheinsprung, side by side, two lordly mansions, but while M. Lucas lived, in the midst of the austere magnificence of the " Blue House," rather a quiet and retired life, M. Jacques had made of his " White House " a brilliant social centre.

How many foreigners preserved grateful memories of that clear and lofty façade topped with chimneys and gables ! Grotesque masks grimaced from the window ledges. And stone parapets adorned with lions' heads, stretched on either side of the gateway.

Though the hosts of the White House entertained, on occasion, Joseph II and Prince Henry of Prussia, they preferred the company of philosophers and artists. True to their Lorraine origin, they spoke French among themselves. But, in fact, Jacques Sarasin was greatly under German influence. It was in German that he wrote his private diary, and that he welcomed Goethe's companions, the first exponents of romanticism, whenever the " Swiss Congresses " brought them together in the country. It was in German that he corresponded with the good friend of the poet, Johann-George Schlosser. And when Sophie von La Roche, a blue-stocking of some reputation, visited Basle, she was received most cordially at the White House. The German acquaintances of Jacques Sarasin were numerous and important.

Nor, when it came to confiding in his best friend, the pastor Lavater, did he use French. Lavater, who lived in Zurich, was, if possible, even more under the domination of German thought. Of an exuberant vitality, irrepressible as water, as fire, as the elements unleashed, he was preacher, fisher of souls, prophet and apostle of a mystical religion, besides being a justly celebrated physiognomist. By his fiery speech and dazzling imagination, he would carry away his audience to the seventh heaven. And though his utterances shocked the sceptics, sorrowing hearts, drawn by his brotherly love and overpowered by the magnanimity of his spirit, yielded themselves to him unreservedly.

. . . .

Since Gertrude Sarasin had begun to fade, little by little, like a lamp deprived of oil, no angel could have watched over her with greater solicitude than the good Lavater. Neglecting his pastoral duties, he would constantly repair to Basle to cheer up his dear friends.

Jacques had broken his right leg in childhood. And the bitter winter of 1754 having aggravated the fracture, the poor fellow had had his marrow frozen. Whenever his old complaint recurred, he had to take the waters at Plombières. But his athletic constitution would soon gain the upper hand, and enable M. Sarasin to get through a formidable amount of work, eat with a good appetite, and go about as usual.

Much more to be pitied was his unhappy spouse. At the time of their wedding, Mlle Gertrude Battier had shown every sign of health: she had a bright complexion, an ample bosom, and a robust, not to say masculine, figure, such as painters and sculptors used to give the warriors of Valhalla.

But many successive child births had slowly undermined her magnificent constitution. She decayed. Her cheeks turned a leaden colour. She seemed to be sunk in some dark abyss from which she only emerged with mysterious and violent starts. The medical men could not make it out at all; with visible diffidence they talked of gout or bilious fever. When the fits came on, eight strong men were hardly enough to hold the poor body on its bed.

Then, after the frenzy had passed, Gertrude would await its return in agony, so that her suffering was only transferred from her limbs to her imagination.

Lavater's eloquence could do no more. Gertrude was scarcely

alive. Haggard, worn out, she longed for the release of death. Yes, the grave, that kind bed which was not shared with fever or sleeplessness, that was her last and only refuge ! To that hope of which she could never weary, she clung constantly, heedless of the prayers and objurgations of her friends. Jacques himself, undergoing treatment at Plombières, alone, condemned by his own troubles to a most cruel exile, received letters from Gertrude which powerfully depicted all those terrible images.

"O my fond love," replied the wretched husband, "you whose tiny hand I counted on holding in mine throughout eternity, I beg you, abandon these melancholy thoughts. Death should never be considered as a deliverance by those who respect the call of duty. Believe me, to them to die means to rise to a higher state. They will prepare themselves for it joyfully. See how the wretched caterpillar, the lowest among created things, toils almost without rest in anticipation of its metamorphosis. . . . If our corporal fetters chafe us, let us reflect that it has pleased the divine wisdom to keep us obedient and humble for the good of our salvation. . . ."

Misled by an appearance of calm, Sarasin composed a hymn of thanksgiving for the eleventh anniversary of their wedding, the 8th January, 1781. But the next day, jaundice appeared. A pain, sharp as a sword, pierced through the right side. Except for sleep and bodily warmth, all natural forces and functions failed little by little. The stomach, too, was disordered, and Gertrude complained of a sickeningly bitter taste in the mouth :

"My wife's condition," wrote M. Sarasin, "is terrible." One of the best doctors in Basle, a very skilful and highly reputed man, cried out desperately that he could wish to stop the passers-by and ask for their advice.

Jacques Sarasin heard then of a man who was being extolled (if, indeed, he were a mere man) for the miraculous cures he had effected in Strasbourg. When the resources of the pharmacopœia had been exhausted, and the doctors pensively slunk away, not daring to return, the Count de Cagliostro would appear at the bedside of the patient. The grim struggle would be started again, and death would relax its hold.

Would that friend of the eleventh hour condescend to take Gertrude under his protection ? Nothing was less certain. He was supposed to be mad and eccentric, gentle to the poor and hard on the rich. But one could find out by sending a messenger to Strasbourg.

Now no one seemed more suitable for this than the most helpful Lavater. And the mission did not in the least alarm him, for he was burning to know Cagliostro. One of his favourite correspondents, the Baroness Elise von der Recke, née Countess de Medem, had long since lyrically recounted to him the prowess of the mysterious philanthropist in Courland. Lavater did not have to rack his mind to recall *this*—that the Count de Cagliostro put his disciples in touch with spirits, after the fashion of the magicians.

God knows what fantasies crowded in his mind as he left Basle, on the morning of the 23rd January, 1781, accompanied by Dr. Hotze and a young man named Toble.

Reaching Strasbourg the next day, the three travellers went immediately to Cagliostro's residence.

Their first interview, unhappily, was spoiled by mutual constraint. If not the effusive outburst of joy with which men who have been long separated greet each other, Lavater hoped at least to be able to exchange scientific ideas with Cagliostro. But the Count only darted angry glances at him. Why has this pastor brought along two companions with him? With Asiatic, nay, African blood flowing in his veins, Cagliostro had to exert considerable self-control not to throw them out. What did they want of him? Medical advice? Good! But then, why this inquiry by a committee of three, this cross-examination? And if these boobies had no faith in him, they had only to go back to Basle or Zurich. . . . His bad humour would not brook any reconciliation. The conversation fell flat. . . .

Next day, Lavater had the courage to come back alone. Ushered into Cagliostro's presence, he put into his hands the following questionnaire:

"What are the sources of your knowledge? How was it acquired? In what does it consist?"

Reading it, while his pipe made blue spirals of smoke, Cagliostro shrugged his shoulders and smiled with pity. However, he condescended to give an answer in Latin: "*In herbis, in verbis, in lapidibus!*"

In other words, he ascribed all his knowledge to ritual formulas, simple recipes, and to minerals. In this cryptic form, the disclosure was useless. But Lavater had to be content with it, for neither his importunity nor his charm could draw anything more out of him. The Titan's pride was inflexible. His contemptuous lips would not be unsealed.

Yet, praise and blame were strangely mixed in the portrait which Lavater, on his return, sketched for his friends. Here, for example, is what he told Goethe:

"Cagliostro's nature is a consistent whole, original, and vigorous, but too often revolting by its triviality. Don't take him for a philosopher! He is rather an alchemist, fascinated by the mysterious, an infatuated astrologer like Paracelsus. Otherwise he has few or no defects. A solid compact block; a massive monument which commands attention. . . . Having heard and seen him for a quarter of an hour, I admit all the testimonies which, notwithstanding the minute details with which Mme von der Recke was careful to support them, formerly used to surprise me so much.

"Cagliostro claims the gift of second sight. He pretends to be able to see the Seven Celestial Angels face to face, and to touch them as though they were human interlocutors. Let it be ! But how his pride leads him to utter boastful words ! . . .

" Remote from vulgar charlatanism though he is, he has yet a taint of it. He trifled with me, by invoking professional etiquette to evade my questions. Another thing puzzles me : for an enchanter, he has surely very little charm, very little physical or sentimental allure. There is nothing seductive about him. And, nevertheless, Cagliostro surpasses the majority of great men. He is a giant monolith, in whose shadow lie a humble group of hovels. What a pity that such incomparable beings should be so badly wanting in courtesy. Some of them splash, and others crush you ! "

Goethe felt more and more interested in this exotic personality. Not that he attributed supernatural powers to him. " But such men," he exclaimed, " reveal certain aspects of humanity which could scarcely be studied elsewhere."

As for Jacques Sarasin, he could not conceal his joy. M. de Cagliostro had agreed to receive Gertrude. And the patient was getting ready for the journey. . . . On the 1st April, 1781, she reached Strasbourg, and immediately put herself in the care of the healer.

Though there was but a faint chance of success, Cagliostro readily undertook to cure her. And as the entire Sarasin household, with numerous servants, was evidently about to move into the Ratzenhausen house, the patient would be assured of every comfort and attention that she might need.

Her fits recurred the next day with dreadful violence, but the Count brought them under control by quite simple methods. While at Basle the accompanying loss of appetite had continued for five days, here it never lasted more than twenty-four hours. True, it was no easy matter to stop the convulsions ; but their intensity and frequency diminished. Little by little, Madame Sarasin took courage again. Her calm and relaxed nerves resisted the attacks. And the poor insomnomaniac who, even at the best of times, had eaten her meals with reluctance, had shivered with cold and tottered and knocked herself against the furniture in her room, nowadays slept for seven hours at a stretch, walked about without effort, and impatiently clamoured for food. Little by little, she discarded her warm garments and the truckle bed. And when she recalled her former miseries, she would offer thanks, with clasped hands and uplifted eyes, to God and the Count de Cagliostro.

The healer's prestige was enormous. His followers abounded in Alsace, proudly led by the royal banker, the Intendant of the province, two field-marshals, the commandant of the King and the governor himself, M. the Marshal de Contades. Could there be more illustrious supporters ?

Cagliostro's all-powerful recommendation had sufficed to introduce the Sarasins, protestants and of plebian origin though they were, to the Bishop of Strasbourg, Cardinal de Rohan. And it was to him that Gertrude Sarasin owed the services of a charming young woman, whom she adopted as her most intimate companion.

This charming lady, the Countess Branconi, was, in fact, one of Lavater's innumerable correspondents. Widow of an Italian, the Count Pessini di Branconi, she had met, at the age of fifteen, the hereditary prince of Brunswick, Charles William Ferdinand ; and without hesitating a moment between the boring English princess whom, for reasons of State, he was expected to adore, and this little marvel of fifteen years, the august traveller had thrown himself at her feet.

When he declared his fervent love for her, the Countess felt her own heart respond warmly. A few months later, she gave birth to a child, who received the title of Count Forstenbourg.

But the prince's instincts were not monogamous, and rather than struggle daily to retain him against unworthy rivals, the young Countess determined to surrender her position. She left him. She led thereafter a nomadic existence, between Lausanne and Strasbourg, consulting doctors, teachers and professors about the health and education of her son. A handsome young man whom she had engaged as a tutor, Carl Mathei, eventually won her love. From then on, she thanked Heaven that she had been released from her fickle lover. All these amorous adventures might have shocked the Sarasins ; but, like them, she doted on Lavater and Cagliostro, and that merit made up for everything else.

Unexpectedly, however, one day the Countess Branconi began to revile Cagliostro. Even in Gertrude's presence she said biting things about him, forgetting that she should not shake the patient's confidence in her doctor. Jacques complained to Lavater :

" I hope to show her my disapproval without beating about the bush, rudely, crudely, notwithstanding her handsome face. So much the worse for her. Why the devil should I fall on her neck ? "

Seeing that Gertrude had cooled towards her, the Countess appealed to Lavater, who at once undertook to plead for her with Mme Sarasin :

" The Branconi, such a noble soul—how noble God alone knows, notwithstanding your husband's prejudices—seems to me inconsolable by your sudden change of attitude. She does not deserve it. Don't judge her by her quarrels with Cagliostro : it would hardly be just. An excellent physician can be vain and full of faults. It were in vain to visit her. I do not ask so much. But why suddenly withdraw your confidence from her ? "

Lavater pleaded in vain. Thereafter his friends concerned themselves solely with their obligations towards Cagliostro. These were considerable. Not only had the sublime Æsculapius restored Gertrude to health, but he had also cured Jacques Sarasin of a fever he had contracted from his wife, then Felix, their eldest son, of a nervous complaint. So, in their eyes, Cagliostro was far more important than anybody else. But was it necessary to sacrifice to him, besides everything else, their old friend Lavater? Could they not hold the scales even between the two benefactors? Alas! the two prophets harmonised with each other with difficulty. Whenever he saw Cagliostro, in the early days, Lavater would express to them his wonder at a physiognomy in which he could read, with the eye of an expert, all the signs of genius. But the charm later vanished. How could he permit this devil of a Cagliostro to monopolise for his benefit not only the affection of the Sarasins, but intercourse with immaterial beings? Little by little, the prophet of Zurich came to declare war on the prophet of Strasbourg. His letters sowed the seed of doubt in weak and irresolute minds. Here is a sample:

"Should we be dupes of Cagliostro? His physiognomy alone is worth, in any case, a dozen ordinary physiognomies. As for his presumptions and his vulgarity, how is it that his disciples don't advise him to behave more decently? Dear friend, don't believe too readily in the Seven Celestial Spirits! If the least satellite of the least of the angels had honoured me with his confidence, would I not be streaming with fire and light?"

No matter! To the Sarasin household Cagliostro's words were as comforting as some elixir of life. That powerful heart set a new blood flowing through their veins. On the 10th November, 1781, Jacques Sarasin wrote to M. Straub what was ostensibly a letter, which, when published in the *Journal de Paris*, caused a sensation. The public learned then with astonishment of the extraordinary maladies of which the Sarasin family had been relieved by the "beneficent hand of M. the Count de Cagliostro."

There was the same astonishment among the people of Basle when they heard that Mme Sarasin had given birth, on the 14th April, 1782, to a son. Never was a baby more healthy and vigorous. He was christened Alexander, in honour of the physician who had made his birth possible. And Cagliostro, seeing the perfect health of the infant and its mother, himself advised them to return to Basle. When the time came to say farewell, he told them how to make his principal medicines, and requested that they should pass on the information freely to whoever should ask for it. The White House became M. Sarasin's laboratory, and he soon mastered the art of preparing Cagliostro's remedies, the Yellow Pills, the Liquid for Women, and the Wine of Egypt.

M. and Mme Sarasin were perfectly happy. But Cagliostro had awakened indefinable yearnings in them. Even while the hard struggle between doctor and disease was being waged, while the malady was being tracked down and vanquished, he let them catch a distant glimpse, first by guarded words, then with irresistible eloquence, of apotheosis. He spoke of how neophytes healed themselves, how the soul conquered its freedom. He exhorted them to claim their supreme heritage. In this earthly prison-house, Cagliostro alone had had the courage to break his chains. Medicine, pharmacy and alchemy itself, the mysterious divinity with the flame-coloured veils, had no secrets for a mind which had cast off the shackles of necessity. He could easily produce those strange phenomena which the vulgar called miracles. He even offered to communicate his secrets to souls tormented by original sin.

A sharp longing at once seized Jacques and Gertrude. Ah! to escape at last from their dungeon! to attain mastery! According to the Count, every well-born soul had a right to its heavenly inheritance. But it was necessary to abjure Promethean larceny. For that inextinguishable spark would be given to those who worked for it patiently, with heroic perseverance. And, when once the test had been endured successfully, what infinite perspectives opened out! . . . Spiritual regeneration gave one boundless power over nature. And the regeneration of the body was in a way equivalent to immortality. . . .

Following these interviews, Cagliostro invited M. Sarasin to build a hermitage where the hierophant could at leisure carry to an end the spiritual and physical regeneration of Jacques and Gertrude. MM. Bischoff and Ritter had then offered their garden for the purpose, and the ground for the kiosk had been broken without delay. That was in 1782, in the summer, and ten years had gone by!

. . . .

It was thus, passing from reminiscence to reminiscence, that Jacques Sarasin finally reached his destination. Suddenly, through the mist, he recognised the compound wall which extended along the Basle road. At the entrance, with the gates open, the gardener was waiting, cap in hand, and a bunch of keys at his waist.

Scarcely had he greeted M. Sarasin than he broke into complaints. He was not exaggerating, he insisted: the pavilion was literally in ruins. Besides, no one at Riehen was surprised, the kiosk had been built with so little foresight. In the thickest fog, and in a miry soil; and without foundations, good heavens, without foundations! It was a miracle that the walls still stood upright. And when he wrote to Basle about it, never a reply did he get from M. Sarasin's office. . . .

As soon as he went in, M. Sarasin realised the justice of these complaints. The saltpetre was crumbling everywhere in whiskers and hairs, trembling in the lightest breeze. The plaster was coated with dust; spectral stains disfigured the paint; the half-rotten Venetian shutters were sinking into the flower beds; the doors were crooked on their rusty hinges; the keys, fixed deeply into the locks, seemed to belong to some old shipwrecked vessel; dust, rust and humidity had deplorably ravaged the hermitage where M. Sarasin had come to confer with the Count de Cagliostro.

M. Sarasin was profoundly affected by the rapid and extraordinary decay of the pavilion, which he had intended for his regeneration. But already, out of horror of vain regrets, he was calculating the cost of the thorough repairs which he desired should be made at once.

Thrifty by nature, M. Sarasin could nevertheless allow himself to be carried away by gratitude to boundless generosity towards the wonderful doctor to whom he and his family owed their happiness. Cagliostro had accepted the dedication of the kiosk as a singularly flattering tribute. The news had spread to the various groups of the cult. Would it not be a sacrilege to neglect that house, and leave it in ruins?

As a matter of fact, no expenditure of money alarmed the enthusiastic disciple, who longed to be Cagliostro's banker. By the most sublime and persistent efforts, the silk merchant had obtained this result: the Master allowed himself to be accredited to the various branches of the Sarasin firm to facilitate the journeys which he undertook with a tireless and indefatigable zeal for the welfare of mankind.

There was nothing bewildering about a bill of exchange to an alchemist who could, at will, enlarge the size of diamonds, or manufacture gold. As he had a very clear insight into character, Cagliostro never confounded his patients with his disciples. The one seemed to his eyes but temporary passengers in his vessel, while the others belonged to the permanent and regular crew. It is only the last that he would permit to render some slight services to him. With regard to Jacques Sarasin, for example, he exclaimed with emotion:

"Oh! As for him, he would give me his whole fortune!"

Perhaps, however, if he had had less facilities to tour Europe, the Count would not have been separated for four years from the affection of his disciples. He would not have left Strasbourg without having proceeded, thanks to the proximity of Riehen, to the regeneration of Jacques and Gertrude. In August 1783, obeying only his impulse, he rushed impetuously to Naples, there to catch the last sigh of his venerable friend, the Chevalier d'Aquino, who was a brother of the Prince de Caramanica, then viceroy of Sicily. Returning to France in the same hurry, he settled at Bordeaux in November. Eleven months later, there was another departure. The Count and Countess moved to Lyons. Would to Heaven that they might remain there! As long as he was in that capital of the silk industry in France, which had such close connections with Basle, Jacques and Gertrude Sarasin felt he was quite near to them. But the Cardinal de Rohan clamoured for his dear Cagliostro. He bombarded him with letters, and then sent the ingenious Ramond de Carbonnieres with instructions to bring him back, by hook or by crook. His insistence had at length prevailed. On the 27th January, 1785, the Count went from Lyons to Paris to rejoin the Cardinal. A melancholy expedition it was, and one which led to many calamities.

Few people felt more keenly than M. and Mme Sarasin the catastrophe which broke upon the château of Versailles on the 15th

August, 1785. However, if the whole truth must be told, their indignation but remotely resembled that of the public. The prodigious folly of the cardinal, the blunders of the Crown jewellers, the villainy of Mme de La Motte, the grotesque pantomime that they had caused a prostitute to execute in a thicket, almost beneath the lighted windows of the Queen, certainly all this upset the Sarasins. But it pained them still more to hear that their erstwhile guest, Baron Frederic de Planta, an honest and worthy soldier belonging to a respectable Grisons family, had been thrown in the Bastille, pell-mell with forgers. And that nothing should be wanting to their consternation, there was involved in the scandal the most sacred authority, the semi-divine personality, the terrestrial manifestation of the angels, the Count de Cagliostro !

But it was precisely then that they gave proof of their fervour. In spite of the anguish in which they awaited the verdict of the Parlement of Paris, M. Sarasin calmly wrote to Lavater :

" Calm and collected, we remain more than ever devoted to our father and benefactor. Should he share the fate of Socrates, we should consider it an honour to proclaim ourselves his disciples."

A hemlock more bitter than that of Socrates was reserved for Cagliostro. No sooner was he acquitted, than he was ordered to leave Paris within three days, and the kingdom within three weeks. The shepherd was separated from his flock, the sower from his harvest, the high-priest from his altar ! No matter ! Anxious to render unto Cæsar that which was Cæsar's, the Count proceeded to obey his orders. Without complaint or clamour, he sailed, on the 16th June, 1786, from Bordeaux to England.

M. and Mme Sarasin soon had an opportunity of sending him a letter through a German literary woman whom they had often entertained at Basle. Sophie von La Roche, on her way to London, offered to hand their letters to the celebrated thaumaturgist. A message was entrusted to her, and the news she brought back was received with pleasure. The master was maintaining in his exile an indomitable spirit and an exalted style. All the same, after so many persecutions, he could not resist a hint of bitterness in his reference to his wife :

" Beloved creature ! But for her, I should have buried myself in the desert, and there at least, among the wild beasts, I should have made friends."

After a few months, the Count complained of being lonely. No doubt, in England, as elsewhere, his patients increased in number ; but of friends, he had not one ! His only disciple among the English nobility was Lord George Gordon, a fanatic whose churlish manners had earned for him an unenviable reputation. What a strange bodyguard ! Happily, the Count had found there some old friends of Strasbourg.

Of them, the one that he met most frequently was a marine,

military and landscape painter by name Phillipe-Jacques Loutherbourg. Son of a Hessian father and a Strasbourg mother, he had readily migrated to England when he found that his canvases sold better there than in France. A member of the Royal Academy of Art, and covered with honours as he was, he could be of valuable help in London. No one professed greater respect for the Count. And who knows ! Interested in occultism, M. Loutherbourg himself perhaps cherished some hopes of physical regeneration.

But Cagliostro had at his command somebody more useful still. M. Rey de Morande, of Lyons, the intimate friend of M. Ramond de Carbonnieres, after having rendered the Count and the Countess inestimable services during their detention in the Bastille, had been eager to be with them in London. Now, under the Master's supervision, he devotedly applied himself to alchemical work.

The name of Morande, formerly so dear to the elect, had been, alas, dishonoured for ever by a French refugee in London. M. Charles Theveneau published in London, with money extorted from the French ministry, a bi-weekly gazette, called the *Courrier de l'Europe*, under the usurped name of Morande. No doubt, all decent people felt nothing but contempt for this spy. But to the great distress of his namesake, the virtuous alchemist of Lyons, " M. Theveneau de Morand," " M. le Chevalier de la Morande," as he impudently described himself, finally rendered famous a name to which he had no more right than to the money of the King of France.

And he was ready to tear the Count de Cagliostro to pieces, at the bidding of the French embassy. The campaign which, with infernal ferocity, he conducted for several months, was more disastrous to its victim than a short imprisonment in the Bastille.

The deed was done : the poison had infected the faithful. Defections multiplied. Even those who had formerly braved with the utmost courage the *lettres de cachet* and the royal anger, could not now read without some sympathy the monstrous libels of the bogus Morande. The exile in London suffered torments unknown to the prisoner of the Bastille. Cowardice, like heroism, has its mysteries. That the giddy and thoughtless Baroness von der Recke, demolishing what she had adored, should dishonour herself so far as to publish in Germany a satire on the Count's sojourn at Mitau—well, she was free to do what she pleased ! Jacques Sarasin had nothing to learn of the fickleness of pretty women. But why had M. Rey de Morande, who was such a sound man, ventured to repudiate their Master ? Why did M. Thilorier, the Paris lawyer, who had until then so zealously and skilfully defended the Count, lend an ear to the calumnies ? And, finally, M. Loutherbourg himself, after thirteen months of devotion, seemed to have lost all enthusiasm. His faith was struggling painfully against doubt. His affection wavered. . . . Some weeks later, he openly declared his ingratitude.

Finally, enigma of enigmas, it was the Countess of Cagliostro herself. Remaining in London, in April 1787, while the Master had gone to Basle by way of Belgium, Serafina de Cagliostro had promised to rejoin him as soon as she had sold their furniture. But one morning she was unexpectedly set upon by that perfidious Theveneau. And she gently told him of her financial difficulties. How mean of Cagliostro to desert her, and take away with him all their valuables and jewels! . . . The poor creature had no judgment at all. Credulous, and jealous to the point of madness, she saw herself at once betrayed, fooled, and reduced to misery. Her despair broke out into recriminations which the *Courrier de l'Europe* did not fail to publish with a seasoning of comments on the morality of the Count.

But as soon as she rejoined her husband in Switzerland, Serafina was ashamed of her blasphemies. She wished to retract them. To the immense relief of the whole flock, the magistrates of Bienne registered her formal disavowal. Jacques Sarasin alone, in spite of the general satisfaction, nourished a secret rancour. He could not forgive the culprit the scandal she had caused. Besides, various details set him thinking. What, for instance, was one to infer from the crass ignorance observable in the Countess? Serafina had only learnt to write when she went to the Bastille. In vain did Cagliostro affirm that Romans of good family were nearly always brought up like that, without the least glimmer of instruction, for the safety of their future husbands. Many people shook their heads; they saw in Serafina the gait and bearing of a rope-dancer rather than that of a great lady.

In society at Geneva, while Mme de Charriere proclaimed her unchanging gratitude for Cagliostro, whose wonderful Yellow Pills had cured her, she did not dissemble her aversion from Serafina, "the Count's evil genius." And M. de Luternau, a very respectable Bernese gentleman, swore that Serafina had, one day, in his presence, torn and burned a letter from Cagliostro, saying:

"Ah! would that I could do the same with the person who wrote me that!"

Mme Sarasin turned a deaf ear to these ugly rumours. She would not tolerate any criticism of her benefactor's wife. In the eyes of this faultless friend, Serafina's crimes were mere peccadilloes. True, Gertrude herself admitted that the sublime Cagliostro deserved a less childish wife. But try and find suitable companions for the eternal hermits, the heroes and the saints!

The very handsome Mme Loutherbourg's rôle was still more suspect. Certain Furies look like the Graces; and this one showed herself terribly efficient at embroiling the relations between old friends. Incensed at her failure to seduce the Count, this painted Circe had, during their stay at Bienne, alienated her husband's affection. And the clever but foolish artist passed overnight from exuberant fervour to an aversion not less frenzied. He uttered terrible threats, which were at first dismissed with a laugh. But when he armed himself with powder and shot, it had become necessary to inform the police. What baseness! Jacques Sarasin, even after a year, could still feel the blood rush to his cheeks at the recollection. Was it for this that he had invited his benefactor to Switzerland? Ah! if he could only suppress this scandal! But there had been too many witnesses at Bienne, and Loutherbourg himself made an infernal uproar. No doubt, the loans of which Loutherbourg demanded repayment amounted, in fact, to an absurdly small sum. But to an unscrupulous woman, like Mme Loutherbourg, it was child's play to magnify and envenom these trifles.

Thank God, the Countess Serafina never repeated her London mistakes. Without really considering her to be a guileless dove, Jacques understood, as he watched her, the paternal indulgence which her husband displayed towards her. No one could bear conjugal discussions so little as Cagliostro. At the smallest quarrel, pale, tremulous, upset, he became a pathetic sight. In regard to the letter that Serafina had burned, he had gently told M. Luterneau:

"Look here, when she does such unseemly things, we must forgive her. She is bored. Never have I been less well off than I am, and never have I been less able to provide her with amusements and clothes."

Clothes? Amusements? In truth, it was all a question of these. Was one going to sacrifice a wonderful work for the futilities of a linnet? What madness! Cagliostro granted himself on his own authority six weeks vacation in honour of the ceremony. Everything was ready, and the altar now awaited its high-priest. . . .

In Switzerland, Cagliostro's first concern was to find a residence. As soon as they had settled in the outskirts of Bienne, the Countess set herself to atone for her blunders in London. Three months were consumed in barren formalities. Loutherbourg's violence had at length rendered inevitable an appeal to the magistrates. Fresh consultations and worries. Oh, the bitterness of these disputes, which exhausted the energy in endless and hateful proceedings!

Nevertheless, during that disastrous sojourn at Bienne, the Master lavishly distributed favours and benefits. At a splendid religious ceremony in the White House, on the 2nd May, 1787, Cagliostro officiated so impressively that the spectators, with tears in their eyes, volunteered to labour with him in the foundation of the celestial Jerusalem.

During the same month, Jacques Sarasin proudly accompanied his illustrious friend to the annual congress of the Société Helvétique. It was then sitting at Olten. Though the conference had no esoteric character at all, Cagliostro's visit produced an extraordinary impression.

The next summer, Cagliostro again deigned to honour with his presence these rural discussions. Master and disciple expected to remain at Olten until the end of May. But the welcome they received but ill corresponded with their hopes. Besides, the hour of separation was approaching. Having suffered much by the humid air of Bienne, Serafina wished to take a cure at Aix-les-Bains. On the 19th July, 1788, fond and sorrowful farewells were exchanged.

After Aix-les-Bains, the Count and Countess went towards Italy. Was it not said that they had been recognised in Turin, Alessandria, Genoa? Jacques and Gertrude wisely reserved their judgment. And in October 1788, a letter in the Count's own hand informed them of their safe arrival at Rovereto. The population had welcomed him as a demi-god: and the good people, he said, were so earnest that they deserved the same favour as the dear people of Basle—he never sold his services to those who seemed worthy of them. The letter concluded in affectionate terms.

Jacques, however, felt a piercing regret. He had hoped that the Count and Countess would spend the winter in Switzerland, after their sojourn at Aix-les-Bains. The scandals and persecutions they had suffered at Bienne had doubtless disgusted them with that city, but why should their aversion extend to the whole of Switzerland? Why did they reject, without consideration, any proposal of a stay at Riehen? In the Chinese cottage, M. and Mme de Cagliostro would have felt perfectly at home.

Nevertheless, M. Sarasin introduced the Count to his bankers at Venice, and to his correspondents in the Trentino, and possessed himself in patience. How often had the Count repeated to him the motto: One should make haste slowly.

In short, since he was bound in honour to put the Chinese cottage in shape, M. Sarasin, tearing himself away from his office, undertook the journey to Riehen that foggy morning of October 1788.

. . . .

"My friend," he said firmly to the gardener after their inspection, "you shall have M. Buschel here to-morrow and the workmen within three days."

In fact, all the time they were in the pavilion, Jacques had been computing the cost of a complete restoration. And now he announced what he wanted in such decisive terms, that the old watchman, slow and stammering like the majority of those born to obey, stood stupefied. . . .

Within three days a group of painters, masons and plumbers were at work. No expense was spared to make the kiosk look exactly as it was originally. On returning to Basle, M. Sarasin at once spoke about it to his architect, M. Buschel. . . .

The knowledge that he had taken wise and timely measures, or at any rate done his best, gave M. Sarasin a very agreeable sensation. While he walked through the small French garden to the gates where his carriage was waiting, the mists lifted. Between the big masses of clouds floating through the air like squadrons, the sun and the blue sky began to show. The rest of the day was going to be bright. So much the better ! It would be fine on the return journey.

But, instead of rejoicing, M. Sarasin heard within him a mournful and hostile voice, bitterly repeating : " In vain, in vain ! Your most judicious measures will be vain, always vain ! "

Not that the silk merchant was yielding to the disgraceful malady which had decimated the flock. Jacques Sarasin clung to the sublime idealistic religion in all its purity, and his devotion to the person of the Count was upheld by an inexhaustible enthusiasm. But, alas, it was the Master himself who was little by little withdrawing himself from the disciple !

Since that deplorable tragi-comedy of Bienne, their friendship had been waning. Did Cagliostro fear that Jacques Sarasin was only serving him half-heartedly ? Anyhow, he made no effort to control his outbursts. On one occasion—and, fortunately, on only one occasion—he had accused Jacques Sarasin of being " interested." The word wounded the generous silk-merchant like a knife-thrust. Interested ? Truly, Jacques knew he did not deserve the reproach, he of whom formerly the Count had been pleased to say : " Oh ! as for him, he would give me his entire fortune ! "

Such a shameful imputation seemed an inexplicable mystery to M. Sarasin, for the Master could penetrate to the innermost recesses of a man's conscience. How could he vindicate himself before one who could, if he wished, at any moment read his most secret thoughts ? But perhaps, in reply to the letter from Rovereto, he should clasp the knees of the Master, beg for mercy, and appeal to his magnanimity as a supremely just father. And even while he was talking to the gardener, M. Sarasin was drafting in his own mind, the essential, the decisive phrases of that letter :

" *Well beloved Father and venerated Master* "—thus he would begin—" *My heart bleeds to find myself so sorely misunderstood.*" And then, at once, he formulated this protestation : " To be ' interested ' has never been and never will be my weakness. . . ."

Near the gates, his glance fell on a caterpillar. Having crossed the edge of the flower bed, the grub was wandering at random. It was brightly coloured : gold, a warm, flaming gold, bristling with bushy hairs and spotted like a leopard. Jacques Sarasin, to save it from being crushed, bent down compassionately and picked it up in the hollow of his gloved hand.

He had acquired, since the days of his apprenticeship in Italy, a wonderful knowledge of silkworms ; nor was he likely to confuse this regal grub, with its luxurious hairs, with the *bombyx muri*, to which the White House and the Blue House owed their wealth. But all these filaments, subjected to mysterious processes by moulting and metamorphoses, exercised a curious and inexplicable fascination on M. Sarasin's mind.

He could not, in picking it up, have hurt the grub, for, instead of rolling itself up into a ball, it simply showed its displeasure by twisting a little on itself. Then, lifting its head up, as though to bear testimony to the violence it had suffered, it slowly displayed all its scaly feet. It began, finally, to crawl over the glove of its gigantic ravisher, not much reassured, it would seem, but still resolved to persevere, and not to be distracted from its task.

One can, without any superstition, have a feeling for symbols. Observing the courage with which the grub followed its vocation, ready to bear everything in order to become an insect, to be worthy of its wings, Jacques thought of the words which he had himself addressed to Gertrude, when she wrote to him about her melancholy forebodings : " See," he had told her, " how the wretched grub, the lowest in the scale of created beings, works with hardly a pause in view of its metamorphosis." It was now for him to reflect on it ! He had the example right under his eyes.

He, too, like the humble insect, was looking forward to his metamorphosis, in spite of obstacles, dangers and the most terrible perplexities. He also had woken up suddenly in the formidable hand of a giant, far above the little world where he had, until then, lived in peace. . . . In spite of this extraordinary incident, he bravely set about the performance of his duties, without trying to plumb the depths wherein his spirit floundered. The Chinese kiosk must be repaired : the original plan must be followed exactly. And on the day when it should please the Master to return to Richen, the chrysalis would emerge as a butterfly. His long persistence would then have its reward : and it would be a holiday, a wonderful holiday of light and liberty, in an eternal youth of love. . . .

III

CAGLIOSTRO AT ROVERETO

DEALING for the first time, at thirty-three years of age, with a living subject instead of old books and maps, Vannetti was diffident and uncertain like one emerging from an ill-lit and stuffy room into sunlight and open air and the roar of human crowds. However, he did not care to enter into personal relations with the Count de Cagliostro; he was content to watch him at public gatherings. But there the noise and the promiscuity distracted his attention from his model, and his thoughts would wander to his fellow citizens whose failings always filled him with a painful astonishment. A singular personality had appeared by chance in their midst. Why not study him patiently and form a considered judgment, instead of discussing for hours, as these chatterers did, whether he was entitled to call himself the "Count de Cagliostro"? A name, a mere name, interested them more than genius itself.

Vannetti shrugged his shoulders. The Count had, no doubt, quite other claims to the attention of intelligent people, but the somewhat childish curiosity of Rovereto was not without its excuse. In that small town, where every passer-by scattered a handful of news, where the gossips in the inn read foreign papers as attentively as their local sheets, the recent revelations of the *Courrier de l'Europe* had stirred up public opinion. It was aware that M. Theveneau de Morande, in his anxiety to expose Count de Cagliostro, represented him to be a certain Giuseppe Balsamo, a Sicilian painter, who was also a London Freemason. In order to throw people off his scent, Balsamo had donned the gold-embroidered satin cloak of the Count de Cagliostro. The Count's chequered career had certainly a dramatic interest, and envious folk eagerly followed every phase of his controversy with the journalist.

In Rovereto, as in London, bets were laid. The mystery must be cleared up: what was there in common between the Count de Cagliostro and Giuseppe Balsamo?

. . . .

Since the memorable evening of the 24th September, 1788, the little square upon which opened the windows of the inn, was rarely deserted. Peasants in multi-coloured rags, and chamois hunters in leather jackets, came from their fields and their mountains, on foot or by cart, to seek information among the townsmen. Was Cagliostro a magician? Or was he rather the Anti-Christ?

The thaumaturge would burst into laughter when these questions were repeated to him. Then he would murmur dreamily:

"How could they know who I am? I do not know myself. My remedies take effect; among the ignorant I distribute my knowledge, among the poor my alms. That is all. For the rest, like them, I grope in the dark. . . . Come, ignore this idle talk; the truth will pierce through of its own accord, on the day when the Count de Cagliostro shall have ceased to live. . . ."

This reticence only sharpened curiosity. Some evil-minded people endeavoured to catch Cagliostro flagrantly contradicting himself, or telling a lie; but, overcome with admiration in their turn, they affirmed that the man could not possibly be an impostor.

Cagliostro must certainly have dealings with the forces beyond. Only supernatural knowledge and supernatural faculties could account for his miraculous cures. He raised the dead, they said, and forced them to speak, and sometimes even brought them together with the living at the same table.

Vannetti was not one to be taken in by these stories. Whether or not Cagliostro was a man of unparalleled greatness, he meant to treat him just like the others whose history he had written: he would apply the same methods.

Cagliostro had been all over Europe. And Vannetti hoped through his connections with learned societies to obtain not only copies of everything published in different countries about the Count, but the depositions of eye-witnesses as well. By a happy coincidence, his illustrious friend, the poet Ippolito Pindemonte, was just then setting out to France by way of Switzerland, and he promised to send Vannetti details of Cagliostro's stay at Strasbourg, Bordeaux, Lyons and Paris. Through the silkworm breeders and agents who were at Bergamo, such as M. Hans-Caspar Steiner, Vannetti hoped to make perfectly clear what had happened in Switzerland in 1787 and 1788. Conscientious scholar that he was, no source was too trivial for him, no pains too great. And meanwhile, his eyes fixed on his model, he mingled with the crowds which gathered round Cagliostro, and became a familiar figure among the habitués.

The academician compared his personal observations with the documents and reports which daily reached him. The most difficult thing was to sort out the mass of information. Out of sheer boredom, the fanatical partisans of the thaumaturge tried to pick a quarrel with him. They looked askance at the diligent and silent onlooker, who never sought to be introduced to the Master, yet noted down in his book every smallest thing he heard fall from him. They accused him of being actuated by hostile motives. Clementino took pains to set their minds at rest. He repeatedly assured them that, far from wishing their Master harm, he inclined rather to a certain admiration. He only desired to relate faithfully what he saw and heard, so as to furnish an accurate report. It was the truth. Once he had overcome his first aversion to his rival, he applied himself without prejudice to his work. His monograph was to create a mysterious sympathy, verging on friendship, between its scholarly readers and its subject. If, hereafter, he had any prejudice, it was in the Count's favour. His personality had captivated him, and he loved it through and through.

In fact, Cagliostro had a very pleasing appearance. Of medium height and with an enormous head, he was yet active, in spite of his stocky figure and premature corpulence. Oriental or Mediterranean blood gave his complexion a swarthy tinge. His black hair, and deep bright eyes, lent him a youthful air. He was dressed respectably, without extravagance or elaborateness, except for a hat over-decorated with feathers and gold lace. And the sound of his voice exercised a singular influence over his patients. . . . On first meeting him, Vannetti had been unable to suppress a thrill : here was the man he had seen in a dream on the night of the 24th September, 1788 ! . . .

. . . .

As the hostelry on the square was small and unsuitable for a prolonged residence, Cagliostro began to look for lodgings less primitive. After many inquiries, he selected the apartments rented by Councillor Giuseppe Festi, who respected the Count highly and congratulated himself on having secured such an august tenant. From the way he drank in the Count's words, one would have thought that he was becoming intoxicated with some delicious beverage. To such enthusiasm the Count and the Countess adapted themselves readily, all the more because Giuseppe Festi was known to be a gentleman whose reputation extended as far as the court of the Prince-Bishop of the Trentino. Clementino, too, was on familiar terms with him, as his tutor had formerly been the Abbé Gottardo Festi, a near relative of the councillor. He was thus able to go into the *casa* Festi at all hours and observe the Count at close quarters.

Cagliostro's was a life devoted, with but intervals for food and sleep, entirely to the public welfare. He would stretch himself in an arm-chair, with his head resting on some cushions, and he would be up before dawn, attending to his work. His patients started besieging him quite early. They came from the heart of the Venetian and Milanese districts, each one as best he might, in cart or litter, or by stretcher, and the more healthy on mules decorated with ropes, tassels, and coral or glass beads to ward off the evil eye. And later, one could see them emerging, radiant, from the *casa* Festi, their prescriptions in one hand and their money in the other, ready for the apothecary.

But there were others who did not pass the threshold without crossing themselves. They shivered, and the chill of a mortal fear would seize them at the throat when consulting the stranger. The wealthier among them were accompanied by their own physicians. It was thus that a cunning old man, afflicted with renal lithiases, came and threw himself at Cagliostro's feet :

" Count," he said, " save me, if it be possible ! "

The thaumaturge replied :

" What, at your age, and afflicted by a deep-rooted malady, you still hope to be cured ? All right, come to-morrow, and I shall have your medicine ready for you."

He reassured him as best he could. And the physician, who was listening eagerly, approved of the Count's instructions, and thanked him. After a few days, as a result of the remedy prescribed, the old man felt some relief. The local doctors were abashed. What could have been that remarkable powder, they asked themselves, and rivalled each other in their efforts to dig out the answer from their pharmacopœias old and new. To the old fellow's physician, Cagliostro gave this advice :

" Do what you can to obtain generous payment for the services you have rendered to your patient. As for me, I have assigned myself the task of fighting death. I believe it has now been checked for the next ten years. After that, I can answer for nothing."

At these words the old man, who overheard them, was extremely glad, for he had not expected to live another ten years.

Cagliostro did not concern himself only with the rich and the powerful. He had a kind word for everyone and a promise to heal them within a fortnight. And to those who distrusted his drugs, he would say gently :

" I forgive you, for you do not know me."

It was about this time they brought to him from the outskirts of Verona, a woman suffering from cancer of the breast. He began by showing her to the most celebrated of the local physicians. Holding the patient by the hands, he told them :

" Look, gentleman, and judge."

And these great specialists, after a meticulous examination, declared that the woman was irrevocably lost, at any rate unless a surgical operation were performed. Besides, the success of the operation was doubtful. After they had made their pronouncement, the Count sweetly murmured :

" My way is not to mutilate my neighbour with a knife. . . ."

Preparing an ointment, he told the patient to apply it properly with a napkin. The unhappy woman cried out :

" My lord, I haven't a napkin."

The Countess de Cagliostro, who was a compassionate looker-on, at once ran to fetch a suitable napkin, and the ointment was applied. That done, the patient begged to know how long she would have to remain at Rovereto.

The Master contented himself with muttering :

" For some time. . . ."

She at once burst into tears :

" Alas ! how can I manage it ? I should have to go into a hospital and I haven't a single sou. . . ."

And he replied in a ringing voice :

" Come, eat and drink without worry ! I'll pay all your expenses."

When, overcome with gratitude, she had gone, the Count arranged with the innkeeper about her bills.

His popularity at once went up. And the doctors, when they visited the patient next day at the inn, found her confident and complaining of nothing. More and more disconcerted, these professional gentlemen began to spy upon the Count, in the hope of discovering his secrets. As for him, he behaved toward them with scrupulous courtesy, always careful not to encroach upon any of their privileges. Never did he consent to hold consultations outside the *casa* Festi. He made an exception only in the case of a demented young woman who used to shriek with clenched teeth and foam at the mouth, and in the case of a soldier of the guard who, with swollen thighs, had writhed in pain for five months. These patients being unable to leave home, he consented to go to them.

It seemed as though his discretion and tact were bound to win over the doctors. Even Clementino Vannetti considered it possible that they might arrive at mutual understanding. But he did not realise the acerbity of professional jealousies. The doyen of the Rovereto doctors, annoyed at hearing the praises of the Count, finally threw off his mask. He sharply called upon the magistrates to do their duty : no one had a right to practice medicine in the town without a diploma conferred by some experienced member of the profession, duly named and appointed by His Majesty the Emperor and King. To ignore that rule was to ignore Cæsar.

Cagliostro was thereupon requested to suspend his consultations. He contented himself with telling the magistrates, apparently calmly, that his ministrations were always given in the presence of the doctors, and with their full consent.

" Every time I prescribe a remedy, I indicate its action in the most precise manner, and you know whether any of my patients have had to complain of my treatment. Meanwhile, prevent your people from besieging my door. Is it my fault that the unhappy creatures entreat me so that I have not the heart to resist their prayers ? "

A cruel predicament for the authorities. If the law were not applied, the powerful and spiteful college of physicians would rise in revolt. On the other hand, there was an angry murmur among the populace, and its voice was in favour of Cagliostro. After prolonged deliberations, they decided to retain the ban as it stood ; but they made it secretly known to the thaumaturge that none of their officials would cause him any trouble.

The Count was disgusted. To show that he cared little for Rovereto, and that Alexander de Cagliostro would be welcome anywhere, one Sunday afternoon he crossed the Adige. At Villa Lagarina, the civic heads welcomed him enthusiastically. Men and women of the highest distinction gathered at the house of a high official named Gaspare. And Cagliostro discoursed to them on the loftiest topics.

Meanwhile, the sick people in the village crowded into the hall, and hemmed in among them was one Joseph, whom strange fevers and giddiness seemed to be leading to the grave. Cagliostro had only left Rovereto for some relaxation and rest, but as the wife of one of the officials very charmingly requested him, he agreed to have a look at the patient.

Joseph came in, leaning on his youngest son. Cagliostro ran forward to meet him, and taking him by the hand, conducted them into a closet, shutting the doors behind them. Having examined the old man, he told him :

" My good fellow, do you know what you need ?—a vermifuge." Dumbfounded, father and son looked at each other ; no one had thought of that.

" It is regrettable that no one had thought of it sooner," continued the Count, " but this is my profession. You shall be healed in eight days, provided you have confidence in God and me."

It was getting late. As dusk fell, some servants began to drive away the crowd, which, clinging to the banisters, resisted their efforts with pitiful cries. The whole company escorted the hierophant, as a mark of respect, up to the city gates. Recrossing the Adige, he returned to the *casa* Festi.

The next day he devoted himself chiefly to his patients, some of whom were feeling a decided improvement. No one talked any longer of shutting up the mad girl in an asylum. She had grown visibly calmer, and her relatives effusively kissed the Count's hands, calling upon him the blessings of Heaven. As for the soldier of the guard, he was, to the general amazement, beginning his convalescence. He had languished for so many months that it seemed certain that he would succumb to what was evidently the plague, that chastisement of the dissolute which had come from the New World. Such cases were all too numerous at Rovereto. Ceaselessly importuned by them, the Count concealed neither his anger nor his disgust.

" Corruption is no more hideous at Constantinople or Paris than here," he muttered between his teeth. " Woe to you, citizens of Rovereto, for your sins will be visited upon you and your offspring."

When the young soldier, now recovered and full of joy, came and threw himself at his feet, the Count lifted him up :

" Instead of thanking me, go to church," he said, " and there, in front of your brethren, proclaim that the Lord has been pleased to extend to you his healing compassion."

This cure caused a great stir. The women, especially, gave free rein to their enthusiasm, seeing some sovereign virtue in the least of his utterances. They constantly spoke to him of their petty troubles, and with tears in their eyes, conjured him not to forsake them ; for no one knew exactly how long he would remain at Rovereto. But when they began to demand of him a certain potion supposed to have the effect of an elixir of youth, he answered smilingly :

" No, I assure you, I have nothing in common with the daughter of the king of Colchide."

To disillusion them, the Count related the story of a woman who had refused to reconcile herself to her decay. He had solemnly sent her a bottle of pure water, which the old hag had since been drinking. Confident of having recovered her charms, she enjoyed such delightful security that she would not even look at herself in a glass. The women who admiringly listened to him did not find this banter to their taste. But finding that he was adamant, they gave up thoughts of the elixir. Besides, the Count had put them on their guard against swindlers who took his name in order to sell their own concoctions.

News came just then of another Cagliostro at Milan, and the gossips began to ask themselves if the astonishing mystagogue possessed, by any chance, the gift of ubiquity or of multiplying himself. But the shrewd ones laughed in their sleeves, confident that one or the other must necessarily be a knave, and that it would not be long before they knew which one. The Milanese impostor was, in fact, exposed before long, and during the brief period of uncertainty, the real Count, indifferent to the gossip, did not for a day relax his philanthropic labours.

Although the leading physician in Rovereto persecuted the Count, some of the others, avid of knowledge, frequented the *casa* Festi. They respectfully invited the sage to try his skill on their own persons. Thus a deaf doctor requested him to restore his hearing. Cagliostro gave him a tonic and breathed vigorously into his ears, assuring him of a speedy cure. . . . But his enemies, hoping to stir up the populace, continued to vilify him. And sometimes, at the end of a harassing day, Cagliostro would sigh sadly :

" It is impossible to do good without arousing jealousy. What an uproar wherever I have been ! And yet, far from returning evil for evil, I shall always try to help and console. For it is only by love that a man becomes the equal of God. . . ."

He would mention the snares laid for him in Russia, in France and England, and then forgive all his enemies without exception.

It was not without interest that the few physicians who visited him listened to all this. But so ardent was their scientific curiosity, that they would much rather that he explained his teachings and his methods. Unfortunately, his principles in medical matters reduced themselves to a few cryptic maxims that were scarcely intelligible. He maintained, chiefly, that every form of sickness was due to a thickening of the phlegm or a corruption of the humours. As he would not recognise any other cause, even the doctors who most loved and respected him, could not profess to agree with him: they merely said they did not understand. An important section of the public was beginning to throw doubt on some of his most amazing cures. The young soldier's cure, the slanderers said, was only superficial. Old Joseph of Villa Lagarina, contrary to the Count's prediction, had not ejected any worms, and his life was despaired of. As for the rich old man who suffered from calculi, it was said that he had rudely snubbed the Count's supporters who urged him to mount his horse and publicly testify to his recovery:

"Are you teasing me?" he is said to have asked; "I am much worse than before, and if I had always been treated in this manner, I should long since have gone to rest with my ancestors."

As though to try his patience, they demanded the most absurd things of Cagliostro. He was generous enough to give his advice to a priest who had come to consult him. But the priest would not be content: he wanted antidotes against future ills. Thereupon, the Count raised his eyes to Heaven:

"Mr. Abbé," he said, "if I came to you to confess, you would doubtless absolve me of my sins. But if I insisted, in addition, on being saved from my future sins, what would you do?"

To his other patients who were complaining that they felt no further improvement, he replied:

"What can I do, my good friends? The treatment which you need is at the other end of the world. Shall we go and find it on the wings of eagles?"

Vannetti noted this down: what they expected of Cagliostro was the impossible. Every enchanter has to face that demand. To subsist, to escape sarcasm and hate, he must ceaselessly multiply his miracles, and like doctors, never permit himself to tell the truth. Vexed by some delays, people turned away from the Master and began to grumble. No more than other benefactors of the human race could Cagliostro avoid the cup of bitterness. When the authorities of the hospital sent asking him to visit their patients:

"What is the use?" he replied. "Whatever I prescribe for them, it will have no effect, for they have no faith in me. If I had the means, I should surely remove them from the hospital, and minister to their needs. But you know I cannot do that. After all, they have their own physicians and surgeons, let them go to them! . . ."

After that, he would only attend strangers. Some writers of Rovereto having been less than respectful to him, he wished to say farewell to that cursed town:

"It is all over," he said to the civic authorities. "By losing me you lose also the advantages of my celebrity. I shall go afar, and restore their parents to the orphans, or rather, for the consolation of fathers and mothers, snatch their children from the jaws of death."

His enemies only asked for his departure, for they were afraid that his penetrating insight might read on their faces the secret of their vices ; and they ceaselessly denounced him as a disturber of the peace.

Yet strangers hastened to the spot, not only from the ends of Italy, but from Germany and countries bordering on the Mediterranean. Coming from afar, they would rebuke the citizens of Rovereto for their indifference, their hardness of heart :

" How is it," they would exclaim, " that we face fatigue and the expenses of a long journey out of love for this great man, while you, who have been lucky enough to have him in your midst, take no account of it, and feel ashamed to pay him homage ! "

But the time had gone when such demonstrations could influence the mind. The doyen and his accomplices had intrigued so effectively that people even ceased to observe good manners, they broke out into criticism and gross abuse :

" Who is this vagabond ? " they asked. " Where does he come from ? Does he really know anything ? None of his patients is what he calls healed. . . . He roams over Europe, distributing gold coins and muttering here and there grotesque formulæ, over which people pretend to go into ecstacies. As a matter of fact, which of us has not that sort of genius ? His miracles are applauded everywhere. Why, then, does he not favour *us* with some ? "

If anyone were to refer to his brilliant reputation :

" All right, but you would scarcely have heard of him but for that affair of the necklace ! His fame was born in gaol, and that strange commotion which accompanies him is that of the chains which they had fixed on him. . . ."

A little while after, the senior physician scored a definite victory. Joseph II, under the severest penalties, prohibited Cagliostro from carrying on his practice at Rovereto. And the ever ungrateful mob applauded this news :

" Long live our Lord the Emperor and King ! like a kind father he watcheth from afar over our welfare. For all those who have had the imprudence to trust themselves to the stranger are either dead or dying. . . ."

Cagliostro who, as he had lately announced in a celebrated pamphlet, invariably submitted to government orders, thereupon sent all his patients home.

. . . .

After a month of patient observation, Vannetti was still without a key to the mystery. How readable were the classical authors even in their most obscure passages ! How pleasant and easy to translate Cicero accurately ! . . . But the Chevalier had observed so many troublesome facts about Cagliostro, that he gave up the effort to form an opinion, and reserved his judgment. Such restraint displeased the vulgar, impatient by nature and grossly dogmatic. An official, a friend of the doyen, and a man who attacked Cagliostro everywhere, was yet anxious to probe to the truth of the matter. He questioned the permanent secretary somewhat brusquely, and Clementino replied with great politeness :

" You must excuse me. I feel incapable at present of judging a man who arouses such diverse sentiments. There are not two citizens who think alike about him."

Assuredly, the Count was a very complex subject. Like the triple Hecate, he had three different aspects. Physician and philanthropist, he was besides a master deeply versed in the occult sciences. Of the three personalities, the philanthropist was the most highly esteemed. The whole province paid a tribute to his generosity, with so unanimous a voice that even his enemies dared not dispute it. Not only did he decline all payment, but he insisted on similar disinterestedness in his servants. One who had been with him for fifteen years, was discharged for having accepted some tips. To which, the irreconcilables would promptly reply :

" All right, we grant you the clever fox takes no recompense, but that is because he prefers to mulct some rich dupe from time to time. See how he has exploited Cardinal de Rohan at Strasbourg and M. Sarasin the younger at Basle. Wherever he goes, he remains only so long as public opinion tolerates him. Then, when his victims begin to find out the fatuity of his promises, when they begin to rebel against him, he decamps hurriedly and wanders from place to place, so that his frauds never cease. He passes himself off as an all-wise doctor, pretending to have captured the mysterious energies which emanate from the spirit world. But if he really had such powers, wouldn't our kings have long since given him a post in their courts ? As for his servant, never has anyone been discharged who showed less contrition. That fellow has gone to wait for his master somewhere, sure of getting back his job one day."

Such insinuations were easily credited in an ecclesiastical province, where the Count had committed the unforgivable mistake of exposing himself to the suspicion of heresy. A few lucky words had at first put them off the scent. Cagliostro caused it to be well known that he advised the young soldier to thank the omnipotent God for his cure. Nor did he forget, every day, when he sent away his patients after their consultations, to make an elaborate sign of the cross over them. Yet, after all, he scarcely ever attended Mass, and he ran away from the Holy Altar. Did he really have a dispensation, as he alleged ? No one believed it. And when they asked him if he were a Jew or a Mussulman :

" What do these denominations matter to you, my dear son ? " he would reply. " Follow me and I will show you the indelible mark left by each of these beliefs in our history."

It was said that he looked upon all religions, beneath their apparent diversity, as the rays of one single and universal religion, varying according to race, customs, climate and age. As for Clementino Vannetti, he refrained from collecting these precepts, for fear of compromising the *Accademia degli Agiati.* But each day, after sunset, zealous neophytes gathered round, to whom the Master would hold forth at great length on his teaching. Among them was Battista, brother of Nicola, and a gentleman from Vicenza named Eligio. One evening they took the Count away to an inn where they liked to meet. The windows were barred, and no sooner had the Count seen them, than he cried out that the vile ironwork reminded him of the Bastille, and ran away precipitately !

Since then, their meetings were held by preference at Battista's, and still more often at the *casa* Festi, in the Count's own apartments. Cagliostro delighted to recount to them the wonders with which he had filled the world. On one occasion, however, Battista feared that the Master was less than truthful. Cagliostro was telling how once, in London, he had annihilated one of his detractors simply by exclaiming :

" By the Grand Architect of the Universe, let him who has taken a false oath among us fall stark dead on the spot ! "

At these words, Battista got up with an extremely annoyed expression :

" Let us go, dear Eligio. The Master is trifling with us to-day."

This anecdote having gone the round of Rovereto, some people made use of it to identify Cagliostro with the lesser impostor Elymas, who had dared to battle against St. Paul at Paphos. But the best judges agreed with Clementino Vannetti, who said :

" The Count is doubtless a member of the brotherhood of Freemasons. They have given him a mandate to heal the sick. And as we are assured that charity is one of their main principles, it maybe his largesses come from their coffers."

The Count was readier to expatiate on alchemy than to explain this point. Skilled in the spagyric art, he told them how metals may be transmuted, how gold may be made fluid as mercury, or inversely, rendered solid. In Switzerland, he said, impressed by the enormous stores of gold and silver and rock crystal concealed behind the eternal snows of the Alps—a treasure better guarded by our indolence than by any gnomes—he had offered to extract those riches at his own risk and peril, provided the magistrates would assign to him, in return, ten years of the public revenue. But the numskulls were appalled at the price he asked for his services, and showed him out of the door.

Someone asked :

" How would you have melted the ice ? "

" Parbleu ! with vinegar. . . ."

And Battista remarked :

" Perhaps the Swiss were afraid that when their snows suddenly melted, the torrents would flood their towns and fields."

" Not at all," replied the Count, after a little thought, " there are plenty of lakes in Switzerland, and I should have diverted the enormous mass of water into them."

The conversation would often turn on the numerous aerial experiments then being made in France. The Count was interested in celestial explorations. In regard to the balloonists, he made the following prediction :

" How to steer the balloons, these flying globes which have been built by an enterprising man ? I will tell you. To steer them as easily as ships, it is necessary to abandon their spherical shape ; but no one knows it at this moment."

Being obliged to give up medicine, he contented himself with sprinkling his listeners with the dew of his mysticism. He talked to them freely of the Egyptian Rite, of which he was Grand Master, and which too many still confused with the dreaded Bavarian sect of Illuminists. A man whom some of Cagliostro's friends tried to sound on the subject, excused himself apologetically. He would much rather, he said, fumble in the dark than let himself be blinded by a dazzling light.

Others were less discreet. Felix Baroni, an ardent Freemason, wished to give a magnificent supper at his house in Sacco in honour of one of his friends. The Count and the Countess were invited to it. The revelry continued far into the night, as was proved by the innumerable candles whose light filtered through the blinds and curtains. At length, unable to resist their curiosity, the villagers had begun to peep through the doors and windows. They claimed that they saw flaming crosses and unsheathed swords, while the company, cloaked in red, were toying with glasses of blood. One was assured that Felix Baroni's little daughter, intrigued by the preparations, had hidden herself in a cupboard, and overheard many strange tales.

Probably an enquiry would have been ordered if the scandal had not taken an edifying turn. The Countess de Cagliostro returned to God. All through Mass at San Marco, the congregation saw her praying and shedding copious tears on the floor. And when the priest spoke of the Kingdom of God, it was with relief that she learnt that the place reserved for the repentant sinner was not less glorious than that of the righteous.

Meanwhile, Serafina was living like a recluse. Confined to her house, with her jewels and her elixirs, she received no one for fear of thieves. The Count's enemies considered themselves bound to hate her as the accomplice of a charlatan. But her simplicity and frankness, her grace, her pretty and regular features, her admirable complexion, prevailed in her favour. Clementino Vannetti himself looked at her benevolently when she entered the thaumaturge's room, immediately transfiguring it by her grace. Twenty years ago she must have been ravishing. In spite of her careworn features, her eyes red with vigils and tears, she had not altogether lost the charm of youth. Her spirit seemed flexible and ardent as a flame. Even though she was timidly deferential towards her husband, she spoke of him with pride.

"He can cure anything," she would repeat, "except death."

Superficially, nothing seemed to disturb the harmony of their household. While opening his letters, the Count would sometimes cry out to her:

"Look, Serafina, come here! . . . the Lord strikes our enemies and rewards our friends. . . ."

And then she would share in his happiness.

All the same, now that their mission was over, they had to leave Rovereto, to help other miserable creatures, and relieve other sorrows, for it is the quality of benevolence to shine indefinitely. The Countess did not conceal her desire to see Rome, her native town, once more, and there embrace her old parents from whom she had been separated for twenty years. But it was not for her to choose. May the will of the Master be accomplished, and not her own!

. . . .

At the beginning of November, Cagliostro crossed the Adige for the last time. He visited different places in the Val Lagarina, where many sick people, afraid to consult him at Rovereto in defiance of the Imperial order, were waiting for him. His inspection over, he returned to the *casa* Festi. Two days after, on Thursday the 11th November, 1788, at nine o'clock in the morning, the Count and the Countess got into their carriage. It was very cold. Between the Monte Baldo and the Pasubio, the *tramontane*, already icy, was blowing violently. Cagliostro was about to seat himself beside his wife when someone pushed through the crowd.

It was the servant who had been discharged a few weeks before. Now the Count knew that the rascal, hiding himself in a stable, had been selling ointments and electuaries, with the words:

"May the peace of God never more descend upon me if I do not effect the same miracles as my master."

And yet here he was, impudent enough to say bon voyage to his master and mistress! The Count waved him aside with an angry gesture:

"Back, rascal! get out of my sight!"

Then standing at the door, he took off his hat to the crowd:

"Gentlemen, please beg your fellow-citizens to excuse their most humble servant if he does not seem to have brought them all the satisfaction that they deserve. At any rate, the Count de Cagliostro applied himself to it with all his zeal, and his heart was to the end sincerely at their service. . . ."

A fanfare of trumpets cut him short. The coachman set the horses going with an elaborate flourish of the whip. As the carriage vanished in the direction of Vienna, the rumour spread that the Count was going to throw himself at the feet of the Emperor. But the same evening it was known that he had reached Trente, and been received very respectfully by the Prince-Bishop.

After that, various persons tried to draw up a balance-sheet for the forty-seven days he had spent at Rovereto. A very difficult business. It escaped any rigorous estimate. One did not even know which of his patients had been positively cured. In comparison with the Count's enormous spiritual attraction, the results seemed but mediocre. But, perhaps, fairly to judge a man so different from others, one must wait until his end was known. . . .

. . . .

Now that his rival had gone, did Clementino Vannetti feel any real satisfaction? True, his beloved Rovereto was his again, but one infidelity had been enough to break for ever the innocent charm of their loves. Besides, his rival having become the subject of his biography, Vannetti would have been quite happy that he should stay until he had finished his work. Information was sent to him in abundance, and the excellent Ippolito Pindemonte had not failed in any of his promises, but, in spite of it all, Vannetti was grieved that the thaumaturge was no longer under his observation.

At the *Accademia*, one never spoke of Cagliostro, whether because the name of the adventurer was unworthy to be mentioned at its sessions, or because the *Agiati* awaited an expression of opinion from their permanent secretary of whose assiduous visits to the inn, and then to the *casa* Festi, they were not unaware. Clementino thus lived in the conviction that his colleagues were not in any way jealous of his eminence.

Imagine, then, his surprise, when, about a week after the mysterious love-feast at Felix Baroni's, one of the *Agiati*, named Gianviglio Giannini, asked permission to recite a poem he had composed! . . . It was a delightful poem, picturesque and facetious, and greatly entertained the scholarly audience. Vannetti himself could not withhold his congratulations.

The first quatrain described Cagliostro in his characteristic surroundings. He was seen among his acolytes, pompously inaugurating an Egyptian Lodge. Upright, with his face towards the altar, the necromancer was officiating. His fillet and stole of black velvet contrasted strikingly with the dalmatic and the mitre of gold brocade. Dressed in white linen, the officiants marched ceremonially between the torches and the naked swords. With their faces turned, in accordance with the ritual, towards the septentrional, they held their oboluses in their hands. And each one, passing behind the high-priest, gave him the obscene and ridiculous kiss which the sorcerers, in the moonless nights of the Sabbath, do not refuse their master, Satan Trismegistus :

E al trismegisto lor con oro in mano,
Chiudendo il rito a l'Aquilon rivolti,
Baciavan d'ambo i lati il deretano. . . .

To Vannetti's great chagrin, the applause at this point was long. He thought his subject was being irretrievably ruined. Until that day, he had avoided taking Donna Bianca-Laura into his confidence. Authoritative and vehement, the old lady would have thought it a crime in him to have abandoned the *Life of Cicero*, which she anticipated would be a masterpiece. Moreover, her piety was so austere that the Chevalier had not ventured to speak to her about Cagliostro. All the same, when he returned, excited, from the *Accademia*, he threw himself into her arms. In the absence of his usual advisers, Ippolito Pindemonte and the Abbé Pederzani, it was to her that he looked for advice and consolation. Donna Bianca-Laura responded perfectly to his appeal. She at once understood what her rôle should be. " No," she declared, in her grave, heroic voice, the voice of a fighting Clorinde, " nothing is lost." The welcome given to the sonnet proved that Clementino's notes must be made use of before the public grew tired of the enchanter. That was all. There was no need at all for a huge tome. What was wanted was a light satire, a good-humoured fantasy like his father's trifles, the *Ninfa del Leno* and the *Barbologia*. Such a work was bound to be a success, and Clementino would find at his feet all those who had burned incense before Gianviglio Giannini.

The permanent secretary agreed with her. That very night he set to work. In a few hours, with an ease and a wealth of vocabulary at which he himself was astonished, he improvised a narrative in Latin. Without love and without hate, careful not to add or suppress anything, he put down all that he had seen and heard, all the rumours that had run through the town during the sojourn of the Count and the Countess. He expressed no personal opinion, but left the reader to judge for himself. And out of scrupulous honesty, Clementino acknowledged that he had never had personal relations with his subject.

To his pure Latin style, he added some naïve phrases which had amused him in the *Life of Æsop*, written by a Byzantine monk named Planude. But the many readers who knew nothing of that old author, took the book to be a parody of Holy Scripture, for it was couched in Biblical style ; and they protested against it. In vain did Clementino cite Planude, his real inspirer ; his timid, ignorant critics invariably cited the New Testament.

" You profane the words of Christ ! "

" Not at all. I neither misuse them nor quote them frivolously, and nowhere do I alter the texts on which our religion is founded."

Clementino added that the process of literary composition had nothing to do with the divine inspiration on which Scripture was based.

" The same stones are used without distinction for houses and for temples. From the same gold, you can make either a cup or a chalice. The Apostles did not change the style of the words they put into the mouth of Jesus, or Simon the Magician, or Theodatus."

" But why have you used precisely this form ? "

" Because of its expressiveness. Nothing else suggests so strongly what many people murmured in the presence of my hero : ' Here is a donkey in lion's skin ! ' Read what Planude the Byzantine has written about Æsop. You will see that no style is the monopoly of Scripture. And do not forget that Planude was a monk. . . ."

But the pious shook their heads, and their hostility exceeded all bounds when the brief memoir came out under the title : *Liber Memorialis de Cagliostro cum esset Roboreti*. Planude, the obscure monk, was ignored. Out of respect for Scripture, they condemned in sorrow what seemed to them an indecent imitation. At first Vannetti pretended to ignore this uproar. He wrote to Ippolito Pindemonte :

" I have written, besides, a kind of Latin chronicle after the manner of Planude, on the exploits of Cagliostro, who spent forty-six days at Rovereto. I shall send you a copy with pleasure."

But some months later, dropping his affected indifference and calm, he told Ippolito the vexations which his brochure had brought upon him :

" The majority of the lettered folk and the ecclesiastics, with the exception of a few friends, cannot forgive me for the style I have used. They say, in their fury, that I have crucified Christ. A little more of this and my book, denounced before the Bishop, would be burned publicly. Some lead the crusade ; others, falling in behind these zealots, fan the flames. Judge for yourself, you who have taken the trouble to read Chapter XV attentively, the stupidity and absurdity of all this uproar. But though the fanatics are angry, reprints have followed one another quickly at Vienna and Milan. There has even appeared in Milan an Italian translation which the journals of Rome, Florence, Pisa, etc., agree in praising."

Confident in the knowledge that he had not parodied Scripture, the Chevalier had a clear conscience. Moreover, Donna Bianca-Laura, who was inflexible in religious matters, supported him warmly. Those who protested to her about the alleged blasphemy, she referred to Planude, or rather to the *Ninfa del Leno* and the *Barbologia* ; for her Clementino, she said, had been much more inspired by these playful trifles than by Holy Scripture.

In the end, extending his powerful hand, the supreme arbiter, Pius VI, shut the mouths of the calumniators. At the first rumour of this affair, His Holiness recollected the wonderful young man who had been presented to him, in 1782, at Rovereto. He ordered his librarians to submit to him the incriminating booklet. And the sovereign pontiff derived such lively pleasure from it, that he condescended to read it four times, and each time with added delight. Immediately, the troubled consciences were stilled, and no suggestion was thereafter made of burning the *Liber Memorialis*.

Nevertheless, good Latinists continued to open their conversations with the question :

" Have you read the Gospel of Cagliostro ? "

That name prevailed, in spite of the author's protests. And the fame of Clementino Vannetti spread through Europe.

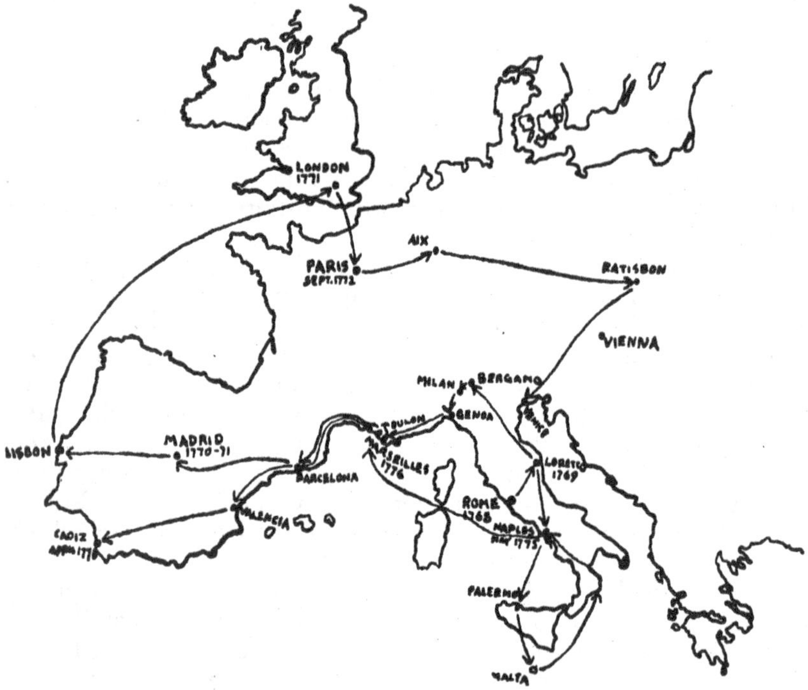

TRAVELS OF GIUSEPPE BALSAMO

IV

EARLY LIFE AND ADVENTURES

LET no one do him the injury of supposing that Vannetti regarded the *Liber Memorialis* with blind complacency: he was extremely critical of his own writings. It is true that, as soon as it was published, his Latin chronicle had completely put into the shade Gianviglio Giannini's little poem, and Donna Bianca-Laura's predictions had been fulfilled in every particular. But such a success, obtained without effort, and even at the price of a scandal, offended his modesty. In his view, those ephemeral sheets, scribbled on the spur of the moment, were no substitute for the big book he was thinking of writing on the Count de Cagliostro. This pamphlet was a mere introduction, a faithful statement by an eye-witness—nothing more. He had not touched upon the essential problem. But he certainly hoped to deal with it at length in his next work, for, to Vannetti as to the rest of the world, the question was whether, as was coolly being maintained by the *Courrier de l'Europe*, the Count Alexander de Cagliostro was formerly known as Giuseppe Balsamo.

Vannetti's idea of his work became clearer in proportion as he accumulated copies of public documents and private letters. By their amount and variety, they formed an inextricable labyrinth, through which he would never have found his way, but for this Ariadne's thread : the flexible and steadfast method he had acquired from his masters. After studying the adventures of Giuseppe Balsamo, one by one, he wished to proceed likewise with the Count de Cagliostro. Then, by putting the two side by side, he hoped to elicit the spark of truth.

Would he thus avoid falling into the common error ? At Rovereto, since the departure of the Count, the followers of the leading physician swore by the *Courrier de l'Europe*. To them this infamous sheet was as the Law and the Prophets. Without any more reliable authority than that for their prejudices, they denounced Cagliostro as an impostor. The best detectives, they affirmed, considered him to be the artist Giuseppe Balsamo, born in Palermo. And upon that, they would crow in triumph, for many inhabitants of Rovereto judged Cagliostro, by his speech and complexion, to be an Italian from the south, a Calabrian or a Sicilian.

The latest issues of the *Courrier de l'Europe* were no doubt disconcerting, but Clementino Vannetti preferred to reserve his judgment. The journalists had gone astray too often. Before discovering Balsamo, they had mentioned other names, and coupled Cagliostro with a certain Tiscio, a certain Balthymore. Warned by these mistakes, Clementino intended to test the latest report thoroughly.

. . . .

According to trustworthy evidence, Giuseppe Balsamo was born in Palermo, on the 2nd June, 1743, to a tradesman named Pietro Balsamo, and his lawful spouse, Felice Bracconeri. On the 8th June, in the presence of his godfather, Giovanni-Battista Barone, a Genoan settled in Palermo, and Giuseppina Basile, who was authorised to act for his godmother, Vincenza Cagliostro, the infant was baptised in the metropolitan church under the names of Giuseppe, Giovanni-Battista, Vincenzo, Pietro, Antonio and Matteo.

In an island where nature was kind and indulgent, Pietro Balsamo, the bookseller's son, led but a pitiable existence. He had neither ability nor fortune, and being, besides, of weak health, he made no more than enough to maintain his wife and his children, for he had also a daughter, Marie-Anne.

Poor as the family was, it consoled itself for its hardships with vague fancies. Among the ancestors of the Balsamos were some dignitaries of the crown of Sicily, and several knights of Malta. The Braconneri, for their part, claimed noble descent; Felice herself, would at times draw, with her untutored hands, the family escutcheon. On her mother's side, she belonged to the Martellos, who were descended from Charles Martel. And as her aunt, Vincenza Martello, had married the Prince of Villafranca's private agent, Giuseppe Cagliostro, the Balsamos, proud of their connections, had eagerly chosen this rich and respectable lady to be the infant's godmother.

Not long after, Pietro Balsamo's health broke down completely, and his business was in danger. Insolvency seemed imminent; whether he was able to avoid it is not known. Only this is certain: he died in his forty-seventh year, and heedlessly the earth opened to receive his remains.

His father-in-law readily gave shelter to his widow and children. Old Giuseppe Bracconeri was, indeed, considered to be a very good man. His sons, Matteo, who was employed in the postal service, and Antonio, a book-keeper in the firm of Gian-Francesco Aubert and Co., had both stainless reputations. He showed much affection for his little grandchildren, and specially for Giuseppe who, he hoped, would one day be able to support his mother and sister.

When the infant was old enough, it was sent to the seminary of

San Rocco where the masters were learned and pious men. But though he had a precocious intellect, Giuseppe shrank from study. He took little interest in sacred history or the catechism.

Old Bracconeri died in 1754, and the child passed under the care of his maternal uncles. He was about thirteen years old when the Father Superior of the Benfratelli, meeting him during a visit to Palermo, was astonished at the as yet undeveloped but brilliant gifts which he discerned in Giuseppe. Hoping to have more success with him than the masters of San Rocco had had, he arranged with the family to remove him from the seminary, and when he left Palermo, took young Balsamo with him.

At the convent of Caltagirone, Guiseppe was given a novice's robes, and put under the care of the brother apothecary, who was very highly esteemed in the community. The Benfratelli, Brothers of Charity, were the guardians of public health, physicians and healers, in the half-deserted countryside. Every day, mortar in hand, the apprentice had to grind and powder and crush the drugs. Under his preceptor's eyes, he mixed unguents and ointments. He watched over the elixirs as they simmered in the crucibles. After having used the pill-machine and the spatula, he would compose the electuaries which, by dint of effort, the monks had brought to a high state of perfection. And the Father Superior rejoiced at having tamed this restless spirit.

But already, tormented by the frailty of the flesh, Balsamo was chafing against the monastic discipline. And when he was required, as a penance, to read aloud in the open refectory, the sinner had the impudence to mingle with the saints of the martyrology the names of the most notorious prostitutes in Caltagirone. Naturally the prank called for correction. But Giuseppe's pride was in revolt. Rather than bend his head and bow his knee, the little Lucifer took to flight. His mother and his uncles saw him back in Palermo with pained astonishment. An attempt was then made to keep him in a Capuchin convent, but his charms did not please the good fathers, and he was soon thrown out. Thereupon, he boastfully said that he meant to become an artist.

He certainly had an exceptional eye and hand, and some of the best artists approved of his desire to devote himself to painting. But he lacked application. His dissolute employments kept him away from the studio. In company with vagabonds who were surely destined for the gallows, he would frequent the taverns where the rowdies and the prostitutes gathered, and if some violent brawl broke out, he would plunge furiously into the mêlée, and, thanks to an exceptional cunning, emerge unscathed. When he had a number of cronies about him, he would attack the police. And what a triumph it was, when, perchance, after thrashing the officers, he could carry some away as his prisoners!

As he paid no heed to their remonstrances, his relatives disowned him, and he took to indecent ways of making a living. Acting as a go-between, he would explain to the lovers that their mistresses wanted fine linen, and wraps, and gloves and lace, and perfumed water, collars and gold watches. And instead of delivering these little gifts into the proper hands, he would keep them for himself as compensation for his pains.

Soon Giuseppe Balsamo had acquired a halo. Every offence committed in the town was ascribed to this scapegrace. Chiefly, he was accused of one form or other of forgery: falsification of a will in the interest of a Marquis Maurigi, the sale of forged theatre tickets, the supply of false permits to monks who wished to leave the cloister. Also, he was supposed to have robbed one of his uncles, and been implicated in the murder of a canon. There was no proof for these suspicions, but they showed, at any rate, that he had a shady reputation. Though he defied human laws, the wicked fellow had not, so far, forfeited his right to divine compassion. The sinner was not yet a reprobate. But some curious events were soon to show him in a more sinister light.

As a novice at Caltagirone, the brother apothecary's lessons had stirred his mind. True, he had not really tried to learn anything. But however uncongenial studies were, a certain kind of knowledge had always fascinated him. In astrology, alchemy, the cabala and magic, he had taken a passionate interest.

Nothing definite was known, but there were some facts which justified the most damaging suspicions. Soon after his return to Palermo, he had tried to steal from a village priest a bit of cotton which had been soaked in holy oils. Why? To exorcise his sister, he said insolently, when he was questioned. But Maria Anna, that big, placid, healthy, somewhat bovine girl, had nothing demoniacal about her. She was just getting ready for her marriage with an honest fellow named Capitummino.

One evening, while walking in the fields with a merry crowd, Balsamo offered to evoke the form of a girl friend of one of his companions. They challenged him to do so. . . . There he was at once on all fours, drawing a pentagon on the ground with a piece of charcoal. Rising to his feet, he gesticulated violently and uttered strange, exotic words. A thin mist at first, then a shadow, a semi-luminous figure, and then, in the end, there appeared an image visible to all eyes. Sitting in a room, a woman was playing *tre-sept* with two men. A solemn silence reigned. Scarcely did the wind moan sweet and sad through the ilexes. And the spectators gazed, and gazed endlessly, transfixed with wonder. When the phantom vanished, they hurried to the lady's villa, which was close by. And there she was, sitting just as they had seen her, with the same expression on her face, in the same attitude, joking and laughing with the same partners. . . .

Giuseppe Balsamo thus gained the reputation of an enchanter,

Religious men avoided him ; others, less scrupulous, tried to turn his secrets to their own profit.

The goldsmith, Vincenzo Marano, a rich and greedy miser, spent his life looking for hidden treasure. In that island, which had often been conquered, and the vanquished had had to conceal their most precious belongings, treasure-hunting was a common pastime. The goldsmith thought he could discover a fortune by digging in likely places. In hopes that the young magician might be of great assistance, he went to consult him. Balsamo first accepted a bribe of sixty ounces of gold, and told him of an enormous treasure hidden at the bottom of a ditch, not far from Palermo. All the details of the enterprise were settled between them. At the appointed hour, that is to say, at the stroke of midnight, the confederates set out, armed with spades and dark lanterns.

Beyond the outskirts there was some enclosed waste land, which they entered stealthily. Giuseppe drew cabalistic signs on the grass. Everything was in their favour : the hour, the solitude, the aspect of the sky, the position of the stars. . . . Balsamo had just begun to intone his formulæ with redoubled vigour when the bewildered goldsmith felt a hard and murderous hail of blows on his shoulder. Ten or twelve devils, more horned than the goats of the Sabbath, thrashed him rhythmically to teach him, as they screamed, what it costs to try to get rich by unlawful methods.

At dawn, when phantoms and all hideous nightmares vanish, Marano, gasping, called out for his enchanter. He expected to find him by his side, covered, like himself, with blood and contusions. There was no answer : Balsamo had disappeared. The poor man was bewildered. Then, with an effort, he seemed to recollect that one of the devils had been remarkably like a friend of Balsamo's. Slowly he began to see light ; slowly he began to suspect that the devils had only been conjured by the magician to repay him those sixty ounces of gold with as many cudgel blows. In short, when he reached home, furious with anger, he told everybody of the trickery to which he had been victimised, and vowed to take exemplary vengeance.

Balsamo became alarmed. It was known that Marano was capable of anything. But never had life seemed so sweet to the youth, never had he less desire to lose it. So the best course, he thought, was to take flight. Pretending to go to Messina to claim a legacy left him by his great-uncle, Giuseppe Cagliostro, Vincenza Martello's husband, he bolted off.

. . . .

From the date of that flight, collate the evidence as he might, Vannetti could not reach even approximate certitude about anything.

Apparently Giuseppe Balsamo left Calabria with two persons as badly compromised as himself in the comedy of the treasure-hunt :

a rascally valet and a licentious priest. More cunning than he, his accomplices had before long deprived him of the money he had extorted from Marano. Finding himself penniless, he had made up his mind to walk to Rome, where painters and draftsmen had, at any rate, the chance of making an honest living. He arrived there early in 1768, and lodged at a low haunt called the *albergo del Sole all Rotonda.*

Vannetti saw all too many gaps in this account. At the time he left Palermo, Balsamo was twenty years old ; when he came to Rome, he was twenty-four. Where had he spent the intervening four or five years ? Had he been travelling in distant lands ? It may be that he went, as he said, to Malta, to gain the goodwill of Don Manoel Pinto d'Alfonseca, for no sooner had he settled in Rome than he conveyed to Baron de Bretteville, the Maltese ambassador, a note of recommendation from the Grand Master. But, as a matter of fact, the rogue was quite capable of forging a signature.

When he went to see the Cardinals of York and Orsini, to whom also he had letters of introduction, the major-domo kept him waiting for a long time, standing in the ante-chamber with the humble folk, who were forbidden to sit on the velvet benches. But his interview with Cardinal Orsini was not long without result. It was rumoured that the Prince of the Church had admitted him into his service. A very respectable person, the musician Ricciarelli, subsequently declared that he had met Balsamo at His Eminence's.

Opinions varied as to his artistic merit. Some said that Balsamo would sell as original work engravings and printed sketches which he had merely touched up with some India ink. On the contrary, others praised his skill. No one knew so much about copying a print, they said. His sketches had the finish of an engraving ; his fans, the delicacy of miniatures. He had not an equal in the world for reproducing a Rembrandt. In that respect, his talent was wonderful. But what a dangerous temptation for an unprincipled man ! Can one imagine an artist whose supreme masterpiece might be no more than a fake ? Whatever it may be, his work was much in demand. A nobleman of Venice, Pietro Zaguri, proudly displayed a beautiful sketch by Balsamo, *Venus et Adonis.*

Creative faculties, thought Vannetti, must soon become atrophied in a lazy man. Balsamo achieved success not in invention, but in imitation, and when he was commissioned to decorate a country house in England, he had failed miserably.

Balsamo was foolish enough to become embroiled with a servant at the *albergo del Sole.* Was protection from high quarters extended in his favour ? In three days he was released from prison, and came out very cheerfully. Emerging, as he did, from a cell infested with cockroaches and centipedes, he relished but the more keenly the beauty of the sunlit Roman hills.

Turning from the Ponte Sisto, he would enter every evening the Piazza del Monte di Pieta by the Strada dei Pellegrini, which was a low and crowded quarter, where poor pilgrims used to halt in the certainty of finding bed and board at cheap rates. But if Balsamo loitered among those clammy walls and sordid booths, it was not by any means to light a candle at San Carlo dei Catinari, or kneel at the Santa Trinita dei Pellegrini. One day he had seen coming out of the half-open doors of San Salvatore in Campo, a lovely child, beautiful as an angel, and, with the volcanic impetuosity of his race, he had immediately fallen in love with her.

The girl, who was about fifteen years old, had a pure complexion, and a delicate, slightly aquiline nose. Very fair, with blue eyes, and hair bright as chestnut, she represented a type of beauty very rare in Italy, and hence the more appreciated.

Balsamo, whom she passed with her graceful walk, followed her as far as the vicolo delle Cripte, where she entered a mean shop, and shutting the door behind her, vanished. When he returned the next day, Balsamo caught sight of her standing, between two pots of basil, at a garret window. He conveyed to her, with his ardent eyes, the feelings she had aroused in him. His advances were accepted, and a conversation ensued.

Lorenza was the daughter of Giuseppe and Pasqua Feliciani. Her father was a copper founder, an unusual and obscure trade, leading to nowhere. Pious and conscientious artisans as they were, the Felicianis brought up their daughter and young son Francesco to be well-behaved, and to observe the law and the precepts of religion. Pasqua Feliciani jealously watched over the virtue of her charming Lorenza. But in spite of everything that the parents might do, the children did not grow up aright.

Besides, ordinary precautions were of no use against a suitor who had, at Palermo, learnt all the tricks of love. A Neapolitan friend of Balsamo lived some distance away from the Feliciani. Out of the kindness of his heart, and for a little money, this man put at their disposal an attic where Lorenza could meet her lover whenever she wished.

"To put the plough before the oxen," as they naïvely say in their tongue, did not seem an unpardonable sin to these simple lovers, for they were really determined to be married according to the sacraments. Besides, Lorenza wished to forestall the opposition of her family by taking an irrevocable step. Otherwise her parents might never have consented to accept as their son-in-law a dirty vagabond whose means of livelihood, notwithstanding the patronage of a Cardinal, remained problematic. When, finally, Balsamo asked for their permission, Lorenza was already being talked about a good deal, and the Feliciani had to give in with the best grace they could. Having commended their daughter to the Madonna del Carmina, their special protectress, they gave their consent to everything. And on the 20th April, the wedding was celebrated at San Salvatore in Campo.

The next day, Feliciani made over to his daughter, in the presence of the notary Guadenzio, a dowry of a hundred and fifty scudi in the shape of a trousseau, jewellery, linen and cash. Balsamo, on his part, in proof of his ardent love, gave his beloved wife an equivalent dowry. Lorenza heard these figures as in a dream. Three hundred scudi in goods and money for her alone! A fortune, immense, inexhaustible, fabulous, worthy of gods and fairies!

The husband, however, was sunk in misery. Would it suffice to meet the bills? To draw from morning till evening, and even at night; to wear out his eyes copying prints by candle-light; then to wander through the town looking for purchasers—and all merely to make both ends meet. Alas, what a prospect! So when his father-in-law invited him and Lorenza to stay with them, he hastily accepted the offer.

But it did not turn out very well. The Feliciani could not bear his airs, his ideas, his impertinences of conduct and speech. And the artist complained that he was bored to death with these stupid artisans. He only had sympathy for Francesco, whose charming sprightliness he relished. This handsome but effeminate boy was like Lorenza in character as in physique. Balsamo could not bear the other members of the family. One fine day, throwing to the winds both economy and discretion, he left the house with his wife. Furious at losing their daughter, the Feliciani revenged themselves by slandering him everywhere. The very week that he married, they exclaimed, the libertine attacked their washerwoman, an honest and good creature who brought in the family washing without an evil thought in her head. Besides, he tried to pervert his wife with horrible persistence. How often had their poor darling had to resist his diabolical influence? No sturdier than their canary, hopping about between its fishbone and its lettuce leaf, Lorenza had to listen to a monstrous string of sophisms. A woman of experience, her corrupter told her, would readily give herself to a wealthy and generous lover, if her husband did not object. Nor would there be any breach of marital vows, for real adultery only began where love began. Where there was none of the delirium and the intoxication of the senses, no passionate connivance of the soul, there was neither perjury nor mortal sin. In the interest of the community, a discreet spouse might therefore condescend to small compliances in which her heart had no share. And in virtue of these fine maxims, the Sicilian exhorted her not to discourage her lovers.

When their funds were all gone, Balsamo himself introduced Lorenza to opulent and libidinous noblemen who might appreciate her supple figure, her innocent blue eyes, and her blonde hair. And if, sobbing, she rejected them, woe to her! Balsamo would jump out like a devil from an adjoining closet, and appal her with his threats and his abuse, sometimes even beating her. Dazed and terror-stricken, Lorenza had not had the courage to deny herself to the Maltese ambassador.

Balsamo liked no company better than that of his own countrymen. Two Panormitans, Giuseppe Cazzola and Gaspare Martelli, had been present at his wedding. These two, at any rate, good men both, did honour to their country. But later, Balsamo became friendly with a scamp named Ottavio Nicastro, who fascinated him with his Sicilian fluency. In Balsamo's eyes, the rogue was as diverting as any comedy. One knows not which Norman or Angevin ancestor had bequeathed to him his red complexion and his hooked nose, his wondering choir-lad expression that was at once so naïve and insolent. His buffooneries set Balsamo roaring with laughter. But when he heard that Nicastro would have been nothing if he had not been befriended by an infinitely superior person, the " marquis " Agliata, the artist begged his friend to introduce him to the great man.

Agliata proved to be as aloof, secretive and gloomy as Nicastro was simple and jolly. He would have received Balsamo's homage but indifferently, had he not at first caught sight of Lorenza. He at once took the young couple under his protection. For the first time since his apprenticeship to the brother apothecary, Balsamo submitted to a stronger personality. The Marquis expatiated on the prospects open to a skilful artist. As Balsamo was unable to earn a living, he should set about copying something else than prints and paintings....

The fateful hour had struck. Whether he wished it or no, Balsamo was entering the sharp and perilous path whither his evil star drove him.

For hours he would be closeted with Agliata. And no one could guess what they were doing. But Lorenza, in spite of her parents' hatred of Balsamo, was foolish enough to speak to them about it.

The Marquis Agliata, she told them, who was a nobleman of commanding appearance, a Prussian colonel and minister plenipotentiary, had offered Balsamo advantageous posts in Germany : either an Italian secretaryship or a captain's commission in the Prussian army, of which he already had the warrant. The good Cardinal Orsini agreed to their journey, even promising to recommend them to the governors of the cities through which they would be passing. Had it not been for the grief of parting from her parents, Lorenza would have loved to travel and see the world. She added mysteriously that her husband and Agliata had shut themselves up for several weeks in a dark closet. What did they do ? She had seen the Marquis come out one day with vignettes which looked like receipts ; comparing them one with the other, he exclaimed that no one could have done better.

Their darling angel was about to leave them. Lorenza was going away with a scoundrel to distant and barbarous lands. No letters need be expected, she could not write. Giuseppe and Pasqua Feliciani threw themselves at the feet of the Madonna del Carmine. Ah ! if she would but deign to turn towards them with her compassionate face, and tell them what to do. . . . When he finished his prayer, the copper-founder's mind was made up. He rushed off to denounce his son-in-law before the papal authorities.

When he accused Balsamo of forging tickets and false rent receipts, Giuseppe Feliciani was not afraid he might be sending an innocent man to his death, for he had had Lorenza's childish words confirmed with terribly exact details by Ottavio Nicastro in person. Ottavio could not forgive his countryman for having supplanted him in the favour of the Marquis. Indeed, Balsamo, who abused his prophetic powers, had once gratuitously predicted that he would die at the hands of the public executioner, and this pleasantry had seemed to Nicastro to be in unpardonably bad taste. Not only did he tell Feliciani everything, but lodged a complaint against Balsamo in his own behalf. As he had just been implicated in a murder, Ottavio thought it very clever of him to put the police off the scent by volunteering information.

But the *bargello* already had his eye on him. When he reached the police station, the public-spirited informer was at once arrested and put in chains. They examined him, and had to apply the queen of tortures, the torture by rope; then, as his guilt was amply proved, he was speedily convicted and hung. His disclosures went unregarded in the midst of these dreadful proceedings.

Neither Balsamo nor Agliata suspected Feliciani. But Nicastro's fate sent a cold fear through them. They decided immediately to leave for Germany, and escaped on the 20th December, 1769.

Thus, a few months after her wedding, Lorenza was fleeing along the high roads in company with gentlemen who turned pale at the mere sight of a police officer. She herself, considering the extreme danger they were in, felt she could not get away too quickly from Rome. Unfortunately, one had to reckon with the coachmen, who could not be persuaded even by tips to drive at more than a snail's pace. Lorenza sat in the first carriage with the Marquis. Dying with fear as she was, she was not the less willing to reciprocate Agliata's caresses. Balsamo complacently rolled behind, in company with an abbé-secretary and the German valet of the Marquis. Thus, making hardly more than three miles an hour, they crossed Umbria, then the Marches, and arrived safely at Loretto.

. . . .

In that uncertain region, full of snares, where Vannetti was following in the wake of the Balsamo couple, the date 20th December, 1769, was a landmark. That was the beginning of his hegira. The only reliable document to which he could refer was a deposition made by Lorenza at Paris, three years later. Long hidden and forgotten in the archives of the French police, it was unexpectedly produced in 1786, at the time the ministry was busying itself to confirm the *Courrier de l'Europe's* assertion that Cagliostro and Balsamo were identical.

According to this account, the travellers, when they reached Loretto, had boldly introduced themselves to the Governor with a letter from Cardinal Orsini. On reading the letter, the Governor hastened to offer them fifty sequins, which the Marquis gravely put in his pocket. He had, with his own hand, added a postscript to the Cardinal's letter designed to provoke this generosity.

They then went to Bergamo, where they lodged at a respectable inn and announced themselves as recruiting officers of the King of Prussia. Lorenza was just beginning to recover from her fatigue when, on the third day, Agliata and his lackeys disappeared as though by magic. That very evening, a dozen soldiers arrived to arrest Balsamo, his wife and the abbé-secretary. Balsamo had just time to slip into his wife's hand some small notes, begging her to try and save her life with their help. She preferred to hide them in her bosom, and as soon as she was alone in her cell, she tore them into little pieces.

The next day they appeared in the dock before the magistrate. Whence did they come? What did they know of the "marquis" Agliata, of his parentage, his means of livelihood, of the forgeries he had committed? Terrified by his skilful questions, the victims fluttered like butterflies in a net. After thoroughly frightening them, the Venetian magistrate declared that they were free to go where they pleased, but in a voice and manner so crushing that they were ready to sink into the earth.

Balsamo hesitated which way to go. Agliata having vanished, he had to give up thoughts of Germany. Farewell to the fine secretarial posts! Farewell to the captain's epaulettes! Still less attractive was Rome. It was just there that his comrade Nicastro had been convicted, and Cardinal Orsini might now wish to prosecute him for misusing his signature at Loretto. As a crowning calamity, Agliata and his valet had run away with the cash, and the Balsamos were obliged to sell some of their least indispensable personal effects to pay their way to Milan.

In that magnificent and luxurious city the vagabonds might have sunk to the depths of human misery, had not Balsamo had one of those gleams of genius which from time to time revived Lorenza's confidence in and admiration for him. He would disguise his wife as a pilgrim. And, himself taking the pilgrim's cloak, the gourd and the staff, he announced that he and his wife were going to Saint-Jacques de Compostelle, to atone for their sins.

No journey could be less expensive. The Balsamos, familiar with the Strada dei Pelligrini, did not expect to find along the road such superb almshouses as in Rome or Loretto or Bologna, where the pilgrims were generously lodged and fed free for three days, but they hoped to put up at the hostels which religious people maintained at different places, and where one could lie down in proper beds, not overrun with vermin. And as they visited the principal shrines and said their prayers, they would also beg for alms. The voice of the lovely pilgrim who spoke with the peculiar charm of a Roman would not be slow in attracting gifts of gold and silver pieces.

They travelled by easy stages from Lodi to Genoa, and along the Mediterranean. There was some trouble at Savoy, which alarmed them considerably, over a counterfeit note of twenty-five ecus, which Balsamo was accused of having forged. After that, the artist did not venture to put Agliata's teachings into practice, and it was for Lorenza to earn the family bread.

She no longer repulsed her admirers with a blushing tear-stained face. Under Balsamo's training, the "marmotte" had awakened. Her good looks and charm met with some success in France, notably among the garrison at Antibes. They admired her ingenuous appearance, and the sadness which spread over her features a certain softness and pallor, and the angelic manner in which she would lower her eyes if she thought her modesty were involved.

Through Toulon, Aix-en-Provence, Perpignan, they passed, arousing curiosity everywhere. In the streets around their inn, the young Italians would distribute among the poor what they could spare of the alms they received, which included at times some ecus, some louis, and some fine Spanish doubloons, which were given to Lorenza instead of the small sou for which she begged. But the pilgrims desired to show that they lived from hand to mouth, relying on Providence to conduct them in safety to Saint-Jacques de Compostelle.

The pilgrimage came to an abrupt end at Catalonia. And the family in Rome, uneasy at having had no news since December 1769, received from Barcelona a letter in which Balsamo begged them to send him an authentic copy of his marriage certificate.

. . . .

On arrival at Barcelona, Lorenza, finding herself penniless, went to the nearest church for confession. Kneeling in the semi-darkness, she pretended that she and her husband were members of the highest Roman aristocracy. They had had, unfortunately, owing to the stubborn opposition of their relatives, to get married secretly and go abroad, and now a delayed bill of exchange, which they were expecting daily, had put them in a serious embarrassment. It was not without some eloquence that this simple story was related.

The priest who listened with bowed head and hands thrust in his sleeves, was touched by it. He begged the penitent to accept the little that he could spare; and by way of making up for the meagreness of the offer, he added to it a tasty ham. When he went the next day to call on the noble travellers, their words of gratitude gave him a sweet satisfaction. However, as the days went by, and the bill of exchange was still held up, he began to have some suspicions. Were the young people really married ? He did not conceal his uneasiness, and, to escape from the awkward predicament, Balsamo had to send for a copy of his marriage certificate. It was a timely precaution; in Spain, the Holy Inquisition would admit no excuse for the rash creatures who set up house without the sanction of the Church.

According to another version, His Excellency the Count de Ricla, Captain General of Catalonia, had condescended to detain the artist in Barcelona. Delighted with his skill, he had given him commission after commission. In reality, the youthful charm of Lorenza had inspired in him a lively craving. But, though she pretended to share his love, this inhuman creature repulsed him like some austere nun. In four months, the pigeon had stopped cooing and become a vulture. Harassed by his menacing inquiries, the Balsamos were obliged to obtain from Rome, as speedily as they could, a properly made out copy of their marriage certificate.

Those who were best informed about it gave a yet different account. By making the Captain General pine for her love, Lorenza had imagined that she could convert his caprice into a rooted passion.

What a foolish delusion ! Brutal soldier that he was, and long experienced in love affairs, the Count gave her a few days in which to decide either to yield or to leave Catalonia. The next time that he saw her in the Palace in Balsamo's arms, he peremptorily asked her to say yes or no. Blushing, she bent her head ; but Giuseppe pronounced an emphatic " yes " on her behalf, and went off to his painting, leaving Lorenza to the Captain General.

This visit was followed by several others ; but they brought the poor child but little financial reward. . . .

But this straw fire was threatening to go out, and Lorenza thought it her duty to look for another lover. Chance brought her the Marquis de Fontanar. This worthy and generous nobleman, infatuated with her, offered to take the Balsamos to Madrid, where the artist would certainly find a numerous and liberal patronage. His invitation was gladly accepted.

The journey to Madrid was accomplished somewhat after the manner of the journeys to Loretto and Bergamo : Lorenza, alone with her lover in a carriage, and Balsamo, on horseback, trotting at the side. But the Marquis de Fontanar, truly in love as he was, did not share Agliata's cynical lack of restraint. Lorenza took advantage of this to practise the strategy which had failed with the Count de Ricla : she rode the high horse.

At Madrid, the recommendations of the Marquis quickly enabled the Sicilian to earn a living. He worked for the Duke of Alba and other great personages. His naïf patron, utterly subjugated and incapable of tearing himself away even for a single minute from his Lorenza, shared their apartment and their table and drove them in his carriage to the bull ring, the theatre and the bal masque. But one day he realised that they were trifling with him. No doubt, Lorenza gladly accepted his gifts. But what did she give him in return? Seized with one of those violent fits of temper which are liable to overpower timid and sheeplike creatures, he made a terrible scene one day, and Balsamo himself expressed the opinion that Lorenza should show herself a little less inflexible. It was thus that, every morning, as soon as the first rays of light filtered through the blinds, upon a sign from the half-asleep Balsamo, a shadow would rise, and Lorenza, wrapped in a cloak, would steal into the next room. . . .

Thus, between 1770 and 1771, the Balsamos lived very comfortably, free from all material cares. But their sojourn at Madrid was spoiled by the wiles of another Sicilian. The liar said such atrocious things about his compatriot that the artist had to sue him. Lorenza went to the Minister to plead for justice. Don Manuel de Roda received her paternally. Feeling an interest in the beautiful Roman, he questioned her at length. When Lorenza finished the story of their wanderings, Monseigneur ardently offered to take the place of the Marquis de Fontanar. He was no longer the same man; he caressed her hand, sighed, and his big eyes shone like an owl's in the dark. Lorenza was shocked, astounded, and could not conceal her embarrassment, which had disastrous consequences. The Minister, who had allowed himself to fall on his knees, rose with a furious air; and with a sinister smile, he said that he would make her regret it. Indeed, a few weeks later, the Marquis de Fontanar deserted her, and Lorenza would have been glad enough to reconquer His Excellency; but his footmen jeeringly shut the door in her face.

At Lisbon, where they moved next with their all too light baggage, they invested their savings in Brazilian topazes. It was not a bad speculation; but Balsamo found it very difficult to sell his sketches. He sold a few at a very high price to some English people who asked him why he did not try his luck in London where so many Italian artists had made their fortune. If they learned the language a little, they would not feel too homesick. The idea appealed to Balsamo. An able young woman was at once engaged to teach Lorenza English. The copper-founder's daughter was eager to learn, but being without the most rudimentary knowledge, these strange sounds merely produced a bewildering confusion in her little head.

The excessive heat of Lisbon tired her without spoiling her charms. How easily she managed to turn the head of the Seigneur Anselmo La Cruce! The old merchant was known as the Crœsus of Portugal, and the highest dignitaries could not rival his magnificence. He took Lorenza off to the country where, in the midst of an orange grove, he had a luxuriously furnished cottage. The entrance hall was paved with black and white stones ; on pedestals of veined marble stood busts of famous kings, soldiers and sailors. Lorenza was delighted with this cool retreat. She went there several times during the three or four months of her stay in Lisbon. Old La Cruce solemnly gave her, after each visit, eight pistoles, with which Giuseppe hastened to buy more topazes.

. . . .

The travellers must have embarked for London towards the end of July. The *Courrier de l'Europe* proved, much later, by careful investigation, that on the 3rd August, 1771, Balsamo had rented a room in Leadenhall Street and engaged an interpreter by name Moses Botibol.

The artist seems to have made, at that period, a supreme effort to live by his brush. Shutting himself up in his room throughout August, he worked diligently at some big portfolios which he hoped to submit to George III.

On the 1st September, a visitor came in, asking to see some of his work. He was a tall man of vigorous build, Moses Benamore by name. Was he really in the service of the Emperor of Morocco, as he claimed ? By his curved profile, it could be seen that he was a Portuguese or Spanish Jew. After having admired his sketches at great length, Benamore declared that Balsamo could roll in wealth if he would but agree to go to Fez. Balsamo, who had no fear of undertaking a long journey, and who had been greatly flattered by his visitor's compliments, said he was ready.

On the 10th September, Benamore sent word begging him to meet him in Fenchurch Street, at the house of one Mr. Plummer, a printer. When Balsamo went there, the Jew repeated his extravagant eulogies, and commissioned him to make two sketches. The first was to be an exact copy of a model. As for the other, he gave *carte blanche*, stipulating only that a luxuriant and graceful imagination should be displayed. The Emperor usually paid sixty to a hundred piastres for this kind of work.

The two pictures were completed about the 25th September. And when he looked at them, Benamore exclaimed aloud. These works rivalled the most perfect productions of the great masters. If he did not pay on the spot, as he sincerely desired to do, it was only because he was prohibited from making any disbursements without formal authorisation. The smallest infringement of this rule would cost him his head in Morocco, where the very gracious Emperor himself deigned, every Friday, after prayer, to chop off the heads of the offenders, for the diversion of his slaves and odalisques. Never mind. That very day, Benamore would write about it to his Court, and the delay would be trifling.

The weeks passed. Balsamo's resources were exhausted. When he sent his interpreter, Botibol, to ask for some money, Benamore swore by the God of Abraham and Isaac and Jacob that he still awaited instructions from His Moroccan Majesty, and could do no more than pay two guineas on account. Angry as he was, Balsamo forced himself to avert a rupture. They continued to be on good terms, on the surface; they even dined together. At Drury Lane, at the Italian Opera in Covent Garden and at the Marylebone theatre, the Balsamos shared the box of the mysterious Israelite, whose haughty bearing and aquiline features suggested rather the turban of an Oriental, than the wig and three-cornered hat. The autumn passed, and still no piastres! During the winter, the Sicilian put his affairs into the hands of a solicitor, Edward Aylett, who obtained a summons against Benamore, and Balsamo affirmed under oath, on the 2nd January, 1772, in the Middle Temple, before Mr. John Evans, Registrar of London and Middlesex, that Moses Benamore owed him truly and lawfully £47 and more for goods and services, rendered, sold, and delivered to him. Upon which a couple of constables bore Moses Benamore off to prison.

In spite of this, the year 1772 opened under unfortunate auspices for Balsamo. He won the Benamore case, but at what expense! The cost of justice in the United Kingdom was ruinous.

Like the sick in their beds, the unhappy Balsamos restlessly moved from place to place. From Leadenhall Street, they moved to St. Albans Street, then to New Compton Street, Soho, to the house of a turner named Brandall. Here they became acquainted with some Italians who lived opposite, the Pergolesis. Mr. Pergolesi, a painter and decorator, welcomed his confrère with open arms. About the same time, they met Ricciarelli, the good old musician who formerly used to frequent the Cardinal Orsini's palace in Rome. But other members of the Italian colony kept aloof from them. In vain did Balsamo beg for the protection of the painter and sculptor, Agostino Carlini, who had attained celebrity by an equestrian statue of George III. Snubbed by this artist, Cagliostro fell back into the herd.

He haunted the filthy smoking-rooms where the lowest Italian immigrants forgathered, and returning home, drunk with gin or beer, he would belabour Lorenza. Woe to the "marmotte" if she began to pray!

"A truce to your mummeries!" he would shout angrily. "Does your God ever think of helping you? Don't you see that he is leaving us to die in misery? . . ."

Although they had often played him false, Balsamo showed an unchanging preference for his compatriots. His crony in London was a Sicilian named Vivona who ruled over a number of swindlers like a monarch over his subjects. Quick-witted and ingenious, he had a fund of gaiety which pleasingly recalled the happy days of Nicastro; and, like Agliata, he made great play with the title of Marquis. Vivona, long familiar with the manners and customs of the English, inspired great respect among the tyros who came to consult him. And it was through him that Balsamo found a way of making money.

It had been noticed for some time that Lorenza's charms were operating on the heart of a Quaker who ogled the young woman, slyly, but hungrily and often. Such was the proverbial severity of his sect that everyone began to chaff Lorenza about her austere lover. Balsamo openly laughed at it. But one day, Vivona told them in all seriousness that the Quaker was an extremely rich man.

The law in England on these matters was then explained to them: it offered every compensation to the deceived husband. Provided the adultery was proved, it permitted them to punish the guilty lover as they pleased—either by suing or extorting money from him. And should it please the outraged husband to ruin his rival completely, he was free to do so: his misfortune gave him every right.

Soon after this, the Quaker obtained an assignation with Lorenza. But while he was deeply relishing the joy of being alone with his idol, Balsamo and Vivona were hiding in an alcove. The Quaker took off his hat and wig for comfort. He removed his coat and vest, out of a love of simplicity. Though he was not young, he had other gifts which could make him interesting, when he chose to exercise them. Everything was going sweetly. . . . But, with a little cry, Lorenza suddenly put her face in her hands. Balsamo and the other witness appeared at the door. And the Quaker, alarmed and confused, but unable to deny the evidence, considered himself lucky to escape a scandal by paying one hundred pounds, which the accomplices immediately divided between them.

Delighted with this success, Balsamo pressed his dear Vivona to help him sell his topazes at a good price. The other hesitated somewhat; he said he did not wish to undertake such delicate responsibilities. However, when pressed, he agreed. But, as soon as the gems were in his possession, the Marquis felt the need of a change of air, and all trace of him was lost.

Betrayed by a dishonourable compatriot, as in Calabria, as in Bergamo, as in Madrid, Balsamo could not escape his fate: he sank to the depths of misery. Impatient creditors were already taking possession of what remained of the Quaker's money, when, hearing of the disaster, a heartless woman, a female Harpagon, Mrs. Wright, had him thrown in prison.

The Sunday following the arrest, Lorenza, disconsolate but still attractive, went to Mass at the Bavarian Embassy. For all her lapses, she remained faithful to what she had been taught at home. She never failed, for instance, to pray to the Madonna del Carmine in her misfortune. Her sighs quickly moved the congregation, which included many lords and ladies, to pity. There was an elderly gentleman who regarded her with particular compassion. Lorenza was aware of it, and, from time to time, through her tears, looked up at him. Sincerely touched, the good Samaritan inquired why she was in distress.

"Alas! sir," she stammered in a constrained voice. "I am the most unfortunate of women. My husband is in prison for debt. When he was free, he supported me by working. But what will happen to me now that I am thrown on myself?"

"How much does your husband owe?"

"Seven guineas."

"Here they are."

He put some banknotes into her hand, and quietly walked off, so as to avoid her effusive gratitude.

Lorenza nevertheless succeeded in finding out the name and address of her benefactor: Sir Edward Hales, who lived in London at 43 Albemarle Street. He was considered to be one of the oldest baronets, and one of the most strongly attached to Catholicism. The poor and the sick whom he relieved, or who lived entirely on his charity, spoke highly of his kindness and generosity. They praised in him, besides, his learning, and his keen interest in art, in the pursuit of which he had not hesitated to undertake long journeys.

On the third day, Sir Edward saw a shabby and commonplace Italian come into his house. The stranger threw himself on his knees, and kissed his hands. After thanking him most humbly, Balsamo, for he it was, begged his saviour to employ him as painter and decorator, or to recommend him to his acquaintances.

Some rooms had yet to be painted in a country house near Canterbury which Sir Edward had restored, Hales Place. Would it be suitable work for Balsamo? He had never done any work of this sort; he had no idea how to draw a landscape, or sketch a portrait. Yet, blinded by vanity, and hard pressed by need, he boldly represented himself to the nobleman as one of the foremost living artists in Italy.

At Hales Place, Balsamo wasted several weeks in useless preparations. And when, at length, he had completed the work, the critics, looking at the clumsy and fantastic daubs, burst into laughter. Sir Edward was furious at the insolence with which the disgraceful trick had been played on him, and railed fiercely at Balsamo. At twenty-seven years of age, the Sicilian could no more tolerate a well-deserved reprimand than in the day of his apprenticeship with the Benfratelli. Pale with anger, he declared in confidence to the valet that if the baronet, the old fool, had dared to say all those things in Italy, he would have plunged a dagger into his heart, a threat which was quickly reported to Sir Edward.

Besides, Balsamo had had the audacity to carry on a liaison with Sir Edward's daughter. Did the young lady actually yield to his seduction? Had she merely been indiscreet enough to respond to his oglings? The episode remains obscure. Whatever it was, Sir

Edward, taking the painter by the shoulders, threw him ignominiously out of the door.

The Balsamos did not care to return to town after this holiday. Besides that the cost of living in London was high, their proceedings against Moses Benamore had ruined them. Edward Aylett, their solicitor, to whom they owed £10, was loudly demanding payment of at least a part of it. Balsamo preferred staying away from London to giving him a penny.

Canterbury was not more attractive. It had a large population, but the scandal at Hales Place having created some commotion, no one would have anything to do with the Sicilian. Disgusted with England, Balsamo and his wife embarked at Dover for Calais.

. . . .

Lorenza who, with the exception of the Quaker, had had little success among the British, suddenly recovered her influence in the packet which took them back to France on the 15th September, 1772. A charming passenger came up to them, and spoke in Italian, to the great relief of Lorenza, who could never manage to pronounce any foreign words.

He introduced himself as M. Duplessis, a lawyer, and the Marquis de Prie's steward. He was fifty years old, and had a fiery complexion, red ears, scarlet lips, a handsome set of teeth, and elegant legs.

In the course of the conversation, Balsamo took out some of his best sketches from his portfolio, and M. Duplessis went into ecstacies. He had never seen anything so fine, he declared, with his eyes fixed on Lorenza. The artist who had produced such masterpieces was assured of success in Paris. The noblemen with whom M. Duplessis was intimate, would deem it a pleasure to present Balsamo at Versailles. Pampered by Court and town, he would never want to leave France. And as M. Duplessis forecast these splendours, he did not for a moment remove his gaze from the charming Lorenza.

The Balsamos thought of stopping for a while at Calais, as they had no money to go any farther. But M. Duplessis protested. Their acquaintance, no doubt, was very recent, but he begged them all the same to treat him like an old friend. His purse was at their disposal. Lorenza, not without a little fuss, agreed to share the post chaise with him, and Balsamo followed on horseback.

The lawyer congratulated himself on the skill with which he had contrived the affair. How disillusioned he would have been had he known that it was the third time that the well-schooled Lorenza was travelling *tête-à-tête* with a lover, and that the experience did not fluster her in the least! M. Duplessis gave expression to one folly after another. He was like a schoolboy all the way. Now imperious, now plaintive, he would demand and implore by turns that which she refused with unruffled calm. As for him, he could not tear his eyes off that mother-of-pearl complexion, that skin which was less that of Southerner than of some child of the mountains, a white skin suffused with the radiance of dawn. It was indeed the skin of a seraph, shining with the light of youth and health ; a mouth vernal and appetising like spring fruit. The eyelids, amber coloured, gave to the blue eyes an inexpressibly languishing air. And a hundred times during the day, M. Duplessis chanted the litany of his passion. Gracious, captivating, irresistible, ah ! how he would not worship her ! He would make her fortune for her if she would but be a little more human. Lorenza listened to these fine words with an obvious air of satisfaction, but without yielding any more to his violence than to his humble supplications.

They arrived at Paris on the 18th September. Under pretext of saving his friends from the rapacity of the innkeeper, M. Duplessis suggested that there was a fine apartment in the Marquis de Prie's house which they could occupy. They went there after dinner. And Balsamo, tired by his long ride on horseback, went to bed at once, while Lorenza accompanied M. Duplessis to the Opera.

The ardour shown by the lawyer, his eloquence, his promises, his numerous little gifts, finally touched the heart of the young woman. Though he was not a rich man, M. Duplessis anticipated and provided for her slightest caprice. Lorenza had expressed a wish, after their visit to the Opera, to learn dancing : the next day, M. Lyon, a ballet-master, arrived to teach her the minuet, the gavotte, the rigaudon, and all the fashionable airs and quadrilles. And every day she received some flowers and trinkets. These attentions were in such contrast to her husband's brutality that Lorenza could feel herself melting. In the end, one Sunday, when Balsamo had left them alone, M. Duplessis had his heart's desire.

Then began a period of intense misery for the three. Though he enjoyed many advantages in this situation, Balsamo was alarmed at the thought of losing a wife whom he had succeeded in making an accomplice. For he guessed that M. Duplessis had awakened in Lorenza a feeling quite different from that inspired by his predecessors, something like a tender yearning. The lawyer, for his part, was wretched at the thought of sharing Lorenza with Balsamo. He could not imagine, he would often say bitterly to her, how she could put up with such a scoundrel. He repeated to her that in France, at least, unhappy women had the means of obtaining a separation.

Lorenza had, for her part, become jealous when she came to know that every evening after supper, the lawyer went to the house of a dressmaker named Foucher, in the rue Saint-Honoré. The disclosure shocked Lorenza. When M. Duplessis begged her to leave Balsamo, with her clothes and jewels, and hide herself in a small room in the faubourg Saint-Germain, under the protection of M. the Prince de Conti, she turned a deaf ear to him. " Such sacrifices," she replied, " ought only to be made for the sake of some exclusive love, some heroic and idolatrous passion." If M. Duplessis gave up Mme

Foucher, she would see what she could do. Upon which, the lawyer, irritated, said she had neither courage nor affection.

Lodged by the Marquis and fed by M. Duplessis, the Balsamos did not care how much money they spent. For household work and for running errands they employed a lad dressed up as a page. They gaily contracted debts to the extent of two hundred ecus. Balsamo, a Sicilian susceptible to the cold, must have proper bedding, and a gentleman's cloak. Lorenza and her husband hired superb costumes to show off at the grand ball that M. Lyon, the dance master, gave for his pupils. But the day after the fête, when the secondhand dealer came to collect his garments, he had difficulty in recovering a richly embroidered cloak; and when at last it was discovered, the ticket that had been attached to the lining was found to be missing. The man at once concluded that he was dealing with some swindlers, and jumped at Balsamo's throat. The house echoed with their screams, and a complaint having been made to the Marquis, M. Duplessis, extremely embarrassed, induced his protégés to move into his own house, in the rue Neuve-des-petits-Pères.

The exiguity of the accommodation made cohabitation very unpleasant. Besides, Balsamo had to complain of the fare provided for him. Some eggs had caused him very suspicious pains in the stomach. Once, when Lorenza made as though to drink from her husband's glass, M. Duplessis pushed her aside with a strange abruptness; he poured out the wine into the chimney, and filled another glass for her out of the same bottle. After four days of this, Balsamo decided to take a furnished apartment in the rue des Vieux-Augustins. . . .

But when he was on the point of moving, M. Duplessis rudely reminded him of the sums of money he had advanced, and absolutely refused to let him take away his big trunk. And as the Sicilian said something about sending for the police:

"Go to the devil!" replied M. Duplessis.

Then he slammed the door with his feet.

Deprived of their principal luggage, the Balsamos lodged a complaint with M. de Sartine, the chief of police. In addition to their undergarments, their warm clothes and their ceremonial costume, the box contained an old "book of secrets" which Balsamo considered to be very precious.

The title of this book is not mentioned in any official document. Was it, as claimed by Jacques Casanova in his *Soliloque d'un penseur*, the treatise *Secrets admirables*, published in 1555 at Venice by Alessio Piemontese? As this erudite conjecture was not based on any fact, M. Duplessis's determination to retain possession of the old book seemed as unjustifiable to Vannetti as Balsamo's unwillingness to be separated from it even for a single day.

Two days later, Lorenza returned to the rue Neuve-des-petits-Pères with a message of peace. As M. Duplessis welcomed her warmly, and even asked her to stay for dinner, she hoped that she was going to get her trunk back. But at the end of the meal, she drank something which threw her into a deep stupor. The clock struck twelve when she recovered consciousness. Standing beside the sofa, M. Duplessis was gazing at her with eyes aflame with love. Could she return, so late in the night, to Balsamo ? What blows and curses would be showered on her ! Trembling with fear, unable to think or to do anything, the poor creature threw herself, crying, into M. Duplessis's arms : she remained there all night. . . .

The lawyer knew very well that he might be sent to jail for kidnapping a married woman. So the next day, his servants, the Morats, husband and wife, took Lorenza to a house in the rue Saint-Honoré, belonging to a Mme Douceur. They confided her to a woman named Theron, who occupied the fifth floor, instructing her to say that she had found Balsamo's wife lost in the streets, and had brought her back to the rue Saint-Honoré by her own consent.

Morat and his wife daily called on Lorenza, and swore that she had nothing to fear. The Marquise de Prie still retained her goodwill for her, and M. Duplessis had promised to exert himself on her behalf " to his last sou."

Besides, some secret agents were busily trying to obtain a divorce for Lorenza. They took her to M. Fontaine, the commissioner of the Châtelet, and King's Councillor, to lawyers and solicitors. The Marquise de Prie asked to see her once more : in a sharp and authoritative tone, she bade her not to compromise M. Duplessis, who was a very good man, to weigh her words carefully, and behave very discreetly ; in return, she would provide her with the means to go back to Rome. But when she said good-bye, the noble lady gave her, with a lofty gesture, the sum of twelve francs. Lorenza showed some surprise, and Mme de Prie murmured indifferently :

" For your cab fare ! "

Balsamo, for his part, was moving heaven and earth to discover his wife. It was alleged that he had conciliated M. de Sartine by painting his portrait. Anyhow, his rights were so indisputable that, on the 26th January, 1773, the Chief of Police wrote to Commissioner Fontaine ordering Lorenza's arrest.

On Monday, the 1st February, Commissioner Fontaine and Inspector Buhot succeeded in tracing the fugitive spouse and arresting her.

Finding herself thrown together with the miserable prostitutes in the prison of Saint Pelagius, Lorenza began to hate the frivolous egotist who had caused her to be put in that hell. Far from protecting him, she reported all the wicked things he had told her. She even went to the length of swearing that her scoundrel of a husband had been sentenced in Rome for forgery, and that instead of doing honest work, he had sought to make a prostitute of her. Alas, that she should be frail enough to utter such lies ! But later, coming to her senses, she was horrified at what she had said, and withdrew them all.

Balsamo was informed that his wife, questioned in detail on Thursday, 20th February, 1773, had disclosed that she had no more resisted M. Duplessis than she had resisted the knaves Nicastro, Agliata or Vivona, but that she spoke of him with love and respect. He was touched by that, and asked to be allowed to see her. She fell at his feet, sobbing ; and he abused her in the most terrible manner, but he could not help feeling moved, for, in his own way, he loved her. Nevertheless, it was several months before he fully forgave her. When at last he consented to take her back, Lorenza was released, and the French authorities washed their hands of the affair.

In the meantime, Balsamo had recovered his trunk, but he could not find his " book of secrets " in it, nor a bottle of carmine and the eight new shirts of Dutch linen he said he had put there. Was it the truth, or was he only trying to extort money from M. Duplessis ? No one can tell.

Balsamo was regretting that he had accepted several commissions in Paris which he had not discharged. But he did not expect anything more there. His wife helped him as best she could to pack up, and they left in the autumn, with little noise but great speed.

There are some facts to support the conjecture that from Paris the Balsamos must have gone to Brussels, then to Aix and Ratisbon. It might even be that they spent the winter of 1774-1775 in Vienna, and later gone toward Venice. But to recover definite traces of them, Vannetti had to pass on to the spring of 1775.

. . . .

The Balsamo family had had no news of Giuseppe since his departure from Palermo. It is true, they had heard of his marriage, and were not unaware that Giuseppe and Lorenza were always travelling about. But these good people had not the time to keep crying over their prodigal son. Without hope or illusion, they dragged on their laborious and painful existence. Giuseppe's sister, Maria Anna Capitummino, had given birth to three fine children, a son and two daughters ; then, her husband dying suddenly and leaving her destitute, she had had to work. If anyone mentioned the absent one, no attention was paid to him.

In the spring of 1775, Antonio Bracconeri happened to be passing through Naples. As he was crossing the Place du Palais, he unexpectedly ran into a ne'er-do-well from Palermo, Davidde La Rocca, a wig-maker by profession who had brilliantly sustained the rôle of a Marquis in Turin, and delighted the whole of Italy with his pranks and rogueries. Bracconeri was very much amused at meeting him. He said he had come to Naples after having been all over Europe. When he was asked if, in the course of his wanderings, he had come across any trace of Balsamo, he said no ; then he invited

Bracconeri to follow him to a house near the Theatre Royal, where they could talk in comfort. No sooner had they stepped on the threshold, than Bracconeri found himself in Giuseppe Balsamo's presence. And as he turned round towards La Rocca to rebuke him for the concealment, Balsamo informed him, with a guffaw, that the rogue was his valet.

Uncle and nephew then embraced each other. By tacit agreement, they avoided any reference to "old, unhappy, far-off things."

Balsamo begged the old man to excuse him a moment, while he went to fetch his wife. He returned with the Signora Lorenza, and introduced her gracefully. After which, they all went to a house that Balsamo had taken. . . .

Antonio Bracconeri thought he must be dreaming : one marvel followed another. The house they went to see was magnificent and spacious as a palace. A sumptuous equipage was waiting for Giuseppe at the door. Numerous servants bowed almost to the ground at the slightest command of M. the Marquis Pellegrini.

Whence did he derive this name ? From Mount Pellegrino, which dominates the bay of Palermo ? From the Strade dei Pellegrini, the scene of his courting in Rome ? Or from the pilgrimage to Saint Jacques de Compostelle which he had not had the perseverance to finish ? Whatever it was, the time seemed to have come for Balsamo to represent himself as a nobleman.

Wishing to be neither a dupe nor an accomplice, the honest accountant of the house of Aubert and Co. declined the hospitality offered him by his nephew. But thereupon, Giuseppe changed his tone. In a touching voice, he protested that his greatest wish was to return to Palermo, and settle there as a law-abiding citizen, if the authorities would but ignore his past follies. Antonino took him at his word. Since Giuseppe, weary of his exploits, was at last repenting, he should not refuse to help him. What a consolation it would be for his sister, who had endured so many griefs and hardships, if he succeeded in bringing back the lost sheep to its fold ! He began to make the necessary arrangements. The Prince de Butera, a high official, wrote to his son, the Prince de Pietre Persia, who was in Palermo, asking him to lend his support to Antonino's nephew. And Antonino, beaming with joy, was soon able to sail for Palermo with the young couple, and their arrival was made the occasion of a grand celebration in his house.

But he was quickly disillusioned. After the first outbursts of repentance, Giuseppe became his old self. His frauds, intrigues, and pranks began again. Thriftless as he was, more and more clothes and jewels had to be pawned. And when the Prince de Pietra Persia became enamoured of Lorenza, Bracconeri saw with horror that their relations were encouraged by Giuseppe himself. The remonstrances he ventured to make were ill received. And after a fortnight, his guests left him without a word of thanks.

CAGLIOSTRO IN THE LODGE OF ANTIQUITY
From a rare caricature by Gillray. Cagliostro is the first person seated alongside table.

Until then, out of consideration for Antonino Bracconeri, whom everyone in the island loved and respected, the goldsmith Marano had kept quiet. But the desire for revenge never dies in the heart of a Sicilian. Marano was incapable of forgetting the nocturnal bastinado he had received. No sooner had the Pellegrini moved out, than he took steps to secure the arrest of the so-called Marquis.

Unpleasant as had been Giuseppe's contacts with the law in England, here in Sicily, as he knew, he would be treated still more harshly. The Sicilian judges had a reputation for stubbornness, ingenuity, and severity, which made him shudder. What would happen if they began to make enquiries in Rome? Would the charge of counterfeiting money be revived? And if, besides, they brought up the case of the will altered in the Marquis Maurigi's favour, or the murder of the canon, could he save his neck?

Under lock and key, shut in by the whitewashed walls of his cell, his thoughts were terrible. He thought of Nicastro's execution, which he had predicted. He imagined he saw him, with his misleadingly honest face, being marched between a double row of soldiers. His wrists were handcuffed and tied behind his back. He wore the white shorts and the white shirt of the condemned. Kneeling round the gallows were the Brothers of Death, bundled up in their sacks, and the Penitents in their blue and white ceremonial robes; they recited the *Miserere*, and the place rang with the sound of their chanting. While Nicastro haltingly climbed the ladder, the father-confessor, hitching up his robes, clambered briskly up a side ladder to hold the crucifix to his lips. The greasy ropes were tickling Nicastro's chin. And suddenly, while they were mumbling the *Jesu Maria*, he was shot into eternity.... The chief executioner jumped on his shoulders, another seized his legs and pulled them violently. Then when Nicastro had finished dancing his last tarantella, the townsmen filed past the corpse, pointing it out to their offspring, with vigorous admonitions, so that they might never forget the sight.

While he was trembling with horror in his cell, a personage with wide athletic shoulders, a bull neck and an apoplectic complexion, dashed into the President Airoldi's offices: it was the Prince de Pietre Persia, who had been summoned to the rescue by Lorenza. Furious at learning that they had dared to apprehend the husband of his mistress, the prince strode straight up to Marano's lawyer, who was in the ante-chamber. He ordered him, in a loud and menacing voice, to withdraw his charges and release Pellegrini. The lawyer pleaded the interests of his client. Then the redoubtable Goliath, with his herculean strength and ferocity, grabbed him by the collar, threw him down, thrashed him soundly, kicked him about, grinding his heels into his body, until President Airoldi, attracted by the clamour, rushed out and intervened. But the magistrate had not the courage to deal sternly with the seigneur. Out of respect for the Prince de Butera, he released the self-styled Marquis Pellegrini, enjoining him to quit Palermo within twenty-four hours. A *spironara* was about to sail for Malta, and as a strong breeze was blowing, it should soon reach Valetta. Giuseppe and his wife went on board, and in their great hurry they forgot to repay poor Maria Anna Capitummino the fourteen ounces of gold with which she had redeemed their jewels from the pawnshop.

This trip to Malta was as definite a landmark in Balsamo's career as his earlier visit to the Grand Master Pinto d'Alfonsea was dubious and problematic.

During his stay at Valetta—about three months—he had the good fortune to connect himself with the Chevalier d'Aquino, the younger brother of the Prince de Caramanica, who had just become viceroy of Sicily. The Chevalier was rightly regarded as a model of politeness, humanity and learning. His friendship was a valuable recommendation among all respectable people. Thanks to such a distinguished patronage, the Pellegrinis made a brilliant re-entry into Naples. And when they settled down there, the past was wiped out of their memory.

The Marquis Pellegrini, the intimate companion of the Chevalier d'Aquino, had nothing in common with that obscure black and white artist, Balsamo. He appeared to the Neapolitans marvellously versed in physics, chemistry, anatomy, botany and the occult sciences. And, through his friendship with the Chevalier, he had learned to speak and carry himself in a way which hardly suggested the hovels of Palermo.

Now that their position had improved, Lorenza was allowed to invite her father and her young brother, Francesco, to Naples. Giuseppe even agreed to pay for their journey, so far was he from suspecting that it was Feliciani who had formerly denounced him to the papal authorities. The copper-founder noted that with relief. Nevertheless, bewildered by all that he saw in Naples, and feeling nothing good could come out of it, he quickly returned to Rome.

Before his departure, he confided the young Francesco to Lorenza's care. Giuseppe himself had asked to keep him. The Sicilian was really fond of his charming brother-in-law. The pretty child of former days had grown into a very handsome youth : he had the soft, milky complexion of Lorenza, a well-shaped figure, and there was, in his voice, as in hers, the soft and elegant cadences of the Roman. Seeing how he himself was getting on, Balsamo thought that, if he should succeed in finding a rich heiress for Francesco's wife, their two households would be well endowed. Francesco was as gentle as a lamb. And there was nothing about him which could have enabled Balsamo to foresee that he was to cause his relatives serious dissatisfaction.

First of all, he fell into the clutches of the Baron de Santa Venera, a pervert who introduced the young man to abominable practices. Balsamo, as a matter of fact, did not object to licentiousness. He did not in the least blame the Prince de Francavilla and other libertines who reawakened in Naples the echoes of ancient Capri. But among those in his charge, no foreign influence must conflict with his own. Francesco had no more right to attach himself to the Baron de Santa Venera than Lorenza to M. Duplessis. Not content with sharply rebuking his brother-in-law, Pellegrini beat him and threatened to send him back in disgrace to Rome. Then he relented, thinking that new sights and scenes might cure this Ganymede of the streets. Indeed, the time had come for Giuseppe and Lorenza to resume their wanderings.

. . . .

At this point, all is enigma and mystery. . . .

His lessons in the Cabala and alchemy brought him plenty of money ; his friendship with the Chevalier d'Aquino gave him safety and prestige ; and yet, why did not Balsamo-Pellegrini stay in Naples ? Was he yielding, once more, to the lure of the unknown ? Did he expect to get rich more quickly on the highways of adventure ? Did his precarious and nomadic existence appeal to him by the violent contrasts which intoxicate gamblers ? The fact remains that, by the end of 1775, he had sailed from Naples for Toulon, accompanied by Lorenza and the too handsome Francesco.

The Marquis Pellegrini—one must no longer refer to him by any other name—once more practised on French soil all those little tricks which had succeeded so well in Paris. His toilet water gave instant satisfaction to decaying beauties. And as he represented Francesco to be a Roman nobleman with high connections, a woman of Marseilles, as credulous as she was infatuated, offered to betroth one of her two daughters to this amiable young man. But Francesco lacked either the inclination or the ability to play his part. The Marquis and Marquise were in despair over it. But their stay in Marseilles was none the less profitable on that account. When his admirers presented him with a fine post-chaise, Balsamo suddenly declared that he was called back to Rome by the serious illness of his father-in-law. Actually, he took the road to the Spanish frontier.

Catalonia was still ruled, in King Charles III's name, by His Excellency the Count de Ricla, but Pellegrini was not very anxious to renew his acquaintance. At Barcelona he sold his carriage, and went on to Valenzia, where he engaged a servant by the name of Carlo Sacchi. Was this medical student, half bone-setter and half dentist, really in a position to perform an operation on Pellegrini ? Had he the ability, as one day he was to boast loudly, to cure him of a venereal disease contracted through intercourse with some Spanish beauty ? Whatever it may be, the travellers soon went on to Alcante, and to Cadiz.

It was here that Francesco Feliciani completely forfeited the confidence of his sister and brother-in-law. The unfortunate wretch showed himself completely unworthy of it. Not only did the party derive no benefit from his fine looks, but they constantly complained of his petty frauds. The religious instruction his parents had given him did not prevail against his instincts. The Marquis Pellegrini, at Cadiz, finding that he had been robbed of several gold pieces, as well as some valuable trinkets, became furious ; he handed over the culprit to the law, and Francesco was sentenced to three months' imprisonment.

While this case was under examination, the Marquis aroused enormous interest by his discourses on the panacea and the philosopher's stone. The most fanatical, carried away by their enthusiasm, handed him a bill of exchange for a thousand ecus, to send for chemical products and apparatus. The alchemist signed notes for considerable amounts. Then he appropriated a very valuable cane with a repeating watch set in diamonds at its top, alleging that this masterpiece of the jeweller's art had been given to him by his disciples. But the firm of Silvestre proved, subsequently, with corroborative documents, that this cane was the object of a formal sale for which he demanded payment.

Towards the spring of 1776, the Marquis and the Marquise, leaving Francesco in the Spanish jail, vanished like shadows. A chasm seemed mysteriously to have opened out to engulf them. . . .

Thirteen years later, they still remembered at Cadiz a complaint lodged against a certain Francesco Feliciani by his brother-in-law ; and the house of Silvestre still sought payment for the cane ; but no one could say what had become of the Marquis Pellegrini and his wife. The tracks of Giuseppe Balsamo also disappeared at that spot. . . .

However, even credulous minds at times protest, and the population of Rovereto would not accept the story of the sudden disappearance of the Balsamos. They threw their imagination forward in pursuit of Giuseppe and Lorenza. Where were they hiding themselves ? What had become of them ?

At the café, whenever Vannetti began to talk about it, the general conversation would stop, and they would all gather round him in a circle. In vain did the vanilla chocolates exhale their flavour on the tables : the pensive eaters paid no heed. The waiters stood still, their hands in their apron pockets. And even the chess players suspended their moves. . . .

Pious people thought of the impenitent blasphemers who were flung alive into the braziers of hell, certain that that violator of human and divine laws, Giuseppe Balsamo, had surely called forth a similar punishment.

But presently, sober men began to make enquiries as to the date when the Count de Cagliostro had first made his appearance. And this definite problem at once diverted attention to a career more remarkable in its way than that of the obscure Sicilian artist.

V

THE EMERGENCE OF CAGLIOSTRO

VANNETTI pieced together Cagliostro's story with as much care as he had expended on the life of Giuseppe Balsamo and with as much detail.

Between his flight from Palermo and his installation in Rome, between his departure from Paris in 1773 and his arrival at Naples in 1774, and then again, after his stay at Cadiz, nothing was known about Giuseppe Balsamo. But at least one knew where he was born, what his parentage was, and the evidence of Antonio Bracconeri was decisive in regard to certain aspects of his early youth.

In the case of Cagliostro, the difficulty was of an inverse order. Details were abundant after a certain date. They were minutely precise. But one could not probe beyond the past twelve or thirteen years. Whence did he come? Where did he acquire his wealth, his knowledge, his gifts, his all-powerful influence? . . . Mystery. One might have said he had dropped from the clouds.

This dearth of information gave wide scope for the imagination. Fantastic tales were in circulation about the magician. Many confused him with the Comte de Saint Germain. That notorious enchanter, they said, had only pretended to die at Holstein in order to baffle the detectives who had been set on his track by certain royal courts whose secrets he possessed. And, naturally, they credited the Count de Cagliostro with all the exploits attributed to the Comte de Saint Germain. Others allowed Cagliostro a distinct personality, but nevertheless regarded him as a disciple of Saint Germain, who had in 1774 conferred upon him the highest initiation.

Cagliostro aggravated this confusion by the stories he told of his rebirths, in the course of which he would recall that he was the occultist Frederic Gualdo.

Vannetti was, indeed, beginning to form an opinion. But determined not to express it until the time should be ripe, he confined himself strictly to the question in hand: what was the date of the first authentic appearance of Count Cagliostro in Europe?

. . . .

In the last weeks of July 1776 the Count de Cagliostro disembarked in London, in company with the Countess, and took rooms at

No. 4, Whitcomb Street, near Leicester Fields, the house of a Mrs. Juliet.

The landlady gained a favourable impression of her guests on account of their liberality. Not content with an apartment, M. de Cagliostro, a little later, rented the whole house. According to his own confession, he had at the time two thousand pounds sterling in Spanish gold pieces, a very expensive assortment of clothes, many objects of value, and jewels which alone amounted to an enviable fortune. Such resources easily enabled him to keep up the appearance of a gentleman.

Without further explanation about his career, he represented himself as an Italian officer, born in Sicily. A captain on his arrival in London, he had subsequently become colonel. In the service of Naples, Spain or Prussia ? It was in vain that one sought an answer, but the ambiguity was not embarrassing to him in an age when soldiers were at liberty to wear their swords in the service of no matter what ruler.

As M. and Mme de Cagliostro hardly understood the language of the country, their first concern, on establishing themselves at Mrs. Juliet's, was to engage an interpreter. The man they chose was named Domenico Aurelio Vitellini. This Italian had been preparing to join the Company of Jesus at the very moment when it was dissolved by the Holy Father. The storm which scattered the reverend fathers over the world, threw him, a miserable waif, on to the banks of the Thames. Happily, Vitellini was educated, and could speak English, French, Latin and Italian with elegance ; he became a language master, and thus managed to earn a living.

Mme de Cagliostro was glad to find in Vitellini a companion in her solitude. She was bored. When she complained about it to Mrs. Juliet, the landlady introduced her to one of her tenants, Mme de Blevary, a Portuguese woman of distinction. This old lady, needy and sick as she was, delighted the Cagliostros with her good manners, with that art of subtle and dignified flattery which one acquires at royal courts, and proved a timely encounter. Since their arrival in London, study, meditation, and chemical experiments conducted in the greatest mystery, had removed M. de Cagliostro from his wife and confined him in the depths of his laboratory. Admitted once into the sanctuary, Vitellini had come out of it so bedazzled that he went about proclaiming his admiration everywhere. From coffee house to coffee house he carried his eulogy of his patron, the most learned of men, one possessed of the sovereign formulæ for which so many alchemists, so many cabalists, ancient and modern, had sighed in vain.

Though Cagliostro smiled at such foolish enthusiasm, he confessed to having made some correct calculations in regard to an impending English lottery, to be drawn on the 14th November, 1776. To subject chance to calculation did not seem to him an absurd thing, for he did not consider the human understanding to be the measure of the possible. An old manuscript in his possession taught him how one could ensure success in every gamble.

As M. de Cagliostro was thus able to be of considerable help to his friends, Mme de Blevary determined to take advantage of it. She began by introducing into the place a Scottish couple of her acquaintance, Lord and Lady Scott, whom the autumn had brought back to London for the education of their children. No doubt, their extremely shabby appearance consorted ill with the idea M. and Mme de Cagliostro entertained of the Scottish nobility. No matter! They found them to be decent people, respected their character, and continued to talk in their presence as freely as before.

For the draw on the 14th November, Cagliostro indicated, half in fun, the first number that would be drawn, and it turned out just as he had foretold. For that of the 16th November, his tip was number twenty. By way of experiment, Scott chanced a trifle on it and won. For the 17th November, Cagliostro gave the number 25, and his prophecy was worth a hundred pounds to Scott. For the 18th, Cagliostro gave the numbers 55 and 57, and he was right again. The Scotts and Vitellini at once shared the profits between them, while Mme de Blevary delightedly accepted a well-earned commission. But after the 18th November, Cagliostro, out of some strange scruple, suddenly discontinued his prognostications.

To the gamblers it was a calamity. Each of them had been counting on the great man's genius to amass a fortune quickly, but now he had abandoned them. Mme de Blevary wept over the ruins of her castles in Spain. Though crushed under the blows of fatality and chance, Vitellini did not turn against his patron. He was hoping to lay his hands on the famous cabalistic treatise and on a certain rose powder which he had seen Cagliostro use in his alchemical transmutations. But of all the rest it was Scott who, possessed by the demon of gambling, became most violently excited. As he could get nothing out of Cagliostro, it occurred to him to offer Mme de Cagliostro a fur cloak, worth at the most four or five guineas. Before another day had passed, Cagliostro sent him in return a golden casket, worth twenty-five guineas. Then, to have some peace, the Count resolved never again to invite the troublesome couple.

Lady Scott, however, contrived to force the barrier. Throwing herself at Mme de Cagliostro's feet, she made the most humiliating confession to her. She said her real name was Mary Fry, and that she had no right at all to the title of Lady Scott, which she had assumed. Having lived for some years as William Scott's mistress, she had had three children by him. That sharper, given over to all manner of dissipation, was her misery and her disgrace. And during this sad recital, her tears ran freely.

Mme de Cagliostro had not a heart of stone. She intervened on behalf of the alleged Lady Scott, and Cagliostro, out of compassion, was good enough to tip her the number 8 for the 7th December, 1776.

Selling or pawning her most precious personal possessions at once, Mary Fry put every penny she had on that number. Her confidence was rewarded. Vitellini, present at Mary Fry's on the day when she returned with the fruits of her investment, himself counted four hundred and twenty-one guineas and four hundred and sixty pounds sterling in banknotes. After which he coolly pocketed a tip of twenty guineas. On the same number, William Scott won seven hundred guineas, showing that there was complete mutual understanding in this false ménage.

Her first transport of joy carried Mary Fry to Cagliostro's house. She rushed to him to render thanks for the fortune which she had won ; not so much of gratitude, perhaps, as in the hope of inducing him to make fresh prognostications. He contented himself with replying :

" Keep it, my good woman ; I have no need of that. Take the word of a friend : go and live with your children in the country."

Vain words ! The plotters meant to exploit his wonderful genius to the full. But how were they to compel him to speak ? They argued that, since Mme de Cagliostro had not actually refused the fur cloak, she could doubtless be won over with some more costly gift.

One day, when Miss Fry was in the drawing-room at Whitcomb Street with Vitellini, she innocently took from her pocket a gold snuff-box, filled with a vegetable powder, which she said was a sovereign remedy for inflammations. Mme de Cagliostro tried some of it. The snuff having delighted the lady with its fragrance, her visitor firmly refused to take the box back. After much pressure and resistance on each side, the little gift was finally accepted.

Mme de Cagliostro discovered later that the box, which had a double bottom, concealed in its inner compartment a jewel in the best taste, a beautiful necklace of sixty-two diamonds. And subsequently it transpired that Mary Fry had bought it for £97 in Prince's Street, at the same jeweller's that she had bought her snuff-box for twenty guineas.

On learning this, Cagliostro was furious and gave full vent to his anger. Yet the trick had been played. Could a gift be returned that was so belatedly discovered ? Having thundered and fulminated, Cagliostro did what extremely busy men do : he acquiesced in the accomplished fact rather than start a tiresome argument. Only, to put an end to such intrigues, he moved out of Whitcomb Street in January 1777, and went to live in Great Suffolk Street. But his interpreter, Vitellini, soon betrayed him. No sooner than M. and Mme Cagliostro had settled on the first floor of the new house, than Mary Fry rented the second, and it became impossible to avoid her.

Her proximity was a torture. At times she talked of returning to the country with her children, but complained that she had made some bad investments, and was at the moment out of funds ; at times she begged for forecasts. Cagliostro's patience was exhausted. Their relations were becoming strained. And it was then that Scott and his accomplices decided on a bold stroke.

On the 7th February, 1777, at ten o'clock at night, when he was peacefully chatting by the fireside to his wife and Vitellini, Cagliostro saw half a dozen police officers enter his house. Their chief, one William Saunders, thrust a writ under his nose, a document which Vitellini hastened to translate in a loud voice. Mary Fry swore that M. de Cagliostro owed her £190 and more for moneys she had lent, advanced, paid and disbursed, and also for goods and effects sold and delivered to him by the above-mentioned deponant. . . . On the strength of this document, Saunders took Cagliostro into custody.

Staggered by this villainy, but confident in his innocence, the victim was getting ready to follow him, when an unusual noise was heard issuing from the next room. Cagliostro asked permission to go and see, and everyone present accompanied him. Horrors! It was William Scott breaking open a cupboard. He had two men helping him, a fellow named Broad, Mary Fry's servant, and a solicitor named George Reynolds. The latter claimed, with an air of assurance, that he was entitled to open the cupboard in his capacity as a sheriff of London. Following to the word the directions previously given them by Vitellini, the pillagers discovered and carried off, under Cagliostro's own eyes, his marriage certificate, the cabalistic manuscript, a gold box containing the rose powder of transmutation, and the receipt for the loan of £200 jointly signed by Scott and Mary Fry.

Cagliostro, an angry witness of the scene, had nevertheless to spend the night at the bailiff, William Saunders's.

But the saddest nights have their lessons. The next day, having made a statement of his defence, he was given to understand that, in default of the sureties required by law, he would have to deposit with the bailiff about £1,000 in cash and jewellery. He deposited accordingly:

1. The necklace and snuff-box given to Mme de Cagliostro by Mary Fry.
2. A cane with a gold repeating watch, set in small brilliants, at the top.
3. His wife's watch.
4. His own watch.
5. Several pieces of Spanish and Portuguese money.

And Saunders gave him a formal receipt.

When she saw him return home on the evening of the 8th February, Mme de Cagliostro imagined that her husband had got out of the affair once and for all. But she was mistaken. The next day, toward midnight, a serjeant, accompanied by several policemen, loudly knocked at the door. By virtue of a warrant, issued on Mary Fry's application by the justice of peace of Hammersmith, the couple were to be arrested as magician and sorceress respectively. The prospect of shivering in a cell through an icy February night was not very cheerful. Some notes, slipped into the serjeant's hand, brought him to reason, and he was glad to allow M. and Mme de Cagliostro to remain in their house until they should be summoned to the court.

One can imagine in what agitation they spent the night. Early in the morning, who should they see coming but the solicitor George Reynolds in person. Paying first a compliment to Cagliostro's learning, he had the audacity to question him as to how the manuscript and the rose powder were to be used. William Scott, hidden behind the door, was overhearing their conversation. When it seemed to languish, the desperado rudely burst into the room. Putting a pistol to Cagliostro's chest, he threatened to shoot him if he persisted in his silence. His victim only replied with a long and contemptuous stare, while Reynolds knocked the pistol aside. In vain they resumed their shameful inquisition. An abyss of silence lay between them and Cagliostro. In the end he told them with a majestic air :

" Fools ! Why do you ask for the impossible ? In vain have you robbed me, for you will never know how to make use of those objects. Better return them to me, and I shall, in exchange, give up the receipt for £200, as well as the articles that have been left with Saunders."

A supernatural influence, an almost divine effluvium, seemed to emanate from that man. Confounded, the rascals promised to do as was suggested. But later they changed their minds, and broke their word. To return the manuscript and the rose powder would have broken their heart.

After they had gone, Cagliostro appeared before the magistrates. He took an appeal to the King's Bench Division, and two securities which he offered saved him in the meantime from gaol.

. . . .

Clementino Vannetti refrained from going into the mazes of English legal procedure. His countrymen would not have followed him. He confined himself, therefore, to the essentials of this tiresome chicanery. Instead of enumerating the different means by which, in 1777, the prophet had tried to protect his life, his peace, his liberty and his honour, he described him denouncing to the police the outrages committed on him, and in his turn, taking a series of warrants against his aggressors. But warned secretly, Scott, the solicitor Reynolds, and Broad the footman, unfortunately had time to make off.

Nor is it necessary to follow the Fry-Cagliostro trial, which Vannetti called the " case of the first necklace." Diamond necklaces, in fact, brought ill-luck to his subject.

Mary Fry dwelt mainly on the fact that her poverty would have prevented her—even had she wished—from giving Mme de Cagliostro such a costly jewel. The soothsayer had assured her that, merely by burying the diamonds for a while, they could be softened, and that it would then be child's play to expand them by an appropriate method, and harden them by means of the rose powder, and thus increase their value a hundredfold. If she had bought these diamonds in Prince's Street, it was only with a view to making this experiment.

Besides the necklace and the gold box, the magician had extorted considerable sums from her under various pretexts. So, on the 24th May, 1777, she obtained another warrant against him, on the ground that he was withholding an amount equivalent to £200 belonging to her, " in a foreign currency called sequins."

Every word betrayed her folly. But her bitterness, and the villainy of those in whose power she was, made of her a dangerous enemy. Her sister, Mrs. Gaudicheau, a shameless and cunning creature, ran a coffee house at Charing Cross ; there Mary Fry was able to consult Scott's gambling companions whenever she wished.

They instigated her to challenge the security furnished by Cagliostro ; they contrived all manner of threats, obstacles, distraints and arrests ; they left no stone unturned. And Cagliostro, alone, unaided and without connections, betrayed by Vitellini and Mme de Blevary, was giving battle in a country where everything, including the language, was unknown to him.

In his profound anxiety, he went to William Saunders for advice. In spite of the natural toughness of a bailiff, this man was not without a certain good-nature. Of his own accord, he put the matter before a solicitor named Priddle, who was an old hand at chicane and whose obstinacy and combativeness were well known. At the same time, he recommended to him a capable lawyer named Mr. Wallace. It was thus that M. de Cagliostro came in touch with these two men.

After much delay, his case was finally posted for the 27th June, 1777. Cagliostro congratulated himself that it was coming up before Chief Justice Lord Mansfield, a judge, they told him, who was universally held in respect.

However, his enemies did not take it in the same way. They quietly got in touch with Priddle, and after some mysterious conversations between the contending lawyers, it was resolved to appeal to an arbitrator. The Chief Justice, on being informed that the parties had agreed to waive their right to plead before him, consented to have the matter sent up to arbitration.

Cagliostro protested. He did not approve of this procedure, which had been manœuvred hastily and behind his back. But they rebuked him. He was told that such was the practice in the United Kingdom, and that his cause would lose nothing by it. Moreover, at that stage, Priddle was still endeavouring to keep up appearances ; it was not until the end of the week that, finally, the mask was thrown aside. On the 4th July, 1777, the parties having assembled before the arbitrator with their respective solicitors and witnesses, to the great scandal of all present, Priddle rudely declined to plead for

Cagliostro. They exhorted him, and they begged him, but nothing availed ; he persisted in his refusal, and Cagliostro, unable to speak English, had to defend himself through the medium of Vitellini. It was thus that this delicate business fell to the cunning interpreter who had been betraying him ceaselessly for the last six months.

The stranger put forward the defence he had always put forward, namely, that the necklace and the snuff-box with the double bottom were, in his eyes, simple thankofferings. Besides, to prove his powers of divination, he offered to give, no matter against how large a stake, the first number to be drawn in the approaching lottery. And far from wishing to keep the secret of his method to himself, his most ardent desire was to divulge it for love of the human race.

But the arbitrator, Henry Howarth, was an Englishman of the old school. He was mortally afraid of clever people who were, as a rule, in his opinion, scoundrels. Devoted body and soul to the sober orthodoxy of custom and opinion, he would have liked nothing less than to injure the prosperity of the English lotteries. Ignoring Mary Fry's accusations, as well as Cagliostro's numerous affidavits, he contented himself with awarding both the snuff-box and the necklace of sixty-two diamonds to the plaintiff. As for the other articles deposited with William Saunders and not claimed by Mary Fry, he ordered that they should be returned to Cagliostro.

The surrender of the necklace could not, certainly, distress the prophet, who had, of his own accord, offered to give it up on several occasions. But according to the arbitrator's award, the jewel was not a gift, but a loan, and, what is more, the seer was condemned to bear the costs. What a disappointment, after all these vexations ! But the pill had to be swallowed ; on the 17th November, 1777, he grudgingly paid the costs.

Thus, from his first visit to London—assuming that he had not arrived there until the summer of 1776—Cagliostro had a foretaste of the hateful persecutions which were to follow him through Europe. And this visit is so important that most of the subsequent events cannot be understood except in the light of this period.

Without taxing their patience, Clementino Vannetti succeeded in pointing out to his fellow citizens the picturesque, savoury episodes which he hoped would divert them. He explained to them, for example, that in the spring of 1777, Cagliostro, tired of being repeatedly arrested on Mary Fry's application, had had the original idea of leaving Great Suffolk Street, and taking up lodgings in the bailiff William Saunders's house. There, as a voluntary prisoner, he was not, under English law, liable to arrest. His person became sacred, and he was at least sure of going to sleep in his own bed. Well lodged and well nourished, he kept open table, for seven or eight guineas a day, and regularly settled his account with his host every evening.

This incident delighted Vannetti's audience. And not less amused were they at a mishap that befell Cagliostro on the 9th August, 1777. A Mr. Badioli, who had stood security for him, having invited him to come for a drive, the soothsayer agreed very cordially. It was a bright morning. At a prearranged time, the carriage stopped in front of a gateway. Badioli got down, and after him, chatting all the time, Cagliostro. A heavy folding door opened into a yard. Badioli, out of courtesy, stepped aside to let his friend pass first. The latter went in, not suspecting anything. But behind him the door closed quietly, and Cagliostro found himself, to his dismay, locked up in jail. His companions in misfortune informed him later that in England, those who offer bail have only to appear in Court for the defendant, or rather, surrender him to the authorities, to be discharged of their obligations.

The imprisonment would have been prolonged over a month had not Cagliostro, at the end of that period, fallen in with a good fellow named O'Reilly. Touched with pity, O'Reilly acted as intermediary, and introduced him to a very active and able young barrister named Mr. Sheridan. From that time the clouds lifted. Lord Mansfield learned, not without indignation, of the frauds by which Cagliostro had been victimised. Fresh bail was found for him, and the Chief Justice himself being at the back of it, it could not be opposed by Miss Fry, and Cagliostro, after an incarceration of six or seven weeks, regained his liberty.

These piquant interludes did not cause Vannetti to overlook the question of identity about which the public was so curious. He displayed with the greatest care the significant coincidences and the troublesome conjectures to which Count de Cagliostro had given rise since his first appearance.

In July 1777, for example, the solicitor Edward Aylett had met in Westminster Hall a foreigner in a military uniform. Impressed by his exotic features, after some little reflection he thought he recognised in them a client of whom he had unpleasant memories; a certain Giuseppe Balsamo, a Sicilian painter and sketcher, who had bolted off in 1772, without paying the costs of a lawsuit that had been started in his name against a Moroccan Jew named Moses Benamore. For five years Mr. Aylett had been unable to console himself for this disappointment, and at last providence had brought his debtor back to him. He immediately commenced his inquiries, and discovered that the fugitive was living in Great Suffolk Street.

On the 12th August, he made out an affidavit saying that Giuseppe Balsamo, self-styled Cagliostro, owed him £10 and more, for his fees as solicitor, as well as for moneys lent and advanced. The claim was subsequently increased to thirty pounds sterling.

How astonished was Cagliostro, therefore, when he learnt, at the moment he was released from jail, that another arrest was impending. He did not understand it at all, he said. Nevertheless, in his extreme impatience to regain his liberty, he at once sent Mr. Crisp some silver plate by way of security ; then, the next morning, he was careful to send him the required thirty pounds. Too late ! The " marshal " replied that the plate had been confiscated by Mr. Aylett. Cagliostro hastened to the solicitor. *He* swore, in his turn, that Mr. Crisp was lying. Which of the two rogues was the culprit ? The quarrel became embittered. Meanwhile, good-bye to the silver plate !

It is hard to understand Cagliostro's weakness in these circumstances. No doubt, disgusted and tired out with worries as he was, he had reached the point at which men readily give up the struggle. But Cagliostro had absolutely lost his head. Why did he not prosecute Aylett for perjury and the " marshal " Crisp for fraud ? There is really something inexplicable in his deplorably passive attitude.

Aylett, for his part, did not fail to produce two important witnesses. John Lowe, his clerk, who had seen Balsamo " fifty times " at the time of the Benamore affair, asserted that he could recognise him in the person of Cagliostro. The painter, Pergolesi, said the same. No doubt, according to the soothsayer, all these depositions had been paid for by Scott and Co. Cagliostro believed he had alienated Mr. Pergolesi, the conceited dauber, by refusing to see him at the time when the exaggerated eulogies of his interpreter, Vitellini, had every day drawn so many importunate visitors to him that he had been obliged to shut his door against them. But his arguments, plausible in themselves, lacked that final and supreme authority which victoriously dissipates doubt.

In the course of these proceedings, Cagliostro did not, in any official document, use the title of Count. There was a deep uncertainty even as to his Christian name. Mary Fry's first warrant attributed to him the curious surname of " Melissa," of unknown origin. Cagliostro's affidavits were not signed Alexander, but invariably " Giuseppe," the same Christian name as that of Balsamo.

The 21st April, 1777, he admitted that he " came from Sicily, his native country." The next day, another affidavit confirmed his declaration : " he was born a Sicilian." A third document, manifestly written under his dictation, began with the words : " The defendant, M. Cagliostro, native of Sicily. . . ." Balsamo and Cagliostro, then, were fellow-countrymen.

The analogy went still further. As Giuseppe Balsamo had shown a taste for chemistry and magic, the Count represented himself to be " a very good painter." So that the taste for plastic arts and for occult sciences made them doubly related.

Was it pure chance that, among the valuable objects that Cagliostro had entrusted, in February 1777, to the bailiff Saunders, they noticed a cane whose top contained a repeating watch, set in diamonds, exactly similar to that which Balsamo-Pellegrini had bought in 1776 in Cadiz at the firm of Silvestre ? A curious resemblance : such an object is not met with frequently. Finally, the money which Cagliostro had brought to London was found to consist exclusively of Spanish and Portuguese coins, as though he had come straight from the Iberian peninsula. Was then the thread so mysteriously broken at Cadiz to be recovered in London?

Aylett and the other persecutors of the soothsayer did not push the comparison home. It was enough for them to make England too hot for him. Incensed by so many injustices, greviously impoverished—the £2,000 which he had on arrival, had dwindled to fifty guineas—Cagliostro prepared to leave with the remnant of his fortune. What he regretted more than all else was his manuscript and his rose powder.

He thought so highly of these two things that, on the eve of his departure, he took care to place in Mr. O'Reilly's hands a power of attorney, instructing him to pursue William Scott until he was definitely convicted. But to this he added another, a confidential note, authorising him to recover the box and the manuscript by no matter what means.

Vitellini, fallen into frightful destitution, languished in Newgate Prison, but his former patron did not go to see him, having learned of his treacheries and villainies. On the eve of his departure from England, Cagliostro retained his esteem for but a handful of friends, those whom he effusively called his liberators: Mr. O'Reilly, Sheridan and Chief Justice Lord Mansfield.

. . . .

Perhaps these good men had intervened on his behalf at the request of an occult society. For M. de Cagliostro had belonged, since the spring of 1777, to English Freemasonry. He had been admitted to it at the same time as Pierre Boileau, a footman, and the musician Joseph Ricciarelli, an old man of sixty-two, whom Balsamo had formerly met at the Cardinal Orsini's. Brother Hardivilliers, an upholsterer, had presided over the triple initiation in the King's Head Tavern, at the corner of Gerrard Street, Soho, where the Hope Lodge, frequented chiefly by artists and petty bourgeoisie, usually gathered. The shoemakers, wig-makers, and lodging-house keepers were not a little proud to welcome Brother Cagliostro, who was described in their registers as "colonel of the third regiment of Brandenburg." On the twelfth day of April of the year 5777 of the Masonic era, in other words, the year of grace 1777, Cagliostro successfully underwent the ritual tests.

These tested the courage, docility and perseverance of the candidate.

By means of a cord fixed to the ceiling by a pully, he was hoisted up in the air, in such a manner that the weight of the body caused an intolerable pain in the arms and legs. With his eyes bound, he had to load a heavy pistol. But when he was bidden to shoot himself in the temple, his courage seemed to fail. At that moment, the pistol was torn from his hands with expressions of scorn, and his chiefs ordered him to repeat the following oath:

"I, Giuseppe Cagliostro, in the presence of the Great Architect of the Universe, before my superiors and the respectable company in whose midst I am, I promise everything that shall be commanded me by my superiors ; to that end, I undertake, under penalties known to my superiors, to obey them blindly, without prying into the motives of their orders, and not to disclose the secret of the mysteries which shall be communicated to me, either by voice, gesture or written word."

Miraculous virtue of this formula ! No sooner had the candidate pronounced it, than he felt himself becoming a different man, full of an indomitable energy. The pistol was returned to him. With a firm hand, he brought it near his temple and released the trigger. A flash, a report, a rude shock, but no pain at all. At that instant, the bandeau was removed. They gathered round him, they congratulated him, they embraced him, and there he was, in one single day, apprentice, companion and master, raised, moreover, to the honour of the "Scottish rank."

A bookseller sold him, soon afterwards, in some obscure circumstances, a lot of manuscripts formerly belonging to a certain George Cofton. The life of this Irish Catholic priest, who had died in the odour of sanctity, had given rise to intricate controversies. There is no doubt that his writings produced a strange transformation in Cagliostro. In meditating over them, he received visions of the means by which Freemasonry could advance to its ideal stage. Adumbrating sublime projects, he dreamed of a purer sect of which he should be the founder, the Grand Master. Thereupon he made his first disciples. Soon after, the presence of the sower not being any longer necessary in the field where the mystic seed had begun to sprout, he did not hesitate to take leave of his proselytes.

. . . .

After having thus described what took place in England between the years 1776 and 1777, Clementino Vannetti remained silent, considering that he had discharged his duty towards his listeners.

But their tongues were soon wagging, and each one began to interpret the story in his own way. The partisans of the doyen of the doctors were certain that Cagliostro and Giuseppe Balsamo were identical ; they triumphantly produced all the analogies they could. Meanwhile, however strong their reasons, their case broke to pieces against the invincible obstinacy of Cagliostro's disciples ; these latter pointed to the infinite distance that virtue, talent and the inspirations of a semi-divine wisdom had put for ever between the two persons. And the pious folk were rather inclined to believe that Balsamo had been swallowed alive by the earth at Cadiz for his sins. All these debaters pressed Vannetti to give the casting vote. But he, smiling, with a finger at his lips, left them to their disputes.

Nor would he consent to relate to them the sequel of the voyages of the Count de Cagliostro. The happenings in London, he explained to them, were recorded in a small number of brochures accessible to the whole world. But the latter career of the hierophant was the subject of an enormous literature. As he had not finished studying the documents which were reaching him every day, Vannetti would not allow himself to offer his fellow citizens an unauthenticated account.

With these words he respectfully bade them adieu with a graceful air and walked out of the café where the gossips continued to chatter away. At home he found Donna Bianca-Laura, also impatient to question him. For the old lady, since the success of the *Liber memorialis*, had felt for Cagliostro a curiosity that her son could hardly satisfy. . . . How that warm, inextinguishable interest, showing itself in all that concerned him, consoled and stimulated Vannetti in his work ! How he felt transported, exalted above his habitual sphere ! And how could he, after this, return to the *Life of Cicero* ?

VI

TRAVELS IN GERMANY AND EASTERN EUROPE

BY the spring of 1789, Vannetti had accumulated an enormous amount of material. Unfortunately, the fame of his *Liber Memorialis*, spreading far and wide, had alienated from him all Cagliostro's supporters. None of them would consent to help the spiteful author of that satire. And Vannetti, though he continued his investigations, was regretting more and more his inability to benefit by the advice of those who had had dealings with the Count and been taken into his confidence. How much enlightenment could he derive from the disciples, especially Jacques Sarasin, who was so familiar with the Count! But there was no use in making friendly overtures. No response ever came from the " White House."

According to the evidence that Vannetti had, the Master, on his way from London, had stopped at The Hague in 1788. The Freemasons of the City invited him to their Lodge, the *Indissoluble*. Standing with uplifted swords at the entrance, they had formed an arch under which he passed when he came to visit them. For two hours he discoursed to them about the sacred and profane sciences, and the glory of the great Architect of the Universe. In their enthusiasm, the brethren, among whom was the Duke of Brunswick, begged him to organise a Lodge for Women, and he agreed. The Countess de Cagliostro, presented with a diploma of membership on the 29th March, 1778, and subsequently appointed Grand Mistress, inaugurated her sacerdotium with grace and dignity.

At The Hague the Master grew fond of a disciple who, being poor, begged him to make forecasts as eagerly as William Scott and Mary Fry in London. With this difference, however, that unlike those swindlers, the Dutchman and his wife willingly put what jewels they had at his disposal for the most expensive experiments. They only had to lend them. By a process only known to him, Cagliostro transformed some tiny pearls they gave him into a few superb ones worthy of the proudest kings. Then, accompanying his friend to the casino in Brussels, he caused him to put about five hundred ecus on some numbers that he had carefully worked out in advance. He himself made up at Brussels for the losses he had incurred in London.

Nevertheless, his enemies maintained that the charlatan, having " plucked " the Dutchman, had gone off to Venice to resume the rôle of the Marquis Pellegrini, which Giuseppe Balsamo had so brilliantly created in 1775.

Promising to make gold, whiten diamonds, solidify mercury and convert hemp into silk, he had extracted a thousand sequins from a rich merchant on the Grand Canal. Then, without saying anything, Pellegrini, once more turning into Cagliostro, had made off as fast as he could via Innsbruck to Germany. . . . But there is no proof for this story.

The Count and the Countess were at Nuremburg soon after. A

TRAVELS OF COUNT CAGLIOSTRO

gentleman connected with the Rosicrucian Order came to see Cagliostro at his inn. With their first greeting, they recognised each other as brethren. And the visitor became profoundly respectful when, having demanded of the Count his true name, the latter silently pointed to the badge he was wearing: a serpent clasping an apple in its mouth, and an arrow piercing it through. Struck with awe at the sight, the gentleman immediately fell on his knees. He had no doubt that he was in the presence of the secret head of the Masonic Order, the depository of the principal truths of this and the next world, who kept himself hidden from human eyes so as to escape the tragic fate of the Templars. Prostrating himself, he begged Cagliostro to accept a magnificent diamond ring, and with a grave smile, the Count deigned to put it on his finger.

After these homages, he could not but have been disappointed with Prussia where Frederick II was maintaining a drab rationalism. Though he claimed to be the protector of the Freemasons, he only controlled them the more effectively. No prayer, no act of faith could issue from such narrow and contracted hearts. The vogue for mystical raptures was not to seize Berlin until the reign of Frederick's successor.

At Leipzig, the ground was better prepared. In fact, Saxon high society was infatuated with the mysterious. It went in crowds to see a young tavern maid who was reputed to have supernatural gifts. Johann George Schrepfer, the innkeeper, locked up his visitors in a dark back room, having thoroughly befuddled them with drink and smoke. And a-quiver with excitement, the enthusiasts would then watch various sinister happenings, dialogues from beyond the tomb, spectral processions, rattling chains, moans, groans and sighs. Schrepfer himself presided over these phantasmagorias, dressed in the uniform of a French colonel, which he would account for by showing a warrant from the Duke of Chartres, the Grand Master of French Masonry. His dealings with the spiritualists was of great financial advantage to him. Among his patrons was Prince Charles of Saxony, ci-devant Duke of Courland. Little by little, however, the illusion wore out ; the dupes revolted, Prince Charles thrashed him, and the police came rushing up. Confounded by this hue and cry, Schrepfer had gone out of his mind.

Four years had passed since then. And the proprietor of the Hôtel de Baviere, a former Freemason, judging by the way they spent money, formed a very favourable opinion of the Count and the Countess. He was somewhat surprised that the Countess should be travelling without a maid ; but as the Count insisted on his servant having lodgings and food as good as those supplied to himself, the absence of the maid was not very serious in the eyes of the hotel-keeper.

It was he who introduced Cagliostro to the Freemasons as a celebrated hermetist. The Lodge *Minerva aux Trois Palmiers*, impatient to behold the lamp of wisdom, gave a banquet in his honour. Under the eyes of the brethren, the apprentices covered the table with a dazzling cloth upon which the dishes, decanters and glasses were stretched in a long row, in groups of three, the sacred number. And that the ministrations to the body may not distract them from their masonic duties, Cagliostro gave a solemn lecture in the course of the meal.

Assuredly, he said, Freemasonry is in principle indivisible, and the different lodges in the world form but one single community. But, actually, schism was triumphant. The Dutch first, then the Germans, had passed from the Grand Lodge of England to the Strict Observance. Secession, sacrilegious in the eyes of those who clung soberly and firmly to orthodoxy ! . . . Dogma had decayed as well as discipline. The creation of the higher grades aroused the jealousy of the rest. Many of the lodges, out of a desire to make money, sold their diplomas, and thus encouraged the grossest ambition. Instead of obediently rendering unto Cæsar that which belonged to Cæsar, the new officials took part in politics. They professed to trace Freemasonry back to the Workers' Guilds and Chivalric Orders of the Middle Ages. What childish inventions! Only the rogues who travelled about, pretending to be great occultists, benefited by these fables. Black magic had taken root in London with Samuel Jacob Falk, the old cabalist Jew. And even in Leipzig, the crafty Seiffert was in league with the demons. Shame and woe to their accomplices! . . . In the midst of a deep silence, the orator predicted that before the end of a month, Seiffert would feel the weight of divine anger.

He next visited Danzig, and was warmly welcomed by the masonic lodges. Then, at Königsberg, on the 25th February, 1779, the inhabitants read in their newspapers that Count de Cagliostro had arrived at the Schenken inn, in the Kehrwiederstrasse. But they took no further interest. To rouse them up, the prophet had been obliged to speak in German and preach in public. Besides, a high official, the Chancellor von Korff, was hostile to him. The traveller's impudent looks and terribly coarse manners prejudiced M. von Korff against him.

"He a Count?" he muttered between his teeth. "Tell it to someone else. Much more likely a Jesuit on some secret mission."

Nothing more was needed to stir up Königsberg, that citadel of Lutheranism, against the so-called revered father. A second encounter only confirmed M. von Korff's enmity.

"By my faith," he exclaimed afterwards, "there, undoubtedly, is a lackey in masquerade! My boys, take it from me. . . ."

Discomfited, Cagliostro refrained from thrusting himself on an unfriendly public. What was there to do at Königsberg, and who to see? Emmanuel Kant was not yet celebrated. In 1879, the only local glory was a Johann George Hamann, surnamed the "Sage of the North," in opposition to Lavater, the "Sage of the South." This religious warrior persistently attacked, in his rough and obscure style, the Berlin rationalists such as Mendelssohn, Reimarus and Nicolai, who made an idol of reason. Hamann defended sensibility, the imagination, all the intimate spiritual faculties which nourish the soul. Human beings, he maintained, could not attain to true grandeur except by the co-operation of all their energies, including the most obscure of them. Opinions quite similar to those, in short, of Cagliostro. Yet Hamann, the suspicious and embittered recluse, scorned the traveller whose volubility he could not tolerate. He let him depart for Courland without seeking to make his acquaintance.

. . . .

Pierre de Biren, Duke of Courland and Semigalle, was grateful to his deceased father for having pulled down the ancient palace of Mitau. In place of that pile, more military than seigneurial, and recalling the barbarity of the Gothic Ages, Rastelli, the architect of the Winter Palace, had erected an edifice as lovely as it was magnificent. Admirable were its gardens, its spacious courtyards, its French-Italian façade. Three hundred elegantly decorated rooms opened their windows on to the impetuous waters of the Aa. Pierre de Biren, an upstart nobleman and prince of recent creation though he was, thus found himself in possession of a residence worthy of the Habsburgs and the Bourbons.

But he hardly took pleasure in it. Though he had in his youth shared his father's disgrace and suffered exile in the fogs and marshes of Siberia, the cold at Mitau was unbearable to him. In more peaceful days, he had dreamed of travelling through Europe, its capitals and watering-places. But since the first partition of Poland, his Russian neighbours had been causing him anxiety. What exactly were they plotting? What dangers threatened the Duchy of Courland? If he could, he would have gone to consult the tavern-keeper Schrepfer at Leipzig, as his predecessor Charles of Saxony had done.

Nor would his subjects have blamed him for it. As the German lodges knew, Courland was the promised land of occultism. Cagliostro had been advised not to rush through Mitau. He should stop there, they said, and convey their greetings to His Excellency the High Burgrave von der Howen as well as the brothers de Medem, the Count and the Marshal. These three gentlemen had been early initiated into Freemasonry in their student days at Strasbourg and Jena. They could not have been better disposed towards the Count de Cagliostro, through whom they hoped to replenish themselves with spiritual energy.

It was in the guise of a colonel in the Spanish service, sent by his masonic superiors on a mission to the north, that the traveller presented himself to Marshal de Medem, who arranged that he should meet at the High Burgrave von der Howen's house his brother the Count de Medem and an intimate friend, Major von Korff. These gentlemen's hopes were surpassed. The enchanter, after transmuting mercury into silver before their eyes, offered to perform a still more difficult feat with the assistance of a small child.

The Marshal de Medem was pleased to entrust to him, for this purpose, his youngest daughter, aged about five or six years, whom Cagliostro himself seated on her father's lap. Drawing certain cabalistic signs over her head and in her palms, he anointed her with a special preparation, the oil of wisdom, which was conducive to psychic phenomena. And no sooner had the little child glanced at the palm of her left hand, than she shivered and her face was covered with sweat.

"What do you wish that she should see?" whispered Cagliostro to the Marshal, after reciting a psalm.

Anxious not to alarm the child, the Marshal asked, also in a whisper, that she should be shown her mother and her sisters. Cagliostro fell on his knees and said a *pater*; then, standing up, he traced with his sword some figures as incomprehensible as the formulæ with which he accompanied them. Ten minutes later the child gave a cry: it saw its mother and its sister Louise, it could recognise them distinctly; sitting on a green couch, they were both in conversation with her cousin, Elisabeth von der Recke.

"What is your sister doing now?"

"She is clasping her throat, as though she was suffocating." Then:

"Oh! Now she is getting up. . . . My brother Charles has come in. They are embracing him. . . ."

At first this seemed improbable. Everyone knew that Charles de Medem, the Marshal's eldest son, was at that moment fourteen leagues from Mitau, and that his business would prevent him from returning before the eighteenth of the month.

After the séance, everybody, including Cagliostro, accompanied Marshal de Medem to his house. Who should be the first to greet the nobleman in the antechamber but his son Charles? A few minutes later, the ladies, gathered round the green couch, told him that his daughter Louise had been seized with palpitations from which she had but barely recovered.

What consternation there was at the news! All eyes were fixed on Cagliostro with respectful admiration. The brother de Medem, the High Burgrave von der Howen and Major von Korff, bowing before him, begged him to found a Lodge at Mitau.

As the thaumaturge did not insist upon secrecy, his exploits were noised abroad that very day. The burghers, the nobility and the Court could talk of nothing else. Women reproached the High Burgrave for not having invited them. But more than by anyone else, the Count de Medem was questioned and harassed in his own family: his eldest daughter was passionately interested in the problems of the hereafter.

. . . .

To awaken the dead, to renew broken friendships with them—no other desire had Charlotte Elisabeth Constance since the collapse of her marital happiness. This sensible, delicate and conscientious young woman was married at fifteen to the Chamberlain Baron von der Recke, and had endured five years of torture. His fierce and violent temper kept her perpetually on the rack. There was nothing in common between the pious visionary and the brutal elk-hunter. She had at length decided to run away. But out of consideration for her only child, a girl, she had deferred seeking a divorce.

As far back as she could remember, Elisabeth von der Recke had heard people around her talking of magic and alchemy. Immured after her wedding in a solitary and dilapidated old mansion in the midst of a wilderness of forests and lakes, she had given herself up eagerly to reading. Her enthusiasm for Lavater dated from that time. From his books she learnt that it was possible to render oneself worthy of supernatural revelations by practising a lofty morality and constantly meditating on Christ.

Her brother, of whom she was very fond, Jean Frederic de Medem, encouraged her in these beliefs. He himself was strongly under the influence of Greek thought. His heroes were Plato and Pythagoras. He had, moreover, like Vannetti, a great esteem for the Alexandrians and the Gnostics. Unhappily, the promising youth had died in June 1778 at Strasbourg, where he was finishing his studies.

This bereavement intensified Elisabeth's passion for the supernatural. She lost all interest in ordinary occupations, and spent her time in correspondence with those who had been her brother's teachers at Strasbourg, including the celebrated Laurent Blessig. She went to Lavater for relief. She wrote hymns and religious songs, some of them so good as to inspire Johann Adam Hiller to lofty music. But nothing, not even in success in these lines, brought a moment's peace to Mme von der Recke. Her deep sorrow, her absorption in departed loves, verged on obsession. At night she would go alone to meditate and weep in the graveyard, hoping, by the power of her tears, to evoke the fugitive shades.

Her aunt de Medem, née Kayserling, and her cousin Louise, shared, if less vehemently, the same tastes. Becoming fervent admirers of Cagliostro, they set themselves to recruit a large number of converts when he announced that he had been authorised by his chiefs to found in Courland not a Women's Lodge as at The Hague, but a Mixed Lodge admitting women on the same footing as men.

Elisabeth von der Recke manifested such extravagant delight at this news that several of her friends were seriously perturbed. The counsellor Schwander, who had a paternal affection for her, tried to hold her back at the edge of the precipice. But the two spoke totally different languages. While Schwander, on principle, rejected everything repugnant to reason, Elisabeth, influenced by Lavater, firmly believed in the boundless power of prayer and its miraculous efficacy. It was in vain for Schwander to warn her against Cagliostro. Finally, seeing that nothing would prevail against her infatuation, he said to her, in an impressively sad tone :

" Dear friend, I am desolated by your madness. You are being victimised by an impostor who excels in tricking himself out with all the marks of virtue. Alas ! I have no further hope of turning you aside from the abyss into which you are rushing. Only allow me to accompany you and help you. I shall come with you to your magician's, as if I had myself fallen under his glamour."

At a meeting on the 10th April, emerging from a brief retirement, Cagliostro made the following announcement to the initiates. His chiefs informed him that a famous magician once lived at Wilzen, which was the property of the Marshal de Medem. Foreseeing that his successor would surrender to evil influences, the holy man had himself buried his wealth and his magical instruments in the forest. Necromancers in the service of the dark powers were actively in search of the treasure. One of them had even settled in Courland on purpose. . . . Everyone recognised in this an allusion to M. Starck, the professor of philosophy at Mitau, who was reputed to belong to some mysterious sect. . . . Nevertheless, Cagliostro hoped that the Grand Architect of the Universe would permit him to discover this fabulous treasure before anybody else. The enterprise was certainly fraught with danger. While it was proceeding, the Enemy would redouble his malice, and try to drive him towards black magic. But what a disaster it would be if Black Magic were to prevail ! What a triumph for Beelzebub ! It would take long centuries of effort for mankind to recover from the catastrophe.

" Pray with me, pray for me," advised Cagliostro to the faithful; " perhaps out of consideration for you, the Eternal Being would be pleased to lend me the strength to resist our common enemies."

He indicated on a sheet of paper the part of the forest where the treasure was hidden, and he gave such a precise, minutely detailed description of it, though he had never been there, that the Marshal could not suppress a cry of wonder.

" It is quite simple," said Cagliostro. " During the half-hour when you left me alone, the spirits under my control carried me to Wilzen. I was able to study the scene at leisure, and the guardian spirits of the treasure disclosed the rest to me."

The Marshal and the Count de Medem listened to him with increasing emotion. They had heard people speak of the legendary treasure from the time that they used, as children, to play in the woods at Wilzen. Besides, though Cagliostro reserved to himself the magic instruments, hidden there, he surrendered in advance the plate and the coins and jewels to the Marshal de Medem. The Marshal was accordingly but too glad to allow the performance of yet another experiment with his little daughter.

Elisabeth von der Recke was, no doubt, like the rest, deeply interested in such investigations ; but she did not lose sight of her main object. On the very first day, she had confessed it to Cagliostro: she had but one desire—to establish communication with the spirit of her beloved brother. Though she had spent nights in prayer and meditation, she had not, alas, been granted this singular favour.

Cagliostro answered her frankly :

" Madame, I have unfortunately no power over the dead. My authority is limited to the intermediate spirits of Creation, who are at the service of mankind, as it is said in Scripture. Assuredly, I can, thanks to my knowledge of the sacred mystery, establish contact with the higher Spirits and receive their teachings, but I should be unable to procure visions in a case like yours. Besides, my miracles are not intended for general amusement. Were I to effect them without good reason, the demons would soon get the better of my guardian angels."

And when she pressed him :

" Be careful," he replied solemnly, " above all, when I am gone, not to enquire constantly the why and the wherefore of things. Christ himself said to his disciples : 'Of how many things would I not tell you, if you could bear them !' What do you suppose is the fall of Adam, the original sin ? They are but allegories to warn us against curiosity, pride and ambition, which would prove our undoing to the thousandth generation."

Thus the Master suppressed in the argumentative young lady her flickering spirit of independence. When she pressed him with questions, he would cry out peevishly :

" Come ! Can't you see that it takes time to acquire knowledge. Let us recognise it, my child ; the Supreme Being imposes limitations on ordinary creatures, and the spirits whom I have reduced to obedience have not yet told me everything."

She would then look at him so humbly, so despairingly, that he would be filled with pity. Finally, to console her, and perhaps also to hasten her spiritual development, he promised that she should have a vision. On the night of the 12th April, 1779, she should have the joy of seeing and talking to her brother.

" Go to sleep," he ordered her, " firmly resolved to speak to him as soon as he should appear. And then, be careful to remember what passes between you, for I shall give your father this evening a question in writing, and it is from your vision that I await an answer."

The Count de Medem received the same evening a sealed triangular note, with the injunction not to open it until the baroness had given an account of her vision before the assembled Lodge.

Elisabeth von der Recke retired to her room at the usual hour. After having gone over the happenings of the day, she fervently prayed to God. Then she waited. . . . It was impossible for her to close her eyes. Her thoughts went round and round in grotesque confusion. When dawn broke, she had not had a moment's rest. Cagliostro said nothing, but when a similar failure was reported to him the next day, he could no longer conceal his irritation :

" I did not think you were so devoid of the mystical energy," he said to her rudely. " So much the worse ; you have lost an opportunity ! Forget all about it."

Elisabeth turned very pale, and seeing her about to faint, Cagliostro repented of his harsh manner. He told the baroness's parents, in confidence, that, in spite of everything, the vision might still occur on the third night. And when, after supper, he was inviting his hosts to a talk the next morning at nine, on the *Barba Jovis*, a medicine which would keep one's energies in equilibrium and prolong life, he graciously extended the invitation to Mme von der Recke.

Before going to bed, the baroness read a few pages of Swedenborg and put out the candle. A violent attack of fever came on about midnight, accompanied with nightmares and convulsions. This extremely severe fit left her gasping and too weak even to call for her maid.

The next morning the Master began by announcing to his disciples that the baroness had not sufficiently strong nerves. In spite of the intercession of the most kindly and favourable spirits, her weakness condemned her to visions which were only horrible or absurd. Thereupon, he bade an old gentleman to go and repeat the invitation he had previously given to Elisabeth :

" You will find her in bed," he said, " exhausted with fatigue, incapable of accompanying you. Don't be alarmed ; this weakness will disappear by itself. Mme von der Recke will be able to get up at three in the afternoon. Confine yourself therefore to telling her how disappointed we are that she is not in our midst, as she had promised to be."

The baroness was in fact in bed, tired out and much distressed. After the messenger had gone, she fell into a peaceful slumber. When she woke up, about three in the afternoon, she was able to dress and go into her boudoir to write.

" Now go back to our dear sister," said Cagliostro to the old gentleman. " She has recovered strength and is at present busy with her correspondence. Bring her here."

It was quite true. The baroness, who was seated at her desk, received the gentleman very graciously, and drove with him to Cagliostro's house. Seeing her enter, Cagliostro ran forward with his arms wide open.

" Ah ! my dear daughter, what a night ! what suffering ! However, is it not partly your fault ? When you are less impatient to see your brother, when you have a physique more suited to the strength of your longings, you shall certainly succeed, and your eyes will plunge into the depths of the Beyond. If you maintain your zeal, you should arrive at your goal ; only, it will be by the main road with others of equal rank. On the day that you joined us, I put you under the care of the angel Anachiel, who vigilantly looks after you day and night. Judging from what he tells me, you have not been drawn to us save by the single desire to see your brother again. Take care ! If it is true, your guardian angel will desert you for ever. Magic should be loved for its own sake."

At that moment, the Count de Medem returned to him the envelope, as the vision had not appeared, and Cagliostro burnt it without opening it.

In short, though he cursed her inwardly for her perpetual questions, Cagliostro treated Mme von der Recke as a superior woman ; as an intellectual queen who had no need of a sceptre to dominate and command. By way of compensation, he offered to conduct an evocation that evening at the Marshal's. On this occasion, he revealed traits such as no one expected from a being so heavenly.

Cagliostro had not fared well at the Court of Mitau. Had Pierre de Biren indulged in any misguided pleasantries ? The fact remained that the enchanter angrily vowed to revenge himself.

On the evening of the 15th April, he began by writing down the Christian names of the Duke and the brother of the baroness. After having interlaced mysterious symbols with their initials, he shut himself up in the Marshal's office where he wrote and burnt some papers.

Then he recalled his disciples. Between two lighted candles on the table, a sheet of white paper covered with cabalistic formulæ was spread out. Dropping on his knees, the enchanter drew toward him Elisabeth's little cousin, embraced her paternally, and rubbed her head with some magical ash. Then, rising, he announced that the child should be left alone in the room.

Everybody withdrew into an adjoining room. Chairs were arranged within a circle drawn on the floor and the disciples sat down quietly, with their faces toward the connecting door, which was shut. Almost at once strange, unintelligible incantations came piercing through the silence.

" *Helion ! Melion ! Tetragrammaton !* "

The three sounds recurred continuously among other Hebraic or Arab names. The magician poured them out with a vehement volubility. Upright, with a naked sword in his hand, he drew emblems in the air or on the panels of the closed door. His shouting, his stamping and his gestures made a horrible din. Charles de Medem, the Marshal's eldest son, thought he would go and see if the doors of the adjoining room were properly shut. But even before he had left the circle, Cagliostro had stopped him. In an unearthly, bloodcurdling tone, he shrieked through the door :

" Wretch ! What are you doing ? Sit down, do not move, in the name of heaven, or you will die ! "

After which, seized with terror, his eyes aflame, he began to stamp and whirl round madly and struggle and shout. When, at length, the ceremony resumed its course, a conversation—perfectly audible to the disciples—began between Cagliostro and the child.

Mme von der Recke heard, with real relief, that her brother Jean Frederic was not at all looking miserable. Dressed in a red uniform, the dead man had his hand on his heart and gave his young cousin an affectionate look. Then, in a remote country, a country of sables, birch trees and the thick fir trees of Wilzen, a handsome boy was seen digging in the earth in the midst of an extraordinary litter of gold and silver ingots, coins and magical apparatus. Suddenly a giant appeared on the scene. With a scarlet cross on his white robe, he stood, a resplendent Saint George, at the edge of the open pit. And Cagliostro, saluting him as an archangel, appointed him as the child's guardian spirit. The child must have felt the heavenly visitor's hand on his lips, for the sound of a kiss was heard.

The Duke of Courland's turn came next. His face was overcast with dark melancholy. Chains were on his hands, his legs, and even his neck, and at each step he made a sinister rattle. Cagliostro instructed the child to stop him and question him, and the answer the child got was that Pierre de Biren, the Duke, on going to his castle at Wurtzau had felt a terrible pain, particularly in his chest. Cagliostro could not dissemble his joy at the information.

"So much the better," he exclaimed with a ferocious chuckle. "His Serene Highness will not any longer doubt my power."

He muttered some formulæ, kicked the door open, and the child, recovering from her spell, came out.

Immediately the thaumaturge began to reproach Charles de Medem violently. How had he dared to come out of the magic circle without permission? Cagliostro's head trembled, his eyes burned with anger and he fell into a swoon.

When, with some difficulty, he was restored, he ascribed his fit to the evil spirits that Charles de Medem had rashly let loose. The demons rebelled, it seemed, every time the good spirits were invoked. And their attacks could not be resisted without the protection of the magic circle.

As for the Duke, he must have been suffering laryngeal spasms at the time the child saw him bound in chains. Cagliostro gave the name of the doctor who had been called to His Highness's bedside. All these details were fully corroborated the next morning.

The old starostine von Korff, Elisabeth's maternal grandmother, who had treated the Count as a charlatan, next incurred his hate. In fact, the opinions of this powerful dowager were not to be despised. Equally important on account of her birth as well as her wealth, proud of what remained of a still arrogant beauty, with enough natural intelligence to supplement the education of which she had no more than any Lettish peasant, she ruled over her family with an iron rod. The mystical curiosities of her granddaughter annoyed her. Not less incredulous than her kinsman of Königsberg, the Chancellor von Korff, she insisted on seeing in Cagliostro nothing but a particularly dangerous swindler. When he went to call on her, the old lady treated him in the most humiliating manner. Cagliostro had at once to go to the Marshal de Medem for consolation.

Pale with anger, he cried, "The starostine will pay dearly for this. She will die on the 13th of next May, before lunch."

Horrified by this prophecy, the venerable old lady's relatives and friends pleaded for her, but in vain: though mollified, Cagliostro declared that the insult was unforgivable. The starostine was destined to die on the 13th May, 1780.

Such a disproportion between the offence and the penalty scandalised Mme von der Recke. Should a sage give way so completely to personal resentments? Besides, though he affected the airs of a nobleman, Cagliostro was so lacking in ideas of propriety that the baroness considered him to be, except in moments of supernatural inspiration, a mean fellow, whose manners were often disagreeable. Other disciples, knowing that his education had been made in Arabia and Africa, deplored the low tone which evidently prevailed at Medina and in Egypt.

Meanwhile, Cagliostro promised the Marshal de Medem and his family that he would go to look for the famous treasure at Wilzen. He agreed that the party should include Elisabeth von der Recke as well as the Count de Medem, von der Howen and Major von Korff. And to her great joy, the baroness was permitted to travel alone with Cagliostro in his carriage. They talked of nothing but the psychic sciences, for Elisabeth was far more deeply interested in them than in the transmutation of metals or treasure hunting.

According to Cagliostro, intercourse with spirits was not an exceptional privilege. All of us can obtain it by means of spiritual exercises and propitiatory ceremonies which give us access to the middle or intermediate stages of nature. The ruling spirits of that zone make it their business to lead us on to ever higher truths. That, in fact, is their duty. And to discharge it, they assume, when necessary, human form. But how infinitely superior are their faculties to ours! To their penetrating eyes nothing is opaque. They read our fate, recommend us to the seven principal Angels, and from ordeal to ordeal, from initiation to initiation, they lead us finally to Jehovah's throne.

JEHOVAH! The echoes of that formidable name roll like thunder across creation. No one had better understood its plenitude, its inexhaustible effulgence, than Jesus Christ. Cagliostro eulogised Scripture as a complete repertory of magic, and the Christ not only as the most divine of beings, but as the first of the thaumaturgists. "Our Lord," he said, "who was initiated in Egypt into the ancient wisdom, was able to work miracles by the virtue of this single word—Jehovah. He was so familiar with its different concealed and superposed senses, its effective value and special privileges, that he could command the Seven Angelic Princes like God himself. The contemplation of that prodigious name, the theory of the numerals 3, 7 and 9, these are the immovable bases of magic. Let therefore our invocations always begin with the sacred name: JEHOVAH!"

While expounding this doctrine, Cagliostro kept making enquiries about a person whose character and conduct he wished to understand better. Elisabeth knew something very important about him. But she had got it from her mother-in-law who, with the exception of two other friends, being the only one to know it, had conveyed it to her under seal of secrecy. And the baroness, faithful to her promise, eluded the Count's questions as best she could. But Cagliostro, throwing fierce glances at her, suddenly dismayed her with this outburst :

" Snake in the grass ! You are hiding from me something that you share with only three others. Swear, swear now, if you dare, that you have not been told about it ! "

Mme von der Recke, alarmed and confused, vainly sought to collect her thoughts, while the magician transfixed her with his fiery gaze :

" Hypocrite ! Quick ! Answer me ! "

Recovering her spirits, the baroness replied with dignity :

" Sir, I am alone in this carriage with you. Why do you make such an indecent scene ? I cannot understand you. You claim to have put me under Anachiel's care. Well then ! If he is my guardian angel, he should be able to read my heart as plainly as God himself. I look, therefore, for my justification entirely to the Supreme Master, in the certainty that he would control the apparent disorders of this world with a view to our salvation."

Upon which, Cagliostro gently shook her hand.

" Dear and noble creature," he murmured, calmly. " You exceed my hopes, you surpass them. Who would have expected so much wisdom of you at your age ? I was ordered by my superiors to put you to this test. If you had failed, you would have been thought capable of any treachery, and fate would have led you to your ruin."

On nearing Wilzen, Cagliostro became absorbed in prayer. Drawing out of his pocket a red morocco Prayer Book, he read to himself in a low voice. Suddenly, at the edge of the wood, he gave a shiver.

" It is there," he cried out impetuously, " yes, there, that the treasures are hidden. Great Architect of the Universe, will you grant me grace to discharge my mission ? "

As soon as they reached the forest, he dashed into it without waiting for a guide. M. von der Howen, the Marshal, and the Count came panting behind. Suddenly he stopped, and pointed out to his companions, who were out of breath, the lightning-riven tree under which for six hundred years gold and silver, maps and magical instruments, had lain concealed.

It was necessary, however, for several reasons to postpone the excavations. Dark, perhaps deadly, influences were at work. Only spirits of a particular class could be pitted against them. Cagliostro did not give battle at once, but effectively barred the approaches to the treasure so that the black magicians could not without special permission approach within three hundred leagues of Wilzen.

That was the main result of his visit. The presence of his ordinary " pupil," the Marshal's youngest daughter, helped his conjurations.

Magnetising a long iron spike, Cagliostro, followed by the whole company, went and planted it solemnly on top of the treasure.

Eight days later, the initiates went to the castle of Alt-Autz, where lived the Countess de Medem, mother-in-law of the Baroness von der Recke, and mother of the exquisite Anne Charlotte Dorothy who was soon to become, by marrying Pierre de Biren, Duchess of Courland and Semigalle.

On the way back to Mitau, the conversation turned on affairs connected with the Lodge. Cagliostro was anxious that the brethren and sisters should devote themselves to the welfare of mankind, a topic to which he referred in terms which would have wrung admiration from his most irreconcilable detractors. He promised Elisabeth that magic, the science by which the soul is suffused by a shadowless light, should enable her to come into touch with the dead, as she was longing to, and that, in addition, she should travel in spirit across the celestial spaces and become, little by little, one of the protectresses of our planet. Finally, she should be carried off to her triumphant apotheosis in a cloud of fire far beyond our petty solar system. What would she see then ? Other firmaments, other abysses, and no doubt a creation less unworthy of the Creator.

The doctrinal expositions of Alt-Autz were continued at Mitau. Cagliostro sat at a table, and his disciples, surrounding him, took notes. He could not express himself correctly in any language ; but his inspired features, his effusiveness, the vehemence of his oratorical gestures, a scarcely intelligible jumble of exclamations and apostrophes, had a powerful effect on the nerves. Professor Ferber himself, the tough-minded realist, the chemist and naturalist whose writings were esteemed everywhere, yielded delightedly to this curious fascination.

Cagliostro laid down as axiomatic the existence of the Supreme Being and the immortality of the soul. Among pagan philosophers, he liked Pythagoras best. Solomon seemed to him a brilliant initiate, but a master rather of material than spiritual forces. Cagliostro showed a profound reverence for the Old and the New Testaments, books which, he said, were as venerable as the *Zend Avesta,* and Greek mythology, and the *Edda.* But the Bible, in its customary and popular form, is shorn of three priceless chapters containing the secrets which rule the world, and of these chapters the occultists alone possessed the authentic and complete text.

Moses, Elijah and Jesus are the spiritual chiefs of our globe. A virtuous Freemason could not set himself more illustrious models. Yet Cagliostro displayed some antipathy for Moses ; though eulogising him in extravagant terms, he would occasionally substitute the prophet Enoch in his place. For millenia, these radiant beings had inhabited the vast spaces of the sky, whence they presided over the birth of the worlds. Their proper sphere of action lies among us, and each of them has his disciples.

The privilege of the followers of Elijah, among whom Cagliostro was proud to count himself, was to rise to heaven in the flesh, like their august Master ; they lost this advantage only if they gave way to the abominations of black magic. But those who escaped the taint were gradually led to supreme perfection through a succession of apparent deaths, and the phœnix rising from the ashes was their appropriate symbol.

Every lodge was, in truth, a school where the neophytes grew in wisdom and virtue. If the Brethren and the Sisters seemed in general but little conscious of it, it was on account of the subtlety with which their spirits were turned away from inferior objects. Their chiefs watched them closely, so as to promote them, when necessary, to the various degrees of the hierarchy.

The process had five distinct stages.

The first stage comprised seventy-two members. Next, the dignitaries of the second rank, the " Forty-Eight," were recruited. These possessed the secret of the rose powder, which was indispensable for the transmutation of metals.

Higher up were the third and the fourth grades, the " Thirty-Five and the Twenty-Four," who possessed still loftier powers. But their responsibility grew in proportion, for the minions of Satan pursued them incessantly from their hiding-places. Blessed are they who attain to the fifth and supreme stage ! The " Dozen " watch their glory shining endlessly through the ages.

Cagliostro himself had not yet passed the third stage. But the impending assumption of one of the " Dozen " was expected, and a promotion would be necessary to fill his place. If, then, the Brethren and Sisters heard it being said everywhere that the Count de Cagliostro was dead, and again, that he was alive, they would understand that their initiator, triumphing over temptations, had attained to the penultimate stage, that of the " Twenty-Four."

His destiny, his apostolic mission, now summoned him to Petersburg. Wishing to make an impressive appearance there, he urged Elisabeth von der Recke to come with him. If she would but support him skilfully, he considered it certain that Catharine II could be won over to their cult, a conversion, moreover, which would be of immense advantage to Courland. Fervent patriot that he was, the Count de Medem, also, exhorted his daughter not to avoid this duty under any pretext. Yet, torn by obscure misgivings, she hesitated.

The final séance astounded and perplexed Mme von der Recke. Alone with the Master, facing the assembly, she was kneeling inside the pentagon, with a magnetised watch in her hand. The " pupil," hidden by a screen, could not see her. And yet, when the thaumaturge began to ask her questions, she described the scene quite accurately : her cousin Elisabeth on her knees, holding a watch. But she also saw, in addition to the usual apparitions, an unknown angel, wearing a golden crown. What was the heavenly visitor's name? Cagliostro wanted to know it, and bade the child put the question. Strange to say, there was no answer. As the pause grew longer and longer, Cagliostro enquired why the angel refused to give him his name. And the reply was instantaneous:

"Because he has forgotten it!"

Cagliostro's indignation was indescribable. He stamped about like one possessed. Asking the spectators to remain absolutely still, he traced with his sword strange figures in the air; he recited incantations in which repeatedly occurred the names *Helion*, *Melion*, *Tetragrammaton*.

Suddenly, he dashed behind the screen and began to write rapidly. A confused and extraordinary noise was heard. The house was shaken as if by an earthquake. Some members of the audience said they felt a hard pinch on their arms. When at length the Master reappeared, haggard, he made this prediction:

"The angel refuses to give his name. I am sorry to say I am convinced of this: there will arise from among you a Judas vowed to my undoing. How can I express the pain it gives me? It is monstrous, it cuts my heart. If I am distressed, it is, however, only for your unfortunate brother's sake. As for me, the Great Architect of the Universe protects me; and the power which knew how to draw Saint Peter out of a twice-guarded cell would not find it difficult to protect me. But for that madman, there is no salvation. Beg though I may with tears in my eyes for his pardon, I should be denied it. You, children of Heaven, faithful to your vows, join with me in my distress. Let us pray together for him who hastens to his ruin, and please also pray for me, for I have to fight against the Evil One unto the hour of my transfiguration."

Later, he gave his followers a lesson in demonology. The spirits whose names ended in *el*, he said, belonged to white magic, while the ending *fer* is connected with black magic. He read out to them in a loud voice the sixth chapter of Genesis, expatiating complacently on the singular love affairs of the angels with mortals. The demi-gods of Greco-Latin paganism, he asserted, had no other origin than this, and not only Christ, but he himself, Cagliostro, was born out of such embraces. Shocked, Mme von der Recke firmly told the Count de Medem that she would never again attend these lectures. Her father had great difficulty in calming her.

However, such tactical mistakes were rare. Warned by a wonderful instinct, Cagliostro carefully watched his words and deportment at Mitau, an unsophisticated town where the slightest imprudence would have led to his ostracism. If they asked him why he went without food and drink, he would reply that physical appetites are blunted by intercourse with angels.

He stumbled on yet another occasion. At a meeting of the Lodge, he started to describe the sorceries by which a magician could triumph over the ladies and win their favours. At once protests broke out on every side ; his words were cut short. And Cagliostro, severely criticised, beat a clever retreat. He congratulated his audience on their purity, saying that he had only intended to test them.

About the same time, the Master quarrelled with his servant and kicked him out. Such brutal treatment increased Elisabeth's misgivings. She thought that devils at times took possession of Cagliostro and that it would be folly to accompany him to Petersburg.

When next he mentioned the project, she confessed that she was not eager to find herself alone in a foreign country with a magician who was liable to succumb at any moment to demoniac attacks. But she promised to go with her father to Petersburg, as soon as the Empress should show the least sign of wanting them. In vain did Cagliostro exert his eloquence. The baroness remained inflexible.

Elisabeth one day asked if she might mention his name to her correspondent at Zürich. Strange to say, Cagliostro did not know of the illustrious thinker Lavater even by reputation. He wanted to consult his chiefs first. Their permission was obtained during a nocturnal interview, and he communicated it to the baroness the next day, but with the reservation that she should not disclose it for a year. In her very first letter, she referred to the " Count of C." Lavater naturally asked if the count was really the great Cagliostro, and the baroness then said " Yes."

Toward the end, Cagliostro disclosed to his friends in confidence that he was not a Spaniard, that his name was not really Cagliostro, and that he had assumed the title of count under instructions from above. On a previous occasion, he had been similarly required to play the rôle of the cabalist Frederic Gualdo. The Lodge would know his real name at some future date. He did not know, either, when the treasure at Wilzen could be dug up.

On the second day before his departure, as they were displaying before him the Duchess of Courland's superb pearls, he could not repress a smile. Those stones, he said, had been made by his own hand in Holland out of some inferior pearls, to oblige a friend who was in difficulty. These words immediately threw the baroness into profound thought. Having need of a considerable sum for some charitable purpose, the very next day, without consulting her family, she took the pearls to Cagliostro. But the alchemist apologetically declined to handle them. Each transmutation of this sort took him at least six weeks, and his chiefs, to whom he owed implicit obedience, had ordered him to leave on the third day. The baroness offered to bring the pearls with her to Russia, where he could melt them at leisure ; but he would not consent. He promised, however, to give her some signal proof of his tender and paternal love. Elisabeth, who cared not at all for earthly goods, begged him only for his spiritual favours. And Cagliostro replied :

" Take care not to reject the other gifts. Jesus, before he undertook his redemptive preaching, was pleased to allow the Prince of Darkness to conduct him to the top of the temple. All the treasures of the world were then exposed to his view, and he observed them dispassionately. Thereafter he judged himself ripe for the sacrifice which was to redeem the son of Adam. Begin then by submitting yourself to temptations. Only when you triumph over them would you have the right to aspire to a higher initiation."

On the day of his departure, Cagliostro did not conceal his grief. Advising his disciples to think of him, to pursue their work diligently, and to keep a discreet tongue, he sighingly kissed them farewell.

. . . .

Among all the masonic obligations, the most irksome to the Courlanders was undoubtedly that of silence. The new initiates would have liked to question the Marshal's daughter about her visions; but Cagliostro had warned them that such curiosity would bring numberless calamities upon them, in spite of the special protection of the archangel Gabriel, and that it would deprive the child of the friendship of the good angels. After his departure, they found their empty days unbearable. Passionate letters were despatched from Mitau by every post, but the sole reply which reached them from Petersburg was a letter in Italian addressed to Mme von der Recke.

The few lines scribbled in a large, childish hand, breathed sorrow:

"Dear daughter and sister, my letter ought to prove to you my singular regard for you. I seldom write to women. . . ." He exhorted her to look after the other initiates as though they belonged to her own family, and to refrain from vain talk.

"Fortified and healed by silence, you can walk upon the veritable Sabine way. By silence, you will be reunited with the heavenly glory in reward for your merits. Dear sister, my heart is unchangingly with you. I watch over your welfare with infinite solicitude. While advising you to be silent, I yet request you to be my interpreter to your father, your mother and your sister. Tell them, as from me, everything that your heart dictates to you. Add that I am in hopes of returning soon to embrace them in person. In the meantime, pray for me; I find myself surrounded here by enemies, and full of grief. This is equally true of your devoted sister, my wife. Whatever may happen, let us bear our sorrows patiently and not struggle against the ignorance of the profane."

The letter ended with a monogram.

However flattering the letter might be, the baroness was distressed to find no reference in it to Catherine II's views. Was there no hope of securing imperial patronage? His reception had apparently been not very warm in Petersburg. And the High Burgrave von der Howen took personal umbrage at it, for he had given Cagliostro several letters of introduction. He raged particularly against a young gentleman of Courland and a Freemason, to whom he had specially commended Cagliostro. How was it that the puppy had not moved heaven and earth in the hierophant's cause?

In fact, the same thing happened with Baron Charles Henri Heyking as with Elisabeth's grandmother and the Chancellor von Korff. The young nobleman had detested Cagliostro at first sight. Nevertheless, subordinating his repugnance to his curiosity, he had gone to the thaumaturge's house to be introduced to the countess.

Cagliostro had extolled his wife, née Princess Santa Croce, and Grand Mistress of Egyptian Masonry. But for all that rhodomontade, Heyking found himself in the presence of an insignificant low-class woman, already fading, with her eyes red with weeping, a woman whose deportment and language recalled those of some wretched circus girl.

What was the object of their journey? According to Cagliostro, it was to visit Catherine the Great and spread the true Light over the territories of the Northern Semiramis.

"I am the chief of the Rosicrucian Princes," the mystagogue declared, showing the baron a turban and a medal. "Here are the insignia of my rank."

The baron permitted himself to remark that the medal was that of the order of Saint Stanislas, and that a king's emblem had been substituted for its red rose.

"You are quite right," said Cagliostro. "Brother von der Howen lent it to me at Mitau to replace my own, which was stolen during the journey. But do you know *this*?"

This was a reproduction of a hieroglyphic emblem such as one may find in any cabalistic treatise.

"I cannot guess its meaning," confessed Heyking modestly. "But I undertake to show you to-morrow, if you like, ten similar reproductions; you would not understand them any more than I do."

For the first time the Count's proud features grew purple with anger.

"I forgive your ignorance and your unbelief," he replied haughtily. "But, let me tell you, Mr. Greenhorn, that I can make you tremble in spite of your Masonic rank."

At that moment a servant came to announce that M. de Normandez, the Spanish chargé d'affaires, requested M. de Cagliostro to call at the legation at his earliest convenience. The words died on the magician's lips. When he had recovered himself, he muttered:

"My faith, I have a great desire to put the wretched chargé d'affaires on the spot; there is nothing to say about ourselves."

"Be careful," replied the baron. "You would soon have the imperial police at your heels if you talk in that strain."

Convinced of the truth of this remark, Cagliostro promised to call the next day at the legation. Then, as dinner-time was approaching, the baron allowed himself to be detained; he had not finished studying the traveller. And at table the conversation turned on the physical and natural sciences:

"What is chemistry?" asked the master of the house. "Child's play compared to alchemy. And alchemy? Nothing to him who knows how to command the spirits. I, for example, have some gold. . . ."

He tinkled some ducats in his pocket.

"—and diamonds."

He displayed a not very elegant ring.

"But it is from my spiritual prerogatives that I derive all my powers. I call up the dead, I compel them to answer me. You smile? Come, then, you would not be the first sceptic that I have converted. Which one among your deceased relatives would you like to see again?"

"My uncle. But on one condition. Let me fire a pistol at the phantom. It cannot harm a pure spirit."

"You are a monster, you wretch! No, a thousand times no, I shall show you nothing. You are unworthy . . ."

He leapt to his feet, furious, and dashed out of the room. The poor countess trembled like a leaf. Cagliostro reappeared in a moment, calmed down, and seated himself, declaring majestically:

"One day you will know the Count de Cagliostro and his omnipotence. . . ."

The dinner was finished in silence; but after this skirmish, the two men had no further desire to meet each other.

At the legation the next day, M. de Normandez urged Cagliostro to cease calling himself a colonel in the Spanish army. Perhaps he even showed him, in connection with a certain cane containing a gold watch, an invoice from Cadiz. Had he not in 1776 stayed there under the name of the Marquis Pellegrini? Cagliostro swore by the great God that this claim had nothing to do with him.

Happily for him, there were in Petersburg other Freemasons than the Baron Heyking, and other diplomats than M. de Normandez.

One of his most faithful followers was a military officer named Peter Ivanovich Melissino. A learned chemist, an excellent mechanician, a skilful pyrotechnist, and a perfect soldier, this Greek from Cephalonia had known how to earn the favour first of the Czarina Elisabeth Petrovna, then of Catherine II. A grand dignitary of the Masonic order in Russia, he had a profound respect for Cagliostro.

His enthusiasm communicated itself to the chargé d'affaires of the French king. The Chevalier de Corberon, also a Freemason, was invited to all the most important séances. He saw Cagliostro deposit his naked sword on a table, between two lighted torches, then write something in an eastern script, with the "pupil" standing at the side. Thereupon the questions commenced, and with remarkable accuracy, the child related all that he saw and heard. After the séance, Cagliostro solemnly burned what he had written.

The violent convulsions he suffered during the ceremony were attributed to the action of the spirits. But the Chevalier de Corberon had some sinister forebodings. He suspected the thaumaturge of being in league with the demons.

While at Mitau the traveller had devoted himself exclusively to Freemasonry and magic, combined with religious sermons, he had here to resort to medicine to attract the public. In this, at any rate, the Russians quickly appreciated his gifts.

The Baroness Strogonow, driven nearly mad by some nervous complaint, recovered her mental balance. Mme Boutorline had prompt and happy accouchements. Senator Ivan Perfiliewitch Yelaguine, the director of the Imperial theatres, paid him homage in dithyrambic terms. And the doctors themselves went into ecstacies over the healing of the assessor Ivan Isleniew, who was suffering from a cancer which they had thought incurable.

This record of success finally drew the attention of Prince Potemkin. After meeting the Count, he professed an enormous admiration for him, in testimony of which he every day sent costly presents to Cagliostro. Not only did Prince Potemkin closely follow the alchemical experiments to which M. de Cagliostro devoted himself in company with General Yelaguine, the senator's father, but he extended to the coterie his all-powerful protection.

On every hand, however, the vulgar protested at the heresy ; the philistines denounced the imposture. However favourable to him his positive successes might be, they were ascribed to an illusion, an optical trick. But suggestion had only a minor place in Cagliostro's system. Beyond the patient himself he usually saw the spirits who were the effective cause of disease. All his art consisted in appealing from nature to the supernatural. And it was precisely by that that the ignorant and the jealous professed to be most scandalised.

Dr. Rogerson, the Czarina's English physician, had given up a case he thought incurable. At the news that the Count de Cagliostro had taken the liberty to cure the patient, Dr. Rogerson was outraged by what he considered to be an infringement of his rights, and called on the thaumaturgist to protest about it. Cagliostro was not disposed to allow himself to be lectured.

" To whom do you address your recriminations, sir ? " he roughly demanded. " Is it to the Count de Cagliostro ? In that case, my servants will throw you out of the window. But if it is to the physician that you address yourself, then I shall offer you satisfaction."

Cagliostro's servants being numerous, Rogerson stammered out that he was only dealing with the physician.

" Very well," replied the Count. " Let us fight, but with our own weapons. Give me some of your deadliest poison and I shall swallow it. As for you, you should swallow in my presence two small pills of arsenic that I shall have the honour to give you, and we shall see which of us fares best."

Dr. Rogerson did not dare to accept the challenge. He revenged himself by prejudicing the Czarina against the thaumaturge.

And that was how the Empress, knowing Cagliostro only through the venomous diatribes of her physician, came to consider ridiculous the infatuation of the Chevalier de Corberon, that "resolute seer of spirits."

Not only did she mock at the French diplomat, but she wrote a farce entitled *The Impostor*, in which Cagliostro was represented under the grotesque name of Kalifalksherton. It was a shallow piece of buffoonery. Some moneyed middle-class women become desperately infatuated with a swindler. He pretends to show them the stars at noon, and robs them methodically of their jewels and gold. In the last act, he runs off with the French instructress of the daughter of one of them, Sophie. But a fine young man, who is in love with the girl, pursues the culprits up to the city gates, stops the cabriolet, and returns in triumph. And the parents show him their gratitude by giving him the hand of the charming Sophie.

As it became certain that the Master could not gain access to the Czarina, his presence in Petersburg, where Rogerson and his cabal continually attacked him, became useless. The countess could not bear the terrible Russian climate. Towards the middle of April 1780, Cagliostro applied for his passports and took leave of his friends. General Melissino gave him some introductions in Warsaw, and the Chevalier de Corberon, still preoccupied with black magic, put him on his guard against one of the most dangerous necromancers, a certain Thoux de Salverte, who was a French officer in the Polish army.

. . . .

Elisabeth von der Recke learnt with painful surprise that the Count de Cagliostro, on his way to Warsaw, had passed through Courland without endeavouring to see her. So the paternal solicitude he had promised had not survived a few months' separation? Since then, Mme von der Recke had lacked the energy to protest against the malicious rumours about the Count.

The High Burgrave von der Howen complained that he had given the hierophant eight hundred ducats and a splendid diamond ring. Another said the same. . . . Yet Cagliostro had refused to take the baroness's pearls with him to Petersburg! What a maze of contradictions! How could one judge such a complex personality?

On the 13th May, 1780, a year to the day since Cagliostro had made his prophecy, the baroness was apprehensive about her grandmother's fate. Happily, the anniversary passed without incident. The old starostine, lunching with a good appetite, could scarcely understand the anxious, tearful looks fixed on her. And Mme von der Recke, overcome with joy, readily concluded that the magician had forgiven Mme von Korff.

Meanwhile, Professor Ferber, in his capacity as naturalist, had been summoned to Warsaw by King Stanislas Augustus Poniatowski. Cagliostro, who preserved happy recollections of their relationship in Courland, hastened to invite the scientist to his hypnotic experiments. And on his return home, Professor Ferber gave the baroness detailed news of the Master.

Elisabeth learnt that, as soon as the thaumaturge had arrived in Poland, he had literally been submerged by a flood of applications. Everyone begged for admission into the Egyptian Masonry. But the appeals were really less disinterested among the Poles than among the Courlanders or the Russians. To solidify mercury or to manufacture gold—such was their sole ambition.

The most instructive meetings were held in the palace of Prince Adam Poninsky, a learned and convinced Freemason. A " pigeon," eight years' old, here replaced the "pupil." The little girl was locked up by herself in a closet, and the questions and answers passed through the connecting door, covered with a black curtain.

One evening, everyone present put down his or her name on a piece of paper which the Master burnt very ostentatiously in their presence. Then he instructed the little girl to pass him the letter which she would find had dropped at her feet. At once, through the half-open door, a tiny hand slipped into his palm a sealed envelope which was hastily opened. It was the document which had been destroyed, or rather, its duplicate; all the signatures were to be found there, complete, in the same order.

Many similar performances excited the King's admiration. Stanislas Augustus then did what the Czarina had not done: he received Cagliostro at Court. And not haughtily and stiffly, like the Duke of Courland, but with affability and consideration. Cagliostro achieved a veritable triumph in His Majesty's presence.

The Princess Charlotte Sanguska, a frivolous and coquettish young lady, having challenged him to tell her of certain events in her private life, he displayed so much knowledge about her that she was staggered. Falling on her knees, the charming sceptic begged him to read the future as he had read the past.

Cagliostro hesitated to reply, but upon the insistence of the King himself, he felt it his duty to explore the immeasurable abyss where time takes shape.

At length, he told the princess that she would go on a long journey. Some stages from Warsaw, her carriage would break down. While it was being repaired, the peasants, fascinated by her hooped skirt, and her high powdered coiffure, would offer her some apples.

" You will go to the spas," continued the soothsayer gravely. " You will there make the acquaintance of a great nobleman. He would inspire in you such a lively passion that you will marry him in spite of your family. I shall myself be in the town where your marriage will take place, and you will try, without success, to meet me. Accept, madam, this talisman. May it protect you from the calamities which threaten you ! But if you commit the folly of looking to it for all your future good, the phylactery will desert you and return to my pocket."

Two years later the princess married, in the circumstances foretold, Charles Henri Otho, Prince of Nassau Siegen, and a high grandee of Spain ; the prophecy was fulfilled, and Cagliostro recovered possession of his talisman.

To the great joy of the Poles, the Master deigned to found a Lodge at Warsaw. The disciples in Courland and Russia heard with a sweet satisfaction that the countess's birthday was celebrated there in great splendour. The Chevalier de Corberon alone was alarmed at the relations which seemed to have grown up between the mystagogue and Thoux de Salverte. The Frenchman, a member of the Strict Observance and president of an " Academy of Secrets," occupied an eminent position in Poland, and Cagliostro had no doubt excellent reasons for wishing to be on good terms with him.

Unfortunately, he incurred the enmity of one much greater, Prince Adam Poninsky, who had, until then, been his protector. Their quarrel broke out at the castle of Wola, where the great nobleman had invited the Count and Countess to manufacture the philosopher's stone in peaceful and tranquil surroundings.

Adam Poninsky was anything but a pure spirit. Carried by the Tempter to the summit of the temple, he had scorned none of the goods of the world. Youth and love were dear to his heart, if one may judge by the furtive glances he cast at the Countess de Cagliostro ; ambition led him into scarcely honourable intrigues, and wealth was essential to his lavish and greedy temperament. He urged Cagliostro to assign to him a personal angel, ready to carry out his orders day and night.

Yet Poninsky was capable of rising, spasmodically at least, to sublime levels. But what a mistake to have chosen Count Moszynsky as laboratory assistant ! He had all the malevolent prejudices of the starostin von Korff and Baron Heyking. Instead of being an impartial observer, he described as imposture everything he failed to understand.

His evil disposition was revealed during the transmutation of mercury. The members of the Lodge having gathered for the occasion in the laboratory, in front of the *athanor*, everyone could see, in the flickering lamplight, the two alchemists at work in apron and shirt sleeves.

The Master and his assistant had prepared the previous evening the Extract of Saturn and a powder called Virgin Earth or Secondary Matter, obtained by distilling rain water. The assistant himself had furnished a pound of refined mercury.

Now, on the 7th June, 1780, Moszynski poured thirty drops of the Extract of Saturn into a flagon containing sixteen grains of Virgin Earth and half the mercury, very carefully weighed. When this mixture was stirred, the mercury was seen to be " redeemed " or fixed. The same quantity of Extract of Saturn was spread over the other portion of mercury ; and as it produced no change, the two portions were mixed in a bigger vessel. When this also had been thoroughly shaken, the mercury took a uniform consistency, of a dirty grey colour. It was then put into a crucible, which it half filled. At that moment, with a solemn gesture, Cagliostro handed to Moszynski an envelope containing two others. The smallest contained a bright red powder, which was immediately thrown into the mercury. And while the Master, to the general astonishment, rolled up the envelopes into a ball and swallowed it, the assistant began to cover up the vessel with plaster.

At once, Cagliostro grasped his hands. It was useless to do it, he declared severely. And, without paying any attention to the protests, he began himself to seal the crucible and did not return it to his assistant until he had carefully smeared it over with plaster. Moszynski let it dry for a moment on a coal fire, then he put it on a heap of ashes. Half an hour later, when it was drawn out with a pair of tongs, and broken open in front of the spectators, everyone could swear that at the bottom there lay a real ingot of refined silver !

Moszynski rubbed his eyes. He knew he had been tricked, and yet everything had been done with his vigilant help. He spent the night in solitary meditation. Furious at what he considered a personal affront, he secretly plotted his revenge.

In his opinion, the transmutation was beyond doubt illusory. The residue must have come from a previous crucible ; the warmth of the ashes would not have been enough to melt it.

Moszynski did not forget either that the alchemist had locked himself in alone one whole night at Warsaw, under pretext of consulting the spirits. And the assistant had found in the laboratory, the next day, that a big basket of coal was two-thirds empty, and that the big pitcher filled with water, had been emptied in the tub.

In short, it was not difficult, in a semi-obscure room, under an apron, before a group of excited and fanatical spectators, to substitute one crucible for another. And Moszynski, so vigilant and so clever, had taken everything into consideration except the possibility of legerdemain. There was not a shadow of doubt about it: at an opportune moment, Cagliostro had seized the crucible and substituted for it another brought from Warsaw.

But Moszynski's companions snubbed him when he ventured to communicate his suspicions to them. What indignant looks ! What shrugging of shoulders ! In vain did Moszynski reveal a conversation he had overheard while passing by a closet : the Countess de Cagliostro, speaking to her husband, was being congratulated for having thrown out of the window, into the drain, a certain mysterious packet he had wished to get rid of. Neither the prince nor his guests would listen to him. More and more audacious experiments were announced. Cagliostro was now getting ready to turn the ingot of silver, impregnated with " germ universal," into primary matter.

He had it filed. The powder being collected in an open phial, double its weight of *aqua fortis* was poured into it, and the solution was put on the stove where, little by little, the liquid evaporated. Moszynski undertook to hold the lamp ; the whole Lodge came to watch over the crucible, in which were taking place those transformations of colour and condition which the alchemists call passages. According to the Master, matter in evolution first took a black colour, characteristic of the first passage. Then followed a series of metamorphoses ending in the brilliant red colour of the seventh phase. Finally, at the eighth or last passage, matter was changed into gold.

The most learned alchemists did not agree among themselves over the duration of the process. Some said sixteen months, others a dozen, but no one less than ten. Cagliostro, for his part, allowed to each passage a period of six to eight weeks. Leaning over the crucible, he would occasionally pour some *aqua fortis* into it. Then, after having from time to time carefully inspected the stuff, he would drive round to visit the sick in the vicinity.

These varied occupations saved him from boredom. But Poninsky and his companions very quickly exhausted the resources of Wola. How they regretted, after that, their seclusion in the depths of a forest ! Loneliness and waiting displeased these ardent creatures. Morning and evening, after reciting the psalm which chased away evil spirits, they gathered round the crucible, happy as undergraduates if they discerned any trace of black ; otherwise, gloomily, they would revert to the deadly monotony of their existence and long to return to their habitual occupations at Warsaw.

A tragi-comic incident occurred to divert them. As they had started unduly to question the " pigeon " he used at Warsaw, Cagliostro had replaced her by a young girl of sixteen. She lent herself so wonderfully to mesmeric experiments that even Moszynski was surprised. Now, on the 16th June, a big uproar was heard : the young woman was accusing Cagliostro of the most disgraceful outrages, and the onlookers found it difficult to soothe her. Moszynski took advantage of this to solicit her confidence in secret. And the " pigeon " finally told him that the ceremonies were prearranged by the mystagogue. Sometimes the answers were given in writing, sometimes it was enough to repeat the first phrase. Never had she been visited by an angel ; and the sound of the kisses which were heard through the door, she herself made by kissing her arms. Triumphantly, Moszynski communicated these confessions to everyone. And his friends, though they still affected an incredulous air, listened to him without annoyance.

These wicked charges reached the Master's ears. He violently railed against Moszynski, the monster to make a fortune for whom he had been racking his wits. The two were quickly brought face to face. When Moszynski had enumerated all the reasons he had for suspecting the imposture, Cagliostro, in the most solemn tone, deplored his ignorance and assured him before God that, notwithstanding his ingratitude, he would make him wealthy. As for the complaints of the would-be Lucrece who had dared to impute profane motives when he had nothing but spiritual ones, he exculpated himself easily. To dispel suspicion, he offered thenceforward to work with chains on his legs, insisting, moreover, that they should put a padlock and seal on the laboratory door. If the eyes of the unbelieving were not opened before the fourth passage, he offered to die by the dagger of one of his disciples. He bent down, touched the ground with his hand, carried it to his lips, and stretching his arms towards the sky, invoked God to confirm his veracity.

But Count Moszynski had the better of him. He discovered in the garden, by chance, the fragments of the crucible which the charlatan had wrenched from his hands on the 7th June and which the countess had tried to get rid of, by throwing it, as she imagined, out of the window and down the drain. There was, therefore, material proof of the substitution, and the news came as a bolt from the blue to those who still defended Cagliostro.

The mystagogue, having assembled them around him, offered to undertake a fresh experiment, but in vain. About midnight, he said, they would go with lanterns to the middle of the park, sufficiently far not to damage the castle by any careless conflagration ; the disciples would then see something more wonderful than any legend. And the next day, he would convert for the benefit of the poor, five hundred pounds of silver ore into refined silver. But they would not even listen to him. The more impudent among them heaped him with abuse. Suddenly, anger mounting to his face, he threatened them with his supernatural powers. Then becoming himself again, he decided to pack up. What was the use of devoting himself to such unworthy pupils ? The next day, the 26th June, 1780, at the early hour when he got into a carriage with the countess, one disciple only came to the door to wish him bon voyage. Cagliostro embraced this dutiful son, this staunch believer ; he blessed him, and encouraged him to persevere in the great work. Then he pointed to the coachman the road to Warsaw.

His erstwhile disciples followed him soon after. After their return to town, Prince Poninsky, Treasurer of the Crown, and Count Moszynski, referendiary of Lithuania, sought to dissociate themselves from Cagliostro. These powerful magnates offered him as much as five hundred ducats to persuade him to go away. But he imperturbably continued his weekly meetings at his Lodge.

As a physician he showed respect for the Salerno school, and praised their prescriptions highly. The apothecaries, however, found it difficult to make them, as they required costly and strange ingredients. Others were extracts from an old book published in Cologne, by an occultist of the previous century—Frederic Gualdo, whose name Cagliostro claimed to have borne in a previous existence.

During this time, his enemies pursued him with their insults. They did not spare even the countess who was accused of trading on her charms. She had thus obtained in Poland, they said, robes and jewels worth two thousand and five hundred ducats, and notably the splendid diamonds which shone at her ears. The same dupes who had thrown away eight hundred ducats in the crucibles and the alembics of Wola had first allowed themselves to be blackmailed by this pretty adventuress.

Some Polish noblemen subsequently boasted that they had made the impostures disgorge. A booklet that Vannetti had before him said so. But was it reliable, this anonymous work, " Cagliostro Unmasked at Warsaw," whose authorship was ascribed to Count Moszynski? It had appeared much later, after six years, at the moment when Cagliostro, a prisoner in the Bastille, was unable to defend himself. Such as it was, it supplemented at many points Elisabeth von der Recke's account. And Vannetti regretted not having something similar to it for the period between the end of July and the middle of September 1780.

For the evidence was sadly conflicting here. According to the author of " Cagliostro Unmasked in Warsaw," the charlatan had taken to his heels before the 27th June. But Professor Ferber asserted not less categorically, that M. and Mme de Cagliostro had spent four weeks at Warsaw after their return from Wola. According to one isolated and dubious statement, the Master had sought refuge with a disciple and protectress, the Countess H——. But who was this noble lady? These reports were all wrapped in impenetrable obscurity.

In Vannetti's judgment, the only certain thing was this: the Count and Countess, leaving Poland, had travelled across Germany; then, after a short stay at Frankfort, they had arrived at Strasbourg in the course of September 1780.

VII

THREE YEARS AT STRASBOURG

AFTER having rested eight or ten days at the Hôtellerie de l'Esprit on the quay St. Thomas, M. and Mme de Cagliostro moved to the Vieille-rue-du-Marché-aux-Vins, joining Saint Pierre le Vieux, where the landlord Vogt gave them the rooms formerly occupied by Jean Frederic de Medem, Elisabeth von der Recke's beloved brother. It was there that a Polish nobleman, the Count Ezewuski, recognised them. He spread the news and the Freemasons of Strasbourg immediately hastened to see the celebrated adept.

Cagliostro dazzled them at first by mentioning all the distinguished friendships he had made in Courland, in Russia and in Poland. But as he subsequently urged them to introduce him to the best society in Alsace, many of his visitors stole away, disappointed.

He was more careful after that. As the only careers open to members of the French aristocracy were the Army, the Church, and diplomacy, he breathed not a word about his medical practice. At most he insinuated that his fame was due rather to his gifts than to his birth, and that, for reasons of State, he was condemned for a time to assume a modest name and rank.

The masonic lodges had quickly broadcast his glory. He possessed, they said, the authentic chemistry and physic of the ancient Egyptians, as well as the philosopher's stone, for the last links between alchemy and the nascent science of chemistry had not yet been broken at this period.

Toward the middle of October 1780, Cagliostro began to give away his balms and elixirs gratis. He could not be reproached with stooping below his rank, for he accepted no payments in any form. On the contrary, he distributed alms and subsidies in addition to his medical advice. In urgent cases, at night, he would rush to the sick bed. The venerable curé of Saint Pierre le Vieux, M. Zaegelins, was so much impressed by him, that he held him up as an example to his flock. His popularity immediately spread beyond the parish. His house, besieged by crowds of patients, was no longer big enough. Sick men of every kind, blind men, deaf men, cripples, dropsiacs, struggled for admission.

In winter, from six in the morning; in summer, from five, his carriage sped about the town up to nine or ten o'clock in the evening. And people noted with approval that his carriage made much briefer halts in front of the superb mansions of the rich than before miserable hovels. Men, women and children knelt around him and sprinkled holy water on him ; some told their beads and made the sign of the cross, and money flowed freely into the hands of the doorkeepers.

About this time, Lt.-Gen. the Marquis de la Salle, second officer in command of the province of Alsace, happened to be deprived of the services of his chief secretary, M. le Monnier. This unfortunate young man was suffering from gangrene, and the doctors expected that he would die within forty-eight hours. Cagliostro was then called in. A few drops of some unknown liquid which he administered to the dying man caused him to perspire freely. He then made him drink some goat's milk, the goat having been fed on a special kind of fodder. The head was released first, then the legs, which had been swollen and paralysed, looked a little less ghastly, the sores began to heal, and finally, to everybody's surprise, M. le Monnier completely recovered but for a toe or two that had to be sacrificed to the gangrene.

The whole garrison warmly applauded the achievement. Several senior officers declared themselves in favour of Cagliostro. Two Field-Marshals, Baron de Flachsland, the third officer in command of the province, and Baron de Lort de Saint Victor, sang his praises everywhere. The example, in fact, was set still higher up, for one of the most illustrious soldiers, the old Marshal de Contades, Commander-in-Chief of Alsace, praised and publicly patronised the healer.

A not less extraordinary case was that of the Chevalier de Langlais, a captain of dragoons in the Lescure Regiment. This officer found himself withering away in the flower of his youth. Some invisible germ was mysteriously leading him to the grave. The only external symptoms were a periodical attack of nausea, with alternations of fever, insomnia, and stomach-ache, over which no sedative had power ; such a complete mental upheaval that the sick man himself began to have doubts of his sanity. The few lucid intervals he had only showed him the abyss which was engulfing him. He would much rather have preferred to be quite blind than see his wife, his brother and his comrades watching over him stealthily and constantly, forcing themselves to hide their tears and taking the most humiliating precautions against the violence to which his despair might lead him. From hour to hour he sank into a more profound dejection, when, finally, Providence sent the Count de Cagliostro to him.

In three months, his gloom was dispelled and normal health restored. M. de Langlais thereafter easily submitted to experiences of which the mere mention would have formerly prostrated him with fear. His heart overflowing with gratitude, he regretted that he had not a pen sufficiently skilled to extol the marvellous gifts of his saviour in the newspapers.

The women, already numerous, became enthusiastic converts to the religion of the new Æsculapius. The Marquise de la Salle and the Baroness de Flachsland and Baroness de Saint Victor, unceasingly sang his praises. And their fervour gradually won over the ammeister de Dietrich, M. de Gerard, the King's banker, M. Chaumont de la Galaisiere, the intendant of the province, and finally the élite of the official class, and the civil authorities.

These notable proselytes almost established themselves in Cagliostro's house. The women, weaving metaphorical crowns in honour of the thaumaturge, chattered happily among themselves. At the stroke of noon, brilliant officers, like the cavalry captain Count de Brivazac, would come and join them from the place du Château.

It is scarcely possible to exaggerate what credulity and fashion combined to make of Cagliostro. A kind of Court was held about the countess. While Mme de la Galaisiere and the Marquise de la Salle held their salons only twice a week, Serafina received guests every evening. At the houses of those ladies, one stayed only for a short half-hour, whereas no one took leave of the countess before eight in the evening. Modest and very timid, she hardly dared to open her mouth when presiding over her circle by the fireside ; yet travellers would beg for the honour of being presented to her. Soon a resounding voice would summon them to the next room. There, standing with his back to the fireplace, Cagliostro himself would welcome them.

He was well built and stocky, with a swelling chest and the shoulders of Atlantis. Under the bushy and yet well-made eyelids, his extraordinary eyes darted fire. The slightly hooked nose had a strong arch, and the nostrils were large and well made. The hands were fine and dimpled ; the feet dainty ; the ears more delicate than becoming in a man. His conversation was generally about the astonishing cures he had effected by his treatment.

The thaumaturge filled the old women with joy by promising them eternal youth. He promised to spare them the disgrace of the senile Tithon, wife of Aurora, who, having received eternal life from the gods, but not youth, saw her limbs becoming stunted day by day. And since his Alsatian friends had none of the scruples of the chaste Courlanders, he guaranteed to them inexhaustible incense for the worship of Cytheria.

Some notable personages were caught by this bait. They were not above serving in the capacity of secretaries. As the Master did not like to write, he made them write his letters and prescriptions. Thus, he could often be seen in the course of his consultation, slapping his disciples unceremoniously on the shoulder, saying : " Friend de la Salle, friend Flachsland, friend de la Galaisiere, write this down ! "

. . . .

Among Cagliostro's followers in Alsace, no one, not even Marshal de Contades himself, equalled the Bishop of Strasbourg in prestige.

The Protestants and the Jews agreed with the Catholics in according the first place in the province to the Cardinal Prince Louis-René-Edouard de Rohan-Guemenée.

It would be tedious, if indeed it were necessary, to enlarge on the causes of his pre-eminence. All Europe knows the dominant position occupied by the house of Rohan in the French monarchy. Showered with honours for centuries, the family fortunes had reached their zenith in the reign of Louis XVI. The Countess de Marsan, lately governess of the royal children of France, took advantage of the services she had formerly rendered to the sovereign and to his brothers and sisters, to advance her favourites at Versailles. She was overwhelmed with joy to find her duties devolve on her niece, the Princess de Rohan-Guemenée, whose husband was Grand Chamberlain to the King. Her brother, the Prince de Soubise and d'Epinoy, duc de Rohan-Rohan, peer and marshal of France, unlucky in battle but without a rival at Court, enjoyed the prestige which everywhere belongs to birth, power and considerable wealth. The Prince de Condé, widower of Mlle de Soubise, never failed to help the relatives of his deceased, though still well-beloved, wife, so that the memory of the alliance benefited in turn each of the Rohans. Prince Ferdinand, Grand Provost of Strasbourg, was Archbishop of Bordeaux. Field-Marshal the Prince de Rohan Rochefort was Governor of Nîmes. The Prince de Camille, Canon of Strasbourg and *tréfoncier* of a church at Liége, was the naval commander, while Emmanuel Jean Marie des Neiges de Rohan was the Grand Master, of the Order of Malta.

Every good fairy seemed to have been present at the birth of Prince Louis. He had charm and refinement. Everywhere that he went, he was adored by lesser men for the gentleness of his character, his friendly manners and his unlimited generosity. His conversation made up in charm what it lacked in intelligence. Not that his brain was empty, but indolence, foppishness and a superficial and capricious temperament had somehow arrested its growth ; so that now in his fiftieth year, Prince Louis, for all his pompous titles and Cardinal's robes, had no more discernment than when he left college.

His indiscretions, his conceit, and his dissolute ways had been his undoing in Vienna, where he used to be French Ambassador. Even Clementino Vannetti, whose feelings were scarcely cordial towards the Austrian Chancellory, felt some contempt for the envoy who had been so badly wanting in ability to please the Queen Empress either as diplomat, prelate or grand seigneur, that Marie Thérèse had eventually asked for his recall in explicit terms.

Since this calamity, Prince Louis's nonchalance had given place to a frenzied ambition. Was it not necessary to wipe out the disgrace, and regain pre-eminence over his execrated rival, Baron de Breteuil, whom he had formerly supplanted in Vienna, and who had paid him back in his own coin by taking his place ? With insatiable greed, he set about intriguing for honours. Having been a member of the Académie Française since the age of twenty-seven, being head of the Abbeys of la Chaise Dieu and de Montmajour, and Bishop of Canopé, was not enough for him. He still sought for the position of Grand Almoner of France, to which belonged, among other privileges, those of being Commander of the Order of the Holy Spirit and Superior General of the Hôpital Royale des Quinze Vingts. Having finally secured it, despite the King's opposition, he also obtained in succession the Cardinal's hat, the episcopal see of Strasbourg, the Abbey of Saint Waast d'Arras, and the highly coveted office of proviseur de Sorbonne. Thus, in an exceedingly brief space of time, he went from victory to victory, followed by the acclamations of the whole province.

It was indeed an old tradition in Alsace to support the Rohans. Since the beginning of the century, three cardinals of that name had held in succession the episcopate of Strasbourg ; and now Prince Louis, who had been coadjutor of his uncle for twenty years, was establishing himself there as the fourth.

What a great day it was when he was enthroned ! Strasbourg had never seen anything so splendid since the Archduchess Marie Antoinette had stopped there on her way to Versailles to marry the Dauphin, Louis-Auguste. Prince Louis, who had received her by his uncle's side, delivered an eloquent address on that occasion. But ten years had passed since then. A troubled life, vexations of every sort, anxieties and disappointments, had cut deep furrows on his noble countenance. But Louis de Rohan had still a grand air. And as the twelve canons and the twelve domiciliaries of his chapter came to welcome him at the entrance to the cathedral, the populace showed by its cheers how pleased it was with the new Bishop.

The Cardinal was an impressive figure in his rich pontifical robes. His cassock of scarlet moire blazed in the sun. The alb worn on special occasions, bearing the arms of the Rohans and their motto, was so fine that one scarcely ventured to touch it. The best experts estimated it to be worth more than a hundred thousand pounds. There was displayed also that other marvel, the Cardinal's illuminated missal, which had a fabulous value on account of its perfection and its age.

Though the bishops of Strasbourg, landgraves of Alsace, were sovereign princes of the Holy Empire by right of their possessions beyond the Rhine, the diocese was no more than a bagatelle for Louis de Rohan-Guemenée. He was so rich that he did not know the exact amount of his revenues. The abbey of Saint Waast d'Arras alone brought him three hundred thousand pounds. And his residences were as good as his benefices. In the rue Vieille du Temple, in Paris, the gardens of the Cardinal's Palace adjoined the Soubise mansion. During the warm weather, the Prince sought refuge among the shades and the delightful waters of his castle of Coupvray. In

Alsace, not satisfied with the palace of Mutzig, he rebuilt on a colossal scale and at a great cost, one which had been burned down at Saverne. Whenever he was in Strasbourg, he stayed in that vast and sumptuous edifice in red sandstone which stood between the cathedral and the Quai de l'Ile. And it would be impossible to enumerate all the pavilions which he possessed throughout the kingdom : cottages, belvederes, gloriettes, rustic hermitages and shooting boxes.

Alas ! the gifts of the good fairies were not inexhaustible, and the Cardinal had had the folly to squander them all in turn. He complained of his health. Certain deceptive forewarnings of decline filled him with anxiety. So as not to reduce his retinue and to carry through to a successful conclusion his manifold enterprises, he mortgaged a part of his property. While Strasbourg was admiring his superb equipages, his runners, pike-men and foreign footmen, the Cardinal, harassed by his banker Kornmann, and his private moneylender, the Jew, Cerf-Berr, grew familiar with all the fears of a hard-pressed family man.

Meanwhile his *amour propre* had been wounded. He had wished to exercise the same supremacy at Versailles and Paris as in Alsace. But the Grand Almoner of France was a nonentity at Court. The Queen scorned him. For years she had not spoken a word, nor given a look to the man who had formerly been unfortunate enough to incur her mother's displeasure. And everyone, down to the lackeys, openly laughed at him. Three supplicating letters, in which the guilty one begged for an audience, had produced no effect. In vain did the Rohans move heaven and earth, strive vigorously to rehabilitate him; his disgrace endured. That, doubtless, was the cancer which was consuming him.

Only a miracle could extricate him from his difficulties. So naïve was his self-conceit that he was absolutely sure the miracle would happen. God, who looked after everyone, could not overlook a cardinal, still less a Rohan. No, his old age was certainly not to be consumed in tears. He remained attached to his Christian convictions. His errors, his follies, his dealings with the materialists, so assiduously cultivated at the time of his election to the Académie Française, had not alienated him from the holy tabernacle. Unhappily, the believer was credulous ; he clung to his superstitions as firmly as to his faith. And in the hopes in which he lived of a miraculous reversal of his ill-fortune, his spirit slipped in spite of himself from religion into magic.

. . . .

At the first rumour of the Strasbourg miracles, Louis de Rohan had felt a strong desire to meet the Count de Cagliostro. But when the Baron de Mullenheim went to call on the thaumaturge on behalf of the Prince, he received this reply :

" If Monsieur the Cardinal is sick, let him come and I shall heal him. If he is in good health, he has no need of me, nor I of him."

After some days, the baron returned to the attack. The Cardinal, he said, was suffering from asthma, and begged to consult him. This time Cagliostro went with a good grace to the episcopal palace. And the sick man was so pleased with this visit, that he begged his new physician to be good enough to come often.

His Eminence had fallen under the charm. He saw in the Count an imposing dignity. By his own admission, he had experienced a religious exaltation on seeing the Count, and his first words had been inspired by reverence. Cagliostro manœuvred it so that he captured the Cardinal's confidence without seeming to.

"Your spirit," he affectionately repeated to him, "is worthy of mine, and you deserve to be entrusted with my secrets."

These effusions, these promises, intoxicated the dilettante who combined with a taste for botany and chemistry an inordinate passion for occultism. No sooner was the palace of Saverne restored than the Count and the Countess de Cagliostro were often invited, and stayed there for three weeks and more at a time.

At the request of this fervent admirer, Cagliostro looked for lodgings closer to the Cardinal. The "House of the Virgin," so named because of a statuette which was hung outside in the rue des Ecrivains, satisfied him perfectly. Without bargaining over the rent, he at once engaged the first floor, of which the windows, five in number, opened on to an elegant iron balcony.

Feather beds, gold-fringed curtains, furniture of inlaid rosewood, and crystal chandeliers were at once moved into the apartment by the furnishers. A sumptuous equipage took the place of the hired coach. Three handsome servants were engaged to wear Cagliostro's green livery with silver trimmings.

And miracle followed miracle. But public opinion was not in every case unanimous about their efficacy. An old spinster, deaf from the age of seven, claimed to have recovered her hearing. Everybody was surprised, however, to find her always asking, "What did you say? What, monsieur? I don't understand you," etc. Shrugging his shoulders, Cagliostro would retort to malicious pleasantries on this subject by saying that it was easier to cure a disease than a habit ingrained since childhood.

On the other hand, there was no difference of opinion at all as to the incredible transformation wrought upon Mme Gertrude Sarasin. It was a resurrection as extraordinary as that of Lazarus.

Baroness von der Recke, learning that the Count was in Alsace, sought news of him through an old Strasbourg friend of the late Jean Frederic de Medem, the Protestant minister Laurent Blessig. In answer, the young cleric sent to her on the 7th June, 1781, a ringing eulogy of Cagliostro. He was loud in praise of the training that the thaumaturge had received in Medina.

Some reservations nevertheless broke through the generous admiration contained in M. Blessig's letter. He criticised the thaumaturge for his excessive optimism :

" He is too sure of himself, and occasionally it is seen that his promise of a cure was given too readily. However, this attitude inspires in his patients an unbounded confidence."

Cagliostro was so contemptuous of orthodox methods that his patients begged him in vain to enter into consultation with the leading practitioners in Strasbourg. The thaumaturge always refused.

" He dubs his colleagues with nicknames taken from the animal kingdom. For their part, our physicians do not mind telling the truth about him, I mean the truth in which there is neither jealousy nor malice."

Sometimes he left his patients in the lurch without any explanation:

" Many strangers, come expressly to put themselves in his hands, have been given up by him in the middle of their treatment ; others have been peremptorily turned out. Extremely kind to some, he is hard and brutal to others, depending on whether their looks please or displease him, and often at first sight."

There was an attractive frankness about his features, but it was not always borne out by his words. A woman of whom he used to make a lot of fuss (in spite of his habitually scornful attitude towards the feeble sex), once heard him murmur, with a sinister look on his face, when she was ecstatically praising his magnificent gifts,

" Yes, but the master-stroke remains in my heart."

What did he mean ? How was this mysterious, even menacing expression, to be interpreted ? How were the manifold veils in which Cagliostro loved to cover himself to be lifted ? His talk was often nothing but unintelligible jargon. He twisted Italian, and still more, French, cruelly out of shape. A man brought up in Medina and Egypt might be expected to know at least the Oriental languages. But one day when the celebrated Upsala professor, M. Norberg, asked him something in Arabic, he remained silent, to the great delight of his enemies. As for religion, though the name, *il Grande Iddio*, was always on his lips, and though he pretended to have a special flair for scenting unbelievers at a distance, some people accused him of treating the priests as badly as the physicians, even of speaking irreverently of our Lord.

People were lost in conjecture as to the sources of his income. He never received money, either in cash, or in the form of letters of credit; nor did he accept any honorarium for his services, at least directly. Yet he paid his bills promptly. Fanatical Protestants in Strasbourg, like those in Königsberg, took him to be a Jesuit spy. But sensible men tried rather to discover his real motive.

" He behaves towards princes like a man who, expecting nothing from them, is yet in a position to render essential services to them. He seems to cherish some deep and far-reaching projects, but Strasbourg would be but a shabby setting for it. Still, our town stands at the entrance to the kingdom, and perhaps he hopes that his fame would reach the ears of the King, and procure him an invitation to Versailles."

Whilst this conjecture and many others went their way, the medical faculty of Strasbourg was beginning to get annoyed. At first they had pretended to ignore the hue and cry which had overturned all their orthodox notions, the more audaciously because, strictly speaking, he had no ideas of his own. But the love shown him by poor people, and the influence he had with the great ones, made them uneasy. This false reputation was spreading rapidly through France. The *Journal de Paris* had twice extolled the empiric. More serious still, the municipal authorities were receiving enquiries about the Count from long distances.

The physicians and surgeons of Strasbourg did their best to control their irritation. Bound by blood or by friendship to their magistrates—the Councils of the " Twenty-One," the " Fifteen," and the " Thirteen "—they had good hopes of ousting the strange usurper little by little. But a resounding scandal fired the mine suddenly.

M. Ostertag, a physician and licensed obstetrician, was called on the 23rd May, 1781, to the house of one Catherine Groebel, the wife of a poor mason. The midwife and the two doctors he found there conveyed to him their apprehensions. The travail seemed suspended, paralysed. It was feared that the baby might be dead. Perhaps it was necessary to perform the cæsarian operation. But Ostertag preferred to temporise.

The terrible crisis was prolonged. The doctor did not dare to interfere. All he did was to prescribe a small dose of medicine in some veal soup.

On the 29th May, at eleven o'clock in the morning, when he came to Catharine Groebel's house, he saw Cagliostro at the dying woman's bedside. It was M. Zaegelins, the curé of Saint Pierre le Vieux, who had taken it upon himself to send for him. The obstetrician looked furious ; it was explained to him that the Count had not even touched the patient, that he had not prescribed anything, and that he had merely put in her hand a coin of six francs. All in vain. Pale with rage, M. Ostertag threw on his hat and dashed out, saying that the Groebel woman was lost, utterly lost.

Cagliostro, left alone on the field of battle, administered to the sick woman that same day a certain red powder dissolved in wine. At eight o'clock in the evening, she felt hungry ; she was given a drop of wine with some bread lightly dipped in coffee. Finally, about ten o'clock the delivery took place : the baby was born within half an hour.

Thanks to a spoonful of water in which the Count had put some drops of his lotion, the mother was able to get up the next afternoon. The infant was taken to Saint Pierre le Vieux, and the curé Zaegelins had the joy of baptising it in Cagliostro's presence.

This episode started a fierce controversy. As against the evasions of the licensed obstetrician, his clumsiness, his disastrous inaction, everyone praised the courageous and salutary initiative taken by the healer. M. Ostertag, distracted with shame, wrote a pamphlet in self-defence. Other physicians, loyal to their *esprit de corps*, came to his support. Too late ! This fresh achievement capped the Count's reputation.

M. Le Monnier, the Chevalier de Langlais, M. and Mme Sarasin and the old deaf spinster, hastened to defend him. Prince Louis, delirious with enthusiasm, began to look upon Cagliostro as a sort of Messiah. And the conviction spread to his retinue. Baron de Mullenheim, Baron Frederic de Planta, a Protestant gentleman in his service, and his young secretary, M. Ramond de Carbonnieres, a gifted writer, shared in his admiration. Only an old companion of Viennese days, an indispensable factotum, the abbé Georgel, vicar general of the Grand Almoner, continued to be obstinately hostile. But the Cardinal did not despair of converting him.

Since March, the rumour of these achievements and controversies had been spreading to Paris. The Chevalier de Corberon, who was there at the time, at once recognised in the extraordinary thaumaturge the Petersburg magician of whom he had heard nothing since his departure from Warsaw. To make sure of it, he wrote to Strasbourg. The answer was delayed ; and the Chevalier was beginning to have some doubts, when he at last received the following letter :

" STRASBOURG,
8th April, 1781.

Monsieur the Chevalier de Corberon will recognise that it is the real Count de Cagliostro who is at Strasbourg, by his habit of not answering letters. However, in order not to let a man from whom he has received so many tokens of friendship, and for whom he has such great regard, suppose that he could be forgotten, the Count has begged one of his friends to assure M. the Chevalier de Corberon that he desires very much to renew his friendship. If, in the meanwhile, there should be an opportunity of doing something to please him, he is requested to believe that M. de Cagliostro would be more anxious to oblige him than he is able to express in words."

Deeply touched by the message, the Chevalier thanked Cagliostro for it on the 25th April ; but he might have gone off to take up a new diplomatic post without seeing the Master if chance had not contrived an unexpected encounter.

Since the end of June, the Marshal de Soubise had been very ill. According to letters from Paris, the trouble was scarlatina complicated with a gangrene in the leg. Was it not also of gangrene that M. de Monnier had been dying ? The Cardinal persuaded himself that only Cagliostro could save his uncle. He asked him as a signal favour to accompany him to Paris and examine the Marshal as soon as possible. Cagliostro did not have the courage to refuse such a pressing request. Giving his wife and some disciples the necessary instructions to see that his patients did not suffer in any way by his absence, he left with the Cardinal, the Baron de Mullenheim, and Ramond de Carbonnieres, on the 29th June, 1781, exactly a month after the wonderful accouchement of Catherine Groebel.

The travellers reached the capital on the 30th. Knowing what it meant to incur the hatred of the local physicians, Cagliostro had no desire to provoke a squabble with the Faculty. That was why he confined himself to the Palais Cardinal, resolved not to interfere until the highest authorities had given up M. de Soubise's case as hopeless. Besides, he was on the spot, two steps from the Soubise mansion, and as the Marshal was improving, prudence counselled patience.

M. de Corberon received an anonymous message inviting him to call at the Palais Cardinal. He hastened over, and it was with no less astonishment than joy that he fell into the arms of the Master.

Having again visited the Palais Cardinal on the third day, the 2nd July, 1781, he wrote an account of that interview :

" I saw Cagliostro this morning. He has given me an ointment for pimples, in which, I believe, he has put some camphor. . . .

Prince de Soubise is still doing well, according to the doctors. I believe they are afraid of Cagliostro. He has refused to see the Prince so long as he is in their hands.

I saw the Cardinal de Rohan at his place, who told me that Countess de Brionne wished to see me about Cagliostro. She wants to entrust him with the cure of the Princess de Vaudemont, her daughter-in-law, whose health at the age of nineteen, is in such a deplorable condition in spite of all that the ordinary doctors can do. . . .

M. de Viviers, whom I found at my place when I returned home at eight in the evening, begged me to take him to Cagliostro, whom he wished to consult about his health. He was received affably and is to go there again to-morrow."

Then, on the 4th July :

"I was at Cagliostro's this morning. His interviews are becoming numerous. Count de Caylus was there, the Chevalier de Luxembourg, many women. . . ."

Cagliostro had little respect for the fair sex. At Paris, as at Strasbourg, fashionable ladies, the highest in the land, vainly tried to monopolise him. He refused to make any distinction between these divinities of Olympus and the poor ones of the faubourgs. Even the Polish lady whom he had formerly known in Warsaw, at the palace of King Stanislas Augustus, and who had justified his prophecy by marrying the Prince de Nassau Siegen, was treated scarcely better :

" The Princess de Nassau sent a message asking him to call on her. He refused, but suggested that she should come to him. The man has created a big sensation. Fanaticism is mixed with it. Madame de

Brionne saw him on behalf of her daughter, Princess de Vaudemont, and was highly satisfied with what he told her about her condition.

I returned in the evening to Cagliostro's. I saw Princess de Montbarey, who was there from eight o'clock, when I went, to ten-fifteen. She was with Baron de Mullenheim, who thinks very highly of Cagliostro. It seems that he has witnessed his magical operations. I wrote down for Princess de Montbarey how to make the Cagliostro decoction. . . .

Madame de Coislin, sister of Madame de Montbarey, is come to talk to Cagliostro, and he has made her write, or rather she has written to him herself, a letter requesting him to come to her house. He has refused, but he has told her that she may come to him."

Sick people, on the contrary, easily persuaded him to visit them. He consented to examine in her own house a sexagenarian, the Marquise de Cucé ; he found her better than he expected, and gave her a prescription.

If he did not run after pretty women, neither did he flatter Ministers and other high personages. MM. de Maurepas and de Vergennes learnt it to their cost, as M. de Corberon observed :

" M. de Viviers came to my house this morning to urge me to persuade Cagliostro to go and see M. and Mme Vergennes at their country house. I immediately went to Cagliostro. He did not wish to talk about it, but when I went a second time and requested him urgently, telling him that a carriage was at the door and everything ready, he said that M. de Viviers had only to appeal to the Cardinal, and that should the Cardinal express the wish, he would leave at once. M. de Mullenheim told me specially that Cagliostro had refused to go to M. de Maurepas' house even when the Cardinal requested him to. Viviers has gone away disappointed."

To tell the truth, the Count de Vergennes, though he was more accustomed to being importuned than neglected, did not at all take offence at this extraordinary treatment. The Chevalier was able to satisfy himself about that when he went to dine at Versailles on the 8th July, at the house of the minister of foreign affairs. M. de Vergennes sympathetically enquired about Cagliostro. Strange things had been reported to his Excellency ; he wished to obtain a medicine that the healer successfully used in cases of gravel. M. de Fontette, the Count of Provence's treasurer, spoke of a Paris doctor, a M. Richard, living opposite Saint Roch, at the Écuries du Roi, who had been laid up for a year with apoplexy. Cagliostro, called in by some friends, had begun by drinking some liquid in front of the patient.

" Richard subsequently took the drug. It burned his mouth. He held it there as long as he could, and swallowed it down according to Cagliostro's instructions. And a little later, his tongue, which had got very thick, became more pliable. It became thick, and some time after free again, without a fresh dose being taken."

Wonderful as these cures were, some people took more interest in the sublime powers that Cagliostro was supposed to have. Mme de Coislin, Princess de Montbarey and still more, the Marquise de la Croiz, always on the look-out for visionaries and mystics, constantly worried him about his supernatural faculties. Another devotee of the mystical, Marquis de Thome, beset him importunately with questions in the hope of discovering in him a Swedenborgian adept. Unfortunately, at the first words which he uttered to that effect, Cagliostro looked at him coldly :

" No, sir," he replied, turning away, " I have nothing to do with those things."

The Chevalier de Corberon, imbued with the same principles as the Marquis de Thome and loyally attached to the teachings of Swedenborg, augured ill of the dryness with which Cagliostro had refused all explanations in this matter. Had the thaumaturge gone astray on the dark paths ? Alas ! in spite of explicit warnings, he had had dealings in Poland with Thoux de Salverte. M. de Corberon was again torn by his old perplexities. He suspected that Cagliostro, whose incomparable erudition in physics, chemistry and medicine he so strongly admired, was dealing in black magic.

He had expressed his misgivings on the subject to Princess de Montbarey. But this gossip could not at all understand his anxiety :

" Madame de Montbarey does not believe that Cagliostro has got the philosopher's stone, and she is right. But she believes that he is on the right path. I told her then what I thought, and the danger which I think the unhappy man is running. She did not agree. She thinks that one can deal in both white and black magic without danger. . . . "

Meanwhile, Prince de Soubise was convalescing, and Cagliostro, anxious to return to his patients in Strasbourg, decided by himself to leave on the 11th July. The good Chevalier was in despair :

" What ! " he repeated ceaselessly through a flood of tears. " We have just begun to renew our friendship, and already I must say good-bye ! "

Cagliostro consoled him by promising to send him from Strasbourg the celebrated specific against gravel, and promised even to return, should M. de Vergennes express the wish in writing.

Obsessed by his *idée fixe*, the Chevalier every day sent his family news about the great man. Happily his letters were preserved, and M. de Corberon had thus the advantage of consulting them later when he was asked about the events of this period.

Was Ippolito Pindemonte permitted to read them when he was gathering material in Paris for his beloved Vannetti ? It is not known. But so many had seen these that Pindemonte doubtless knew one decisive fact.

There was at the Palais Cardinal about that time, among the visitors who crowded together between the panelled walls, an

Englishman named Bousie. This rich London merchant, a Freemason, smitten with a passion for occultism, had installed himself in Paris, in the rue du Petit Bourbon Saint Sulpice, out of admiration for Cagliostro, whose genius he sincerely esteemed. As he liked M. de Corberon, Mr. Bousie had offered to dictate to him Cagliostro's recipes, provided the Chevalier kept them secret. As for himself, this queer person said, he had tested them one by one, very carefully, when Cagliostro was living in London under the name of Pellegrini.

In 1781, there was nothing remarkable about this last detail. Caring little for the name of Cagliostro, the Master himself had owned willingly that he had formerly gone about under various designations. But six years later, Mr. Bousie's account suddenly assumed importance. It became known then that the adventurer, Giuseppe Balsamo, had strutted about in Naples in 1775 under the name of Marquis Pellegrini. And M. de Corberon thereupon bethought himself of Mr. Bousie. As Count de Cagliostro had originally called himself Pellegrini in England, certain comparisons became obvious, and one can guess what conclusions were reached by Pindemonte and Vannetti.

Though in 1781 the name of Pellegrini did not arouse any suspicion, the most extraordinary rumours were circulating about Cagliostro. The old Marshal de Biren, entertaining a large company at dinner, declared that the magician was the son of a Portuguese Jew, a director of the Brazil mines, named Radjo.

Others had it on Cagliostro's own authority that he was born in the middle of the Red Sea and that a kind old man had initiated him into occult secrets among the ruins of the Pyramids. The true devotees alone scorned these petty tales. To them, the Count's birth seemed an august mystery that one must worship and not seek to explain. Cardinal de Rohan, when asked why he threw away his respect on an unknown stranger, contented himself with saying :

"M. de Cagliostro is a scientist who must not be treated like ordinary men."

To his friendship and regard, the Cardinal hereafter added fervent gratitude for the Master's self-abnegation in accompanying him to Paris. Besides, the prophet-apostle having covered himself with glory in the capital, his success was something like the first smile of fortune to the Prince in disgrace.

All the more cruel was the mortification of the travellers when they arrived at Saverne on the 13th July. The obstetrician, Ostertag, had published his self-defence, and this apology, it was said, was as malignant as a speech for the prosecution. Cagliostro the next day bought in Strasbourg a very handsome pamphlet decorated with a cover and tail-piece, of which the typography did honour to the presses of Levrault, the government printer. But never was there a more acrimonious pamphlet. After denouncing the absurd infatuation caused by a certain "oriental doctor" in Strasbourg, and relating in his own fashion the case of Catherine Groebel, Ostertag appealed to the magistrates :

" Gentlemen, you who have entrusted to two obstetricians the delicate and difficult duty which they have the honour to discharge, see to it, in order that their work may not be interrupted, that they are not hereafter exposed to public insults ; avert, sirs, the sad consequences to which, for more than one reason, women in childbirth are exposed by the administration of alleged panaceas. . . . God forbid that I should constitute myself a critic of the physical and medical knowledge of M. the Count ! I formally declare that, provoked beyond reason, I write this solely to protect the mothers and the children, to give you, sirs, a report of my conduct, and to enlighten a public whose faith has been betrayed."

What was particularly painful to Cagliostro was to see that the pamphlet had official sanction. The head of the college of physicians having, "at the request of the Magistracy and by their orders," examined the memoir and found nothing objectionable in it, the ammeister had accorded his permission to print it, so that the diatribe now flaunted the official seal.

The Cardinal de Rohan was much distressed by it. Was it not scandalous that they should have taken advantage of his and Cagliostro's absence to play this dirty trick ? After talking it over with Marshal de Contades, he wrote a letter of protest to M. de Gerard, the royal banker.

But already the banker, angered by the scandal, had summoned an extraordinary meeting of the Chamber of Fifteen. The magistrates decided to send for M. Ostertag and tell him that they emphatically disapproved of the concluding passages of his pamphlet. So that there might be no doubt about it, at the wish of the Cardinal de Rohan and Marshal de Contades, M. de Gerard published in the newspapers—and notably in the *Variétés haut-rhinoises*, which had attacked Cagliostro—the following announcement :

" Though M. the Count de Cagliostro is indifferent to the attacks made on him in M. Ostertag's pamphlet, he cannot so remain to what the Magistracy of Strasbourg think about him : he desires that the Magistracy, which had neither read nor approved of the pamphlet, should say so formally," and that is what was very flatteringly done in the decree published by the Magistracy on the 16th July, 1781. After which, M. the royal banker was requested to inform him, on behalf of the Magistracy, that its members unanimously disapproved of the printing and publication of the pamphlet, and that they were far from sharing the impression which that work sought to propagate about him.

No sooner had Cagliostro emerged triumphant from the duel with the physicians, than he got involved in another, this time with some military officers. In spite of the high patronage of Marshal de Contades and his staff, many of the younger ones among them ridiculed the " sorcerer," and regretted the influence he had obtained over their chiefs. The Princess de Montbarey came to know of it before long. After he had called on her on the 7th August, M. de Corberon wrote :

"We had a private talk for an hour and a half about Cagliostro. She has received a letter from him dated the 1st August, which has disturbed her considerably. He complains of having been treated as an enemy by her son, without any further explanation. It seems that he wishes to leave France. The Princess has written to Saverne, to the Cardinal de Rohan, asking what it is all about. . . . I again told the Princess, on this occasion, that poor Cagliostro was going to the bad, and that I feared he would remain there. She said that he could be reclaimed ; I hope so, but I fear it is unlikely."

Had, then, Cagliostro fallen out in Alsace with the Prince de Saint Mauris, Mme Montbarey's eldest son? Not with him exactly. In the light of all the facts, this is how the Chevalier de Narbonne, a colonel in the second regiment of Angoumois, had caused the whole trouble.

About the end of July, while they were staying with the Cardinal at the palace of Saverne, the Count and the Countess de Cagliostro met several young men from the Strasbourg garrison, such as Prince de Saint Mauris, M. de Chatenay and the Chevalier de Narbonne. They played charades, and everybody was happy.

One day, when he was seated at dinner by Mme de Cagliostro's side, M. de Narbonne made some indecent jokes about her manner of speaking French. Cagliostro, who, from his place, had not lost a word of this, controlled himself with difficulty. A glass of wine was then brought to Mme de Cagliostro ; the Chevalier, by his petulant gestures, spilt some of it on his neighbour's dress. Still Cagliostro managed to keep himself under control. After the meal, he went to his wife and advised her never again to sit by the side of the young idiot. Unfortunately, M. de Narbonne overheard this expression, and cried out rudely :

" Eh ! monsieur, you insult me. . . ."

The other answered with a gesture which the Chevalier interpreted as a threat. Apoplectic with rage, M. de Narbonne seized Cagliostro by the arm, saying :

" Do you want to try cutting throats with me ? "

" Monsieur," retorted the Count, " I am not used to fighting, and besides, it is neither proper nor possible for a stranger to give you satisfaction in this place. However, I am returning to Strasbourg. I shall be at your service on the other side of the Rhine."

Cagliostro having retired to the cottage where he was staying, the Cardinal tried to settle the quarrel. As M. de Narbonne had already offered his excuses to Mme de Cagliostro, why did he not wipe out his injuries by an equally loyal and magnanimous gesture towards the Count ? But the Chevalier was obstinate. The so-called Count, he said, was only a charlatan unworthy to cross swords with a gentleman like himself, and he would see that his servants gave him a good beating. In vain did the Cardinal protest that the gentleman was his guest and that he thought very highly of him.

"That is what surprises me!" bitterly replied the Chevalier. "I must say I did not expect to see you protecting a quack peddler. I thought you would chase him out."

"Gently, Monsieur le Chevalier," retorted the Cardinal, touched to the quick; "you are too young to talk like this. M. de Cagliostro is staying with me and he will stay as long as he likes."

Then the young ladies came looking for M. de Narbonne, to make him repeat some proverb.

When the impetuous Chevalier had returned to Strasbourg, he consulted his comrades: could he really fight with Cagliostro? And these oracles declared with one voice that a man of his birth should not accord such honour to a swindler. Cagliostro waited in vain for his opponent's seconds.

Such was the Cardinal's version, given in an interminably long letter which the abbé Georgel had to write not only to the Princess de Montbarey, but to Mme de Maurepas and de Vergennes. These ministers severely condemned the Chevalier's rashness. And the Princess, ashamed to find her son among the ringleaders, did not fail to send an apology to Cagliostro. But she was soon assured that a general reconciliation had been effected in Alsace, in the palace of Marshal de Contades, in the course of a special dinner.

A deluge of lampoons and libels broke on that occasion over Strasbourg. On the morning of the 4th August, the baker living opposite the Petits Capuchins was surprised at the unusually large crowd that had gathered round his stall. A placard had been posted outside during the night.

"The Count Cagliostro.
A quack doctor in Malta, after having arrived there as a Turk, a charlatan in Toulouse and Rennes, cheat and impostor in Russia, liar and adventurer at Strasbourg, an insolent knave at Saverne, shall be regarded everywhere the same."

Having communicated to the public prosecutor a copy of this document, with instructions to find out who wrote it, the ammeister Lemp believed he had discharged his duty. But the next day, an imperious note summoned him urgently to the Ile de Jar, to which every year Marshal de Contades withdrew at the approach of the warm weather. There M. Lemp found the Commander-in-Chief *tête-à-tête* with M. de Lort de Saint Victor, and it was not long before the bomb exploded. The old soldier, almost eighty, blamed M. Lemp for the fearful scandal which was dishonouring Strasbourg, the obscenities and infamies which were breaking out there every day. At that moment, the police brought in a new placard, torn from the doorway of an inn, which read:

"Flachsland the scoundrel protects Cagliostro the knave."

Thanks to M. Lemp's negligence, that was how at Strasbourg they treated a field-marshal and a respectable philanthropist. The person of the Commander-in-Chief himself would not be spared long if judicious and energetic measures were not immediately taken. After half an hour, the Marshal turned to a different subject, declaring emphatically that if the culprit were not discovered, he would be obliged to lodge a complaint at Versailles.

To crown his misfortunes, M. Lemp, poor fellow, found on returning to Strasbourg, a third piece of villainy verging on madness. In this crisis, he hastily summoned a meeting of the Council of Thirteen, in order to get ready, with their help, the reports which would have to be sent to the Ministry, in case M. de Contades actually carried his complaint to Versailles.

Happily, the agitation subsided little by little. Only, as the mischief makers were still at large, police patrols continued to explore the roads and alleys every night, looking for seditious placards. And the Marshal de Contades complimented M. Lemp on this activity, and admitted, while thanking him, that the Strasbourg authorities had satisfactorily discharged their duties towards an illustrious and beneficent stranger.

. . . .

Thus Cagliostro at length received from his enemies that consecration which even his most resolute champions had not been able to guarantee him up till then. There was a delicious moment for his vanity. What did it matter if the doctors said that he did not know the first principles of their art ? No witness of good faith denied to him an original and profound learning. Imaginary or actual sick persons, tradesmen with broken-down health, beautiful if asthmatic women, rushed to Strasbourg from all parts of the kingdom. At the end of his visit to Paris, five or six fashionable women had insisted on accompanying him to Alsace, " in order to put themselves under his care."

Viscountess de Faudoas, for example, in August 1781, congratulated her dear mother, the Marquise de Boulainvilliers, for having followed her example. She even urged her father to do the same :

" I hope, my dear father, that you will consult him about your health. I have heard it said that it is enough simply to hear him talk ; that he has an easy and agreeable fluency ; that it is, in fact, difficult to speak more charmingly. It is a gift that the medical profession does not usually encourage."

How could the Cardinal have foreseen the melancholy consequences this visit was to have ?

He knew, like a number of others, that the Marquise de Boulainvilliers supported out of her own funds three unhappy orphans, descendants of a bastard son that Henry II had had by a lady of Saint Remy. Deserted by everybody, these great-grandchildren of a king had been dying of hunger, misery and dirt. Mme de Boulainvilliers was touched by their plight. Filled with pity for these feeble offshoots of a stock once all powerful, she had lavished her care on them. Thanks to her, each of them received a pension of eight hundred pounds a year from the royal treasury. The boy was at sea as a naval ensign. And Mme de Boulainvilliers solicited the most influential personages in favour of the two young girls. Suddenly, the elder, Jeanne, became infatuated with a rascal named De La Motte, who had not a penny in the world and had a detestable reputation, yet whom she wished to marry in spite of every remonstrance. The Marquise, thereupon, rightly annoyed, had broken off relations.

But the young Mme de La Motte did not intend to alienate such a generous benefactress. Accompanied by her young sister, Anne Marie, with whom she could do what she pleased, she left for Alsace. By a strange whim, Jeanne de La Motte Valois had put on male clothes and looked like an impudent page. When they reached Strasbourg, Mme de Boulainvilliers was no longer there, and the two sisters went to make enquiries at Cagliostro's house. Crowds of people had come to see the thaumaturge that day. Instead of receiving the young ladies in the *salon*, he went out and talked with them on the stairs, not suspecting that his visitors were the great-grandchildren of a king of France. He informed them that the Marquise had been for the past few days at Saverne, with the Cardinal de Rohan. Jeanne and Anne Marie immediately went there, and the excellent Mme de Boulainvilliers, seeing them arriving unexpectedly, did not have the heart to send them away. She embraced them, and all their errors were forgiven in the joy of reconciliation.

Later, when they were driving along the road from Saverne to Strasbourg, the ladies met the Cardinal de Rohan. The Marquise gladly seized this opportunity of introducing her protégées, and the prelate seemed to be no less impressed by the name than by the bewitching voice and intriguing looks of Jeanne de La Motte Valois.

Mme de Boulainvilliers having come to Alsace when her illness was too far advanced, Cagliostro despaired of curing her ; he had to be content with giving her temporary relief. Soon after her return to Paris the poor woman passed away, but with so little suffering that M. de Boulainvilliers remained eternally grateful to the thaumaturge.

To the sceptics, the art of Cagliostro, like that of all healers ancient and modern, consisted only in a nervous influence. Diet, certain heroic remedies, a blind faith in the miraculous powers of the Master, the mysteriously solemn air with which he excelled in surrounding himself—these alone produced, according to them, such extraordinary results. Be it so. But then, how to explain the rapid convalescence of a consumptive young woman of twenty ? In this case, the empiric had at first set himself to stimulate the confidence of the patient, to encourage her ; a diet of jellied snails and nature's beneficent influence had done the rest. Everything seemed to be effected through the help of the spirits ; and to Cagliostro, medicine seemed but a branch of magic. Though on one occasion, he said, at a meeting of the Strasbourg Lodge :

" A Mason who, when he falls ill, cannot do without doctors, is not a true Mason."

Again, he told one of his patients :

" Madame, the Count knows absolutely nothing about your malady. But there is a God in heaven who can extract an efficacious juice from the most useless herb. Very well ! the Count de Cagliostro will prostrate himself before Him to obtain it."

He generally expressed himself in the third person :

" The Count thinks. . . . The Count de Cagliostro considers that you will be healed. . . ." His oracles thereby acquired a sybilline accent.

Each of his patients introduced to him twenty others. Thus, M. and Mme Sarasin, for their part, had brought a strong contingent of Swiss. In November 1781, a young Zurich couple was welcomed at Strasbourg, the poet Johannes Burkli and his wife ; both were eager to consult the illustrious thaumaturge. Nevertheless, their first impressions were discouraging. Burkli found in Cagliostro the airs of a charlatan. He could not see in his features anything remarkable at all, save a magnificent eye, the eye of a hawk gazing on its prey.

However, no sooner had Mme Burkli described to him her stomach-aches, her nervous attacks and her hiccoughs than she and her husband perceived in Cagliostro a skilful practitioner, and what was better still, a sagacious philosopher, a profound observer of men, an infallible physiognomist who could easily pass from visible effects to their invisible causes. He could penetrate through a disease to the very roots of a person's character, and its main features ; and could therefore suggest rules of conduct as judicious as his drugs and diets. Thereupon, M. and Mme Burkli felt ashamed of their hasty judgment. The Count prescribed for Mme de Burkli a whole set of remedies ; he called on her the next day, and in a general way, was so affectionately generous with his advice to the young couple, that they began to see the friend of mankind in his best colours.

The treasurer of the republic of Basle, M. Wielandt, and his daughter, came to speak to Cagliostro on a still higher level. Like Gertrude Sarasin, Mme Wielandt had aroused grave anxiety among her friends. In her case, the want of sleep and appetite, and frequent fits, were aggravated by terrible nervous headaches and a dry, wheezing cough. Ulcers covered her mouth, her tongue, her throat and even the inside of her throat. No doubt her attacks were not as terrible as those of Gertrude Sarasin ; but every evening, from ten o'clock to midnight, though she had a burning thirst and a severe fit of coughing, the spasms which seized her would prevent her from swallowing even a tiny drop of water. Her jawbones moved up and down convulsively. Her diet was restricted to thin milk, with, at times, though rarely and in tiny spoonfuls, some vegetable soup.

On the insistence of her friends the Sarasins, Cagliostro went to examine her at Basle. His prescriptions took such good effect that, towards August 1782, it was possible to bring the patient by river to Strasbourg, she being still too weak for the journey by coach. Welcomed at the " House of the Virgin " as kindly as Gertrude Sarasin had been, she enjoyed an equally attentive treatment. The Count had the happiness of saving this young and delicate leaf from the storm which threatened to tear it from its stem. On the disorders of matter, on nature in revolt, Cagliostro victoriously imposed his law. The cure was not complete until the last months of 1782, and then Mlle Wielandt's father wrote to his cousin such an intensely interesting account that his testimony had the honour of being reprinted in the *Journal de Paris*.

Before they fell out, the Countess de Branconi had sung Cagliostro's praises at Lausanne, where she stayed for a part of each year. The Baron de Planta had set himself to convert the nobility of the Grisons. And his sister, married to M. Rilliet, carried on at Geneva a propaganda which was the more active because she cherished for another of the prophet's fanatical supporters, a very tender passion. Switzerland thus being filled with their eulogies, distinguished people like Mme de Charriere and M. de Luternau left for Strasbourg to seek a cure.

The echo of these acclamations reached him who had been the first herald of the new Æsculapius in Switzerland, who had been the first also to consult him in regard to Mme Gertrude Sarasin. Lavater was, in fact, alarmed at the rapid advance which this sect was making. It seemed to have a tyrannical and irresistible influence over people. In October 1781, learning that the Count had arrived with Jacques Sarasin at Basle, Lavater thought of joining them there. An unhappy thought. This second encounter, more painful than the first, ended in a brutal altercation. No doubt Jacques intervened between the two mystagogues and managed to reconcile them. All the same, and in spite of his host, it was with a sad heart that Lavater left the " White House."

What an acute and distressing dilemma he was in ! His spirit hesitated between an instinctive antipathy and the thought that the enchanter had, in a supreme degree, the wonderful privilege of communicating with the Beyond. Lavater exerted himself to avert a rupture in the hope of obtaining perhaps a ray of light, and perhaps even, at length, of seeing one of the Seven Angels who stand before God ! In the end, he wrote to Jacques Sarasin, sending him a list of detailed questions with the urgent request to hand them personally to Cagliostro.

On the 6th July, 1782, Lavater, bound for Germany, did not fail to stop at Strasbourg. He had on that occasion the pleasure of being invited to sup with Jacques Sarasin at Cagliostro's house.

In the course of this repast, the thaumaturge severely condemned the impious folk who dared to attack the sacred principles of the Christian religion. And the next day, at the hour of parting, Lavater received such a solemn promise from Cagliostro that the traveller believed he was, after all, going to obtain his heart's desire.

A month later, Lavater begged his friend Jacques to remember him kindly and respectfully to the Count. But Cagliostro's thoughts were elsewhere. . . . Lavater, more and more discomfited, knew not what to think of an apostle who scattered his promises so lavishly and yet deigned to take no notice of his humble and entreating reminders.

As though to aggravate his distress, Mme Lavater acquired a strange infatuation for Cagliostro. Not that this poor woman had mystic ambitions. She did not by any means long to hold converse with the Seven Archangels. But afflicted with a painful disease which the physicians despaired of curing, she could not help thinking continually of her friend Gertrude Sarasin, of Cagliostro's remedies and prescriptions, and of that extraordinary resurrection which had set all Switzerland wondering. Even at a distance, the thaumaturge exercised over her an irresistible fascination. Lavater decided to consult him by letter. And the prescriptions that the next post brought to Zurich had such a powerful, such a salutary effect, that the crisis appeared to have been conjured away. On the 9th February, 1783, Lavater wrote to Sarasin :

" Salute Cagliostro in my name, and give him the assurance that I have increasing respect for the wonderful physician that he is. Shall we never see him in Zurich ? I am not making an appeal ; only expressing a timid wish. But, if he would come, I should welcome him with humble and joyous gratitude."

This " timid wish " had nothing chimerical about it. Since the definite return of the Sarasins to Switzerland, Cagliostro went frequently to Basle to inspire his followers and preach to the group which met at the house of his friends. At that time, the flock consisted of the pastor Touchon, the physician Socin, the Hagenbacks, the Merians, Mme Sarasin's own family, that is, the Battiers, and MM. Bischoff and Ritter, who had so kindly offered the site for the kiosk which had been put up for the spiritual palingenesis. And Lavater longed to be present one day at a séance at the " White House " where the little Felix admirably played the part of " pupil."

The Count therefore used to go often to Basle. But how could he have leisure to go as far as Zurich ? France was disputing his presence bitterly with Switzerland. The Strasbourg Lodges had set Freemasonry going throughout the kingdom. But for the warm recommendation of the Masons, the Marquis de Boulainvilliers, himself an initiate, would not have entrusted his wife to Cagliostro. About the same time another Brother, Jean Benjamin de la Borde, paid a magnificent tribute to the healer, after having visited him at Strasbourg. His *Letters on Switzerland* emphatically corroborated the evidence published from time to time in the *Journal de Paris*.

Hoping to recover peace of mind and heart, the Duc de Caylus took his place in the ranks of the grand seigneurs who came to consult the illustrious magician. In 1782, he went thrice to Strasbourg. Not satisfied with studying Cagliostro, he strove to make the acquaintance of his principal disciples. On the 30th October, he travelled to Basle with the Count and Countess, the Baron de Planta, Ramond de Carbonnieres and M. de Luternau. Meanwhile, the Duc was in a pitiful state. By a strong effort, Cagliostro released him from his hypochondria; but these triumphs were evanescent. When the Duc was away from the Master, dejection gained the upper hand. They were not greatly surprised, therefore, in Strasbourg, when at length the news arrived of his suicide. This is how M. Straub, director of the royal arms factory in Alsace, communicated it to the Sarasin household:

"The poor Duc de Caylus is dead, and from what the papers say, he poisoned himself. This sad news, which, knowing the man's state of mind, I should have anticipated, has nevertheless dealt me a severe blow from which I have not yet recovered. Poor fellow, how I mourn you! Why did you not await the hour prescribed for you by the Creator? Why take your own life? There is something in the idea I cannot bear. I am sure you mourn for him, my dear friends: thoughtless and extravagant though he was, he had a good heart. That is what bound me so closely to him."

As the Duc had always been regarded as a tiresome and melancholy fool, his death did no great harm to the magician's reputation.

But a fatality undeniably more regrettable was that of Lieutenant-General the Marquis de Cambis. In view of the patient's rank, the papers had, since the 9th April, 1781, begun to publish a daily bulletin of his progress. On the 1st May it was known that the Marquis, losing all hope, had recalled his ordinary physician. The journalists rejoiced at the news. "If M. the Count de Cagliostro has no greater success than this," they wrote maliciously, "it is to be feared that his reign will not be very long." These insults hurt the thaumaturge cruelly. In vain did the Chevalier de Langlais, best beloved of all his friends, strive to comfort him. Cagliostro shed tears over the fate which had removed M. de Cambis at the very moment when everyone was rushing to congratulate him on having cured him. Discarding all prudence, he accused the physicians of having, in their blind fury, poisoned the Marquis. And they, in turn, reproached him with having himself poisoned the Marquis. True, M. de Cambis, who was suffering from a venereal disease, had no chance of recovery. But was it necessary, in the state in which he was, to deal him the death-blow?

Following this disaster, many of the physicians regained their lost practice. They could then be heard angrily denouncing the utter ignorance of the prophet. They particularly condemned his lamentable misuse of the Extract of Saturn. This lead salt, they said, was without doubt very effective in cases of plague and extreme urgency ; but, taken in huge doses, it was liable to induce a very dangerous rigidity as well as a horrible colic.

The Alsatians also suspected him of having packed off into the next world M. de Waldner de Sierenz, a young man of eighteen. And the Swiss, in their little colony in Strasbourg, could not forgive him for having given up their worthy compatriot, M. Orell, after cramming him with medicines. It was, in fact, with the utmost coolness that the Count received, on the 13th January, 1782, the news of the death of this good man.

The anger and annoyance of the public began to ferment. And the wits were delighted when the Prince de Ligne, passing through Strasbourg, took a malicious delight in deceiving Cagliostro. He pretended to consult him about his daughter-in-law, and though the young Princess was in perfectly good health, she was given a phial of Yellow Pills. And the thaumaturge thereupon recounted in detail how, summoned once to the harem of an African sovereign to attend several of the sultanas, he had merely raised his eyes to heaven with this short prayer :

" Great God, who art so much blasphemed by Voltaire, Rousseau, etc., thou knowest what a slave thou hast in the person of the Count de Cagliostro. Do not, then, desert him now ! "

And the Great God—*il Grande Iddio*—had, in fact, miraculously come to his aid.

About a hundred people were patiently waiting in his antechamber when he had finished recounting his achievements. And the Prince de Ligne, seeing in this man " the figure, the dress, and the accent," and about him " the big crowds which follow quack doctors," could not understand how he managed to fascinate so many dupes.

To tell the truth, Clementino Vannetti did not take this account too seriously. As a witness, the Prince de Ligne seemed to him little capable of rendering justice to the truth. Were not wits too, in their way, charlatans, obliged at any cost to maintain their reputation ?

But, and for much stronger reasons, he rejected the evidence of underlings who slandered their patrons. He had himself seen a discharged servant denouncing the Count at Rovereto. Another had done the same in Courland. At Strasbourg, it had been worse.

At the end of the year 1781, during a public meeting, a stranger came pressing through the crowd and threw himself at Cagliostro's feet. Everything about him announced the most extreme degradation. Glibly, he poured out some incoherent story. His name was Carlo Sacchi. An Italian by birth, he had been a burgher of Amsterdam, and had had to quit that town as a result of some terrible misfortunes. He affirmed that he had once, at Valenzia in Spain, received various benefits from the Count. Cagliostro recollected having been in that city, when he had stopped at the inn of the "Three Kings," kept by a Provençal; but, as he told his friends, he could not remember this man at all.

Boastful, obsequious and plaintive, Sacchi strove to win the Count's goodwill. He humbly begged him to take him into his service. He offered to wear his livery. He gave a list of all the small services he could render the sick. Had he not, for example, earned his living during the ten months he had been at Strasbourg, as a surgeon-dentist? Notwithstanding the vagabond's repulsive features, Cagliostro, amused and sympathetic, took a certain relish in his fluency. On the afternoon of the 27th December, he definitely engaged him; and as he did not want his future assistant to go about in rags, he caused him to be measured for a suit of clothes. Six days later, the Count was informed that a self-styled surgeon in his employ had been holding forth against him in the cafés. The news was confirmed the next day by an honest citizen who came to him and said:

"Monsieur le Count, since you have restored life to my wife and daughter, allow me to discharge my debt of gratitude. Let me tell you that you are nourishing a snake in your bosom. Your Sacchi is a scoundrel. There is no doubt of it; he is spying on you at the bidding of the local doctors, your implacable enemies. He extorts money from your patients, to destroy their respect for you; he swears that you yourself ordered him to do so."

Moreover, Sacchi was selling for money "Yellow Pills" that he had himself manufactured, and that had nothing in common with the Count's elixir.

Brought face to face with his employer, the culprit made a full confession and gave notice to leave that very day.

As the rascal had uttered some fierce threats, the Marquis de la Salle ordered him, at Cagliostro's request, to leave Alsace within twenty-four hours.

As soon as Sacchi was safely beyond the Rhine, he wrote an insolent letter to the thaumaturge, in which he demanded a payment of five hundred pounds for the six days he had spent in his employment. Should he fail to receive it, he threatened to publish a pamphlet which could scarcely please the Count. At the end of a week, seeing that his attempt at extortion remained fruitless, Sacchi set to work. With the connivance of a French lawyer named Rochebrune, another gaol-bird who had hid himself at Kehl, he at once wrote a scurrilous lampoon.

Cagliostro was shocked by it. Embittered by the treachery, he made matters worse by unjustly charging a respectable man, M. de Tournay, with counterfeiting his pills. Strong in his innocence, M. de Tournay wrote a crushing letter in protest. And the Princess Christine de Saxe, Abbess of Remiremont, and the King's own aunt, as well as the Princess Christine de Hesse Hombourg, found themselves implicated in the scandal in a manner most unfavourable to Cagliostro.

Owing to this misadventure, he resolved to give a monopoly of his medicines to M. Hecht, who had a pharmacy, " At the sign of the Virgin," and who was henceforward to be the only person allowed to sell his purgative powders and drinks, his oil of sugar-candy, his pomade for the complexion, and all the long list of his stomach pills, from the Balm of Canada to the terebenthine. As for his Wine of Egypt, his Yellow and White Pills, the specifics against epilepsy, deafness and gravel, Cagliostro had them prepared under his own eyes, at the rue des Ecrivains.

These innovations were unpopular. The Count was blamed for ceasing to hold more than one public audience a week, on Friday mornings, from eleven to twelve or half-past. And there was much bitterness when the healer transferred his responsibility in part to an employee named Jacquot. This ex-shop assistant had not even Sacchi's knowledge of medicine. Yet it was he who went and visited at their houses such of the patients as were unable to come to the Count ; he reported on them, after his own fashion, to the Master, upon which the latter would entrust him with drugs and prescriptions to be distributed among the patients. Many protested at this. It was thought monstrous that the life of the citizens should be at the mercy of an ignorant dunce. The surgeon Marechal having lodged a complaint, Jacquot was fined and prohibited from engaging in medical occupations. But the Council of Fifteen, under pressure from higher authorities, hastened to annul his sentence, and the employee recovered his former liberty to go about his duties.

It was further charged against the Count that he had begun to flatter the great, whereas formerly he had pretended to despise their ribbons and their medals. If the poor wretches who came to him without recommendations complained that they were unable to take his medicines, what an outburst there was ! He abused them, said that he thought it pretty insolent of them to pester a great nobleman like him, and treated them like fools unworthy of his attention. Repulsed in this fashion, the poorer people no longer made an escort for his coach. Among the celebrities, some had already beaten a timely retreat, and Cagliostro's voluntary secretaries were now only private individuals, such as the Sarasin family, M. Ramond de Carbonnieres, M. Straub, and M. le Barbier de Tinan.

At this period, the police sent one of their most skilful agents, M. de Brugnieres, to Strasbourg, to watch his activities. But this cunning sleuth had to return to Paris without having been able to catch him in the wrong.

Sometimes, suffocated by this network of intrigue, Cagliostro would take refuge in the country, in the school-house of the Ban de La Roche, where the pastor Oberlin generally offered him rustic hospitality. What a relief it was for the philanthropist to pour out his confidences to this virtuous ecclesiastic, an honour to the priesthood, a man who had a taste for the marvellous, who read Swedenborg and cited Lavater as well as the famous mystics, and had himself had remarkable visions ! At night, when their guest had gone to explore the ruins of the castle of La Roche—just as he had done in Courland in the forest of Wilzen—Oberlin and his wife would force themselves to keep awake in case the angel Anachiel should bring them a gold or silver vessel on behalf of the Count. But no such thing ever occurred.

It was not the will of Providence that the thaumaturge should lack the strength to bear all these worries and affronts to the end. Returning home one evening, to the rue des Ecrivains, he was surprised to see his most cherished friend, the Chevalier d'Aquino. Reading in the papers that Cagliostro was in Strasbourg, this venerable gentleman had at once undertaken the long and fatiguing journey from Naples to Alsace in order to renew the ties of their old friendship. The Chevalier called on the civic leaders. He told each of them what he thought of Cagliostro and vouched for the distinction with which he had seen him invariably treated in Italy.

This account, coming from Cagliostro himself, was in Vannetti's eyes a document of capital importance. For it provided yet another link between Alexandre de Cagliostro and Giuseppe Balsamo. The Chevalier in question was, in fact, the Chevalier d'Aquino, the younger brother of the Prince de Caramanica and great devotee of occultism, who had taken Balsamo under his patronage at the time when that adventurer had sought his fortune at Malta and in the kingdom of Naples. Such a coincidence could not fail to impress the secretary of the *Accademia degli Agiati*.

But had this visit of the Chevalier really taken place ? For all that Cagliostro might say, no one had any recollection of it in Strasbourg. In any case, it was clear that the Count, wanting to make a boast of some flattering friendships, had named precisely the gentleman whose protection had formerly been so helpful to Giuseppe Balsamo.

Sacchi's pamphlet certainly swarmed with lies. Vannetti refused to believe that the Master was the Neapolitan barber Tiscio, son of one of the coachmen of the Duke of Castropignani. Nevertheless, the fact that Sacchi and Cagliostro had met at Valenzia in Spain, a town which also figured in Balsamo's itinerary, was a clue to be kept in mind.

When Balsamo vanished in the spring of 1776, he was calling himself the Marquis Pellegrini. Did not Mr. Bousie say that the same name had been Cagliostro's in the early days in London ? And when the Count and the Countess arrived in England towards the end of July 1776, soon after the disappearance of the Balsamo couple, they possessed more than two thousand pounds sterling in Spanish coin, as though they came straight from that country.

Clementino Vannetti also took into account that, in the proceedings against William Scott and Mary Fry, the Count, like Balsamo, had declared himself to be a native of Sicily, and that his Christian name was, also like Balsamo's, Giuseppe.

Finally, many people in Strasbourg knew that Cagliostro owned an elegant cane, containing in its top a repeating watch encircled with precious stones, exactly like that for which the firm of Silvestre, of Cadiz, had claimed payment from the Marquis Pellegrini. . . .

. . . .

The Cardinal de Rohan admired this cane so much that Alexander de Cagliostro could not avoid offering it to him. They were, in fact, in the habit of exchanging small gifts. On receiving a gold casket, the Count had rejoined with one still more beautiful. When the Cardinal sent the Countess Serafina a portrait of Cagliostro embellished with diamonds, the Count addressed to him by way of thanks a huge solitaire, engraved with the Rohan arms, a superb jewel, valued by the experts at more than twenty-five thousand pounds. The Cardinal did not fail to show it to his visitors :

" He made it himself," he repeated rapturously, making the gem glitter. " He made it out of nothing, do you understand ? I was present at the time, with my eyes glued on the crucible."

During three years of a close friendship, the Cardinal had not experienced any fraud. As on the first day, Cagliostro continued to fascinate him by the multitude of his gifts. This alchemist who was also a doctor, this doctor who was also a prophet, had announced in November 1780, the death of the Empress Marie Thérèse five days before the news reached Strasbourg. In October 1781, he had predicted that the Queen of France would give birth to a son. The predictions were invariably right. Thus the confidence and enthusiasm of the Prince Bishop of Strasbourg, far from cooling, as in the case of some ardent devotees, were continually growing.

Seeing that the thaumaturge, tired out by his worries, took refuge more and more frequently at Basle, with the Sarasins, the Cardinal exerted himself to obtain letters from Versailles which would silence the sycophantic and the envious. In collaboration with the Marshal de Contades, he emphasised the loyalty and devotion shown him by the Count de Cagliostro during the illness of the Prince de Soubise ; the continual services which the philanthropist rendered to the town of Strasbourg by his charities and free medical advice as well as by the considerable crowds which his fame attracted to the town. Such arguments prevailed with the Keeper of the Seal and the Minister of War. As for the Minister of Foreign Affairs, he had already been won over. M. Ramond de Carbonnieres had thus the pleasure of conveying to the " White House " on the 19th March, 1783, three official letters.

The Count de Vergennes wrote to M. de Gerard, the King's banker, in these terms :

"VERSAILLES,
13th March, 1783.

I am not personally acquainted, Sir, with the Count de Cagliostro, but all reports which I have received since he came to Strasbourg are so favourable to him that humanity demands that he should find respect and tranquillity there. His position as a foreigner, and the good which he accomplishes in all he does, are qualifications which entitle me to recommend him to you and to the Magistracy over whom you preside. M. de Cagliostro only asks for peace and security; these hospitality must guarantee to him, and, knowing your natural dispositions, I am persuaded that you will endeavour to enable him to enjoy it, as well as the conveniences which personally he might deserve.

I have the honour to be, Sir, your humble and obedient servant,
DE VERGENNES."

"The Sieur Count de Cagliostro has employed himself zealously since he came to Strasbourg in the relief of the poor and the unfortunate, and to my knowledge there are many humane actions done by this foreigner which entitle him to special protection. I charge you to give him, in whatever concerns you and the Magistracy over whom you preside, all the support and all the protection which a foreigner ought to enjoy in the King's territories, especially one who makes himself useful.

MIROMESNIL."

Finally, the Marshal de Segur, Minister of War, thought it his duty to arouse the zeal of the Marquis de la Salle, the second officer in command of Alsace:

"The good conduct, Sir, which I am assured the Sieur de Cagliostro has constantly observed at Strasbourg; the respectable use he has made in that town of his knowledge and his gifts, and the manifold proofs of humanity which he has there given to private citizens suffering from various diseases who have appealed to him, entitle this foreigner to the protection of the Government. The King bids you see not only that he is not troubled in Strasbourg, when he should think fit to return there, but also that he enjoys in that town the respect which the services he is rendering to the unfortunate ought to ensure.

I have the honour to be, etc.,
SÉGUR."

It was thus in triumph that the thaumaturge returned to Strasbourg amidst the blessings of the sick. Several of them were living at that period below the new apartment which the Count occupied in the house of the woman Lamarche. In this vast building, which had been converted into a house of healing, they formed a community like that of the primitive Christians. A caterer named Bourgard purveyed food to them. The little parish endeavoured to foresee and satisfy in advance the slightest desires of Cagliostro. "When one has seen this with one's own eyes," admitted a German, "and how this man holds so many wealthy men so absolutely in his power that they have no thought but of him, then truly everything becomes clear, everything explains itself."

The young Count Leopold von Lamberg, cured by Cagliostro of worms, wished to persuade his sister, the Canoness of Cologne, who was suffering from a nervous disease, to come to Cagliostro too. Yielding to her brother's importunity, Eleonore von Lamberg arrived at Strasbourg on the 5th June, 1783, in a bad humour and with the strongest prejudice against the empiric.

Treatment began at once. Cagliostro's visits were repeated several times a day. The attacks grew less frequent, soon they were less violent. And the Canoness, delighted, subjugated, fell in love with her physician. Within a week, she was trembling at the thought of losing him.

How much more lively still were the Cardinal's apprehensions! No one had more need of Cagliostro than he. His disgrace had never been as cruel as it was now; only this divine man could tell him when it would be over. Even after the solemn baptism of the Dauphin in the chapel at Versailles, the Queen had not wished to take the Grand Almoner of France back into favour. Was his cause then lost? Prince Louis refused to admit it. Being unable to approach Marie Antoinette and make her acquaintance personally, he was reduced to seeking information about her among the menials of the household and the departments. He did not even despise what the pamphleteers said about her peccadilloes, her avidity for pleasure and luxury; he forced himself to believe it. In fact, unless these knaves were utter liars, some magnificent gift offered at the right moment might perhaps soften the sovereign, flatter the beautiful woman. . . .

The Cardinal, who was thought to be rich, though a part of his fortune had been squandered away, was counting on Cagliostro's genius to avoid bankruptcy. This sublime alchemist possessed the secret of the philosopher's stone. That is why a laboratory was kept always in readiness for him at the palaces of Strasbourg and Saverne. That is why the Cardinal had given him for assistant his most capable secretary, M. Ramond de Carbonnieres, the intimate councillor of his Most Serene and Eminent Highness. Their labours had begun at Saverne on the 8th August, 1781. By transmuting mercury, a metal half gold and half silver was obtained, of which the weight, singularly enough, remained close to that of mercury. Though he presumed that the small lump of metal contained many air-holes, M. de Carbonnieres did not on that account entertain such suspicions as had Count Moszynski. The rumour quickly spread that the Count had made five to six thousand pounds of gold for the Cardinal and that the latter was going to be the richest prince in Europe.

Louis de Rohan depended on his wonderful friend for other things as well. The Count de Cagliostro had promised to impart to him some of his powers. Nor did the occultist refuse to share with his favourite disciples the gift which he had of holding converse with the angels. But the development of the soul must precede physical regeneration. Accordingly, the spiritual initiation was commenced on the 22nd September, 1781, at Saverne, in the presence of MM. Straub and Le Barbier de Tinan. Two days later, a supernatural séance was held at Strasbourg, with the assistance of M. Straub's daughter, who proved as satisfactory to the spirits as little Felix Sarasin had in his rôle of "pupil." The meetings were held at night in Cagliostro's house, and sometimes at the episcopal palace, where M. de Luternau was made a Mason on the 31st January, 1783.

No doubt, the Cardinal had persuaded himself that the Egyptian Rite did not fall under the scope of the bulls which had been fulminated against Freemasonry by the Popes Clement XII and Benedict XIV. In this careful culture of the highest virtues of the soul he could see nothing opposed to the dignity of a prince of the Church or to his duties as a simple Christian. Why should not Cagliostro's Rite one day receive Papal sanction on the same footing as the Order of Malta, of which Emmanuel Jean Marie des Neiges de Rohan was Grand Master? Optimistic and confident, Louis de Rohan already caused to be built at Basle a kiosk for his physical regeneration. Nominally, the work was carried out in the name of the Count de Cagliostro. But it was the Cardinal who bore all its expenses, and more, in two payments of 22,000 and 20,000 pounds each.

In order to detain the mysterious wanderer, the Cardinal promised that Louis XVI should personally authorise him, for the good of mankind, to practise his gifts at Strasbourg. In this hope, M. le Barbier de Tinan prepared a draft, or warrant. But Cagliostro said that at Strasbourg a foreigner like himself would only be building on sand. His good deeds never brought him anything but insults. He was treated everywhere as the Wandering Jew, the anti-Christ, the "man of 1400." Tired of these insults, he was seriously thinking of going away.

Where to go? As he and his wife debated the question secretly, each expressed a preference for England. Letter upon letter came to them announcing the defeat and punishment of their old persecutors. William Scott was in prison. As his thefts were no longer in doubt, it was certain that he would be sent to the gallows. Mr. O'Reilly, armed with Cagliostro's power of attorney, had offered to set him at liberty, and give him five hundred guineas, if he would return the manuscript and the rose powder. But the rogue, almost at the foot of the fatal ladder, fiercely refused to part with them. Surprised, the attorney wrote for fresh instructions. Those which he received from

Strasbourg were such as one might expect from a philanthropist. Rather than hand a man over to the hangman, the Count would abstain from pressing his charges. But Scott, for his part, must give up his demands for compensation and bear the costs. The affair was thus settled amicably.

Before packing up, Cagliostro wished once more to see his friends of the "White House," whose loyalty and fidelity he had learned to esteem. Besides, he loved their children. How many times had their eldest son, Felix, acted as his "pupil"! And the little Alexander born at Strasbourg, thanks to his skill, did he not bear his name?

While he was away, M. le Barbier de Tinan sent to him through Jacques Sarasin a report of the patients who were housed at Mme Lamarche's:

"Madame Chambrier is going on well, and has had nothing since his departure. Little Cogel had a slight attack, not severe. Yesterday the Canoness had a violent attack; she was well in the afternoon; she went down to Madame the Countess and later took a drive. I do not believe that she has had anything since. Bourgard has had nothing more than slight pains in the head and it has not been necessary to give him an injection. His wife is well. Mlle Vanderbrock last evening had a violent fit; she continues to take what was prescribed for her. These are the details of the patients. Nothing else new which could interest M. the Count."

Cagliostro did not linger in Basle. With his customary insight, he detected in M. and Mme Sarasin certain aspirations which he was not very anxious to satisfy. No sooner had they been cured, than these good folk asked to be regenerated. They were excessively preoccupied with the pavilion at Riehen. But the time was not ripe. Jacques and Gertrude no more deserved this supreme reward than the Cardinal de Rohan. After five days, the Master left them. And to save them tears, or to forestall their questions, he scarcely mentioned his departure, and avoided saying good-bye. The next day, the 12th June, Lavater arrived, distracted, at the "White House." His wife had had an alarming relapse.

In the fits in which the patient was convulsed, her only hope lay in a visit of the great man. If only he would come to Zurich, he would undoubtedly cure her as he had cured Gertrude Sarasin, as he had cured so many others. . . . Lavater was disconsolate at learning that the Count had already left; but he resolved to catch him at Strasbourg, and put before him forcibly his troubles. Alas! on the 14th June, when Lavater presented himself at Mme Lamarche's, the man he was looking for was no longer there.

The Count and the Countess must have gone away on the 13th June, 1783. A terrible excitement prevailed in the house. The proprietress repeated to everyone who came in that she would await his return calmly, even if it took ten years. The Count Leopold von Lamberg wrote in the most pathetic tone to his family:

" Here we are now, like deserted children. He has vanished suddenly and no one knows where he has gone. We still hope that he will return soon. Many here are in the same predicament with ourselves, and await for him. No doubt he has left with his friends a certain diet for my sister, but it is not necessary to put the same trust in them as in him."

Where was the Master ? In the African seraglio where he had formerly cured the sultanas ? In the Arabian deserts, where the very brigands held his name in veneration ? Was he in the heart of a pyramid, pondering the mysteries of ancient Egypt ? Should one look for clues in Europe, or Asia, or Africa ? . . . The uncertainty continued for three months. At length, on the 4th September, Jacques Sarasin discovered among his letters, with a joyful cry, one from Naples, whose contents he hastened to communicate to the Swiss and the French brethren.

Everything was clear now. Persecuted by the envious, who could not forgive him his success, Cagliostro had been arranging to leave Alsace when, on the way from Basle to Strasbourg, a message was brought to him. It was from his friend the Chevalier d'Aquino who, dangerously ill, had summoned him to his bedside. The Count and the Countess immediately set off on the journey. But quickly as they went, death was quicker. They had arrived in Naples only to hear the last sighs of the initiate.

All the disciples were touched by this story. Nevertheless, the arrival at Strasbourg a month later of the servant La Pierre cast a chill over them. This man had quarrelled with his master at Naples, and the things he said on his return to Alsace were deplorable.

Instead of waiting for Cagliostro for ten years, Mme Lamarche invited M. Straub to drop in the next day. And in his presence, she got a locksmith to open a chest of drawers and a cabinet which were both found locked in Cagliostro's apartment. There was nothing in them save a plaster bust of little Alexander, Cagliostro's godson, which M. Straub offered to return to M. and Mme Sarasin. But the proprietress furiously declared that she would keep as compensation everything found in the apartment. And M. Straub, who would have liked to take the oil-portrait of Cagliostro hanging in the salon, despised the avaricious termagant too much to engage in a dispute with her. He consoled himself by writing to Jacques Sarasin at once :

" We shall see what the dear Count thinks of it when he returns. It seems to me she ought to have more respect for him. Bourgard is just like her. When self-interest is at an end, farewell to friendship ! "

VIII

THE GRAND COPHTE AND THE GRAND MISTRESS

THE Sardinian Ambassador's indiscretions compromised the incognito under which Cagliostro hoped to conceal himself in Naples. And the French chargé d'affaires, M. Vivant Denon, took it into his head to persuade him to resume his consultations. But Cagliostro, deprived of the only friend whose affection could have detained him in Naples, was not at all anxious to expose himself once more to the persecution of the doctors. He resolved to avoid all these importunities by a sudden departure. The moment seemed to have come for his return to England.

Instead of embarking from Naples, the Count and the Countess travelled rapidly by way of Rome and Florence to Lerici, whence a felucca safely transported them to Antibes. Formerly, on their way to Saint Jacques de Compostelle, Giuseppe and Lorenza Balsamo had stopped at this small town on the Corniche. Alexander and Serafina Cagliostro drove through southern France as far as Montpellier, by the same route the two pilgrims had taken. Then bearing north-west, they arrived on the 8th November, 1783, at Bordeaux.

At the theatre that very evening, an officer in uniform fell on their necks with cries of joy. It was the cavalry captain Count de Brivazac, Chevalier of Saint Louis, one of their old friends of Alsace. Thereupon, a Freemason, the Chevalier Roland, who had been watching from a distance this touching scene, took the liberty to approach and salute them. With expressions of the most profound respect, he told them that his Lodge would always be open to them, whenever they should be pleased to attend a meeting. Besides, he begged Cagliostro to be good enough to give all his attention to the sick, as he had in Strasbourg.

The thaumaturge could not remain deaf to these pressing requests. Postponing his departure, he consented to render the people of Bordeaux the services he had denied the Neapolitans. And at the first news of this decision, so impetuous was the rush of the sick and the poor, that the authorities had to establish a traffic service in the neighbourhood of the Hôtel de l'Empereur, near Saint Seurin, where the Count and the Countess lived.

This commotion, this tumultuous excitement, was distasteful to the medical faculty. They complained about it. But already Cagliostro had his supporters, and among the most enthusiastic of them could be cited the names of the Marshal de Mouchy, Commander-in-Chief in Guyenne, the Count de Fument, second in command, the Duc de Crillon and Mahon, and the Viscount du Hamel, not to mention several other gentlemen who warmly befriended him. Innumerable sonnets and epistles were dedicated to him by the poets. And it did not surprise anyone to read, on the 9th December, 1783, in the *Affiches de Bordeax*, this hyperbolical acrostic :

Chiron has descended from the skies.
Friends, he is in this town.
Great herbalist and skilful doctor.
It is said he has received many secrets from the gods.
The public should, while paying him tribute,
Observe too that he is a sage.
His gift and his gold are for all mortals.
Keep silent, foolish critic,
Blush to say that he is an empiric :
Altars should be set up to Chiron. . . .

Equally naïve couplets echoed through the streets :

To Bordeaux has come
A wonderful worker.
By him the whole world is saved,
Open your eyes and your ears,
The Count and the Countess of Cagliostro
Are come to cure of all vertigo :
Bravo, bravo, bravissimo !

A young gentleman of Lyons, M. Rey de Morande, looked after the Count's correspondence so efficiently that the good news was regularly sent to Strasbourg and Basle. The arrival of these long letters, sealed with the arms of the Count, with his motto in Italian : *Bisogna festina festinare lentamente* (One should make haste slowly), was thereafter a sweet satisfaction to the faithful.

They learnt, by this means, that their spiritual father moved from his furnished apartment to a private house which had been offered him by his admirers. Two spacious rooms in the new residence were used in the mornings for public audiences : the well-to-do came on Mondays and Wednesdays, and the poor on Saturdays. As the Count employed his time after dinner in visiting at their homes those of his patients who could not be moved, he scarcely saw his friends before seven in the evening. In brief, he led a life of strenuous charity, exactly as at Strasbourg.

Nothing more was needed to arouse public curiosity. The whole of Guyenne longed to know the great man. His portraits were sought for throughout the province. But the prints ordered from Alsace had not yet reached the local shops, and Cagliostro had to distribute the last of his personal copies between M. Rey de Morande, the Duc de Crillon and the Marshal de Mouchy.

Fortunately M. Sarasin soon sent a trunkful of prints and busts, as well as a selection from the poems that had been composed in Alsace and Switzerland in honour of the philanthropist.

Thereupon, a notable citizen, M. Boyer, wishing to obtain some information before entrusting his wife to Cagliostro, wrote to M. Sarasin to enquire about Mme Sarasin's treatment. In reply, Jacques Sarasin sent him a copy of the letter he had formerly addressed to the *Journal de Paris*, supplementing it with the following statement :

" My occupations do not permit me now to expand this any further. But if there are wicked people to confound, doctors to be silenced, command me, and I shall be with you heart and soul. After what I have told you, sir, it only remains for me to congratulate you on putting your wife in such excellent hands."

To judge by M. Boyer's reply, the Count de Cagliostro must have been deeply impressed by this message.

" On the evening of the 9th, the Count asked me for your letter, and he told me the next day that he wished to have it printed. On the 10th, the 11th and the 12th, he did his best to obtain permission —but in vain. It is true he is a little too obstinate in refusing to consent to a few deletions ; such, for example, as the phrase : ' if there are doctors to be silenced, and wicked people to be confounded, command me, I shall be with you heart and soul.' It is desired to substitute for this : ' if there are ill-intentioned people, command me, and I shall be with you heart and soul.'

That letter is now an important public issue. The matter has been put before the Parlement. But whatever may be the outcome, it is bound to be unfavourable to M. the Count, for, if he succeeds in his claim, he would increase the number of his enemies while it would really be a humiliation to the magistrates who have been opposed to the literal reprinting of the letter. If he does not succeed, he will become a laughing stock."

The conflict could have been avoided with a little tact. But the impulsive and excitable nature of the Grand Cophte, and his invincible obstinacy whenever his vanity was touched, exposed him to the most bitter disappointments.

He fell ill in May. Fever, at first continuous and bilious, developed into *fievre tierce*. Worn down so much as to cause alarm, he had to be confined to his bed. After the 8th June, M. Rey de Morande admitted how anxious he had been, in a letter to M. Jacques Sarasin :

" M. the Count has at last shaken off the fever, and is now recovering the embonpoint of which his illness had deprived him ; he has not now half the paunch or jowl he had when he came. I may confess it to-day : I felt extremely anxious during the first three days."

Strange rumours went round at the time. It was alleged that the thaumaturge was suffering mortal humiliation at having been driven ignominiously out of the house of a woman with whom he was madly in love. He was also accused of turning the head of the Marquise de Merville while pretending to raise the shade of her late husband. From another widow, he had filched five thousand ecus under the pretext of finding for her some treasure hidden in a field. But level-headed men did not accept such insinuations without proof.

What admits of no doubt, however, was the premonitory vision he had in Bordeaux. . . .

During the weary and painful aftermath of an attack of fever, the Master imagined he saw two giants who, seizing him by the collar, dragged him into a cave. A door suddenly opened in the thickness of the wall. His assailants pushed him into a hall lit with a thousand candles, and gleaming with gilt like a royal apartment, where a large company seemed to be waiting for him. Each of these elect was wearing a mantle of dazzling white, in accordance with the apocalyptic text : " There is in the Church of Sardis, a small number of the faithful who have not soiled their vestments." Cagliostro, dressed likewise in a pure and radiant robe of linen, received the Sword which the exterminating Angel brandishes over the threshold of Paradise. A delicious joy filled him. Imagining that he had been transported among the blessed, he was about to pour out his joy in prayer, when a dazzling orb of light threw him on his knees. And from the heart of this incandescence there issued a voice, gentle but overpowering, which said :

" Such will be your reward one day. But until then, you must toil ! "

. . . .

Toil ? In truth, the founder of the Egyptian Rite—the Grand Cophte, as he must be called—asked for nothing more. He longed with his whole being to propagate the true faith, to carry on his apostolate. To serve the Higher Wisdom, to assert it triumphantly, and to transmit it to his successors, such was his dominant ambition. Why, indeed, had he fled from the miserable Neapolitans who had begged him to heal their tortured and impure flesh, instead of begging him to fortify their souls ? Solely in order to reserve for spiritual ends the miraculous powers he held from the Great Architect of the Universe.

The greater part of the tasks he had assigned to himself were of a symbolical nature. Besides prayer and contemplation, he preached obedience to the Grand Lodge of England. Without union and concord there could be no mystical communion. If there is no reversion to the primal principles, the most solemn deliberations must ridiculously miscarry. That had been proved at the French Convention in 1778, and in 1782 at the general Convention of Wilhelmsbad. Only the Egyptian Rite had sufficient strength to assure liberty and dignity to Masonry.

With what respect did not M. Rey de Morande look upon such

wisdom ! It addressed itself with equal ease to the healing of diseases, to prophetic divination, to the evocation of shades, to the research of hidden treasure, and to the manufacture of the philosopher's stone ; and always through the mediation of the Seven Celestial Angels. Like the Cardinal de Rohan and the Sarasin family, M. Rey de Morande, deep in his heart, cherished the hope of being one day regenerated. Even as he went about the petty pharmaceutical or alchemical tasks with which he had been entrusted, he took an infinite delight in the contemplation of these sublime perspectives.

Like him, the people of Bordeaux took a passionate interest in occult investigations. Proud as they were of sheltering within their walls the Order of the Elect-Coens of the Universe, they were in no haste to disavow Martines de Pasqually. His initiates still kept their catechisms ; and wore their triangular talismans. But their decline had rapidly followed the amalgamation at Lyons of twelve flourishing and famous branches into a vast spiritual federation.

For, in fact, more than Strasbourg or Bordeaux, it was Lyons which, next to the capital, exercised the most powerful influence on the Masonic centres of France. It was at Lyons that the Vicar-General of the Strict Observance, Baron de Weiller, had inaugurated with great pomp the chapter of the province of Auvergne. The brethren of Lyons were distinguished, above all, by their knowledge, their fervour and their munificence. In this wealthy and powerful city, whole families joined the Masonic Lodge. Jean Baptiste Willermoz had converted his brother, his sister and his nephew, while M. Rey de Morande brought the light to his mother, his brother, M. Rey de Colonge, his sister Anne Marie, and his brother-in-law, Gabriel Barthelemy Magneval. No other French city gave such a favourable reception to esoteric novelties. And to this promised land it was that M. Rey de Morande endeavoured to lead Cagliostro in 1784.

Cagliostro had no desire to settle in Bordeaux. What was the use of marking time in a province where his preaching had already borne fruit ? Mme Boyer, cured of her nervous affection, was very proud of being pregnant again, after eight years of humiliating sterility. Cagliostro was now at his apogee. Each of his medical and spiritual consultations added to his glory. But he could not forgive the magistrates for having lately suppressed M. Sarasin's eulogistic letter. As for the voyage to London, it was a useful, indeed, an indispensable project, but it could wait.

Towards the autumn, the execrable Sacchi took it into his head to come to Bordeaux and sell his pamphlet. Great excitement among the disciples. In great indignation, the Marshal de Mouchy was preparing to expel the scoundrel, but Cagliostro himself prevented him.

" What is the good," he said calmly, " and why trouble oneself ? The mad dog can bark away as he pleases." His indifference in this matter was genuine, for he was getting ready to pack off. On the

11th October, 1784, in fact, he departed, with his entire household, in the direction of Limoges. And M. Boyer, overcome with grief, could not but unbosom himself to M. Sarasin :

"He carries with him the regrets and the gratitude of many of the inhabitants of Bordeaux, and the gap which he leaves in the relief of the poor is beginning to be felt. He has achieved an endless number of truly miraculous cures."

. . . .

It was through the Cardinal de Rohan that the faithful in Alsace and Switzerland had communicated with Bordeaux during the last eleven months. His Eminent and Serene Highness was likewise the first to make known to them that the Grand Cophte, under the incognito of "Count Phœnix," had arrived on the 20th October, 1784, at Lyons, at the Hôtel de la Reine, kept by the Misses Foret, on the quai Saint Clair, in the parish of Saint Pierre et Saint Saturnin.

The correspondence between the Prince's secretary and the thaumaturge's secretary did not cease. If M. Rey de Morande was not as good as M. Ramond de Carbonnieres in point of style, he had at any rate a fluent pen, and the Grand Cophte judged him worthy to translate into French, under his supervision, the rules and regulations of Egyptian Masonry.

But the Cardinal was no longer content with a mere exchange of letters. He was on the eve of grave events, and sighed for the free confidential exchanges as well as the delight and benediction which are the prerogatives of friendship. He did not mind having to wait still longer for his regeneration if he could but consult the supreme arbiter immediately about an affair in which he was engaged, and on which depended his return to favour, and even, perhaps, to fortune.

That was why M. Ramond de Carbonnieres had been sent with a message to Cagliostro. On the 30th November, M. Rey de Morande informed M. Sarasin of his arrival :

"We have the pleasure of having with us, since the last two days, M. de Carbonnieres at the Maison Tolozan, quai Saint Clair."

The former laboratory assistant rejoiced to meet once more his beloved Master, a year and a half after their last experiments. Cagliostro looked well. As he no longer took patients, the medical faculty left him in peace, and the doctors themselves at times came to him for help. When a rich landowner, M. J. B. Delorme, nicknamed "the American," was at the point of death, his doctor, de Labruyere, appealed to Cagliostro, and the latter was able to secure for the dying man a respite in which they imagined they saw the first signs of convalescence.

As M. Rey de Morande had foretold, the citizens of Lyons, always fond of occultism, admired the hierophant's gifts, which were somehow multiplied tenfold by their calm and exalted fervour. At that time, they were mourning one of their aldermen, M. Prost de Royer, but recently "Venerable" of the Lodge *La Bienséance*. This old man had died in a destitution verging on misery, owing to having imprudently distributed his wealth among the poor. Cagliostro attempted to evoke his shade, and the disciples had the consolation of seeing, upright on a cloud, their beloved brother, M. Prost de Royer, who graciously gave his blessing to them. Other marvels followed—the only bright features of that dark year, 1784, so extraordinarily full of trials. Death deprived the Strict Observance, one by one, of its Vicar-General, the Baron de Weiller, and its founder, the Baron de Hundt. Now the papers were publishing, amidst general excitement, the decree which the Elector Charles Theodore of Bavaria had promulgated on the 22nd June, 1784, against secret societies. Would this example be followed by other governments? It was greatly feared so. The followers of the Grand Cophte alone remained imperturbable. Cagliostro had never attacked monarchial principles. And in Lyons, they admired him greatly for this prudent attitude.

Throwing themselves at his feet, they begged the Master to allow them to have a Lodge in Lyons. They undertook to dedicate to God a magnificent, stately temple, truly worthy of His name. The apprentices' room would be on the left; that of the companions on the right; and that of the masters in the middle. An appropriate site was just then for sale on the right of the avenue des Brotteaux, a little beyond the pond. The fund which was opened for this purpose had an enormous success. And Cagliostro, impressed by this unanimous display of generosity, promised to come and consecrate the edifice in person, on the great day of the inauguration.

Twelve brethren of acknowledged merit swore obedience to him. While setting before them as examples the twelve apostles of Christ, he told them sadly that one of them was going to betray him. In vain did these good people protest, saying that they felt themselves incapable of such baseness. In the course of the next year, the richest among them, M. Finguerlin, rudely declined to pay his subscription. A terrible scandal; but, in fact, his punishment was more terrible still. A thief having robbed him one night of £408,653, this rich and pompous banker found himself reduced within a few hours to bankruptcy.

The new Lodge, denominated *la Sagesse Triomphante*, was given the title and the prerogatives of the Mother Lodge. In the absence of Alexander de Cagliostro, it was to be presided over by two masters, who were to be called respectively Alexander II and Alexander III. The supreme authority devolved on M. Sain Costart, Venerable and Acting Grand Master. He chose as his coadjutors, Messrs. Journet, Auberjonois, Alquier, Rey de Colonge, and the two Magnevals, Gabriel Barthelemy and his younger brother, Phillipe. Their uniform was of green satin, edged with gold. An emblem of a snake, transfixed by an arrow, was stamped on the certificates of membership which were decorated, moreover, with the Grand Cophte's monogram. And after M. Rey de Morande had deposited the manuscript of their ritual in their archives, the Master gave the initiates an account of the extraordinary vision he had had at Bordeaux. After a sublime discourse on the mysteries of the faith, the " pupils " and the " pigeons " were interrogated, and various conjurations were accomplished through their innocent mediation.

Who would believe that the thaumaturge, surfeited with material prosperity and spiritual adulation as he was, had yet had the folly to defraud the Lodge of £500, under pretext of carrying out alchemical experiments? Why should he obtain by devious methods what was offered so readily and willingly? In the person of M. Sain Costart, the Grand Cophte had a banker at Lyons as devoted as M. Jacques Sarasin had been at Basle.

The Lodge was solemnly declared open on the 26th December, 1784. And M. Ramond de Carbonnieres, a young man of an ingenious and daring spirit who felt a special attraction for these strange rituals, was present at the ceremony. But under what pretext had the Prince Louis's secretary lingered at Lyons for over a month?

Did he speak to the Count of the revolution which had taken place at the Palais Cardinal? Did he deplore with him the growing influence of the Countess de la Motte Valois, whom perhaps the Master remembered having once seen in male attire in his antechamber at Strasbourg? The wheedler had promised to restore Prince Louis to the Queen's favour. In fact a preliminary reconciliation seemed to have taken place in the gardens at Versailles. At dusk, on the 12th August, 1784, the Cardinal had slipped into a bush close to the orangery. And the Queen, seeing him on his knees before her, pushed aside with the end of her fan the veil which covered her face, and, not without some trepidation, showed him the rose she was holding in her hand.

" You know what this means! "

Alas! What had been the consequence of this encounter? Demands for money; again and again, and always demands for money. Who would have thought that a great queen could be so short of funds? In August, Marie Antoinette solicited through Mme de la Motte fifty thousand pounds for a necessitous family which she desired to honour by her kindness; in November, a hundred thousand. The Cardinal could scarcely meet the demand. And yet his disgrace in the eyes of the Court remained exactly as before. How explain this discrepancy? The Prince's secretary and Cagliostro asked themselves the question in bewilderment.

Besides, M. Ramond de Carbonnieres informed the thaumaturge of the extraordinary doings in Paris. The *Philalethes* of the Lodge *Les Amis Réunis*, had invited different Masonic delegations from Europe to a meeting on the 25th February. The renewal of the conversations broken off at Wilhelmsbad was contemplated, and two questions on their agenda seemed to interest Cagliostro specially.

"Has masonic science any connection with the sciences known as the occult or secret sciences?"

"With which science or sciences has it the greatest connection? And what is the nature of the connection?"

The organisers had by no means forgotten Mesmer, who had been invited in accordance with the rules. But the question of inviting the Grand Cophte, debated on the 23rd December, 1784, provoked such violent disagreement that the meeting had in the end to be adjourned. This news spread very quickly, owing to the close relations which subsisted between the provincial lodges and the metropolitan headquarters. Cagliostro, indeed, affected to despise any consideration that vulgar Freemasons might show him. But this attitude threatened to cause trouble among his followers, and it was of that that he complained to M. Ramond de Carbonnieres.

The young secretary, thereupon, showed him that he could have easily saved himself this affront, if he had sown the good seed in Paris as he had at Strasbourg, Bordeaux and Lyons. The secretary's devotion to the Master inspired in him persuasive eloquence and irrefutable arguments. Why indeed was the Cardinal burning to see the Count? Was it to hasten his metamorphosis? Not at all! This reward, which had been so generously promised, and was so patiently awaited, Louis de Rohan did not wish to have save at the mystagogue's pleasure. But where else could the divine wisdom be propagated more worthily than in Paris? If the critics dared to say nothing against Mesmer, it was because he was himself on the spot to answer them. It was therefore essential that the Count should appear on the Parisian stage, the most important in the world. For the propagation of the Rite, as well as for the glory of God, it was indispensable that he should do so.

His dialectic triumphed over the obscure hesitations which afflicted his friends. They got ready for the journey. And on the 27th December, 1784, when M. Ramond de Carbonnieres took his place in the open cabriolet which was to take him to Paris, the Count and Countess promised to rejoin him before long.

Towards the end of January 1785, M. Rey de Morande despatched his last letter from Lyons to M. Sarasin:

"Hereafter letters should be sent not to this town, but to Paris, care of the Prince. . . . I am very happy to say that I shall be going with him."

. . . .

M. Ramond de Carbonnieres quickly set about to engage for his friends the first floor of the "Hôtel de Savigny," belonging to the Marquise d'Orvilliers. This convenient and spacious residence stood at the corner of the rue Saint Claude and the boulevard, not far from the Vieille-rue-du-Temple, where the Cardinal lived. But the furnishers and other workmen were still pottering about when the new tenants arrived in Paris, on the 30th January, 1785, at nine in the evening.

Instead of staying in the Cardinal's palace, the Count and the Countess preferred to wait patiently for some weeks in a furnished apartment near the Palais Royal, where the *pension* was no more than fifteen louis. M. de Carbonnieres came there regularly to submit his accounts ; the Grand Cophte gave him the money with which to make his payments, and the young man thereupon paid the furnishers what he thought they deserved.

Though he did not stint his praise of the intelligence and energy of his secretary, the Cardinal reserved for the Countess de la Motte Valois his most enthusiastic dithyrambs. This lady, he affirmed, served him with incomparable skill in his efforts to win the Queen's favour.

On the 1st February, 1785, the Count and Countess saw him come in with a box in his hand. Beaming with joy, the Prince told them that he was just on his way to Versailles with an extremely precious article destined for the Queen. Cagliostro, out of discretion, refrained from asking any questions. But Louis de Rohan seized a moment when he was alone with the Countess, to show her, as a most profound secret, what the box contained. Hardly had the lid been opened than she saw some huge diamonds, dazzlingly bright in a velvet case. Trefoils, festoons and rosettes, prolonged with four shining tassels, made up a many-stringed necklace of fabulous wealth. And Serafina de Cagliostro was nearly blinded by its brilliance.

A few days later, Louis de Rohan frankly told Cagliostro what he had gone to Versailles for.

Thanks to Mme de la Motte, he had come to know that Marie Antoinette had set her heart on a magnificent jewel. With some diamonds of extraordinary size and perfection, MM. Boehmer and Bassenge, the Crown jewellers, had created a masterpiece, a superb diamond necklace, for which they demanded sixteen hundred thousand pounds. The royal coffers were empty. And Marie Antoinette, thinking of the crushing burdens of the State, and the privations which the King gladly imposed on himself for the sake of his navy, had at first told the jewellers :

" For that price, we could get a ship."

A reply worthy of a great sovereign. All the same, Her Majesty loved the jewel so passionately that, when her pregnancy revived within her, in spite of herself, her regrets and her desires, she finally yielded to a longing which was indeed worthy of her rank. Cost what it may, she had resolved to acquire the ruinous necklace. To tell the truth, the sixteen hundred thousand pounds had still to be found, and Louis XVI, so good-natured in other respects, absolutely insisted on her paying cash for the jewel. No matter ! she would buy it on credit, and the King shall know nothing of it. It remained still to choose a sufficiently reliable intermediary for negotiating with MM. Boehmer and Bassenge without causing much fuss. When consulted, Mme de la Motte had had the hardihood to suggest the Cardinal's name, and the tact to get it accepted. Marie Antoinette overcame her hesitations, and wrote to the Prince, entrusting him with the business.

His Eminence, delighted at being charged with such a confidential mission, immediately opened negotiations. On the 29th January, 1785, that is to say, on the very eve of Cagliostro's arrival, the Cardinal had made a contract with the jewellers which Mme de la Motte hurriedly carried to Versailles. The Queen wrote " approved " against each article, and then signed her name.

Cagliostro listened to the story with astonishment. His feelings were reflected on his expressive countenance. No doubt the nocturnal meeting at Versailles, as M. de Carbonnieres had described it at Lyons, had already shocked him. But this story he now heard seemed incredible. Would a nobleman to whom the Queen never addressed a word in public be commissioned by her to execute such an important transaction, covertly, and despite the King's irrevocable ban?

Nevertheless, Prince Louis, overwhelmed with joy, was already seeing himself as first minister. He enjoyed in advance the confusion of his enemies. What a bolt from the blue it would be for the Baron de Breteuil, his *bête noire* ! In vain had this intriguer assumed control, since his return from the Viennese Embassy, of the Royal household and the department of Paris. Moreover, once he was in power, Louis de Rohan would present the Grand Cophte at Court; he would see that he had a position more in keeping with his genius.... But why was he listening to him so impassively?

" Have you advanced the sixteen hundred thousand pounds?" asked Cagliostro bluntly.

" No," replied the Cardinal, " but we have made arrangements with the jewellers which have given them satisfaction. The necklace is to be paid for in four instalments, each of which would be of four hundred thousand pounds, beginning with the first of August next."

He added:

" I myself took the necklace to Versailles. A man in black came into Mme de La Motte's room after a moment. He had a written order from the Queen, directing the jewels to be handed to the bearer. He was then given the casket, and he went out."

Cagliostro could not believe his ears. What inconceivable thoughtlessness! He demanded further explanations. But the Cardinal merely replied that it was done, and there was an end to it.

" In that case," retorted Cagliostro drily, " there is no use in my saying anything more."

He had, in fact, graver preoccupations.

. . . .

From the middle of February, curious Parisians began to besiege his chambers in the Palais Royal. "Who is he? What is his real name?" The eternal questions were repeated endlessly among the crowds, and they noted the reply Cagliostro had given to the most daring of them:

"*Sum qui sum!* . . ."

The sensation was immense. Little by little it affected even those who had been recalcitrant. The *Philalethes*, for instance, who, in November 1784, had decided to be aloof, changed their minds in February 1785; they could not, they said, deliberately ignore a phenomenon which fascinated the whole of Europe. They must summon him, and listen to him, if only to expose him. Accordingly, on the 10th February, the Marquis de Chefdebien presented himself at the Count's lodgings with an official invitation.

Cagliostro welcomed him without rancour. Pretending, out of dignity, to have forgotten the scandalous debate of the preceding November, he named at once those of his spiritual sons whom he intended to bring with him to the Convention, for the Grand Cophte, founder of a famous and autonomous Rite, could not appear before the assembly like any private individual. His claim was eventually admitted; but the consultations having taken time, Cagliostro complained of it in haughty terms:

"The unknown Grand Master of the true Masonry," he wrote to the Convention, "has his eyes already on the *Philalethes*." Certainly he would condescend to teach them. But on two specific conditions: they should become affiliated with the Mother Lodge of his Rite at Lyons, and deliver to the flames, in proof of the sincerity of their conversion, those memorials of ignorance, their manuscripts and printed archives.

So as not to break with him, the Freemasons tried to explain to Cagliostro that the invitation came not from the *Philalethes* but from the Convention as a whole, which had no archives of any sort, and could not, accordingly, destroy them.

Then the Grand Cophte demanded that three delegates should go immediately to Lyons to become members of his Rite. Even before these neophytes had arrived, the *Sagesse Triomphante* conveyed to them their fraternal exhortations.

The reply from Paris was very cordial, but, in between these courtesies, the Freemasons of Lyons could see very well that the Convention regarded the initiation of the three members as a strictly individual matter.

All these subtleties finally exasperated Cagliostro. On the 13th April, he severely lectured the false friends who came to him with loyalty on their lips and perjury in their hearts:

"We offer you the truth, and you scorn it. We have offered it to you out of love for you, and you have refused it out of love for forms."

Was it a declaration of war? The Convention sent three of their members to him. These gentlemen exerted so much eloquence that the thaumaturge was mollified to the point of showing them his catechism of Egyptian apprenticeship ; and the delegates, duly edified, returned to testify that the new doctrine seemed to them sublime and beneficent.

But how could these crafty intriguers cleave loyally to this dazzling genius, this force of nature ? Their quibbling went on indefinitely. Cagliostro could no longer conceal his indignation. On the 30th April, 1785, he fulminated against them the anathema of anathemas:

" God alone can decide between you and me. Since you prefer a mass of puerile books and writings to the happiness to which I would destine you, and which you should share with the Elect ; since you are without faith in the promises of God or of his vicar on earth, I abandon you to your own devices, and I tell you this, in all truth : I shall no longer consider it part of my mission to enlighten you. Unhappy Philalethes, you sow in vain ; you will reap but thorns."

After three months, the Convention, like its predecessor, broke up and was adjourned. In Bavaria, the Elector Charles Theodore issued a fresh decree against secret societies. Those of the brethren who were associated with the Illuminists, left Paris muttering the abhorred names of Nero and Diocletian. But actually their bitterness was wholly concentrated on Cagliostro. Towards this traitor, this heretic, this apostate, they solemnly vowed implacable hatred, and God knows what dark plots were hatched at that period !

The Master did not care. The Seven Celestial Angels made his ways smooth. Thanks to their help, the supreme council of Egyptian Masonry was firmly organised in Paris. Its Grand Master Protector was the Prince de Montmorency-Luxembourg. Its Grand Inspector: Jean Benjamin de La Borde, the same who had glorified Cagliostro's virtues in his *Lettres sur la Suisse*. Its Grand Chancellor : Baduard de Saint James, the extremely wealthy Treasurer-General of the Navy. And its Grand Secretary : the Marquis de Vismes.

Besides, many able men, such as M. d'Epremesnil, the lawyer, were eager to offer their services. Though he did not repulse their advances, the Grand Cophte insisted on such a high code of morality, that M. d'Epremesnil decided to take for his second wife his good friend Mme Thilorier, so as to be worthy of the celestial favours.

Meanwhile, an envoy from the King of Sweden, Colonel Toll, came with a message to the thaumaturge from Gustave III. Towards the end of the interview, Cagliostro gravely assured him :

" You will discover them, my son, the truth and the light which you seek ! The Swedes are specially favoured by the Masters of the Wisdom. Write to your King that I promise to give him that for which he thirsts, and much besides. You will know what I mean before you return to your country. No need to tell me by which route you are going. I shall reach you, whatever your road."

Then he added :

"Inform your master, the King, that I am not a Count, that my name is not Cagliostro. Who I am, some day he will know."

With outstretched hand, he blessed him. And then, addressing himself to God, he prayed that he might have a speedy and successful transfiguration: the world would then know who the Count of Cagliostro really was.

. . . .

Since the end of February, the Grand Cophte and his wife had been living in the rue Saint Claude. Their servants were Jean Baptise Pecquet, a young French valet who had been recommended by the Cardinal's household; Françoise, the Countess's maid; and, in an indefinable capacity which included both that of confidant and factotum, an Italian jack-of-all-trades named Agostino.

Every morning, M. Burlandeux, the expert hairdresser of the rue des Tournelles, came to curl and powder Cagliostro. A woman named Boissonier, also a tenant of the Marquise d'Orvilliers, proved a very useful neighbour for the Countess. Besides, there was a ceaseless exchange of notes between the Hôtel de Savigny and the Hôtel de Strasbourg. Nearly every evening, his Serene and Eminent Highness would drop in familiarly to have supper with the Count and the Countess, and partake of an excellent meal. Besides delicious macaroni, they would offer him beef *à la mode*, which was cooked in half an hour by some culinary magic, and melted in the mouth. Sometimes, the Cardinal had one or two dishes brought over from his own kitchen, but did not in any other way contribute to the expense.

To help in reorganising the Egyptian congregation in Paris, M. Straub, director of the royal factory of arms in Alsace, was invited to come over, and was promised a salary of twenty-five pounds a month in the office of the Treasurer-General of the Navy, M. Baduard de Saint James. And this honest official, selling all his furniture, came at once from Strasbourg, accompanied by his wife and children. He was received with open arms by the Cardinal, and lodged in his palace until he found a permanent residence. M. Straub sensed such an exuberant optimism in his new surroundings that he wrote to M. Sarasin:

"The Prince told me the other day, that he was the happiest of men, and it made me really happy."

Only one thing was wanting to the Cardinal's perfect felicity; a *rapprochement* between Cagliostro and the Countess de La Motte. Without stopping to consider whether these two soothsayers could get on with each other, he desired with all his soul to bring them together.

An opportunity soon offered itself. About the beginning of March, the Queen, who was about to give birth to a son, had some terrible dreams. They seemed to suggest that she would meet with the same end as one of her friends who had died in childbirth, and already Marie Antoinette saw herself being carried to Saint Denis. Could not the Count de Cagliostro, that sublime genius who had so accurately foretold from Strasbourg the birth of the Dauphin, make a similar forecast and allay the Queen's apprehensions? Mme de La Motte made enquiries of the Cardinal.

She herself, besides, happened to be ill. So the Cardinal warmly urged her to consult Cagliostro about her own case. She was not to forget to remind him of their brief encounter in Strasbourg, as it would make a very good impression. Mme de La Motte promised to do all that he asked her, and the interview took place in the Cardinal's palace.

After shedding some tears to the memory of the poor Marquise de Boulainvilliers, Mme de La Motte spoke of her recent indispositions. Cagliostro gave her a prescription which the Cardinal eagerly noted down in a book. They then talked of the sinister forebodings which were tormenting the Queen. Mme de La Motte said that she was privileged to have the key to a small room situated below the great apartments at Versailles, where Her Majesty would often meet her for a private talk. It was in the course of one of these intimate conversations that Marie Antoinette had bidden her to put the matter before the soothsayer.

The Grand Cophte bowed. One does not refuse anything to the Queen of France. But instead of performing a transcendent operation, he modestly suggested a mesmeric experiment.

"Madame," he said frankly. "I have only studied medicine; and although I have no great faith in mesmerism, I believe it has some effect on children. We may be able to discover something by inducing a catalepsy in them. To-morrow, I shall bring with me a child, someone perfectly innocent, and we shall make an experiment."

The Countess de La Motte at once raised an objection. "If the thaumaturge himself brought the child, the Queen would suspect that it had been coached up previously." Accordingly, Mme de La Motte pressed the claims of her niece, Mlle Marie Jeanne de La Tour, who was a wise girl, discreet, and of an irreproachable character. In the end, it was agreed that the séance should be held the next evening, at ten o'clock, in the Hôtel de Strasbourg, with this niece. . . .

At first sight, Cagliostro thought he had been tricked. For they introduced to him, instead of the little girl he expected, a young maiden of about fifteen. Nothing could be less favourable to the experiment. If the fluid was to act strongly, it was necessary to have an ingenuous and naïve soul. However, fearing that he might distress the Cardinal, he forbore to protest, and gravely proceeded to ask her a few questions.

"Was she of stainless character? Had she a submissive heart, and was she devoted to her parents? Did she believe in God and scrupulously follow the precepts of religion?" When the maiden had given an affirmative answer to each of these questions, he told her:

"In that case, request God to disclose to you what is preoccupying us. If you are innocent, you will see a great many things; but if you are deceiving us, nothing."

With the help of the Cardinal he tied a small white apron on her, and made her repeat diverse formulæ; then he led her behind a screen where a table had been placed, with two lighted candles on it and a carafe of clear water between. The Grand Cophte told her to put her hands on the table, and repeated continually:

"If you are virtuous, you will see. . . ."

Later, he rejoined the Cardinal and Mme de La Motte who were waiting for him on the other side. With the naked sword in his hand, he gave himself up to his usual gesticulations, and one might have imagined that the scene was again the Lodge at Mitau or Petersburg, so exactly did he reproduce the way in which he used to shout and stamp:

"What do you see in the water?" he demanded in a loud tone.

As the answer was delayed, he rattled the screen:

"Speak!"

"I can see nothing," stammered the "pigeon."

"Are you not innocent? Look here, my child, listen. I stamp on the floor. Like this. . . . Do the same with your small innocent feet."

At once she uttered a cry:

"Sir, I see, I see . . ."

"Good, what do you see?"

"The Queen. . . ."

They were all amazed, for no one had so far mentioned that august name. In a low voice, Cagliostro asked if Mlle de La Tour had ever met the Queen. Mme de La Motte indicated that she had not. Then loudly:

"How is she dressed?" he asked.

"In white. . . . She is pregnant."

The description she gave of Queen Marie Antoinette was very realistic. And visibly excited, the Count continued:

"If she bends her head, it means that you are innocent, and that she would have a safe delivery. Look now. . . ."

"Yes, sir, she is bending her head. . . ."

Thereupon, turning towards Mme de La Motte, Cagliostro said:

"You may reassure the great lady whom you love. I think she is certain to have a successful confinement. I even foresee that it will be a boy."

The séance was adjourned. Marie Jeanne, emerging from behind the screen, took some refreshment with her aunt and the Cardinal. M. Ramond de Carbonnieres, happening to come in, joined them.

Had they failed to conform strictly to the ritual? Had Marie

Jeanne's hair, had her vestments been in disorder? Cagliostro seemed to be dissatisfied. However conclusive the experiment may have been, he said he was determined to begin it over again. At these words, the Cardinal slipped three double louis into Mme de La Motte's hands so that she might buy her niece a fine new dress.

Three or four days later, Marie Jeanne de La Tour returned, dressed completely in white, down to her shoes. She wore no blue at all, except a belt, which had been prescribed by the Count, and a large ribbon from which a silver star was suspended. She again saw the great white lady whom she called the Queen. And when she left, her aunt accompanied her instead of remaining with Cagliostro and the Cardinal.

The experiment, repeated the next day with a child of six years, brought the same results. There could be no uncertainty after that. Mme de La Motte undertook to reassure the Queen. . . .

On the 27th March, 1785, special messengers flew in all directions to announce throughout the kingdom that Her Majesty the Queen had happily given birth to a son at the Château of Versailles. Once again, Cagliostro's predictions had been fulfilled.

. . . .

Such an achievement, when it became public, could not fail to impress the few French princes who were at the time dabbling in occultism. But they all worked separately and in the greatest secrecy. The Count de Provence claimed to be able, alone with his favourite, the Count de Modena, to raise the devil. In the Orléans family, they spoke of the strange episode in which an enchanter had shown to the Regent his double, wearing a crown which was neither royal nor imperial. At first this seemed incomprehensible, as the son and grandsons of Louis XVI were still alive. Nothing less than a succession of bereavements could make this prophecy intelligible. The Regent's great grandson, the Duc de Chartres, shared the dangerous and illicit curiosities of his forbear. He was mad over talismans, and constantly wore on his chest a phylactery consecrated by the famous Jewish cabalist, Samuel Jacob Falk. And after he became Grand Master of the French Freemasonry, he discharged his functions with a meticulousness that one would not have expected of such an easy-going prince.

The Grand Cophte was becoming convinced that it would be useful to have his Egyptian Rite approved by the Grand Master of French Freemasonry. The Duc de Chartres, for his part, was everywhere making enquiries about Cagliostro. It was then suggested to him that he should meet the Grand Cophte. But wishing to avoid any trickery, the Count was present incognito at one of the meetings of the Lodge, accompanied by a " pupil " of six years, whom no one could have coached in advance. The conjuration took place forthwith. In the presence of the Cardinal de Rohan and the Prince de

Montmorency-Luxembourg, this innocent child, when questioned by Cagliostro, described the Palais Royal, which she had never seen, the gentlemen who were there, their dress, their occupations, and even reported their conversations so fully and so well, that the illustrious visitor, subjugated, admitted that Cagliostro was a supernatural being.

While her brother ruled over the Freemasons, the Duchess de Bourbon was Grand Mistress of the Women's Lodges, for she also was passionately interested in the mysterious and the sublime. But she saw and judged everything only through the eyes of the Marquis de Saint Martin ; and as that theosophist had an insurmountable aversion for Cagliostro, the Grand Cophte had no chance of approaching the Duchess. As for the Count de Provence, his aunt, the Princess Christine of Saxony, sent him from Strasbourg very unfavourable accounts of Cagliostro, and he considered it prudent not to seek the prophet's acquaintance. Thus it was that the Royal Family pretended to be unaware that the thaumaturge had, from Alsace, predicted the death of the Empress Marie Thérèse, the birth of the Dauphin, and then again, from Paris, quite recently, the birth of the Duke of Normandy. Never did the Count and Countess de Cagliostro gain access to Versailles.

In spite of this ostracism, the Egyptian Rite prospered. Half religion, half chivalric order, it sought to serve the Catholic Church in entirely new ways. The hierophant consecrated his " pupils " to the Great God—*il Grand Iddio*—with three insufflations before every ceremony.

Wherever he went, the Protestants reverted to Catholicism. At that very moment, a well-known Calvinist gentleman of Paris, the Baron Frederic de Planta, was preparing in solitude and penance to abjure his errors.

These wonderful reports, borne out by facts that could be easily verified, carried to its peak the enthusiasm of Cagliostro's disciples. The Cardinal de Rohan was deeply interested in a project which had already been discussed at Strasbourg and at Saverne : to obtain Papal sanction for the Egyptian Rite. Cagliostro's initiates, once they were recognised and approved by the Pope, would have equal privilege with the Knights of Malta. But as a prince of the Church, even though he were a Rohan, could not by himself prevail over the political inertia of the Roman Court, his Eminence sought the assistance of the principal members of the French episcopate, and his appeal was particularly successful in the case of Louis Phelypeaux d'Herbault, Archbishop of Bourges. The latter showed great interest in Cagliostro's proposals and in his Egyptian Ritual, which M. Rey de Morande had translated into French. And Cagliostro, who had not refused to show his catechism to the delegates of the Masonic convention, was only too happy to explain it to the Archbishop of Bourges and the Cardinal de Rohan. He told them of the vision he had had in Bordeaux, with details of which even the disciples had never heard. Freely throwing open the stores of his spiritual wisdom, he omitted to explain nothing concerning either the apprentices, the companions, or the masters. But it was not till the end that he referred to the teachings which he knew would most impress the Cardinal's imagination. Only then did he explain the articles relative to the immortality of the body and the soul :

"Having been fashioned in the image and similitude of God," he declared, "we have received from him the capacity to make ourselves immortal, to command spiritual beings and rule over the earth. The Eternal One has destined this planet for his sons, the humans ; but they cannot enjoy it until they have penetrated into Nature's sanctuary. That is precisely what the Egyptian Rite seeks to do. To possess spiritual immortality is to possess wisdom, intelligence, the gift of tongues, and the power to mediate between God and our fellow-men."

The two prelates enquired how this privilege could be won.

"By withdrawal into one's self for forty days," replied the mystagogue.

The Grand Cophte would put up a suitable building at some lonely spot, then confine himself secretly in it with twelve of his brethren. By means of the tools of the different crafts, by means, namely, of the sword, the trowel, the knife, the dagger, the nail, the penknife, the three needles, the compass, the rule, the metal inkpot, and the plumbline, they would together draw the sacred pentagon.

Cagliostro did not, at the moment, say what the sacred pentagon was ; but he asserted that, when this wonderful figure had been drawn, each of the twelve participants would recover his primitive innocence :

"Not only everything that had occurred in the past and the present, but the whole future would be perfectly revealed to them. When the immurement should be over, the pentagons should be effaced, and each of the twelve sages would receive the primary matter, with the privilege of sharing it with whomsoever they chose."

The Cardinal could not conceal his impatience to hear more. "How were the forty days to be employed ?" he asked. And what was the diet to be followed ?

"Invite a true friend to shut himself up with you in a country house," Cagliostro replied. "Take a room facing south, containing two beds in a deep alcove, perfectly sheltered from the outer air. The candidate for regeneration should never leave the room. His friend should store there, in advance, the necessary food, as well as the ingredients for the preparation of the primary matter. The undertaking is to be carried out in May. No other nourishment during the first sixteen days but light soups, fresh and laxative vegetables, and, to end the meal with something solid, a simple biscuit or bread crust. To drink, distilled water, or better still, rain water. Put this drink in a demijohn or in a big varnished earthen pot, and keep it for a day or two in an ice-box, so as to impregnate it with nitrogen: it may be used thereafter for the soup, as well as for drinking. Never eat with an effort; always leave the table hungry. Do not eat things that are sour, or strongly seasoned, or hot or too sweet; abstain from wines, acids, salted or fresh meat, aromatic herbs, etc."

After a short pause, Cagliostro continued:

"On the seventeenth day, at cockcrow, some blood should be drawn from him, and he should begin to take the White Pills in one or two spoonfuls of water: five in the morning and six in the evening. Seven should be taken the next morning and evening. And thus successively, one pill more each morning and evening, until the thirty-second day, when, at sunset, more blood should be drawn. On the thirty-third day, the patient, still keeping to the same diet, should be confined to his bed. He should swallow a mouthful of water, and a grain of primary matter, and keep himself warmly covered. His friend should expect to find him losing consciousness and speech at three o'clock or so, with a violent nervous convulsion, followed by copious perspiration and a general evacuation from all parts of the body. When the patient recovers consciousness, his friend should carefully towel him, and help him to change his bed. He must be extremely careful not to let him catch cold while he was being cleaned, or during the perspiration. The second bed in the alcove, furnished with the necessary sheets and rugs, should be kept ready to receive the patient. Having put him in bed, his friend should give him a soup of beef liver, without fat or bone, and laxative fresh vegetables, to which might be added by way of seasoning, some celery, salt, and leaves of rosemary. . . .

And the cure would proceed smoothly. The next, the thirty-fourth day, the patient should take a second grain of primary matter in a cup of soup. Again, loss of consciousness and convulsions more terrible than on the previous evening; but immediately after, a gentle and refreshing sleep would follow, accompanied by six hours of free perspiration. The friend should then redouble his attention and zeal, for the slightest chill might be fatal. He should wipe his face from time to time with a linen handkerchief. His hair should fall, and his skin peel. Every time that the patient moved his lips during sleep, the attendant should put his finger into his mouth, and help to remove the teeth, which would drop off by themselves. At the end of the slumber, which should not be interrupted at any cost, a violent delirious fever would supervene. Should the patient be thirsty, he should be given some distilled water; should he feel extremely weak, he should have some soup. The fever ceasing after six hours, the patient changes his bed and clothes. If his gums pain him much, they should be rubbed with the Grand Master's liquid ointment.

On the thirty-fifth day, the patient would feel sufficiently strong to take a bath of aromatic herbs in the morning. He should remain there for an hour, while the bath water was being continually poured over his head. The rest of the day, he must spend in bed.

No treatment on the thirty-sixth day : rest in bed.

On the thirty-seventh day, the third and last grain of primary matter in a glass of soup, or, if it seem advisable, in a glass of old wine. The hair and the teeth would begin to grow again. After a sound sleep, the patient should have a second aromatic bath for an hour and put himself back in bed in case he should perspire unexpectedly. And if hungry, he would be entitled to a little soup.

On the thirty-eighth day, for an hour, a bath in ordinary water, in which a pound of nitrogen should be dissolved. The patient should then dress himself, and take a little exercise in his room.

On the thirty-ninth day, in the morning, he should be given ten drops of the Grand Master's balm, in two spoonfuls of good red wine. He may be allowed to go out for a little walk, if he is careful and does not strain himself overmuch. He offers thanks to God for his regeneration. His friend and he mutually promise to observe the most profound and inviolable secrecy about the affair.

" And on the fortieth day," solemnly concluded Cagliostro, " the resurrected adept, leaving the hermitage, will commence to do whatever he thinks best to propagate the truth, annihilate vice, and glorify the Eternal. He should, however, renew this treatment every fifty years, until it should please God to remove him from the world, and gather him unto himself *per omnia soecula soeculorum.*"

During the whole of this detailed exposition, Louis de Rohan had not breathed a word. Where was the need ? His looks expressed rapture. On the contrary, the Archbishop of Bourges vigorously protested, as it seemed to him that palingenesis was incompatible with the teachings of the Church. His disapprobation was so vehement, and so emphatic, that the Grand Cophte had to promise never to make the attempt. As the Archbishop found nothing else that was liable to censure, he expressed the opinion that they might request the Holy Father to authorise the Egyptian Rite.

. . . .

After they had met three or four times at the Hôtel de Strasbourg, in the fortnight preceding the birth of the Duke of Normandy, Cagliostro and the Countess de La Motte had no more desire to see each other ; but they remained in touch through their friend the Cardinal.

Louis de Rohan went from one to the other of them, confiding his anxieties. They had become serious. He was worried to death about the wonderful necklace he had purchased in Marie Antoinette's name. The Queen gave no sign of gratitude. And why, after having coveted the jewel so much as to buy it surreptitiously, did she not wear it ? Mme de La Motte suggested that a jewel which had been acquired secretly could not be shown to the King so long as it was not paid for. "True, but that is exactly what perplexes me," said the Cardinal. "A Queen ought to pay her bills promptly." But since July, Her Majesty had been constantly evading her promises. When the first instalment fell due, she asked, through Mme de La Motte, for a big reduction on the price, and it had to be brought down from £1,600,000 to £1,400,000. In return, Messrs. Boehmer and Bassange were assured that they would be paid in two, instead of four instalments. They were to receive £700,000 on the 1st August, 1785.

At the end of July, the Queen informed them that, having spent the £700,000, she was obliged to postpone the payment until the 1st October. Meanwhile, she paid them £30,000 on account of interest.

From that time, Paris became a hell for the wretched Cardinal. The jewellers themselves, harassed by their bankers, began to blame him. Was it not he who had approached them on behalf of Marie Antoinette? Did he not boast that he had direct relations with the sovereign? "Well then," they insisted, "they ought to be paid on the prescribed dates, and in accordance with the most formal stipulations they had made. They wanted no interest. If they had accepted the £30,000, it was on account of the capital."

After enquiries at Versailles, MM. Boehmer and Bassange became convinced that the Queen did not have the jewel. Her Majesty had never wanted it. She knew nothing of their negotiations, their notes, their ridiculous and indecent haggling. But what, then, was one to make of the Cardinal? Was he a dupe, or a knave? . . .

On the 3rd August, Louis de Rohan, looking pitifully haggard, came along to confide his troubles to Cagliostro. Could the augur extricate him from the tangle? Where *was* the necklace? Mme de La Motte swore she had given it to the Queen's footman, but no one had seen her giving it. Yet there she was, professing to be watched by the police, and begging the Cardinal to shelter her under his roof, at Coupvray or Saverne. . . . What a terrible mess!

The Grand Cophte, after a moment's reflection, asked him:

"Are you quite certain of what has happened?"

The Cardinal then produced the contract where the words "approved" could be seen in the Queen's own hand, as well as her signature—"Marie Antoinette de France." And instantly, by an extraordinary insight, this foreigner from the depths of Asia and Africa, this traveller who was ignorant of the usages of royal Courts, put his finger on what was the weak point in the whole case. "The signature seems to have been forged," he said. "The Queen would not have signed her name in that way. What could be easier for the Grand Almoner of France than to verify it?" But the odds were that Mme de La Motte had been betraying his confidence for a long time. And the Grand Cophte regretted that the Prince had put his faith in an adventuress, a low-bred intriguer.

Stunned by the blow, Louis de Rohan tried to defend himself. But Cagliostro continued more emphatically :

"Of course, she is deceiving you. Go and fall at the King's feet and tell him the truth : that is your last resort."

"Do you wish, then," asked the Cardinal, "that I myself should denounce and ruin this woman ?"

Cagliostro was unmoved.

"If you cannot bring yourself to do it, a friend would do it for you."

But the Cardinal, disgusted with the whole affair, stammered painfully :

"I can see quite well that I have been fooled. I must pay for it. . . ."

A moment later, he asked pitifully :

"What shall I do ? Mme de La Motte thinks, if the Queen refuses to see me, that I should retire to Saverne, where I have been all these years. For my part, I would rather stay here and clear up the matter."

"In that case," said Cagliostro gravely, "put your faith in God."

The Cardinal told him of some still more alarming things. Mme de La Motte was coolly repeating everywhere that if his Eminence frequented the Court and the town, it was only to be able to load the Count and Countess with his gifts—diamonds, and much besides. What did she mean ? Did she intend to drag them, too, into the abyss ?

Cagliostro calmly replied :

"I don't care. I am above reproach."

. . . .

All the same, not wishing to be caught unawares and become implicated, he a foreigner, in a despicable fraud, or perhaps even treason, Cagliostro carefully watched the course of events. He had means of keeping himself fully informed. Messrs. Boehmer and Bassange's principal banker was found to be the Treasurer-General of the Navy, M. Baduard de Saint James, who was Grand Chancellor of the Supreme Council of Egyptian Masonry. In that capacity, he had long and frequent talks with his hierarchical chief, the Grand Cophte.

On the morning of the 5th, M. de Saint James told him of an interview that the jeweller Bassange had had with Mme de La Motte on the 3rd August. At the very moment that the Cardinal was pouring out his griefs to the mystagogue, the descendant of the Valois had been explaining the matter to the jeweller. As she was on the point of leaving Paris, the room where she had received him was unfurnished save for a bed and a sofa. She had begun by telling him that Marie

Antoinette, who was determined to ruin the Cardinal, denied that she had received the necklace. The contract must be a forgery : one had only to look at some genuine example of the Queen's handwriting to be convinced of it. Then, quite abruptly, she had asked :

" Do you know M. de Cagliostro ? " There were rumours, she said, that the Cardinal was constantly at the house of the prophet who pretended to be able to manufacture gold. As Louis de Rohan was devoted to the hermetic sciences, Cagliostro promised to teach him the secret of the philosophers' stone, and many others.

" What do we know for certain, Monsieur," she continued, " about all the diamonds which M. de Cagliostro has ? Where do they come from ? The man has certainly got a lot of them. It is to be suspected that the Cardinal gave them to him. That, perhaps, has been the fate of your casket."

In proof of the charlatan's dishonesty, she told him that after she had left her niece, Mlle de La Tour, alone behind the screen, Cagliostro had made her say that she saw some wonderful things. The girl, in fact, had seen nothing, but merely repeated what Cagliostro had told her to say.

" Finally, I urge you," concluded Mme de La Motte, " to compel the Prince to come to terms with you. He is enormously rich, he should make amends."

Nothing was clearer, then, than that that vixen had been attacking Cagliostro.

But he, firm in his faith in the tutelary Angels, felt uneasy only about his disciple. He wished to save the amiable and magnificent Prince who was one of his most devoted spiritual sons. Louis de Rohan was compassing his own ruin, a victim of his own gullibility. This one defect spoiled his other exceptional qualities. Cagliostro had, for a long time, thought him to be no match for the Baron de Breteuil ; and, far from inflaming his ambitions, he had preached moderation and contentment to him.

Besides, the thaumaturge had detected in Mme de La Motte a secret jealousy against the Countess de Cagliostro. As everyone in the neighbourhood knew, and could see, every day the Cardinal went to dine with the beautiful Roman lady. His evenings were usually spent with her. Had this intimacy offended Mme de La Motte ?

. . . .

Thank God, few people suspected the yet more important rôle played by the Countess de Cagliostro in Paris. Serafina was, in fact, no longer the insignificant creature who, too timid to talk to the great ladies who called on her, used to sit silently, knitting or sewing by the fireside.

By a special dispensation of the Grand Cophte, she ruled over a female flock. A Women's Lodge had been opened in Paris on the model of the Lodges at Warsaw and the Hague, and the hierophant, who had solemnly inaugurated it, appointed as its Grand Mistress, not the Duchess of Bourbon, who was but a tool in the hands of theosophists and mesmerists, but his own wife, Serafina de Cagliostro.

What a transformation there was! In the Lodge, furnished in white and azure blue, Serafina sat on a throne covered by a royal canopy. In the middle of the hall, representing the Earthly Paradise, stood a stately Tree of Life, and entwined in its branches was the Serpent holding the fatal apple in its mouth. The core of the apple was primary matter. A brazier, filled with some spirituous liquor, was burning on a tripod. Opposite the throne was a huge picture of the Temple of Solomon, and on the walls were painted in big letters, mottoes such as: "Glory or Death! . . . Benevolence or Death!" Behind the Countess was a triangle adorned with the heads of seraphim.

Her four grand officers, the Oratrix, the Guardian of the seals, archives and cash, the Secretary, and the Sister Terrible, who was in charge of general arrangements, stood around her respectfully. A little distance away were the other sisters, dressed uniformly in the *talare*, a kind of loose white tunic covering them to their heels. The Grand Mistress's costume was distinguished by a big blue sash edged with silver, worn across the right shoulder, with a medal on which was embroidered in azure silk the Grand Cophte's monogram, and the word: "Silence!" She carried a sword in her right hand, and on the table before the throne was a rose.

There would be a triple knock at the door, and the Sister Terrible having opened it, one could see standing on the threshold a woman with her eyes covered with a white handkerchief, and her hands tied with a ribbon of the same colour. Seizing her by the ribbon, the Sister Terrible would lead her in front of the Grand Mistress:

"Who are you? Who ventures to introduce you?" she would exclaim in a ringing voice. "Are you actuated by a profane curiosity?"

"No," the candidate would say. She humbly begged for the light of the veritable Egyptian Adoption, and the Grand Mistress, appeased, would begin to test her with appropriate questions:

"I come from the depths of the Occident," the stranger would reply, trembling.

"What did you learn there?"

"To know myself. . . ."

The questions followed one another until at length Serafina would declare, if she approved of the candidate:

"Enter, then, and learn the truth."

After five minutes of deep silence, to break which was to incur a heavy fine, three sisters would intone from afar, to a low accompaniment, the psalm *Laudate nomen Domini*. The bandeau would then be removed from the candidate's eyes, and Serafina would address her again :

" My daughter, here, in this holy place and before this respectable assembly, this is what you must swear. First, love of God. Secondly, respect for your King. Thirdly, veneration for religion and its laws. The fourth, love of your neighbour. The fifth, secrecy. The sixth, a limitless loyalty to our Order. The seventh, to conform scrupulously to the rules and regulations of our dear Founder."

The last point required much explanation, for a blind obedience was exacted from the candidates. The oath having been taken, the Grand Mistress would rise to her feet and say :

" The knowledge which you will attain among us is the assurance of God's existence and of your own immortality. The Eternal, having created man three times, and with three breaths, knows that his work is already perfect ; but one breath is enough for us to be able to create in our turn. This breath, we give it to you as it has been conveyed to us by our Founder."

She would then breathe over the candidate's face, from the roots of her hair to her chin.

" May our principles be instilled into you by this breath ; may it strengthen the spiritual element in you, and confirm you, according to your vows, in the faith of your brethren and sisters."

Then, taking up a pair of scissors, Serafina would say :

" Until now, my child, your days have been spent amongst the profane. But our sanctuary is God's sanctuary. Since you have sworn obedience to your chiefs, as a mark of voluntary surrender, you should now sacrifice your hair. Let us see if your heart has ratified your vows. Sister Terrible, cut off her hair ! "

During this test, the Grand Mistress would watch her closely, as if to read her inmost feelings, while the sisters had to stand motionless, and refrain, above all, from laughter. With the consent of the victim, a lock of hair would be cut :

" When they come to us," Serafina would continue, " all our initiates begin by throwing off their pride, in emulation of the Queen of Sheba, who, before entering the Temple of Solomon, was dressed, by order of the great king, in a penitential garb. My sisters, come, purify this robe. . . ."

The sisters would spread incense on the fire and hand her the *talare*, which Serafina would hold up towards the sky, saying :

" Condescend, Great God, to purify this garment. . . ."

After lightly passing it over the flame, she would dress the candidate in it :

" In the name of the Grand Master Founder, and in the presence of the Eternal, I confer upon you physical and moral purity, so as to enable you to live according to our laws."

She would hand her a pair of gentlemen's gloves :

" Be careful to have your hands always clean when you come

here, and wear these gloves that the Lodge bestows on you as an allusion to your future purity. Our Order does not forbid you to love your fellow-creatures. Here are a pair of gentlemen's gloves, and here likewise, the hair that has been cut off your head. Give them both to him whom you love and admire. May he share with you the thoughts and feelings which you would acquire in our shrines!"

Then, giving her the rose:

"This rose, the emblem of innocence and virtue, represents the first flower of truth which you would gather among us. Solomon, when he showed to the Queen of Sheba the temple of the Eternal and the interior of his palace, also presented her with a crown of roses. My child, may you earn by your diligent labours an equally fine crown!"

The Countess kissed her on both cheeks and handed her over to the care of the Sister Terrible. The latter introduced her one by one to all the sisters, to each of whom the apprentice communicated the sign and the password, and was kissed in turn by each.

As one rose in the hierarchy, these emblems and words became charged with an increasingly profound meaning. The companions and, above all, the mistresses, had the most imposing ceremonies. Each of the twelve senior mistresses received the title of Sibyl. They were called respectively the *Persique*, the *Hellespontique*, the *Erythrée*, the *Samiènne*, the *Libyque*, the *Tiburtine*, the *Agrippine*, the *Phrygienne*, the *Americaine*, the *Européene*, the *Delphienne* and the *Cumée*. Each wore round her neck a silver star on which was engraved, besides the Grand Cophte's monogram, this device: *Ego sum homo*. The Grand Mistress would say, as she put it round a candidate's neck:

"These three words round the monogram of our Father signify: 'I am man.' In fact, the spiritual part, which represents your own essence, is male and not female. Or rather, it is sexless. One day you will understand what I mean. You will then be distinguished, not by your sex but by your spirit, which should be continually developed so as to be ready for its future position."

For the glory of the Eternal, and out of regard for the fair sex, Cagliostro enjoined all his followers to prepare their wives gradually for the grand and sublime verities of the Egyptian Adoption. In place of the slavery in which masculine prejudices had held them, he promised women emancipation and knowledge through a progressive course of teaching. Their Ritual, besides, was very similar to that which M. Rey de Morande was thought to have written, in collaboration with the Marquis de Vismes, for the Men's Lodges. The ladies, therefore, could hope equally with the men for spiritual and physical regeneration.

Among all the new initiates, Cagliostro took special note of the Marquise de Flamarens, the Archbishop of Bourges's niece, who was companion to Mme Adelaide. The Hôtel Phelypeaux, where she lived, in the rue de Greneille Saint Germain, was generously thrown open to the members of the Women's Lodge. Just as M. Sain Costart had taken the place of the Grand Cophte at Lyons, Mme de Flamarens in Paris agreed to officiate for the Grand Mistress.

Meanwhile, Serafina was discharging her duties wonderfully. This ignorant and unlettered woman would explain, without faltering for a moment, the subtle and manifold allegories of the Egyptian Adoption. The authority and the unction which she brought to her priestly functions, were admirable. And the delighted Grand Cophte would cast proud and fond glances on the Grand Mistress, like a Pygmalion enamoured of his own statue.

About the middle of August, the Marquise de Flamarens took charge of the Paris Women's Lodge, for, as M. Ray de Morande informed the faithful, the Grand Cophte and the Grand Mistress intended to go to Lyons for a short visit, and stay at the Hôtel des Fermes, in the Place de la Douane.

"It is there, or at my mother's house, maison Tolozan, that you can apply for information from the date that he gets there. M. the Count is to leave this town on the 17th, and there is every probability that he will be at Lyons on the 21st. I do not imagine that he will remain there more than seven or eight days at the most."

Their journey was connected with the dedication of the new masonic temple, built to the glory of God by the *Sagesse Triomphante*, and containing a marble bust of Cagliostro, executed by the Freemason sculptor, Antoine Houdon. The principal disciples looked forward to attending this grand celebration. The Marquis de Vichy and the Marquis de Lezay-Marnesia joined the Grand Secretary, the Marquis de Vismes, at Lyons. Jacques Sarasin came along too. He was very happy to meet the Master, after two years of separation, and to put on the splendid green satin uniform edged with gold which had been prescribed for him. All the pilgrims fraternised informally in M. Rey de Morande's mother's house. How eagerly M. Rey's two other sons, MM. Rey de Colonge and Rey de Cadiz, were looking forward to their beloved brother's arrival!

They awaited him in vain.

. . . .

Did the Grand Cophte, to whom the angels revealed everything, suspect that Marie Antionette, surprised and indignant at the incredible story told her by her servants, had herself interviewed M. Boehmer at the Trianon on the 9th August? The Crown jewellers had then been ordered to state their case in writing, which they did on the 12th.

If the Cardinal de Rohan had taken his friend's advice, he would have thrown himself at the King's feet on the 15th August, before the Assumption services. At ten in the morning of that day, His

Majesty held an important meeting in his chamber, which was attended by the Queen. The Keeper of the Seals M. de Miromesmil's prudent counsels, did not, unhappily, prevail against the violent and implacable insistence of Baron de Breteuil. It was resolved to arrest the Cardinal.

Cagliostro was in the meanwhile reassuring his flock who, afraid to lose him, begged him to settle in Paris for ever. " Nowhere," said the disciples, " would the Grand Cophte be in a better position to carry on his negotiations for the recognition of his Rite by the Holy See. Did he not have, in Paris, the support of the Archbishop of Bourges and the Cardinal de Rohan ? "

Unexpectedly, towards evening, the terrible news was published. And on every tongue was the announcement that the Prince Louis Rohan-Guemenée, Cardinal of the Holy Church, Grand Almoner of France, Bishop of Strasbourg, a member of the Académie Française, proviseur de Sorbonne, head of the Hôpital Royal des Quinze Vingts, president of the administrative bureau of the College of Louis the Great, had been arrested in his pontifical robes, as he was about to leave Versailles. The excitement was tremendous. Since the long-forgotten exploits of the Cardinal de Retz, no one had ever heard of a great man being arrested like this.

On the second day, the 17th, M. Rey de Morande wrote to Gertrude Sarasin :

" I have to confirm, Madame, the news of the sad calamity that has overtaken M. the Cardinal. Doubtless you know that his disgrace has been brought about by some canard about a necklace worth sixteen hundred thousand pounds. M. the Cardinal has evidently been duped."

The Count and the Countess were prevented from leaving Paris on the 17th, because the police had ordered that no horses should be put at their disposal. And M. Rey de Morande regretfully wrote :

" M. the Count's journey having been postponed, and it being unlikely to take place in the near future, he directs me to inform you not to wait for his arrival in Lyons. It would have been an honour and a pleasure to him to come. He begs me to assure you that the visit has only been postponed, and that he would have the satisfaction of discharging it some other time."

Dramatic moves followed each other in quick succession.

On the 20th August, Mme de La Motte was taken to the Bastille, and Cagliostro, who, since the warnings given by the Cardinal and M. de Saint James, had no illusions about the prisoner's feelings towards him, was expecting to be arrested any day. And, in fact, Mme de La Motte accused him at once of having stolen the necklace, cut it to pieces, and sold it.

On the 21st, the King and the Baron de Breteuil sent the Marquis de Launay two *lettres de cachet*, bidding him to arrest the Count and the Countess de Cagliostro, and detain them until further orders in the Bastille.

Finally, on the 22nd, Louis XVI and his ministers ordered M. Chenon the elder, commissioner of the Châtelet, to go with Inspector de Brugnieres, and carry out a search at Cagliostro's lodgings.

IX

THE QUEEN'S NECKLACE

IT was seven in the morning of Tuesday, the 23rd August, 1785, when the commissioner of the Châtelet, Marie Joseph Chenon and Inspector Brugnieres—the same as had previously been spying on Cagliostro at Strasbourg—appeared together at the hotel in the rue Saint Claude. When they entered the bedroom on the first floor, accompanied by a couple of clerks and a few policemen, Cagliostro received them quite calmly. He told them with a detached air that he had been awaiting them for the last eight days, that is to say, ever since the Cardinal had been arrested.

All the papers contained in a bureau in an adjoining room were seized pell-mell, and M. Chenon put them in an envelope which he sealed twice with red Spanish wax, inviting the Count and the Countess also to put their seals on it. The Countess consented without much fuss, but the Count flatly refused. Nor would he sign the statement presented to him.

Subsequently, M. de Brugnieres had no difficulty at all in taking him to the Bastille, saying that the Lieutenant of Police was waiting to have a short talk with him. A cab stood at the door. They bundled themselves into it, and it was thus that the Grand Cophte arrived at about eight o'clock in the morning at the Bastille. The formalities of jail entry took place in the Salle du Conseil, where the serjeant took charge of the jewels and other things worn by the prisoner. Each of these articles were meticulously recorded in the "book of entries." Cagliostro watched the big envelope with the red seals being registered. He was then taken to his new apartments, and M. de Brugnieres returned by cab to the rue Saint Claude.

The Countess was waiting for him in the hall. Surrounded by constables, the Commissioner Chenon, and a man named Lechevin, the Inspector's clerk, she was trembling and weeping. Her servants, Agostino, Jean Baptiste Pecquet, and the maid Françoise, consoled her as best they could, helped by some kindly neighbours, among whom Mme Boissonier distinguished herself by her effusiveness. But on his return, the Inspector sent everybody away save the maid, in order to carry out a second search, this time of the Countess's belongings.

Serafina, in fact, had been scarcely less compromised than her husband by Mme de La Motte's accusations. Every bit of furniture was examined carefully. In a sideboard in the bedroom a lot of jewellery was found, some rolls of louis, and two bags which seemed to contain gold. All this harvest was gathered together in a packet bound several times over with a silk tape. M. Chenon double-sealed it with red wax, and requested the Countess to seal the other end of the tape. Serafina would have liked to use her customary seal, which was artistically engraved, and was difficult to imitate; but as it could not be found, and time was pressing, she had to use another, depicting an old man's head, which she considered to be less safe. As she could not sign her name, she had to trace a simple cross on the police papers. Finally, she was invited to rejoin her husband at the police station, and weakly consented. In such a state of confusion was she that the police had to press her to take certain precautions for the safety of her property. She was advised to take away the door keys, as the servants would not need to use all the rooms. Doors and windows were properly closed, and as Serafina left, she slipped into her pocket two big and two small keys. M. Chenon put her in the cab with the Inspector, and after asking them to guard the packet carefully, went home on foot.

Ten o'clock was striking at the Bastille as Mme de Cagliostro, in her turn, deposited her jewels and other possessions at the Salle du Conseil. The packet containing her money and jewels was noted down in the "book of entries." The four keys were put in a separate envelope under the Countess's seal.

Out of humanity no less than prudence, the minister had ordered that Cagliostro was not to be informed of his wife's presence in the Bastille. They were kept apart, he in the Comté Tower, she in the Liberty Tower. Names were never mentioned in the Bastille. Each prisoner was given the number of the floor and the name of the tower where he was receiving the King's rough hospitality. And since the top floor of the Bastille, which was vaulted, was called the "Calotte," the jailers referred to the thaumaturge in their jargon as the "Comté Calotte," and to Serafina as "the fourth Liberty."

The next day, M. Thiroux de Cresne, Lieutenant-General of Police, came to examine them separately, assisted by the old Commissioner Chenon who at times acted for his son in Bastille cases. The Countess freely told them everything she knew. The Cardinal had shown her the necklace one day, but she had never heard anyone say that Mme de La Motte had been commissioned to sell the diamonds. As for the forecast made by her husband with regard to the Queen's confinement, no one had breathed a word about it to her. The cardboard box was then opened in her presence for a rapid inspection, after which it was sealed up again both by the police officer and the Countess.

Having taken Serafina out, the guards brought in the Count de

Cagliostro. At that very moment, the Marquis de Launay, Governor of the Bastille, leant over to the police officer, whispering :

" Aren't you afraid, sir, that the prisoner might recognise this as belonging to his wife ? "

And he pointed to the cardboard box bound with green tape, which had been left on the table. M. de Crosne hastened to remove the treacherous object, but it was too late : Cagliostro with his first glance had noticed it.

The questions asked him related mainly to the documents contained in the big envelope with the red seals. Out of that jumble of bills, receipts, and useless notes, the Lieutenant of Police only concerned himself with two slips of paper : a message from M. Straub announcing that M. de Sainte James will call in at the Count's on the morning of the 5th August, 1785 ; and a letter from Sweden, written in March of the same year, on which some suspicious signs could be noticed. On both points Cagliostro answered without embarrassment. M. Straub was an honest Alsatian official who worked in the offices of M. de Saint James, a gentleman who came to see him frequently. The other missive emanated from a man who was head of a masonic Lodge in Sweden, and among the devotees of Hiram these apparently bizarre emblems had quite a harmless significance. After some further explanations about his origin, his occupations and his travels, he spoke of the Cardinal. Certainly, his Eminence did not disdain to work with him in the manufacture of his pills and ointments, medicines which shortened illness and prolonged human life. A mesmeric experiment, a simple social pastime, had, it is true, been held in March at the Hôtel de Strasbourg. But, as a matter of fact, no oath had ever been exacted from Mme de La Motte. The contract, annotated and signed by the Queen, was shown to Cagliostro during these last weeks, quite recently, when His Eminence had at length begun to feel some doubts. As to what had happened to the jewel, Cagliostro knew nothing about it, absolutely nothing.

On the 5th September, the elder Chenon came to the Bastille, at the King's special order, to take a proper inventory of the contents of the cardboard box. The Count and the Countess having been accused of breaking up the necklace, it was but fair that an authentic and complete list should be made of the jewellery found in their possession. The work was carried out in Serafina's presence, and all the objects noted down were put back in the box under the Countess's seal, and entrusted to the Governor.

Formerly the matter would have remained secret. But times had changed. The smallest details of the cross-examinations and the official reports leaked out with disconcerting speed. True, the rigorous regulations of the previous century were still enforced in the Bastille : the inner system was scarcely changed. In the course of the night, heedless of the sleeping prisoners, the sentinels would, as before, ring their little bell every quarter of an hour to show that they were awake. If the soldiers on guard happened to meet a prisoner on his way to or from the Salle du Conseil, they were required to push their hats over their eyes at once, so as not to notice his features. But these rules had become mere matters of etiquette. In spite of the military punctilio of the Governor de Launay, in spite of the zeal of his adjutants, M. de Puget and Major de Losme, little by little the discipline had relaxed. The ancient ramparts of the Bastille, formerly so fearful, had lost their gloomy influence.

As a result of the disclosures, the faithful were enabled to admire the coolness of the Grand Cophte and the Grand Mistress, and the frank and convincing answers that they had given. Suddenly, distressing news came. Gnawed by the ingratitude of a nation which he had favoured and loved above all others, and on which he had heaped his favours, the Master had fallen into a dejection which caused alarm for his health. He asked for a guard who could amuse him and help him fight these gloomy fits. On the 29th August, at ten o'clock, there entered his cell one Dory, a young officer with a gentle and firm character, who was to share his captivity until October; thereafter his place was taken by his brother officer, Chatel.

Serafina was even less able to bear her solitary confinement, and, on the morning of the 25th August, joyfully welcomed the arrival of her maid, Françoise, accompanied by the Governor himself. She had arrived at the Bastille without any luggage at all, and was soon in need of clothes. The keys deposited in the Salle du Conseil were then brought out. Major de Losme went with the sealed envelope to the rue Saint Claude, where Mme Boissonnier solemnly broke open her friend's seals, so as to fetch some of her belongings from the apartment. The officer returned to the Bastille with another envelope, sealed by Mme Boissonnier, and Serafina, having identified her neighbour's signet, confided her keys once more to the care of the officials. This was the method subsequently followed whenever necessary.

A more complicated procedure was adopted in the case of the Count. Had not his wife's presence in the Bastille been concealed from him? The jailors repeatedly assured him that she was free and in perfect health. Soon he had permission to write and receive letters which were censored by the authorities. Since Serafina was incapable of writing a single word, Mme Boissonnier informed him on her behalf that she was still in the rue Saint Claude, assiduously negotiating in his cause, and that he would soon be released. Recognising the familiar seal, he had no doubt at all of the authenticity of these messages.

Three letters in Italian which the Governor thought it his duty to intercept and preserve, bore witness to Cagliostro's sufferings. The first was dated the 14th December:

"*Cara Serafina sposa amata*, I say it with regret: I feel very ill. Although I force myself to take the air, my condition becomes worse day by day. Meanwhile, dear girl, I implore you to take what steps you can. Tell our friends to pray to the great God for me. Do not fail to send me news about yourself through Mme de Flamarens. Let me have at least that consolation. May God do me the favour of letting me die in your arms! I embrace you. Adieu.

Your unfortunate husband who is dying for love of you! . . ."

A month and a half later on the 28th December, his sorrow was still in evidence:

"My beloved wife, every day I only suffer fresh pains. My only joy is to write to you and receive your letters on Mondays, Wednesdays and Fridays. However, even these have been failing me. I cannot believe that Mme Boissonnier could have the cruelty to add to my misery. She seems to have improved her handwriting, and I am glad. Yet I find in her letters an altogether new style. I beg her in the name of Heaven to reply to me; otherwise my misery will become so acute that it were better for me to die. For the rest, dear Serafina, I repeat to you, I have experienced, and very thoroughly indeed, every sort of misery. When all is said and done, I can only tell you that Providence will have pity on my innocence. All our friends, I am assured, are thinking of us; especially the lady from Bordeaux who is working for our relief, and I ought to keep calm. Therefore, my soul, what is the use of my agitating myself, and yielding to painful and gloomy thoughts? Dear girl, we must be patient, consider all the good that has been done, the friends who are thinking of us and God who protects you. We shall yet weather the storm.

I end by straining you to my bosom and lavishing on you all the affection in my soul. Be blessed in the name of the Eternal God! I greet all our friends, particularly Mme Boissonnier, whom I clasp to my heart, Morande, and La Borde. Regards to Françoise and Agostino. Your wretched husband who loves you more than himself. I beg Luxembourg and Mme de Flamarens not to make me suffer any longer and I commend myself to their generosity."

His anxiety continued to increase until the last letter, dated the 17th January, 1786:

"Dear wife, I have received at last, *con impazienza*, your letter. I cannot recognize Mme Boissonnier's writing in it; I should be happier if they would reassure me on this point. As for the rest, I am not at all satisfied. For fear that I may go mad, I commend myself to God. My friends, those whom I see, exhort me to eat well. But I have lost appetite as well as sleep. I thank La Borde for the pie, Mme de Flamarens for the partridge and the woodcock and the chestnuts and the oranges; still, I beg her not to forget us. I have received the two books on Switzerland I had asked for. Finally, remember me to all my friends and specially to the Prince de Luxembourg and Mme de Flamarens. I greet them with all my heart. I beg Morande not to keep me waiting for his letters, for I despair at the passage of time.

I end now, dear girl, by embracing you tenderly and blessing you in the name of God. I do the same for Mme Boissonnier, her children and her dear friend. I am very sorry to inconvenience them. All the same, I should like to know who it is that writes to me, as the characters are no longer formed by the same hand. I greet Morande and Grille, and I commend myself to God. Also, I salute Françoise and Agostino. I want some macaroni. Is it a crime to enquire about my supply of shirts?"

So, then, many celebrities, either famous or wealthy, like the Prince de Luxembourg, M. de La Borde and Mme de Flamarens, were faithful to the Grand Cophte. But they were powerless to secure his release from the Bastille. His fate was indissolubly linked to that of the Cardinal.

Louis de Rohan, preferring the justice of the Parlement to the King's mercy, had jolted an enormous and heavy legal machine into motion. The Councillor Titon de Villotran, rapporteur, could be seen arriving at the Bastille, evidently anxious to gather his data as quickly as possible. Towards mid-December, the Parlement issued warrants by which the King's prisoners were handed over to the ordinary law. At last on the 30th January, 1786, after a detailed examination, Cagliostro was permitted to select a lawyer to defend him.

No one was more enthusiastic or more suited to play that part than M. d'Epremesnil. Ever since Cagliostro's arrest, he had heatedly protested at the Parlement sessions. Unfortunately, as he was himself a member of that body, M. d'Epremesnil could scarcely defend the accused before a tribunal of his own colleagues. It was therefore suggested to him that he should appoint in his place his son-in-law, Thilorier, a gifted barrister, whom he promised to help and guide until the end. Cagliostro accepted the offer gratefully. Visiting the "Comté Calotte" several times after this, M. Thilorier prepared under his client's eye his *Memoire pour le comte de Cagliostro*, of which the first copies were ready, opportunely enough, on the 18th February, 1786.

Although the cardboard box bound in green ribbon contained not the smallest trace of the necklace, Mme de La Motte was obstinately clinging to her charges. According to her, Cagliostro was really at the back of an abominable plot to ruin her. Taking advantage of the illegitimate fascination which he exercised at the Hôtel de Strasbourg, this empiric, this charlatan, had, after a séance, made her entrust to her husband two boxes of diamonds for sale in England. That was why no fragments of the necklace were to be found in the possession of the self-styled prophet, but he was none the less culpable.

Only two witnesses confirmed this ridiculous fabrication. Mme de

La Motte's niece, Marie Jeanne de La Tour, questioned by M. Titon about the séances, gave an account of them which was hardly creditable to Cagliostro. And the master hairdresser, Burlandeux, thought he had heard the Grand Cophte say, one day, while he was curling his hair, that he was ready to buy a mansion for fifty thousand ecus in Paris. How could a stranger without visible means of support, have come by this sum? Evidently, by profitably selling some diamonds.

An experienced and aged barrister, M. Doillot, was foolish enough to take this nonsense seriously. In his *memoire* for Mme de La Motte, Cagliostro was painted in very dark colours. Besides, the diatribe was based on Sacchi's old pamphlet in which the absurd and the loathsome were equally mingled. If M. Doillot had had some common sense, he would have warned his client about the danger of such tactics. He would not have allowed her to invoke a suspected authority, and disgraceful arguments. But like so many others, M. Doillot felt the maleficent influence: he could not hold his head against the Circe. Their behaviour scandalised the magistrates no less than the public.

M. Thilorier, on the contrary, started off with a master stroke. Thanks to him, Alexander de Cagliostro seemed to have a reply for everything. The alleged charlatan enumerated his friends, and they were among the greatest names in Europe. He quoted his letters of recommendation, and these were found to have come from the Marshal de Ségur, Miromesnil, the Keeper of the Seals, and the Count de Vergennes. The Minister of Foreign Affairs had written:

"M. de Cagliostro asks for nothing more than peace and safety: hospitality should assure him those."

M. Thilorier, seizing this sentence, used it as the epigraph to his memoir.

In vain did Jeanne de La Motte-Valois, carefully confusing the dates, represent the Grand Cophte, in her pamphlet, as having arrived in Paris at the beginning of January 1785. It was well known that the thaumaturge was then staying in Lyons, and that, on the evening of the 30th January, while he was arriving at the Palais Royal, the necklace had already been purchased. To cap it all, Brother Jean Alquier, keeper of the seals, archives and funds of the *Sagesse Triomphante*, despatched an affidavit from Lyons in which the Misses Foret, licencees of the Hôtel de La Reine, swore that the Count and Countess had been their guests up to the 27th January, 1785.

Parts of M. Thilorier's memoir read like an apology. Those, for example, which attempted to extenuate the mesmeric séances in the Palais Cardinal. Was it necessary to denounce these amusements as if they were exhibitions of witchcraft? In any case, Mme de La Motte had never been urged, in the course of these entertainments, to have some boxes of diamonds sold in England through her husband. In no matter which country he was, bankers like M. Sain Costart of Lyons, or M. Jacques Sarasin of Basle, advanced him the necessary funds for his charities, as they were sure they would obtain, one day, a more than adequate recompense. It was thus that the Count had been able to scatter his largesse, always giving and never taking. Besides, various secrets that he alone possessed, assured him of a superabundance of resources. His expenses remained constant —liberal, but prudent. Whatever his hairdresser might say, he had never desired to own in Paris a house worth 50,000 ecus. But one day when M. Burlandeux was dressing him, the conversation had turned on a mansion which M. de Bondy and some other friends were hesitating to buy, finding it too dear at 50,000 ecus. Cagliostro, who thought it was a fine house, had exclaimed that he would be glad enough to take it at the price. Mere words, as one could see, binding him to nothing.

Allowing for the interest aroused by his disciples, how can one account for the enormous success of his *memoire*, which almost immediately became the topic of every conversation? More than two thousand copies of it were sold. The fact was, people hoped to find in it some definite information about the wonderful history of the magician. For a long time Cagliostro had evaded their curiosity. But as he was in chains, as the French laws demanded of him an explanation, he consented to draw aside a fold of the mystic veil under which he would have preferred to conceal himself. Here was an authentic biography, dictated by himself to his counsel; in that consisted the principal attraction of the pamphlet. No doubt several magistrates had examined him. On the day of his arrest, he professed not to know his age, or to remember where he was born. On the next day, his memory was a little awake. Born at Malta, he said, then brought up in Medina, he belonged to the Catholic religion. His age? About forty. His chief occupation was attending to the sick, medicine always having been his favourite pursuit, although he had no diploma or degree. He was familiar with Asia and Africa, had travelled widely in the Archipelago, in Turkey, in Malta, in Sicily and then across Europe. But such disconnected and enigmatic pieces of information were quite different from the full confession now published.

. . . .

Glory to Holy Asia, cradle of the Earthly Paradise, inexhaustible mother of religions and legends! Having been brought up under the name of Acharat, at Medina in Arabia, in the harem of the Mufti Salahaym, the Count Alexander de Cagliostro loved that continent with an almost filial affection. He had lost his parents at an early age, and knew nothing of them, save that they were aristocratic and Christian. He believed himself to have been born in Malta, and this he hoped to confirm at the first opportunity.

His entourage at Medina consisted of a white *valet de chambre*, and two blacks, of whom one or the other was in attendance day and night. These three men implicitly obeyed the venerable Althotas who, more like a father than a guardian in the touching solicitude with which he constantly surrounded the precious child, was about seventy years old. Having travelled everywhere, he had distilled the essence of human beliefs and ideas. No one could have more skilfully and lovingly developed the gifts which he discerned in his pupil. Under his direction, Acharat made extraordinary progress in botany and experimental physics, without neglecting Oriental languages. Whenever a lesson bore on the ancient wisdom, Althotas would enthusiastically describe the Pyramids, the immense *hypogeums* where Egypt had wished to conceal the incalculable treasure of a divine heritage. Often the lesson would be interrupted by a visit of the Mufti Salahaym, who invariably showed great respect for Althotas and affection for his pupil. Both Acharat and Althotas wore Mussulman robes, and professed the Moslem religion. But in their hearts dwelt the true faith. Young as he was, the child had learnt to revere the great God, to love and serve his neighbour, and everywhere to respect the laws and religions.

Such an education was calculated to mature the mind rapidly. At twelve years of age, Acharat had become disgusted with games and trivialities ; Medina had no longer any attraction for his ardent spirit. The marvels of which he had been told haunted his dreams. Althotas, noticing it, got a caravan ready. And one fine day, the child was informed suddenly that he was to begin his travels at once. His sole regret was at leaving Salahaym. The good Mufti was inconsolable at losing Acharat and his guardian ; he could not hide his grief. . . . Then began distant journeyings from town to town, from kingdom to kingdom.

At Mecca, the Sheriff offered them hospitality in his palace. Acharat felt a curious agitation from the moment he saw him ; his eyes filled with tears, and the Sheriff, delightedly embracing him, tried in vain to restrain his own. What was the secret of their mutual agitation ? Many years later, the traveller experienced a similar emotion at the very memory of this encounter. Each day the Sheriff demanded to see him, each day their friendship gained in intimacy and affection. There grew up between them a habit of long and silent contemplation during which the Prince would gaze on the handsome youth, like one in ecstasy, and raise his eyes to Heaven as if in prayer. . . . The puzzle of his origin constantly tormented Acharat. To what soil, to what race did he belong ? Why did his tutor evade his questions ? Were not orphans entitled to know of their parentage ? What was more natural than this curiosity ? The child is attracted by the mystery of the cradle, as the aged by the mystery of the grave. That night Acharat questioned the negro who slept by his side. But the faithful watchman would not divulge the secret. Once, however, harassed by questions, he declared with a solemn air :

" My Lord, great calamities threaten you, if ever you leave Mecca. . . . Avoid, ah ! above all avoid the town of Trebizonde ! "

In spite of this sinister warning, Acharat grew tired, after three years, of the monotonous existence he was obliged to lead in Mecca. His love of adventures prevailed over prudence and even gratitude.

One day, the Sheriff committed an unprecedented breach of etiquette by calling in person at Acharat's house. He greeted Acharat with more than ordinary tenderness. He advised him to be humbly submissive and bear to the end his misfortunes.

" Adieu," he cried, " adieu, wretched child of nature ! "

This strange and pathetic exclamation, this heartrending and solemn tone, Acharat, now the Count de Cagliostro, imagined he could still hear. And never would this fatal memory be effaced from his mind.

Next day, a caravan, organised at their wish, carried away Acharat and his tutor. Neither of them was to see Mecca again. Their interest in Egypt being what it was, they directed their steps straight to the foot of the Pyramids. To the profane, who cannot conceive their purpose, what could be more futile than these colossal constructions ? But Althotas knew that hidden in their slopes lived the last priests of a vanished cult. He knew how to approach them. And these pious officiants, recognising in him a superior initiate, immediately admitted him and his disciple into their sanctuaries.

Their travels continued for three more years. Finally, in 1766, a French vessel conveyed them from Rhodes to Malta. Like all travellers from the Levant, they were put into quarantine, but two days later they were unexpectedly discharged on the receipt of a message from the Grand Master. Don Manoel Pinto d'Alfonseca informed them through the messenger that he was impatiently waiting to see them. Like the Mufti of Medina and the Sheriff of Mecca, he housed them in his monastic military palace. His hospitality was, in truth, magnificent. Acharat found himself lodged in a sumptuous apartment, close to the laboratory where the Grand Master daily devoted himself to alchemical research.

The most delicate attentions of the Mufti and the Sheriff were thrown into the shade by the unaccustomed privileges which the travellers enjoyed at Valetta. The young man, dressed hereafter in European style, gave himself out to everyone as Alexander de Cagliostro. Althotas had exchanged his Oriental robe for a clerical garb, decorated with the Cross of Malta. A high official, the Chevalier d'Aquino, of the princely house of Caramancia, who was appointed to look after them, presented them with the Grand Cross of the Order. The Count de Cagliostro had thereby the honour of dining with the head of the Rohans, Emmanuel Jean Marie des Neiges, since Grand Master of the Order of Malta, without suspecting that twenty years later, he would expiate his deep affection for a prince of the family by going to jail.

The Grand Master, apparently aware of his origin, spoke to him at times about Trebizonde, but always in veiled terms. As a long-sighted and prudent parent would preoccupy himself with the future of his son, he guaranteed Acharat a very rapid promotion if he would but make up his mind to take the vows of the order. But recognising his true vocation in travel and medicine, Cagliostro did not care to settle as a priest in Malta. Besides, since the loss of his tutor, his best friend, the venerable Althotas, the island had become unbearable. A few minutes before he expired, the sick man clasped his hand, stammering in a dying voice :

" My son, guard always in the depth of your soul the fear of the Eternal and the love of your neighbour. You would but too well experience the truth of my teachings."

The Grand Master unwillingly consented to Alexander's departure, and unable to detain him in Malta, he made him swear to come back without fail. The young man repeatedly gave him this assurance, and set off in company with the Chevalier d' Aquino, who had offered to take the place of Althotas.

Concerned above all with the trial and his defence, Cagliostro did not here go into the detail of his voyages ; it would have taken volumes. But, from what he said, he had moved on familiar terms with the Sicilian nobility. At Naples, the native city of the Chevalier d'Aquino, he had had to separate from his mentor, whom urgent affairs called into the country. Acharat-Alexander thereupon went by himself to Rome, provided with excellent bills of exchange on the banker Belloni.

He lived incognito in the capital of Christendom until the Cardinal Orsini, having discovered him, overwhelmed him with attentions. His Eminence introduced him at his table to the Roman princes and the members of the Sacred College, including the Cardinal of York, Henry Stuart, and the Cardinal Ganganelli, since Sovereign Pontiff under the name of Clement XIV. The then reigning Pope Clement XIII, asked likewise to meet him, and several private interviews which Cagliostro had with the Holy Father, increased still more his prestige.

In 1779, in the twenty-second year of his life, Acharat-Alexander had had the good fortune to meet accidentally in Rome, a maiden of quality, Serafina Feliciani. In her he found the charms and the solid virtues which were to bind him for life to this irreproachable wife. And the narrator melted at the memory of their idyll :

" She had scarcely emerged from her childhood ; her budding charms kindled in my heart a passion which sixteen years of married life have only strengthened. . . ."

Here ended the romantic part of the memoir, the definite cause of its success.

But his followers, carried away by enthusiasm, were not content with ranking this confession with the best Oriental tales. They insisted that Alexander de Cagliostro should be considered to be the natural son of Don Manoel Pinto d'Alfonseca, Grand Master of the Order of Malta. And for these reasons :

Towards 1743, as they claimed, the galleys of the religion had captured a Turkish caravelle carrying to Constantinople five or six distinguished virgins destined for the imperial harem. One of them, the daughter of the Governor of Trebizonde, had scarcely disembarked at Malta, when she captured the heart of the Grand Master. He confessed to her his desire. He even succeeded in making her share it. Only too visibly did she bear its marks when the time came to send these captive beauties back, at the request of the French Government, to the Sultan. The Grand Master's beloved one suffered the common fate. But on board ship, before arrival at Constantinople, she gave birth to a son. The crime leaking out, she was sent back in disgrace to her family. Now the Governor of Trebizonde was a Moslem of the old school ; he believed it his duty to avenge his religion and his honour by the most barbarous methods. Three months later his daughter died. From grief or by poison, no one knew. Thus perished, ravished by the storm, this young rose of the gardens of the Black Sea. Fortunately, the infant son was saved from his murderers. Althotas was already supervising his education, and the Sheriff of Mecca, a relative of the deceased mother, regularly conveyed news of him to the Grand Master.

In the second half of the memoir, M. Thilorier gave an account of Cagliostro's itinerary across Europe, as well as a peremptory refutation of the calumnies piled up by Mme de La Motte. Doubtless a work of great merit, but of more interest to the magistrates than to readers of mysteries and adventures.

Clementino felt like the rest the seduction of these strange adventures, but he did not lose sight of his principal object, which was continually to confront Alexander and Serafina de Cagliostro with Joseph and Lorenza Balsamo. He certainly forgave the Count for totally ignoring the regrettable years of 1776 and 1777, the years of his tribulations in London. The prisoner in the Bastille was not bound to claim, in self-defence, that he had been in an English jail. Nor was this the occasion to reveal to the French authorities the prosecutions which another necklace had brought him in England.

Also, the Count had the best of reasons for not saying anything on the subject of his apostolate. His Egyptian Rite was not at all in question in the Cardinal's trial, and there was no need to mention it. Besides, should not the Grand Cophte set an example of the discretion he preached to his disciples ?

The most astonishing thing, however, was not what he concealed, but what he openly admitted. For the first time in fact, in a document avowedly authentic, he furnished a hint of his close and very compromising relation with Giuseppe Balsamo. In rendering homage to Serafina, Cagliostro had cited her maiden name. Now that name belonged equally to Lorenza Balsamo. The Countess and the Sicilian painter's wife were both born Feliciani. Romans both of them, and of the same age, they had received the nuptial benediction at nearly the same date. Besides, they were equally unlettered ; the Countess had scribbled in the Bastille registers a clumsy little cross like an uneducated person, just as Lorenza Balsamo had formerly done on entering Saint Pelagius. True, the patrician and the daughter of the copper founder had different Christian names, the one being called Serafina, and the other Lorenza. . . . But Clementino Vannetti had under his eyes, thanks to Ippolito Pindemonte, a document less common, less widely circulated, than M. Thilorier's memoir. It was a report of the first examination which the Countess had undergone at the Bastille, on the 24th August, 1785. According to this, the prisoner declared, in the presence of the Lieutenant-General of Police, that she was called Laurence Seraphine Feliciani, aged about thirty years, native of Rome. . . . Laurence ! . . . But then the two Feliciani had the same Christian name—Lorenza ! Any other would have hastily drawn his conclusion and published his discovery with a great to-do. But the permanent secretary of the *Accademia degli Agiati* continued his verifications quietly and without haste.

True, a careful consideration of the memoir showed that the links between the Count and the Sicilian painter were not as plain as those between their wives. But analogies were not wanting. Mysterious voyages about the twentieth year ; journeys to Naples, in Sicily, above all to Malta, to visit the Grand Master Pinto ; a long sojourn in Rome where each of them had married a Feliciani, and frequented the Cardinal Orsini's palace. And here was the Countess innocently giving her name and Christian names to the magistrate, and enabling one to establish a new link between Cagliostro and Balsamo ! Perhaps, after all, the secret of the Grand Cophte would be obtained through the Grand Mistress.

. . . .

While working at his memoir, Cagliostro was astonished to learn from M. Thilorier that the Countess was also in the Bastille. She had entered there on the 23rd August, 1785, only two hours after him. What ! Serafina at the Bastille ! His poor dear wife in this place of horror and pain ! And they had had the heart to hide it from him ! Alas, between the " Comté Calotte " and the " Fourth Liberty " what an infinite distance there was ! What thickness of gates, bolts and walls ! . . . This disclosure worked a transformation in Cagliostro. Suddenly he recovered all his energy.

On the 24th February, 1786, he caused a petition to be put before Parlement, begging for the release of his wife. She had been neither charged with a crime nor arrested by a warrant. Why, therefore, prolong a detention so trying to her delicate constitution? The assembled Houses heard the petition with obvious emotion, and the President d'Ormesson de Noyseau took it upon himself to obtain her release. As no charge was preferred against Mme de Cagliostro and she was suffering in health, the justice and the mercy of the King seemed equally to demand her prompt liberation. M. d'Ormesson de Noyseau did not spare his pains. He appealed to M. de Vergennes, to whose department Mme de Cagliostro, as a foreigner, properly belonged. Had not M. de Vergennes lately written to the Strasbourg authorities in favour of the Count de Cagliostro? M. d'Ormesson reminded him of it, and his letter finished with the words:

"The general interest which this woman has aroused since the publication of her husband's memoir cannot be imagined."

At Versailles, before the prisoner could be released, it was asked why she should be. Was she really ill? By order of M. de Crosne, Commissioner Chenon went to inquire at the Bastille. And the Governor, touched to the quick, replied that had Cagliostro's wife had the slightest indisposition, the Lieutenant-General of Police would have been informed of it, as he was informed of the smallest details of happenings in the castle. This woman, far from being confined to her bed or even her room, was at that very moment taking a stroll on the balcony round the towers. The ministers consequently refused to let her go. But a few days later, Louis XVI, with his habitual magnanimity, cancelled this rigorous decision and the drawbridges of the Bastille were lowered for the prisoner on the 26th of March.

So many people called at the house in the rue Saint Claude that a visitor's book had to be opened. Portraits of the beautiful Serafina were sold in all the print shops. One evening, when she was taking a walk in the garden of the Palais Royal, the women of pleasure at once abandoned their occupations to heap flowers on her, and blushingly the Countess accepted these tributes from Vice to Innocence. But to the great disappointment of the public, when questioned about it, she emphasized the decent treatment she had been given by the Governor of the Bastille, and the sergeant-major. Her maid Françoise had helped her to pass the time, and this long imprisonment had, in fact, enabled her to learn to write: in short there was little cause for complaint. . . . Such restraint was disappointing; they had hoped for a more lurid picture.

Cagliostro for a moment had imagined that he might also be set at liberty. But he was a foreigner, involved in a case that had been referred to Parlement, and his answers respecting his birthplace, his age and his funds having been suspiciously conflicting, he was treated like a lost child which it was best to detain at the discretion of the authorities.

Nor did he succeed in having his property and furniture in the rue Saint Claude put under seal, a precaution that " by a terrible and inexplicable oversight " had been omitted on the day of his arrest. Coming after an interval of six months, his request aroused suspicion, and M. Joly de Fleury, the prosecutor-general, rejected it in view of the fact that the property of the applicant had neither been seized nor inventoried.

What troubled the prisoner, above all, was the cardboard box he had caught sight of on the 24th August in the Salle du Conseil. What did it contain? The Marquis de Launay affirmed that he had found in it only two rolls of twenty-five double-louis and some jewels. Now Cagliostro had drawn up from memory a list of the money, papers and other effects he had had at home, in his desk, on the 23rd August, 1785. It was a fortune by itself. Fifteen rolls of fifty double-louis; a bag of brown linen containing more than twelve hundred sequins; a sealed roll of twenty-four Spanish quadruples; and in a green portfolio, forty-seven notes of the Caisse d'Escompte, each of the value of a thousand pounds. What remained of all this in a room which had been put to pillage?

Meanwhile, the judicial proceedings ran their course, and what the Grand Cophte was capable of, became evident. Prisoner though he was, he obtained over the accused, the witnesses and the magistrates themselves, an incontestable ascendancy. Confronted with Louis de Rohan in the Bastille, he spoke to him as he used to at the Hôtel de Strasbourg: deferentially, but in a tone which did not exclude a certain affectionate condescension. True, had the Cardinal followed his advice, neither of them would have been arrested. But the Master refrained from reproaching his beloved disciple.

As for Marie Jeanne de La Tour, he formally challenged her. Was she not the niece of his cruellest traducer? This young person had enlivened her depositions with various compromising details which the thaumaturge categorically denied. He treated her like a little liar; he called upon her to prove that their mesmeric experiments had been anything more than a pastime. She finally admitted that the evocations held at the Cardinal's palace had really seemed to her a joke and, had it been otherwise, she would not have ventured to mention the Queen.

Cagliostro likewise crushed the hairdresser Burlandeux—a vile spy hired by Mme de La Motte, this fool was not even capable of accurately reporting what he had overheard. It was above all in the presence of Mme de La Motte that his anger broke out. In a new diatribe which went beyond the first, this villainess, this abandoned creature as he called her, had actually repeated in her own name all the abominable things alleged by Sacchi. She had torn the Grand Cophte's defence to shreds. She believed not a word about the unfortunate child of nature, neither the birth of the wonderful orphan, nor the attentions which he had enjoyed at Mecca, nor his arrival at Malta. Their encounter, after this, could not but be a fearful collision. But all apprehensions were exceeded in ferocity. That same evening the Cardinal wrote to his advocate, M. Target, with whom he was carrying on a secret correspondence :

" To-day she had a scene with the Count de Cagliostro ; this woman was all arrogance, ferocity, blasphemy. And yet, her absurd tale crumbled bit by bit. Each day, with her heart full of hate, she has to yield a little more ground." On the 5th April, weary as a hunted beast, she stammered finally that Cagliostro was not " in any way guilty in this dreadful affair of the necklace."

Another of the Master's exploits was to lead a hardened forger to confess his crime. By dint of investigation, the magistrates had established the fact that the word " approved " and the alleged signature of the Queen on the contract, were the work of Retaux de Villette, a former gendarme, and a robust athlete, who was Mme de La Motte's specially favoured lover. He was pressed to confess it. But even thieves have a sense of honour, and Retaux de Villette, rather than disgrace his mistress, preferred to be obstinately silent on this point.

When he was confronted with this fellow, Cagliostro asked him why he persisted in clinging to such an indefensible tale. Retaux muttered between his teeth that he had meant to harm no one. Then, as he recounted it later, Cagliostro had a gleam of genius :

" For an hour and a half I preached to him on the duty of a man of honour, the power of Providence and the love of one's neighbour ; I induced him then to hope for God's mercy and the mercy of the Government. My discourse was so long and vehement that in the end I was speechless. The rapporteur was so touched by it, that he told Villette that he must be a monster if he was not moved by my words, for I had spoken to him like a father, like a man full of religion and morality, and that what I had said constituted a heavenly discourse."

Retaux de Villette thereupon burst into sobs. Yes ! it was he who had written on the contract, at Mme de La Motte's request, the word " approved " and the signature at the bottom, " Marie Antoinette de France ".

The mystery was cleared up from then. The Parlement could pass judgment. Also, from that day, the regulations of the Bastille were relaxed in Cagliostro's favour. On the 4th May, he was permitted to invite his counsel, M. Thilorier, to dinner. As, unfortunately, the permit did not include the Countess, marital love had to contrive some expedient.

Four great towers of the Bastille overlooked Paris, four others the faubourg Saint Antoine. Every morning Serafina clambered up to the top floor of a house in the rue Saint Antoine, at the hour when her husband usually took a walk on the balcony round the towers.

The unfortunate couple had to communicate their thoughts and feelings to each other in the language invented by the Abbé de l'Epée ; they gesticulated as best they could, and this pathetic scene, reported in the newspapers, aroused in sensitive minds as much respect as pity.

The Master was not the less consoled by the devotion of his disciples. At the Bastille, under the shadow of a terrible charge though he was, Cardinal de Rohan constantly inquired after the Master. He exhorted his defenders to emphasize in their final memoirs that Mme de La Motte and Retaux de Villette had both fully admitted the Count's complete innocence.

"If the fact has been omitted, tell M. Target that I beg him at once to have it included ; and if it would be more convenient, put it in a footnote."

Did the public prosecutor Joly de Fleury strike out the title of Count from the documents relating to Cagliostro, Louis de Rohan in desperation would urge his lawyers to use this title all the more frequently in *their* documents and memoranda.

The great majority of the public pitied Cagliostro and warmly wished him success. The fact having been established that the Count had never been implicated in a swindle, it was thought scandalous that he should not have been released at the same time as the Countess. The mystery of the necklace was one thing, the mystery of Cagliostro was another. And it required a truly extraordinary perversity obstinately to confound the two.

. . . .

At four o'clock in the morning of Tuesday, the 30th May, 1786, Messrs. Sergent and Regnault, ushers of Parlement, came to look for Cagliostro and take him to the Court in a public coach.

All day the thaumaturge waited at the conciergerie to be called up before the tribunal. But the examinations of Retaux de Villette, of Mme de La Motte and of the Cardinal having monopolised the first session, towards four o'clock in the afternoon, when everyone was exhausted with fatigue, it was decided to put off Cagliostro until the next day. As he got into his carriage in the Cour de Lamoignon to return to the Bastille, a large crowd cheered him. He was all the more heartened by this, for he was just launching, on M. d'Epremesnil's advice, on an extremely bold move. In a pamphlet entitled *Requête a joindre au memoire du comte de Cagliostro*, he had taken issue with Commissioner Chenon and the Governor of the Bastille, accusing the one of having connived, by his failure to lock and seal the rooms, at the removal of a considerable sum in gold and specie from the rue Saint Claude, and the other of having extorted from Mme de Cagliostro, on the day she was released, a receipt for jewels and money which had not yet been returned to her. Serafina, in fact, had not been able to take away from the Bastille her cardboard box bound with green tape, and Cagliostro based upon this an action for damages and interest. So thirsty for scandal was the reading public that it admired the prisoner who was audacious enough to attack even the King's officers. Besides, the moderation of the form compensated for the bitterness of the substance.

Alexander de Cagliostro wished to dress himself sumptuously for his appearance in Court on the 31st May. His suit of green satin embroidered with gold resembled the regulation uniform of the *Sagesse Triomphante*. His hair, elaborately dressed, hung loosely over his shoulders in long curls. And this coiffure, unusual in France, at first surprised the public. Evil-minded men declared that it betrayed the charlatan at once. But Cagliostro disconcerted them by the dignity of his bearing before the judges. When he was asked who he was, he replied briefly :

" A noble traveller."

At these words, faces brightened. Silent merriment was added to sympathy, without weakening it ; and Cagliostro noted the change. Satisfied, he began his defence in a strange, disconnected jargon, intermixed with Greek, Arabic, Latin and Italian. After six minutes, the members of the Parlement had had enough of it. The thaumaturge was begged to withdraw. And at seven o'clock when he started on his way back to the Bastille, the cheers of the previous evening were repeated. The judgment came late at night, after stormy deliberations. The Count de Cagliostro, as well as the Cardinal de Rohan, were acquitted on all charges. As for the Count's petition against the younger M. Chenon and de Launay, the Parlement rejected it peremptorily. In this matter, Alexander de Cagliostro was put completely out of court.

The next day, the 1st June, at a very early hour, the Governor of the Bastille received this message :

" His Majesty has commanded me, Sir, to order you to release this evening from the Bastille, M. the Cardinal de Rohan and M. Cagliostro, and to instruct you to tell them that his will is that they shall remain at home and receive no one but their relations and business men. Kindly inform me when these orders have been executed.

I have the honour to remain, Sir, your very humble and devoted servant,

Baron de Breteuil."

The same day, by order of the King, Commissioner Chenon came to the Bastille to make sure that the cardboard box was returned to Cagliostro. It was returned at ten in the evening, in the Salle du Conseil.

It will be remembered that the Countess, at the time of her arrest, had been obliged to seal the cardboard box with the seal of an old man's head, which she used very rarely ; with a puzzled expression, Cagliostro refused to recognise it. It was therefore necessary for the

Marquis de Launay to send an express messenger to the rue Saint Claude to fetch the seal, which was immediately brought by the faithful Agostino himself. Cagliostro accepted this evidence, and signed the statement, following the Commissioner and the Marquis de Launay.

Nevertheless, his heart bled at having to sign without reserve, notwithstanding his petition, the document which declared that the goods seized in his rooms were no more than some jewels and two rolls of twenty double-louis each, and thus proved the Governor to be right. But Providence arranged for him the sweetest of consolations. . . . At eleven o'clock in the evening, his carriage was surrounded by a wildly excited crowd. Thousands of Parisians escorted him up to the rue Saint Claude where drums and trumpets waited for him at his door. A few neighbours had illuminated their houses. In their mad enthusiasm, the demonstrators did not hesitate to invade the Hôtel de Savigny. The courtyard, staircases and rooms were packed with a tumultuous rabble, and the Master, without resisting the well-meant violence of his admirers, appeared on the terrace overlooking the boulevard and repeatedly bowed to the ecstatic and jubilant multitude which clapped their hands in acclamation.

The morning of the 2nd witnessed similar demonstrations. The Count appreciated the popular effusion, which was more precious to him than any official compensation could have been. And his disciples exclaimed : " Now then ! You see ! He has emerged from all this only greater and more worthy of himself."

But suddenly a sinister apparition troubled the feast : Inspector de Brugnieres appeared with a paper in his hand. His Majesty had himself written to Baron de Breteuil : " You will order Cagliostro to leave Paris within eight days and the kingdom within three weeks. You may show him my letter."

Dismayed by the turn events had taken, M. Thilorier played for time. After long conversation with the Lieutenant of Police, the only concession the Master obtained was permission to stay for a time in the village of Passy, where M. de Boulainvilliers, in memory of the trouble he had taken over the late Marquise, was glad to offer him a refuge. The thaumaturge, fearing Government reprisals, only asked to be left in peace. But his zealous followers did not share this view.

While the Countess, dazed by so many catastrophes, was supervising the removal from the rue Saint Claude, M. d'Epremesnil, whose fervour bordered on frenzy, was vigorously pursuing his controversies. He imperiously demanded the expedition of the decree of the 31st May, 1786, which would serve M. de Cagliostro as a passport throughout the world. He also took it upon himself to bring to Passy La Salmon, a poor girl whom the Parlement of Rouen had at first condemned to be burnt alive for the crime of poisoning, and who had later been acquitted by the Parlement of Paris. He made her dine with Cagliostro. What a striking picture! Two innocents at the same table with their supporters! M. d'Epremesnil was overcome with emotion.

Mme de Charriere, no less grateful than M. de Boulainvilliers for medical treatment received at Strasbourg, went to see the thaumaturge at Passy. She laughed to scorn the fanatical disciples who watched over him like mamelukes and janissaries. But Cagliostro touched her by a mixture of sensibility and courage which was altogether unaffected. Forgetful of himself, he lamented over the tribulations of his wife. At once, Mme de Charriere could feel all her former antipathies reviving in her:

"As for her, nearly twice as fat as before, I found her as at Strasbourg, a common and disagreeable woman. It is there that I saw Mme de Flamarens and La Salmon, and a priest who was whispering something to her. This roomful, thus arranged, remains in my memory one of the most pleasant pictures I have ever seen."

M. Brenner, a Swiss settled in Paris, a great friend of Jacques and Gertrude Sarasin, was surprised one day when he was passing through a country lane in Passy, to find a long row of carriages standing there, a very unusual sight among those peaceful gardens and cottages. He thought it must be a wedding. But he was undeceived: these vehicles belonged to Parisians who had come in crowds to visit M. de Cagliostro. When he heard this, M. Brenner was seized with the desire to take his chance and go in with the others: the Master received him with open arms. And M. Brenner hastened to convey to Gertrude Sarasin an account of the interview:

"All France is coming to see him. Paris speaks only of him, and wishes that justice had been done to this man, and compensation paid for his wrongs. One sees here nothing but snuff-boxes and fans à la Cagliostro. I have lent a portrait of him printed in Strasbourg, as the best of them all, to a fanmaker who has had it reproduced, and sells as many of them as he wishes in Paris and abroad. The Marquis de Vichy, who introduces everyone who comes to see our friend, has begged me to tell you, my beautiful lady, a lot of things. . . ."

On the 13th June, 1786, the exile went, skirting Paris, to dine with a number of friends at the "Epée Royale," at Saint Denis. Malicious tongues alleged that the fifty merrymakers present had raised a collection to provide Cagliostro with a travelling fund of five hundred louis. And yet the Grand Cophte had insisted on paying for the dinner himself, and when the innkeeper protested, saying that the banquet had been ordered by the others, Cagliostro cried out emphatically:

"Do you not know that wherever the Count de Cagliostro is, he must be the only one to pay?"

However it may be, the travellers took leave of their friends at four o'clock in the afternoon. They embraced most particularly M. Rey de Morande, who was going to his family at Lyons for a holiday. Accompanied by the Marquis de Vichy and the Marquis de Vismes, the exiles left for Boulogne-sur-Mer whence, on the 16th, they embarked for Dover, blessing the faithful who, kneeling on the wharf, waved good-bye to them.

X

THE BASTILLE

CLEMENTINO VANNETTI would never have understood the state of rapturous enthusiasm in which Cagliostro left the majority of his French disciples, had it not been for the numerous documents which testified to it. The prison, the triumphant acquittal, and then the Master's expulsion, had combined to inflame fanaticism. In England the Grand Cophte received letters which had all the fervour of a declaration of love.

In the house of the Councillor Festi, at Rovereto, Vannetti read out one of these written from Boulogne-sur-Mer and dated the 20th June, 1786 :

" Sir and Master, N. . . . has told me how I could send you the homage of my respect. The first use I make of the information is to throw myself at your feet, to surrender to you my heart and to beg you to help me raise my spirit towards the Eternal. I shall not tell you, O my Master, the grief which I experienced at the moment when the tides of the ocean carried away from France the best of Masters and the most powerful of mortals : you know that better than I. . . .

My pen is refractory to all the impulses of my soul ; but my heart is full of the most respectful sentiments. Settle my fate ; do not leave me too long to languish away from you. The felicity of my life is what I ask of you ; you have awakened the need for it within me, O my Master, and you alone can satisfy it. . . ."

The *Sagesse Triomphante* raved in the same strain. Deception was rife at Lyons, and hopes were entertained that, after his acquittal, the Grand Cophte would be able to attend the ceremony which was postponed upon his arrest. M. Gabriel Barthelemy Magneval wrote sadly to Jacques Sarasin :

" God hath removed from us him whom the Government had restored. What a loss, what a grief ! "

The Mother Lodge was consecrated in the Grand Cophte's absence, on the 25th July, 1786. And, in the course of the ceremony, the Grand Inspector exhorted his fellow-believers to resignation :

" Privileged ones like us should know that our weakness prevents us from penetrating the secrets of the Supreme Being. Abraham consented of old to make a sacrifice of his son ; it is for us to-day to make a sacrifice of our father. And let us say with Job : 'The Lord gave and the Lord hath taken away.' . . ."

Such resignation had a speedy reward. The "pigeon" had a clear vision of Moses, Enoch and Elijah, and the Grand Cophte himself, soaring between heaven and earth, entrusted her with a message :

"Tell them that I love them and shall always love them."

Filled with joy, an official of the Lodge hastened to report these proceedings to Cagliostro. Europe, he said, had never witnessed a more impressive ceremony.

From London, Cagliostro supervised not only the *Sagesse Triomphante* but his female disciples as well. For example, the Lodge of Adoption being unable to meet in Paris on the last Sunday in July 1786, a day inconvenient to many of the companions, the Marquise de Flamarens had begged to be allowed to hold the meeting on a week-day. The mystagogue refused permission. For, he said, it was exactly to sanctify the day of the Lord, to tear away weak and changeable creatures from the theatre, from the gossip of the salons, from all their useless and mischievous dissipations, that he had instructed his spiritual daughters to meet on the Sunday.

Notwithstanding the apparently flourishing state of his Egyptian Rite, Cagliostro was full of apprehension. The future seemed uncertain. His celebrated exploits and his unfortunate entanglements with the French Government had, no doubt, attracted attention to his small flock. But, in this notoriety itself, an eye as practised as his could discern a threat to a religion which, before fully developing, had to ripen slowly in the silence of tabernacles and the half light of consecrated lamps. They made, in fact, too much fuss about him personally.

Scarcely had the Grand Cophte been incarcerated in the Bastille than the booksellers had put on sale a licentious fantasy, the *Memoires authentiques pour servir a l'histoire du comte de Cagliostro*. This lampoon, ascribed to the Marquis de Luchet, was so favourably received that a second edition was announced in January 1786, and then a third at Strasbourg. Subsequently M. Manuel wrote a *Lettre d'un Garde du Roi*. Much later, the public were disputing over the *Confessions du comte de C. . . . avec l'histoire de ses voyages en Russie, Turquie, Italie et dans les Pyramides d'Egypte*. It was in vain to warn them of these lies, this incoherent mass of fables and obscenities—people continued to revel in them, all the same. True, no one took seriously the account of the ceremonies to which it was alleged the Egyptian apprentices had to submit as the *Loge d'Isis*, in the rue Verte Sainte Honoré. But such publications indicated a thinly veiled hostility to Cagliostro and his disciples.

Some weeks before the decree of Parlement, a pamphlet entitled *Lettres du comte de Mirabeau a M. M. . . . sur M. de Cagliostro et Lavater* had created a sensation. Under the direct influence of the Berlin rationalists, the author started a crusade against these two visionaries, the alleged heralds of an imaginary Gospel. He aptly differentiated between the two. The one, he said, was absurd, the other suspect. Of the one, he condemned the opinions, and of the other, the character. He held Cagliostro to be innocent in the trial which was proceeding, but the reason he gave was more terrible than any accusation could have been : this strange man might well have been an impostor all his life without being a swindler in the notorious affair of the necklace. *All his life an impostor !* Such a sentence, from the pen of a Mirabeau, could scarcely pass unnoticed.

Besides, it was being fully confirmed by a pamphlet written by Count Moszynski, *Cagliostro demasqué a Varsovie.* This was an account of the thaumaturge's exploits, and represented him in a most unfavourable light. Six years after he had been deceived, the laboratory assistant of Warsaw and of Wola was avenging himself on the alchemist whose secrets he had been unable to discover. But his hate carried him beyond decent limits. The public turned away from the exaggerated caricature.

Cagliostro was at the time in the Bastille, and the smallest imprudence might have provoked his undoing, when the Baroness von der Recke, after years of silence, suddenly threw her accusations into the scale. Happily, her letter, written at Mitau on the 22nd March, 1786, was not reproduced in Berlin until May ; too late for the news to spread to France before Cagliostro's acquittal. She referred to her former spiritual guide as an impostor and a cheat. And the following year she wrote a detailed account of the experiments performed by Cagliostro at Mitau in 1779. She described her recantation as an act of penance. Numerous friends, she alleged, had pressed her to tell what she knew of Cagliostro, and her grandmother, the starostine von Korff, who had always been hostile to the thaumaturge, had called upon her to confess her mistakes publicly so as to protect others.

According to the Baroness, Cagliostro had cunningly got control of Marshal de Medem's son. The poor child, encouraged by his parents to venerate the magician, had become genuinely fond of this strange but kind man, who fondled and caressed him like a father. Cagliostro had promised him no end of wonderful things if he would but follow his instructions to the letter. He undertook to make the fortune of the whole family. Woe to him, on the other hand, if he should disobey ! At the first sign of a prank he would be hacked to pieces with a big sword. That was why the " pupil's " cheeks were aflame after every séance : he was afraid he might have recited his lesson imperfectly ; he trembled, and the blood mounted to his face. In short, the little fellow had been forced to repeat at the séance everything previously told him by Cagliostro in the intimacy of the Medem Palace. Although the Baroness did not support these charges with any proof, their effect, nevertheless, was considerable. In German-speaking countries, her book had the same resounding success as M. Thilorier's memoirs in Paris. Everybody wanted to read it. It was found in the dressing-rooms of the fashionable as well as on the work-table of Goethe. For want of translations, France and England knew it only in dull summaries. But the majority of the papers had already come out against Cagliostro.

In the Russian Court, Catherine II's *Impostor* was put on the boards. The Tsarina, proud of the success of this farce, informed one of her correspondents, Dr. Zimmerman, of it :

" I must tell you that two Russian comedies have appeared here, one is entitled *The Impostor* and the other *The Dupe*. The first represents Cagliostro (whom I have never seen, still less his wife, although they were here) as he is, and the other, his dupes. Our public is crazy about these two plays which are in fact very amusing."

On arrival in London, the thaumaturge had received an ominous welcome from the Press. On the 23rd June, 1786, the *Courrier de l'Europe* paid him this double-edged compliment :

" Letters from Boulogne have informed us of the departure of the Count de Cagliostro who for the last few days has been in this capital, where he is well-known on account of his former visits. This extraordinary man has come, they say, to exercise his talents in London. Only a great theatre seems to suit his activities ; it is evidently some vast scheme that has brought him here."

. . . .

Notwithstanding this disagreeable welcome, Cagliostro could scarcely foresee the terrible calamities which awaited him in London. Why did he take refuge in a city where, between 1776 and 1777, he had suffered so many cruel misunderstandings ? His flock there was small. M. and Mme de Cagliostro would have been quite alone in London had it not been for the constant pilgrimages of the French who crossed the Channel to see him, to consult him, and to maintain around the Grand Cophte and the Grand Mistress a sort of service of honour.

Though the affair of the Queen's necklace was closed to all the world, Cagliostro's lawyers officiously reopened it. The Marquis de Launay and Commissioner Chenon, who thought they had for ever got rid of the troublesome magician and his tricky brood, were surprised to find themselves hauled before the Civil Court of the Châtelet, for the exploit of the 21st June, 1786. £100,000 were claimed from them as compensation for the funds stolen from the rue Saint Claude, by their failure to seal up the place ; £50,000 for manuscripts mislaid or stolen for the same reasons, and another £50,000 as damages for the violence which M. Chenon had done the prisoner. Total : £200,000.

The same day there appeared in London a long pamphlet, *Memoire pour le Comte de Cagliostro contre M. Chenon le fils et le sieur de*

Launay, in which the thaumaturge tried to justify his demands. As a matter of fact, M. d'Epremesnil and his son-in-law Thilorier were pursuing a bold policy. They were trying to work up a campaign against the *lettres de cachet* on the strength of a great and terrible scandal. And loftily M. d'Epremesnil spoke of "debourbonising" France, and making Parlement supreme. Though it was given wide publicity and was as popular as his previous writings, M. Thilorier's latest pamphlet had little effect. The King, much better informed on this occasion than in the affair of the Cardinal de Rohan, was forewarned of the trap being laid for the monarchy. As his own officers were implicated, His Majesty considered that he alone was qualified to judge of the mistakes committed in the execution of his orders. He therefore referred Cagliostro's claim to the *Conseil des Depêches*, that is to say, to himself, and the parties were forbidden to apply elsewhere. By a decree of the 2nd July, 1786, they were allowed three weeks to submit their papers to M. de Boisgibault, the registrar. An expeditious and discreet procedure, that had the advantage of avoiding all publicity and hence all scandal.

On the 4th July, Baron de Breteuil wrote to the Count d'Adhemar, the Ambassador in London :

"His Majesty has ordered me to beg you to inform the above-mentioned Cagliostro, if he is now in London, that he is permitted to return to Paris, and that he may stay there freely while his case is being tried."

But as he could no longer count on creating a scandal, it was thought that Cagliostro would have nothing to gain by his return to France. July passed in obscure negotiations. Finally, in the first days of August, he caused to be circulated in Paris manuscript copies of a memorial : *Traduction d'une lettre écrite par M. le comte de Cagliostro à M. . . .* by which the exile gave it to be understood that, notwithstanding the fine promises of Baron de Breteuil, he would not be safe in returning to Paris :

"Someone has asked me if I shall return to France if the ban against me were lifted. 'Assuredly,' I replied, 'provided the Bastille has become a public promenade. May it please God to make it so!'"

This document, soon to become celebrated under the name of *A Letter to the French people*, ended with an extraordinary prophecy :

"Yes, my friend, I announce it, there will rule over you a prince whose glory it shall be to abolish the *lettres de cachet*, to summon the States General and above all to re-establish the true religion. . . ."

In the composition of this manifesto M. d'Epremesnil had made use of a letter written in Italian, in which the Master freely gave expression to his republican ideas. But after so much publicity, a man who openly wished for the demolition of the Bastille, who predicted the abolition of the *lettres de cachet* and the convocation of the States General, could no longer run the risk of entering Paris. Realising this, Cagliostro determined to settle in London.

He took a house in Knightsbridge, adjoining that of a Mr. Swinton, proprietor of the *Courrier de l'Europe*, with whom he was on good terms. Well-known in London as he was, and speaking French and English equally well, Mr. Swinton was in a position to be of the greatest assistance to the exiled philanthropist. Newly arrived in London, Cagliostro was not yet aware of Mr. Swinton's connections with the French Embassy. Redoubling his zealous attentions, the Englishman seemed anxious to familiarise him with London. No view was more impressive, he repeated, than Greenwich Hospital and the shipyards ; nothing more pleasant than a trip down the Thames. Contemplative and sedentary by nature, Cagliostro was astonished at this insistence. Too preoccupied with his griefs and his meditations, he declined to take any part in pleasure. Mr. Swinton, who was founding some inexplicable hopes on the thaumaturge, suggested that he should hold medical consultations ; but when Mr. Swinton naïvely expressed his desire to act as his apothecary, Cagliostro declined.

One day, in his neighbour's house, he met the co-proprietor of the *Courrier de l'Europe*, Theveneau de Morande. This man had in his pocket, at that moment, several letters from Chevalier d'Agay, the attaché at the Embassy, instigating him to attack the charlatan Cagliostro, and thus help M. de Launay's case. Theveneau affirmed later that the Count's behaviour in the Swinton house was ill-mannered, and his treatment of others discourteous. Meaning to treat him in the same way, Theveneau very rudely questioned him about his two previous visits to England. The Count turned colour :

" I, Sir ? . . . I have been in England only once."

" Excuse me, sir, you have been here twice, and the same persons whom you knew when you called yourself . . ."

Here, his memory failing him, Theveneau fumbled :

" When you called yourself Balthymore, you know now under the name of Cagliostro. . . . M. Pergolesi and his wife frequently had the honour of your presence at dinner on your first visit. You fell out with them on your second ; but none the less, they have had their eyes on you for several months."

Beside himself with rage, the Count replied that this Pergolesi must be a notorious scoundrel.

" And if I should have been in England twenty times," he added, " have I wronged anybody ? "

A great deal was being said, replied his tormentor ironically, about his former trial. Had not the Count to return a certain necklace, after some weeks in jail ?

" I don't care what is being said about me," cried out the victim, " the Count de Cagliostro is known all over Europe."

After Theveneau's departure, the Master explained to his hosts that as this regrettable scene had occurred under their roof and in their presence, it was they who should consider themselves to have been insulted. As for Alexander de Cagliostro, God be thanked, he could suffer no insult from such fellows.

A few days later, Mr. Swinton himself unmasked his batteries. He dictated to one of his daughters a letter to the Count saying that, as he was burdened by a numerous family, he was finding it difficult to make both ends meet. The thaumaturge had helped lots of people to make money. If Mr. Swinton should have the good fortune to share in similar favours, he would gratefully befriend the learned Cagliostro, the sublime Cagliostro, and the *Courrier* would eulogise him twice a week. Otherwise. . . .

The only reply the Count gave was to slam his door in the face of the virtuous publicist when next he called on him. Mr. Swinton was subjected to such rebuffs that, in spite of his impudence, he dared less and less to take advantage of his proximity to Cagliostro.

On the 21st August, Cagliostro himself went to the French Embassy in Piccadilly to fetch the permit enabling him to re-enter Paris and watch the proceedings he had instituted. For fear that some snare might be laid for him, two trusted friends went with him, a French ex-officer, M. Bergeret de Frouville, and an Englishman, Lord George Gordon. Lord George had an execrable reputation. Whether it was due to his aggressive sectarianism, his eccentricities, or his violent manner, nothing seemed to justify it more in the eyes of the French than the fierce hatred which he invariably displayed towards their country. The first inclination of M. Barthelemy, the chargé d'affaires, was therefore to have this firebrand thrown out of the window. But he restrained himself sufficiently to tell Cagliostro, with icy politeness, that he was authorised to permit him to return to France. But the only safe conduct which M. Barthelemy gave him was a simple letter from Baron de Breteuil.

At this the Count protested. Was a minister who had cruelly persecuted him because he was loyal to Cardinal de Rohan qualified to revoke the positive orders of the Sovereign? As he had been exiled by a note from Louis XVI, Cagliostro haughtily declared that he would not run the risk of returning save on the strength of an explicit and personal authorisation from His Majesty. This attitude was excusable in one embittered by prison and exile. But the *Public Advertiser* announced it the following day in language that was scarcely prudent :

"The thousands of good citizens whose cheers caused the Bastille to shake when his innocence was proclaimed, have perhaps confirmed his exile by aggravating the jealousy and fear of an arbitrary Government. . . ." These comments were renewed two days later in a more mischievous tone. When information was sought about it, it was learned from reliable sources that the articles had been written by Lord George Gordon, under Cagliostro's inspiration.

Now the French Embassy held the mortgage of the *Courrier de l'Europe*, which was published in London twice a week. The proprietors of this French journal, Mr. Swinton and M. Theveneau de Morande, could refuse it nothing. The King's agents were therefore in a position to attack their enemies in London whenever they chose.

. . . .

Cagliostro had already experienced how virulent their attack could be when he was visited at Knightsbridge by Sophie von La Roche, a German authoress, sent to him by Jacques and Gertrude Sarasin to find out how he was getting on. The traveller scrutinised the house in Sloane Street in order to describe it to her friends. She found it well-built, with a garden of rolling lawns and shady trees, through which ran a stream. The door was opened by a gigantic negro dressed in Oriental fashion. He motioned to the visitor to descend from her carriage. The silent neighbourhood, the mysterious house, and the swarthy colossus recalled to the mind tales of enchanted castles. Mme von La Roche, stepping from her carriage, could not help whispering to her companions :

" Let us hope we shall come back safe and sound ! "

The ladies were graciously welcomed by the Master, whom they found exactly like his portraits. With him that day was a strange man, dressed in black, tall and thin, with short blonde hair, pale complexion, and dull blue eyes of a sinister look.

" To what confession do you belong ? " brusquely demanded the hierophant.

" I am a Protestant."

" Ah ! so much the better for you. Lord George Gordon, who is here, has a horror of papists. He would have driven you out at once, and in spite of me, if you had been one."

Sophie von La Roche began to laugh. A fanatic Englishman introduced to a German novelist by an Asiatic magician—was not here an intriguing adventure ? The Countess came in a little later. The charming Serafina shuddered when she talked of the Bastille, the French police, and the barbarous treatment to which she had been subjected in Paris. In this connection the Master said :

" As long as I was spending a hundred thousand pounds a year among them, the French did not ask me how I got the money. But now that I am claiming some of my own back, they show a great concern about it."

Then, when Mme von La Roche confessed her interest in pedagogy, he said :

" Education does not change men. They die exactly as they were born. . . ."

Nevertheless he considered the different religions to be so many systems of education, and each of them seemed to him on that account worthy of respect. The Catholics alone he criticised for the enormous power with which they invested their clergy, as well as for their unnecessary repression of natural tendencies. Returning the next day to Knightsbridge for luncheon, Sophie von La Roche once more met Lord George Gordon. The table service was half English and half Italian. While the Master consumed a prodigious quantity of macaroni, his guests were served with a quarter of lamb, fresh cod, stewed vegetables, roast veal, potatoes, salad, sweets and watercress. The table was covered with a beautiful damasked cloth on which everybody, in default of napkins, wiped their hands and lips, in the old English way. The dishes were of silver, the plates of fine porcelain, the glasses and carafes of English crystal. The negro Goliath, assisted by another servant, waited on them, and generously served them with the rarest of wines.

Sophie von La Roche gathered from certain expressions that the exile mistrusted his lawyer, M. Thilorier. Cagliostro, gloomy from his misfortunes, stayed indoors all the time. London offered him but a barren field. In Paris his immense success was due above all to the drugs by means of which he prolonged not only life but the capacity for pleasures. But such secrets did not in the least interest a dour race to whom life itself seemed to be a wearisome burden. The Prince of Wales and some noblemen had at first fêted the exile on account of his misfortunes and his romantic halo. But in September 1786, Cagliostro had already gone out of fashion. His friends were thereafter reduced to Lord George Gordon, Miss E. Howard, who was begging him to regenerate her mother, an old woman incurably wasting away, the artist Loutherbourg's family, and his faithful friend Mr. Bousie, whom he frequently visited in St. James's Place.

. . . .

Yet, in spite of sorrow, in spite of bitter disappointment, never had his genius shone more brilliantly. When Theveneau began to revile him in the *Courrier de l'Europe*, what was his rejoinder? An invitation to lunch. He asked him to come on the 9th November, 1786, at nine o'clock in the morning, and taste a sucking pig that the Grand Cophte undertook to fatten by a special method. One of three things would happen the next day: either they would find themselves face to face in the other world; or they would both be alive; or else one of them would have failed to digest the *plat de résistance*, in which case Cagliostro wagered five thousand guineas that that little mishap would happen to M. Theveneau de Morande rather than to him.

The journalist declined the challenge hastily, as Dr. Rogerson, the Czarina's physician, had formerly declined it in Petersburg. But his alarm raised a laugh at his expense. Furious, Theveneau wagered five thousand guineas that he would, before long, show up the self-styled Cagliostro.

From that date, the question of identity in which the public had for so long been passionately interested, was rigorously defined and relentlessly pursued. Having got hold of authentic copies of some legal documents, the *Courrier de l'Europe* proceeded to unfold before its readers an extraordinary tale. It was the interminable wrangle between Cagliostro and Miss Fry. These sordid incidents did not redound to the Grand Cophte's credit, but the disclosures only related to the period between 1776 and 1777. To fill the cup of scandal to the brim, it was necessary to prove that Alexander and Serafina de Cagliostro had stayed in London between 1771 and 1772 under the names of Giuseppe and Lorenza Balsamo.

In this respect, Theveneau was unlucky. To begin with, he confused the names, referred to a certain Balthymore, and had later to protest that he had meant Balsamo. A lucky chance had enabled him to discover the painter, Pergolesi, who loudly asserted that Cagliostro was no other than Balsamo. But instead of sticking to this valuable witness, Theveneau committed the blunder of bringing the miserable Carlo Sacchi, at considerable expense, to England. And just as Mme de La Motte's lawyer had done, he vainly sought for the fictitious Tiscio, the Duke of Castropignani's coachman. The journalist lost a lot of money in this affair, his inquiries miscarried, and Balsamo was still at large.

But it happened that the name of Balsamo, seen again in the columns of the *Courrier*, after a lapse of fifteen years, strongly impressed the Commissioner Fontaine in Paris. Balsamo ! . . . Balsamo ! . . . A young Italian of that name had once been locked up in Saint Pelagius, accused by her husband of immorality. M. Fontaine pieced together his recollections. By scrutinising the portraits of the Count and the Countess de Cagliostro, he imagined he recognised in them the features of Giuseppe and Lorenza Balsamo.

The authorities still had in their possession the files relating to the case. Soon after, the French police were instructed to furnish the Count de Vergennes with a detailed and systematic comparison of the respective histories of Balsamo and Cagliostro. It was evident from this document that the two men were identical. The most characteristic features of the Sicilian painter were recognisable in the Grand Cophte. For example, Balsamo had boasted to the Commissioner Fontaine that he could fatten a sucking pig with arsenic, and extract a deadly poison from it. Did not this already foreshadow his famous challenge to M. Theveneau de Morande ? Two letters from Balsamo were found in the police archives, and the experts having compared their signatures with an authentic letter from Cagliostro, written in the Bastille, pronounced the writing to be identical. As a result of the Commissioner Fontaine's zeal, this report, as well as the chief papers in the Balsamo dossier, were reprinted verbatim in the *Courrier de l'Europe*.

The Grand Cophte felt it necessary to reply without delay. His

Lettre du comte de Cagliostro au peuple anglais pour servir de suite a ses memoires, was printed in the second half of November 1786. Although deeply hurt by the controversy, the Master put a bold front on it. What were they accusing him of, after all? Of having frequently changed his name and rank? Of having concealed the name of his native country? A fine pass things have come to! Was not a personage of distinction entitled to travel incognito? His disciples, his friends knew it well, for he had told them a hundred times: he was neither count, nor marquis, nor colonel, or even Cagliostro. And still less was he Balsamo. He insisted on that repeatedly, though the unfortunate artist seemed to him more to be pitied than blamed. Certainly, had the Master been obliged formerly to live by his feeble talent for painting, he would not blush to admit it. He had told the French people from his cell in the Bastille that his investigations with regard to his birth had given him an inkling of the truth, but that it was vague and uncertain. To the English he said the same:

"Is my real rank superior or inferior to that which I have given myself? One day, perhaps, the public will know."

In the meantime, a mysterious fatality avenged for him his persecutors. The woman de Blevary, who had repaid him with the blackest ingratitude, had died. His implacable enemy, Mary Fry, had suffered, before breathing her last, the hardships of extreme poverty. Dead, Mrs. Gaudicheau, the worthy accomplice and conscience of this dangerous vixen. Dead too, the sneak and perjurer Broad. Dead, Mr. Dunning, Mary Fry's dishonest lawyer. Dead, Cagliostro's own counsel for defence, Mr. Wallace, who had delivered him helpless into the hands of Henry Howarth, the arbitrator who had been bribed by his opponents. As for the latter, in punishment for the iniquitous award he had given, the Thames had long since rolled his corpse down to the sea. The Hammersmith J.P. who had caused the Count and Countess to be illegally arrested was similarly struck down. For having swindled Cagliostro out of his money, Mr. Crisp had died in a public hospital, reduced to beggary. And each of these victims, with the exception of the old Blevary, had died in good health, in the prime of life.

A few stray survivors were, according to trustworthy reports, leading a miserable and obscure life. Without relatives or friends, William Scott had taken refuge in the depths of Scotland, with the manuscript stolen from Cagliostro, and the rose powder which he could neither give up nor make use of. The usher, Saunders, was atoning for his lies in a prison cell. Reynolds, the evil genius of Scott and Mary Fry, had had to own up to his perjuries in the pillory. And ere long, Mr. Edward Aylett, the errant scoundrel who had thought to identify Cagliostro with Balsamo, met with the same fate.

On the 21st November, 1786, the solicitor could have been seen, mounting a scaffold put up in the middle of Palace Yard, facing the main entrance to Westminster. His black dress, his round wig, and above all his tight-fitting boots, immediately aroused the laughter of the populace. He was locked up in a wooden frame, moving on a pivot, thanks to which Mr. Aylett could survey at leisure, from the corner of his eye, the whole of the open space in front of Westminster Hall. After having been thus exhibited, he was taken back to Newgate Prison amid the jeers of the crowd.

Count de Cagliostro ended his *Lettre au peuple anglais* by summoning his defamer Theveneau de Morande before the tribunal of God. And more than one reader was thrilled when he read the dreadful indictment.

But the journalist was made of hard stuff. He retorted immediately by printing an arraignment extending to twelve columns. If Cagliostro had nothing in common with Balsamo, why did he visit York Buildings, No. 20 Villiers Street, and call on the solicitor John Lowe, who was so much with the Sicilian about the year 1772 ? Why did he never meet Carlini, the keeper of the Royal Academy archives, who had so rudely shown the door to the shabby painter Balsamo ? And why did he never set foot in No. 43 Albemarle Street, the residence of Sir Edward Hales, whose castle he had so artistically daubed ?

As for Serafina, Theveneau declared that he only spared her at the request of two persons who had come and pleaded on her behalf. In fact, this unfortunate creature received a thrashing every time that the Count imagined he could trace to *her* indiscretion the extraordinary disclosures published in the *Courrier de l'Europe*.

The Grand Cophte's temper, no doubt, was only too easily aroused, but he could not contradict one by one all the follies attributed to him. According to Swinton and Theveneau, he had bragged about his ability to make water as inflammable as naphtha, and thus enabling the City of London to save £50,000 a year. He had, again, offered to swallow in a single gulp five grains of arsenic ; after which, taking a spoonful of a marvellous antidote in his possession, he alleged he could have gone back to his ordinary work. . . . But of all these stupid stories, none was more unjust to him than the alleged misadventure of some Swedenborgians, who, it was said, had tried to raise the Seven Celestial Angels according to Cagliostro's formulæ. Suddenly, in place of the seraphim in azure robes and silver that they were hoping for, there appeared a fearful horde of wild orang-outangs whose grimaces, insults and unworthy promiscuity the chaste idealists had had to endure all the evening.

At this period the Grand Cophte was, in fact, on very good terms with the Swedenborgians. He frequented the Theosophical Society, commented on the Apocalypse, and sought for the new Jerusalem. But the orthodox Freemasons had given him a cold reception at their Lodge *Antiquity*, where brother Mash, the optician, had even had the insolence to sneer at him. They refused to come to Reilly's tavern in Great Queen Street, when the hierophant invited them there in the name of the Jehovah Jesus. An announcement in the *Morning Herald* of 2nd November, 1786, exhorted them to come to lay the first stone of the true Church. All in vain! The English did not care for his celestial Jerusalem. And Mr. Bousie himself, when the Grand Cophte suggested that he should have an annual salary of a thousand guineas if he would act as Secretary to the Grand Egyptian Lodge in London, contented himself with a smile.

This hostility was also evident in the cartoons. One of them showed Cagliostro standing in the midst of some open-mouthed dupes of his Egyptian Lodge. He was breathing out lamentations which could be read distinctly in a pennant issuing from his mouth: Holy God! I am found out, etc. . . . His disciples were moaning in a similar vein. Another caricature showed his unhappy patients occupied in taking yellow and white pills, elixirs, purgatives and restoratives right and left. And these outrageous couplets, very different from those which had formerly gone the round of Bordeaux and Paris, only made the ridicule worse:

> Born God knows where, kept God knows how,
> Master or servant, labourer or gentleman.
> Here is the friend of Lord George Gordon
> Here he who was made Free Mason
> Under a false name. Child of imposture,
> He says: "I am the child of nature," etc. . . .

January 1787 was somehow reached. M. Rey de Morande, faithful to his promise, then came to take the place of the Marquis de Vichy as companion to the Grand Cophte and the Grand Mistress. He brought the most distressing news from France. The written defences of M. de Launay and the younger Chenon had now been published. The general opinion was that the King's officers had satisfactorily defended their conduct. Cagliostro's reply was entrusted to a M. de Joly, and published in France as *Requête au Roi par le comte de Cagliostro*.

The style was vigorous; the arguments copious and well-knit. But what was the use? The Marquis de Launay had only to dig out an important document from the archives of the Parlement—the list of Mme de Cagliostro's jewels, dated 5th September, 1785—and his opponent was confounded. On a comparison of this list with the inventory taken on the 1st June, 1786, it was established beyond dispute that Cagliostro's possessions had in no way been affected by his imprisonment in the Bastille. The two rolls of twenty-five double-louis, found intact in the cardboard box when he was set at liberty, had been registered as such at the time of his arrest: it proved that M. de Launay was right. As to the fortune, including jewels and money, which the plaintiff estimated in all at £200,000, no trace of it was to be found in the list dated 5th September, 1785.

M. d'Epremesnil retorted with a *Réponse a la pièce importante de M. de Launay* as well as by a new *Requête.* He pointed out the inexplicable difference, even the flagrant contradictions, between the report on the day of arrest and the list that had been so providentially recovered : according to him, this important document might well be a forgery. But the differences, after examination, were reduced to insignificant shades of meaning, and the reaction in France was instantaneous. Believing itself to have been hoaxed, the public did not wait until the decision of the Conseil des Depêches to withdraw its confidence finally from Cagliostro.

These deplorable happenings produced an irritated and stormy atmosphere in Knightsbridge. In the loneliness of a gloomy exile, M. Rey de Morande had not, as at Bordeaux, a constant flow of visitors to distract him ; nor had he, as at Lyons, the wonderful spectacle of evocations and transmutations. His principal occupation in England was preparing medicaments. The Count not having been able to come to terms with the Knightsbridge apothecary, Mr. Jackson, his prescriptions had to be made up by his disciples. To reward the exemplary fidelity of M. Rey de Morande, the Master initiated him little by little into the secrets of the philosophers' stone.

He thus assumed the same functions as Count Moszynski had discharged in Poland : he supervised the alchemic crucible and constantly improved the projection powder or the primary matter.

The Master and his disciple had been absorbed in this task for two months when they got wind of an infernal plot. Instigated by the *Courrier de l'Europe*, M. Silvestre of Cadiz was coming to London to insist on either the return of the famous cane with the watch, or the payment of the bills signed by Marquis Pellegrini at the time when the noble traveller had not yet begun to call himself Count de Cagliostro. The Grand Cophte, at the first rumour of this conspiracy, sought refuge in Hammersmith Terrace, at the house of his friend, Loutherbourg. In the end, weariness and disgust triumphed over his constancy. He resolved to quit this inhospitable land. Some good Swiss friends offered him refuge in Neuchatel, a Prussian principality. But before any decision was taken, Jacques Sarasin wished to consult Prince Henri of Prussia, whom he had entertained at the "White House." His Royal Highness sent rather an embarrassed answer on the 15th March, 1787, which stated that the Prussian Government would not oppose the entry of the Count de Cagliostro, but neither would it oppose his extradition if a foreign power should demand it. M. and Mme Sarasin did not insist any further. Their inquiries now turned in the direction of Bienne.

While they were still looking for a refuge, a dramatic event occurred in Hammersmith. Cagliostro, hidden in Hammersmith, gave his hosts lessons in elementary alchemy, which their Chiswick neighbour, Miss E. Howard, a fervent admirer, also attended. Wishing to show this old spinster an experiment in silver transmutation, the Count wrote to Rey de Morande, about the 2nd March, asking him to send a grain or two of primary matter.

What was passing in the disciple's heart at the time? What temptations were assailing him? For some weeks, he had had suspicions. In order to set them at rest, he ventured to send a mixture of ash and tobacco instead of the primary matter. Yet in spite of the fraud, the Master was able to accomplish his feat. The transmutation took place without a hitch, under the eyes of the astounded Miss Howard. By the help of the Seven Celestial Angels, Cagliostro had been able to change three copper pennies and one pound of mercury into twelve ounces of fine silver.

At this news, which he received the next day, M. Rey de Morande should have withdrawn into himself, and recollected that the Grand Cophte did not act directly on matter, but only through the agency of the Spirits who owed him obedience. Unfortunately, passion confused his mind. Imagining himself to have been for four years the dupe of an impostor, he flew rather than ran to Hammersmith. Trembling with anger, he accused the Master of cheating, revealed to him the trap that had been laid for him, and set himself to work this alleged transmutation in front of the old English fool. Then, without listening to the protests of the thaumaturge, he hastened back to Knightsbridge.

Meanwhile, the Marquis de Vismes and his brother-in-law, M. de La Borde, disquieted by the turn the Grand Cophte's case had taken in the Conseil des Depêches and still more disgusted with his continual appeals for money, crossed the Channel to ask for an explanation. Yes or no, did he or did he not possess £200,000 in jewels and gold at the time of his arrest? Did the Egyptian Masonry exist elsewhere than on paper? Would he perform, for the edification of his followers, a physical regeneration? Finally, was he quite sure he had never been Giuseppe Balsamo? They demanded an immediate explanation.

The Grand Cophte, forced into a corner, did not hesitate a moment. He bid his wife wind up the establishment in Knightsbridge, and without giving any answer to the preposterous questionnaire, he left for Basle with M. Gerard Teise, an intimate friend of the Sarasin couple. The two men, travelling all day, arrived at the "White House" on the evening of the 5th April.

No sooner had he recovered from his fatigue than Cagliostro went with Jacques and Gertrude to visit an estate situated at the entrance to Bienne. This country-house, called Rocaille, or Rockhalt, was comfortable and pleasant. A beautiful pavilion furnished tastefully, though not lavishly, abundant verdure, some vines, gardens and lovely waters, added to the delights of the retreat.

The local authorities, Sigismond Wildermett and his eldest son Alexander, who was Mayor of Bienne, welcomed the celebrated Aesculapius with open arms. Charmed with what he saw, Cagliostro decided to settle in Rocaille, on the arrival of the Countess. The magistrate evinced great delight at this, and Sigismond Wildermett begged him to convey their compliments to the " White House."

The message, and the warm reception given to him the next month at the Helvetic Congress at Olten, somewhat consoled the fugitive, even though the *Courrier de l'Europe* continued to harass him. Theveneau, a prophet in his turn, was predicting the total suppression of the Egyptian Rite. Nothing would remain of it, he announced triumphantly to his readers. He nevertheless shed a few tears over the Countess, whose martyrdom was to be pitied. The infamous Cagliostro, she declared, had run away with their most valuable possessions, leaving her in absolute destitution in London. But in fact, Theveneau was mistaken. Serafina had both jewels and cash at Knightsbridge. And if she pretended to the contrary, it was on the advice of Cagliostro himself, to avoid a distraint. Alas ! there were other lies which were not dictated by conjugal loyalty. The Countess, left to herself, ignored Cagliostro's instructions and seemed to be actually in league with his enemies. As soon as she was left alone, she consented to receive Theveneau, and pushed her folly to the point of disclosing to him their most intimate secrets. Still less did she conceal her lively affection for M. Rey de Morande, although he had broken the Grand Cophte's heart. And this strange weakness in her enabled the apostate disciple to peddle about her alleged confessions, representing the Count de Cagliostro as being undoubtedly Giuseppe Balsamo and Pellegrini, a monster of hypocrisy and baseness, a hundred times more vile than his most ferocious detractors could imagine.

MM. de Vismes and de La Borde, failing to obtain the explanations they sought, made common cause with M. Rey de Morande. At Paris MM. d'Epremesnil and Thilorier ostentatiously deserted the man whom they had for so long elevated to the ranks of the gods. They both cursed him for an impostor, for each had been in it only for the money. Strangely enough, Serafina did not deny them entrance into her house. Such of them as were in London held mysterious consultations with the cook Agostino, who was ready to sell himself to the highest bidder. M. de Breteuil promised Serafina a pension from the King of France if she would say that her husband's charges against MM. de Launay and the young Chenon were baseless and calumnious. The Countess did not wish to sign the statement which would have been so damaging to Cagliostro, and which was intended for publication, but even so, she was not at all discreet. The Swiss disciples wondered if she would ever consent to return to him.

Happily, M. Gerard Teise, returning from London, announced

soon after that Serafina was reckoning on leaving for Basle with the Loutherbourg couple. She was only waiting to sell at Christie's the mahogany furniture in the Knightsbridge house, her tapestries, her Turkish bed, and her piano.

Serafina's journey was accomplished without incident. On the evening of the 17th June, Cagliostro had the joy of embracing her again. After the many scandalous rumours that had gone round, the Count and Countess were anxious to show themselves for a while in Basle, fully reconciliated. Besides, they had to wait for the completion of the repairs at Rocaille. The Baslians took advantage of this delay. Some time before, their group had been constituted into the Mother Lodge of Switzerland, and at its enthusiastic meetings, so marvellously favourable to the manifestation of miracles, only the absence of Lavater was regretted. In order to coax him, Cagliostro dipped into the French translation of the *Physiognomie* and was loud in his praise of it. But Lavater did not care for these tardy tributes. At the moment he was crazy over animal magnetism, over Mesmer, over the Count de Puységur. And the magician who had too long refused to communicate to him his teachings, ceased to exercise an attraction over the visionary of Zürich.

As the Master said nothing about the Riehen kiosk, M. and Mme Sarasin waited the hour of their regeneration without murmur. But with what vanity did not some of the new disciples vaunt their claims! It was a purely selfish friendship which had brought the Loutherbourgs to Cagliostro. The Grand Cophte had been weak enough to let them invite themselves to Rocaille, and their visit worried M. and Mme Sarasin in advance. To make room for the Loutherbourgs, who had now become their rivals, Gertrude thought she would let their eldest daughter, Suzette, sleep in the Countess's room. This child was to be the symbol at Rocaille of their silent and faithful hopes.

. . . .

On the 29th June, 1787, a sumptuous banquet was held in Cagliostro's honour at Sigismond Wildermett's house in Bienne. There Cagliostro met, after six years, Mme de Branconi, who had been his fervent admirer in Strasbourg and who was hoping to be reconciled with him. Party after party was given in honour of the Count and the Countess. One of the most brilliant of them was the soirée given by the Mayor Alexander Wildermett. Serafina showed herself on that occasion to the celebrities of Bienne "all shining with diamonds." Meanwhile, the gathering crowd of sick persons was noted with satisfaction.

Before everything else, a sworn notary from Bienne was asked to come to Rocaille to draw up a legal statement. And on the 5th and 6th July, 1787, the Countess de Cagliostro, acting on her own account, freely and spontaneously, expressed her wish to retract the words she had allowed to escape from her in London, in condemnation of her dear husband. He had never ill-treated her, much less beaten her ; in no way did he prevent her from practising her religion. It was the Marquis de Vismes who, on the occasion of his last trip to England, had tried to turn her from the right path, and poison her mind against the Master ; at the same time, he had tried to lure her back to France with the offer of a pension. In spite of his insistence and that of M. Rey de Morande, the Countess had refused to sign the insulting letter, the language of which M. Thilorier had, nevertheless, dared to quote in the newspapers. As for their old cook, who was an accomplice of the plotters, she thought him capable of every treachery.

Cagliostro was getting ready to distribute copies of this document and thus triumphantly crush the calumnies against him, when he received a letter from the latest of his advocates, M. de Joly, complaining of being left without instructions. Jacques Sarasin replied to the lawyer on the 9th July, indicating to him bluntly that the Count reserved his communications to his chief defenders, MM. d'Epremesnil and Thilorier. He concluded his letter with these threatening and enigmatic phrases :

" In vain do those with whom M. Thilorier co-operates, according to his own admission, take advantage of the insinuations that they have made about the Countess. Everything has been found out, proved, and put into a legal and voluntary declaration drawn up in the most formal manner. . . . Kindly inform M. the Count if you please, of the success of his case, and let Monsieur Thilorier know that it is not M. Rey de Morande, nor M. de Vismes, nor M. de Lansegre, but the Count de Cagliostro whose cause he has to plead and watch over, and that it is not the business of the husband's lawyer to persuade his wife to divorce her interests from his. . . ."

The Count's case came to an end on the 14th July, 1787, at Versailles. The King, sitting in his council, declared that Cagliostro was not entitled to damages, that his claims were ill-founded, and that he should pay the costs. The suppression of the memoir signed " Thilorier " was ordered as being injurious and calumnious. Thus MM. de Launay and Chenon emerged victorious from the combat into which M. d'Epremesnil had imprudently led the Grand Cophte.

Few people were surprised, so little chance did the thaumaturge seem to have in the Conseil des Depêches. But there were fresh disclosures to startle the public mind. A mysterious correspondent, learning that Commissioner Fontaine had recognised Cagliostro to be the Sicilian painter Giuseppe Balsamo, communicated to him the evidence of Giuseppe Balsamo's own uncle, Antonino Bracconeri, who declared that he knew his nephew called himself Count de Cagliostro. The anonymous letter came from Palermo, and was dated 2nd November, 1786. When its revelations had been verified on the spot by M. Cuggino, chief justice of the Island of Sicily, Antonino Bracconeri wrote a biographical account of his nephew which was printed in the *Courrier de l'Europe* on the 15th June, 1787.

The French Embassy in London now paid Theveneau an honorarium of £2,400 for his anti-Cagliostro campaign, and the journalist redoubled his zeal as a sign of gratitude to the minister of foreign affairs, M. de Montmorin.

In spite of this commotion, Cagliostro tried to live quietly. The Bienne magistrate having proceeded to make a census of the local tax-payers, in preparation of the impending arrivals, every precaution was taken to enable strangers to live according to their means. The crowds were so great that the hotel accommodation was not enough. The innkeepers and the tradesmen gave thanks to Cagliostro for the rain of gold which he drew upon the town, and were perhaps also inspired by a certain superstitious fear.

It was not long before Cagliostro, always irritable and quarrelsome, fell out with the principal chemist of Bienne, M. Schaltenbrand, and then with the laboratory assistant whom he tried to initiate into the method of preparing his medicines. But a still more disastrous scandal broke out among the inhabitants of Rocaille. Perhaps the outburst was inevitable in a house where there were two husbands, two wives and two groups of servants. M. and Mme Loutherbourg blamed the Count for not working towards their physical regeneration. In September, the painter fretted and fumed against the small talk at Rocaille, and found that the interests of the Egyptian Rite were much neglected there. A month later, the two households could scarcely bear each other. Sigismond Wildermett wrote to Jacques Sarasin about it in an uneasy tone :

" There is a new source of pain and grief. All this is a sure proof that it is not yet given to the Count to be happy and that there is something in his destiny, or in the manner of his life, that is firmly opposed to it."

The visit of the young Prince Edward, son of George III, precipitated the catastrophe. Cagliostro, when presented to his Royal Highness, had had the bad taste to speak to him with excessively democratic familiarity :

" I drink to the health of your father and mother, because he is a good man and she a good woman."

The Prince showed no sign of irritation ; but the next day, having gone to see Loutherbourg at Rocaille, he did not inquire after Cagliostro, who became furious at the slight.

At the beginning of December, after a number of quarrels, M. and Mme Loutherbourg left Rocaille. But the initial disagreement seemed to have been smoothed out between the two men. It was apparently but a trivial squabble about money. On an acknowledged debt of 170 louis, the Count agreed to pay Loutherbourg £30 in settlement, and he was given quittance. But the painter had taken a dislike to the Countess. She, on her part, accused the intriguing Lucy Loutherbourg of having wished to turn Cagliostro's head.

Recriminations were exchanged. The Master allowed his guests to leave without saying farewell to them, without the smallest sign of regret, to the great consternation of Sigismond Wildermett, who deplored the rupture. He wrote to Jacques Sarasin :

" Here then are two men fallen out for ever, in spite of their agreement over principles which ought to render their friendship eternal ! . . . I sympathise, like everyone else, with the position of your daughter, in the midst of these domestic alarms and excitements. She is too young to witness such regrettable scenes."

As Cagliostro's patients had monopolised the inns, M. and Mme Loutherbourg asked shelter of the Mayor Alexander Wildermett, who had not the heart to refuse. Besides, the painter was only waiting to give the last touches to a picture that was already near completion, before he left Rocaille definitely.

What evil motive caused Loutherbourg to decide not only to settle in Mayor Wildermett's house, but to resort to violence ? It was whispered that the beautiful Lucy Loutherbourg consoled herself for Cagliostro's coolness by flirting with M. the Mayor, who was suspected of an incurable fondness for ladies. Loutherbourg had had wind of it. And as he was already furious at losing all hopes of physical regeneration, his anger knew no bounds. An incredible rumour suddenly buzzed over the little town : Loutherbourg had challenged the thaumaturge to a duel. His seconds had been seen at Rocaille—Messrs. Wildermett and Dachselhoffer, the son and the son-in-law, respectively, of the Mayor. And doubtless the Grand Cophte good-temperedly showed his visitors out with a smile. He only fought with arsenic, he told them, and that was why M. de Narbonne and he had not cut each other's throats, in their time, at Saverne. . . . But the furious painter declared that, at the promenade hour, he would look everywhere for the perfidious enchanter and shoot him dead, like a dog. Cagliostro then realised that he was dealing with a madman, and put himself under police protection.

Criticism had until now been directed solely against Loutherbourg. It was on this madman, this fanatic, this brutal aggressor of a philanthropist, that public reprobation was heaped. But Cagliostro did not know how to maintain his advantage. He covered himself with ridicule when he accused the young Wildermett and Dachselhoffer of having plotted with the Loutherbourg couple to take his life. The citizens of Bienne went into ecstasies over this new development, and the quarrel grew more bitter every day. According to local custom, the Mayor was entitled to settle the dispute, but Cagliostro was ill-advised to challenge his right, on the ground that the Loutherbourg couple were living with M.

Alexander Wildermett, and that he was the father of one and the father-in-law of the other of his young agressors.

The Mayor, pained by this affront, wrote to the "White House" complaining about it. Jacques Sarasin was indeed the only man who could clear up the imbroglio. Unhappily, he was detained at Basle by the all too recent accouchement of his wife. Gertrude, who was still very feeble, had been able to read at the foot of a letter from their daughter Suzette, the few lines that Serafina had addressed to her in Italian :

"*Carissima figlia*, I have learned with great pleasure of your happy accouchement, which is a very real joy to me. As for the rest, these wretches are trying to torment us. I hope that your husband can immediately start on the journey. My poor husband and I are enduring great tribulations. *Caro amico*, if I do not write well, it is not my fault, I learnt to write without a teacher. I embrace you fondly, as well as my dear daughter, whom I love and shall always love with all my heart.

Serafina Cagliostro."

At last, on the 10th January, 1788, Jacques Sarasin arrived in Bienne. Without any delay he questioned in turn Cagliostro, Sigismond Wildermett and the Mayor ; then he consulted his brother-in-law M. de Gingin, and the doyen Gibolet, who had followed the whole episode. As for Loutherbourg, although his recent letters were obviously those of a madman, he recovered his senses as soon as anyone talked business to him. The promise that his accounts would be settled acted like a spell on this madman who had been foaming and reddening for a month. A lucid interval enabled Jacques Sarasin to conclude a judicious transaction in four days. As a result of some pecuniary sacrifice, which the negotiator willingly made out of his own pocket, it was the Grand Cophte who emerged as victor.

Returning to Basle on the 16th January, M. Sarasin was not a little satisfied with his conciliatory activities. Besides his daughter Suzette, whom he did not like to expose any further to the stormy atmosphere of Rocaille, he was now carrying off in his carriage the Count and Countess, who had been persuaded that a change of air would cheer them up.

During the new sojourn at the "White House," which was to be the last, Cagliostro held numerous séances at the Swiss Mother Lodge. Gertrude Sarasin, scarcely out of bed, insisted on discharging her duties as Acting Mistress. In one of these, the little Felix saw Loutherbourg distinctly, armed with a dagger : the painter was drawing from his pocket a two-chambered revolver, then, opening his vest, he showed, in the middle of his heart, a bloody gaping wound.

Gertrude could not bear the description, she fainted. When she was brought to, she murmured in a thin voice that it was nothing. But she had recognised in Loutherbourg a diabolical power which horrified her. The Grand Cophte reassured her paternally : so long as he was present, there was no risk at all.

Meanwhile, surrounded by the respectful devotion of the Lodge, the Count began to regret the Bienne compromise. Why had he not crushed his enemies ? The blame apparently fell on the maladroit Jacques Sarasin, who had carried the spirit of conciliation too far. The want of firmness annoyed Cagliostro as though it were want of love. . . . It was not long before Jacques Sarasin observed that the Master was being alienated from him.

At the same time, certain obvious inconsistencies distressed M. Sarasin. For example, he openly disapproved of the rehabilitation of the cook Agostino. What a picture had Cagliostro lately drawn of this rascal ! And here was Agostino come from Knightsbridge to rejoin his master, and the Count, who never ceased to regret his loss, had, to Jacques Sarasin's great scandal, installed him without any further reproaches in the kitchen. At Basle, neither he nor his brother would have re-employed an unfaithful workman.

The Count and the Countess returned on the 8th February to Rocaille, where, after so many jolts and disturbances, life resumed its peaceful course. Pilgrims came from all over Switzerland. Mme Herrman of Bienne agreed with Mme Bertrand and M. Bourgeois in singing Cagliostro's praises. The *avoyere* of Bienne, Mme Berseth, blessed him for curing her of a convulsive nausea. Mme de Champvent et Carard, as well as Mlle de Pourtales, summoned from Yverdon by Mme Vos de Nivelit, joined in similar expressions of gratitude. The fame of these cures soon spreading far, M. Haldimann hastened from Turin and, from Marseilles, Mme de Traytorrens, with her daughter who was afflicted with a club foot.

Sigismond Wildermett, delighted with this influx of visitors, wrote to Jacques Sarasin :

"I wish he would always engage in such occupations. It keeps him busy and distracts him. He is much better in every respect since they have all come here."

But Cagliostro was suffocated between the little lake and the high mountains. Seized by his eternal longing for change, he frequently spoke of going to Yverdon, to Lausanne, to Berne, or even to Italy, a country where, as he affirmed, he had never had any trouble. Recollecting the cheers with which he had been greeted the previous year, he was determined to go again on the 6th May, 1788, to the Helvetic Congress at Olten. Sigismond Wildermett sought to dissuade him, foreseeing that Mme von der Recke's recent accusations would have profoundly changed the temper of the assembly. Without even listening to his warnings, the Count got into the carriage, but as soon as he reached Olten he recognised his mistake. Distrust, contempt, anger, were visible on every face. Jacques Sarasin, disconcerted, was wondering how to neutralise such an unfortunate beginning. Cagliostro saved him the trouble. He returned the next day to Rocaille. But on account of this abortive excursion, he had for a long time a grudge against his unfortunate disciple. And when Jacques Sarasin complained about it to Sigismond Wildermett, the latter recalled to him the Eastern education which the Master had received :

" You and I, we can see very clearly what is the Count's misfortune. Be assured that his early education was not designed to fit him to live in Europe ; I can discern therein marked vestiges of oriental principles, so different from our own, above all in persons of high distinction, that that alone convinces me of the truth of his singular antecedents."

After this rude experience, Cagliostro kept quiet. He did not budge until the moment when the Countess expressed a wish to take the cure at Aix-les-Bains for a respiratory complaint she had developed by living close to the Lake of Bienne. On the 19th July, M. Sarasin went to take his leave. The travellers explained to him their plans. They would go with Mme Carard as far as Aix-les-Bains where they were to meet Mme de Traytorrens. Five days later, M. Sigismond Wildermett announced that the Grand Cophte and the Grand Mistress had left on the night of the 23rd and 24th July, 1788 :

" The Count left Rockhalt at six in the evening and came to spend the evening and sup with me. Until about eleven o'clock we were able to keep up our gaiety quite well. From that moment, the Count and Countess and all of us, felt the pain of separation, after having known each other intimately. It was a touching scene when they got into their carriage at about twelve-thirty. I never thought the Count was susceptible to emotion. He could scarcely tear himself away from my arms, and though we were at the door, he did not stop saying to us : ' My friends, do not forget me. You are in my heart, and I shall be with you everywhere.' He was accompanied by Mme Carard, whose carriage was occupied by Augustino and her chamber maid. . . . When left to the guidance of his own heart, we may see in the Count a man of extreme kindness and sensibility. It is that aspect which has most powerfully drawn me to him. I shall always remember him as a man unique in our century for his gifts, his generosity, his weaknesses and by his triumphs, as well as for his misfortunes."

Cagliostro wrote to no one from Aix-les-Bains. But it was known that from there he had gone towards Turin. A Sardinian officer, the young M. de Vos Nivelit, a son of one of his most enthusiastic patients, was surprised to see him pass through Alessandria, where he was stationed. In that same town, Major Burcher had spoken to the Count for a moment, while some repairs were being made to his coach. The thaumaturge talked of pushing on as far as

Venice, if he should find the welcome at Turin not sufficiently cordial.

. . . .

Subsequently, fresh details were received through Mme Carard about the sojourn she had made at Aix-les-Bains with the Count and the Countess. In forwarding them to Jacques Sarasin, Sigismond Wildermett expressed his foreboding as to the dangers to which the Master exposed himself by the eccentricities of his character :

" If his knowledge and good heart had not outweighed his difficult temperament, I do not believe that you or I would have borne with him for long. As he is not able to adjust himself to the proprieties, to the prevailing tone of our small but impérious Europe, as he is not even able to be intimately known save by a handful, while he offends the majority of people, I fear, my dear friend, that all this may end badly."

. . . .

The news about Turin was correct. On the 23rd August, M. de Lalande had sent to M. de Montmorin the following despatch :

" The King of Sardinia is giving a proof of his regard for His Majesty by issuing an order to Cagliostro to leave his territories within twenty-four hours. He has been engaged to come to Turin to practise medicine there. But since the King of Sardinia was informed of his arrival, he has indicated to him through an officer of the government that he may not remain within his territories. And as I have conclusive evidence that His Sardinian Majesty has been principally guided in this by what has happened in Paris, I have requested the first officer of foreign affairs, who is attached to the King during the indisposition of the minister, to convey His Majesty's gratitude to the King of Sardinia, in the conviction that my action will not be repudiated."

In his reply of the 23rd September, 1788, the Minister of Foreign Affairs stated that the King was very deeply touched by the decision of his brother-in-law, Victor Amedée III :

" We have been enabled, sir, to gather together documents relative to Cagliostro, and they have furnished us proof that since his early youth he has led a criminal life ; that he knows no medicine save what he learned during some months when he was a monk, and that, wherever he has gone, he has lived by the basest and the most culpable methods. The King has learnt with appreciation that His Sardinian Majesty has determined to forbid his dominions to this swindler, after his behaviour in France, and you have done well to announce in advance that His Majesty will regard this as a new mark of the friendship of His Sardinian Majesty. But you can assure him that wherever Cagliostro has been tolerated, there has been cause to regret it."

Thus the terrible scandal of the necklace pursued the thaumaturge from town to town, long after the Parlement had acquitted him of every charge. From Alessandria, the Master first went to Genoa. But the Freemasons of this city seeming to him unworthy of the benefits of his Rite, he departed after a few days for Verona. According to his original intention, it might be thought that he would go to Venice. But perhaps he was afraid of being confused there with the Marquis Pellegrini, of questionable repute. To avoid complications, he went North, although prudence warned him against approaching territories ruled by Marie Antoinette's own brother, the Emperor Joseph II. Nevertheless he determined to risk it. It was thus that Clementino Vannetti saw him arrive at Rovereto on the evening of the 24th September, 1788. . . .

XI

ALL ROADS LEAD TO ROME

THE conviction to which Vannetti was led, after a minute comparison of all the evidence relative to Giuseppe Balsamo and the Marquis Pellegrini, to the orphan Acharat and the Count Alexander de Cagliostro, would have developed into certitude if he had known the movements two years earlier, at Palermo, of the great German writer whom he had been unable to meet at Rovereto.

Goethe, after a short stay in Rome and Naples, had sailed for Sicily, where the campaign conducted by the *Courrier de l'Europe* against the Count de Cagliostro was naturally arousing exceptional interest.

Was not indeed the thaumaturge suspected of being a native of Palermo? the artist Giuseppe Balsamo? The controversy was raging when Goethe arrived in Sicily. A fluent lawyer assured him at dinner, volubly and confidently, that in the opinion of the Sicilians, the identity of Balsamo and Cagliostro was unquestionable. The relatives of Balsamo-Pellegrini-Acharat-Cagliostro were actually living in Palermo. And the speaker himself had once had occasion to visit them on behalf of the French Government. He had since then been on excellent terms with the magician's mother and his sister Maria Anna, the widow of Giovanni Battista Capitummino.

Goethe listened to him eagerly. How ardently had he explored, in his early youth, these kingdoms of the spiritual world, alchemy and the cabala, divination and magic! Later, he had had personal experience. Jacques Sarasin, Sophie de la Roche, Mme de Branconi, his own brother-in-law, Johann George Schlosser, had each tried to make him share their admiration for Cagliostro.

The case of the Queen's necklace and the attacks of the *Courrier de l'Europe* had a singular fascination for him. Mme von der Recke's first diatribe which appeared in the *Berlinische Monatschrift*, had impressed him strongly; likewise the reply published by his brother-in-law Schlosser in the *Deutsches Museum*. That was why, after a number of questions, Goethe begged the Sicilian lawyer to introduce him to Balsamo's mother and sister.

It was not a very discreet request. One of the two daughters of Maria Anna Capitummino was in the convent of Santa Caterina;

but the other, of marriageable age, was living at home. A foreign gentleman's visit to these poor women might have given rise, considering the state of local opinion on these matters, to very unpleasant rumours. So, for fear of alarming them, Goethe disguised himself as a Mr. Wilton, an English gentleman with a message from Giuseppe Balsamo.

This poor family lived in a lane turning off from Palermo. On the 13th April, 1787, mounting a squalid staircase, Goethe and his companion reached a big room with but a single window in it. It had a high ceiling, and the walls had once been painted. It was so well kept that it looked quite pleasant. Against the wall were two beds without testers or curtains. No furniture of importance save a wooden wardrobe, some cane chairs of which the gilt was peeling off, and some holy images in black. It was here that they greeted Balsamo's mother, an old woman with a vigorous and noble countenance.

Leaving her saucepans, Maria Anna Capitummino put on a hair-net and a clean apron. Her young son and daughter, whose features were disfigured by small-pox, clung to her skirts and attentively listened to the conversation, of which the best part fell to their mother.

Mr. Wilton pretended that he had met Giuseppe in London. He and his wife were in good health, lacked nothing, and were only too happy to have escaped from the Bastille. Goethe's interlocutors listened to him gratefully, for they had never expected such an affectionate message : so often had they heard that the Count de Cagliostro was ashamed of his relatives ! They begged Mr. Wilton to return the next day to take back a letter for Giuseppe.

When he called again the next day, the old lady said :

" Tell my son how glad I am to have good news of him. Tell him that I clasp him to my breast," she opened and closed her arms in a gesture. " Every day I pray God and the Holy Virgin for his safety. I send him my blessing, him and his wife, and I have but one desire : to see him again, before closing these eyes which have shed so many tears for him."

The charm and modulation of the Italian tongue gave to these words an unforgettable accent. And the vivacity of her gestures emphasised her meaning. Goethe was deeply moved when he said good-bye. He shook hands, and as he went down the stairs, the two young Capitumminos, the nephew and the niece respectively of the thaumaturge, rushed to the kitchen balcony and cried out to him, as they waved farewell, to come back without fail.

As Maria Anna Capitummino confided to him that Giuseppe, after his last visit to Palermo, in 1775, had had to go away in a hurry, without returning to her the fourteen ounces of gold she had paid, in accordance with his wish, to the pawnbroker, Mr. Wilton had an impulse to offer her the money. But returning to the inn, and examining his funds, he found that they had run low. He had yet to visit the interior of the island, where communications were slow and uncertain ; so he decided, on reflection, not to give away any money just then. But at the end of the year, the Balsamo family received a subvention to which both the ducal houses of Weimar and Gotha had contributed. The English merchant who, in pursuance of imaginary instructions from Cagliostro, had paid the amount into the proper hands, conveyed to Goethe the touching messages of gratitude that these good folk addressed to Giuseppe on Christmas Day, 1788.

What a revelation it would have been for Clementino Vannetti if he had cast eyes on the pages dated the 13th and 14th April, 1787, in Goethe's diary ! But these travel notes were not published until later, when the curtain had fallen on the tragedy of the last act. And Vannetti, reading them, was surprised at the method which the great poet had employed in introducing himself to the Balsamo family. Were not these oblique manœuvres more suited to Balsamo ?

Besides Goethe's diary, there was another document which might have confirmed Vannetti's conclusions : a letter written from Rome on the 6th June, 1787, by the copper founder Feliciani to his daughter, then at Bienne.

He said that the whole household of the vicolo delle Cripte were relieved to get her last letter. For they had been greatly distressed to read in the papers that she had been deserted in London, and that her husband had taken to his heels. They could then do nothing but throw themselves at the feet of the most holy Madonna del Carmine. . . .

Thanking her for a bill of exchange for twenty-five pounds which she had sent them, he invoked on her the blessings of Heaven :

" Your mother sends you her solemn blessing and desires nothing more than to see you again soon. As for me, I am, by God's grace, in fair health.

As for your husband, I foresaw but too clearly what you are now telling me. I advise you, as a devoted father, to return straight to us, if you can, for our house is always open to you. You know, *carissima figlia mia,* the soul is immortal and the world is as nothing. I have already taken the necessary assurances from the authorities, so that when you come here, you will be sheltered and defended. If your husband does anything violent, if, for example, he prevents you from fulfilling the commandments of our Catholic faith, he will be punished for it. . . ."

Feliciani requested her to put the date on her letters, as well as the name of the place where she was, and commended her fearfully not only to our Lord but to the most holy Madonna del Carmine.

And the brother whom Lorenza had formerly so lightly abandoned in a Cadiz jail, Francesco Feliciani, added some fond words of his own to his father's letter. His health, which had long been uncertain, was improving :

" *Carissima sorella*, I send you a heartfelt and tender kiss. You are constantly present in my thoughts, and I ask nothing else of God than to see you again some day. Every one of us prays to the Most High to extend his protection over you."

So that was why Serafina had learnt, while in the Bastille, to write ! Certainly, if they had had any suspicion of this secret correspondence, if they had had an inkling of the shameful plots which Serafina was hatching with her parents, the members of the Egyptian Rite would have thought it still more rash of the Grand Cophte to carry out the astonishing project upon which he seemed to have set his heart.

. . . .

Hardly six leagues separated Trente from Rovereto. Vannetti soon heard how the hero of his *Liber Memorialis* had been welcomed in the neighbouring city. Giuseppe Innocente Festi, a member of the Aulic council, had introduced him to the Prince-Bishop, Pierre Vigil Thun. And at once, the Grand Cophte, in a last flicker of fortune, regained in the valley of the Adige the prestige which he had formerly enjoyed on the banks of the high Rhine. A great Austrian nobleman, the Prince-Bishop of Trente, condescended to take the place of a great French nobleman, the Prince-Bishop of Strasbourg.

At Trente, the Count and the Countess rented a fine apartment for forty florins a month. Their landlord, Franceso Trentini, was a rich merchant who was hoping to recover from an attack of apoplexy by the incomparable skill of his tenant.

A young physician of Trente, named Bacca, fresh from his studies in France, served as Cagliostro's assistant. The pharmacist Bommer agreed to make up his prescriptions without keeping a copy of them. One was assured that the councillor Lodovico, an old man of sixty-seven and a notability, was already feeling much improved by the treatment he had undergone. Besides, Cagliostro's patients and supporters were of a rank or fortune calculated to impress the public.

What influenced this town more strongly than anything else was that the Count, charlatan or not, seemed to be a rich man. Cagliostro lived like a lord. He changed his linen every day, paying ten soldi for each shirt washed. He had his food fetched from the *osteria dell'Europa* for four florins a day. And the jewels and ornaments of the Countess struck the simple townsfolk with wonder.

Like Louis de Rohan at the house in the rue Saint Claude, the Prince-Bishop loved to come round familiarly in the evening to the casa Trentini. There was such a close intimacy between them that the Master once offered to introduce a gentleman passing through the town to Pierre Vigil Thun, whose visit he said he was expecting. The stranger pointed apologetically to his travel-stained clothes, and instead of a supper, it was arranged to have a small dinner. Then the stranger presented two Saxon gentlemen to the prophet, Count Witzthum and Count Bunau, who were staying with him at the *dell'Europa*. Knowing that the great man also sent for his meals to this hostelry, they asked to be allowed for once to pay for his dinner. Cagliostro accepted their invitation, and they sat down to an excellent repast. Before the roast-partridge was served, the young men listened with much curiosity to the stories and explanations of the thaumaturge.

But in the course of his talk Cagliostro committed some bad mistakes. The gentleman to whom he particularly addressed his remarks, had visited the *Sagesse Triomphante* at Lyons, and Cagliostro openly showed his pride while listening to his description of the beautiful marble rotunda in the middle of which stood his own bust. After dinner, the *casa* was invaded by a crowd of blind men and others suffering from fever, in examining whom the Count showed himself to be a quack, prescribing to all alike a certain drug of his own preparation which he offered to supply them gratis for fourteen days. This uniform treatment seemed absurd to the visitors. And when saying good-bye, Cagliostro greatly astonished them by disclosing his intention of going to Rome.

Three days later, the *Postiglione* referred to the thaumaturge :

"The Lord Count Alexander de Cagliostro, who continues to devote himself to the sick people of this town, has cured with his free medicines the wife of Giuliano Emanueli, an apothecary of Pery, who was suffering from a cancerous ulcer in her right breast that the physicians and surgeons had declared to be incurable. He has also relieved Bartolomew, the son of Baldasare Felin, of a *spine ventosa*. We confine ourselves to mentioning these two surprising cures, of which we have had authentic proofs."

But at Trente, as elsewhere, the inherent fatalities of his churlish and impetuous nature pursued Cagliostro. When the tailor Mundig brought him a suit he had ordered for his servant, and presented his bill, Cagliostro, who considered the price exorbitant, foamed with rage and threatened to beat him to death. The tradesman hauled him up before the *podesta*. And breathing fire and smoke, the magician declared that the rascal would not address him as Count. He appealed to the Chancellor Centilotti ; but the latter replied coldly that justice would be done to him whenever he should submit proofs of his allegations.

The physician Bacca and the pharmacist Bommer were soon repelled by his violence. The woman whose cure the *Postiglione* had trumpeted abroad, was stupid enough to die. And the passing away of old Lodovico Lutti also discredited the magician. When the accusations increased, the Councillor Barbaroni thought it his duty to carry them even to the gilded chambers of the Castello del Buono Consiglio : he warned the Prince-Bishop against the intrigues of the charlatan.

It was not solely for his supernatural powers that the Prince-Bishop had sought out the thaumaturge. True, Pierre Vigil Thun shared the reverence which most of his courtiers felt for him, and it is to one of their oral consultations that the following note must be attributed :

"To the Count Giuseppe Innocente de Festi, Councillor of the Aulic Council of the Prince-Bishop of Trente.

Most illustrious Lord Councillor.

Here is the oracle of Delphos. Here his reply. I commend it to your sober reflection, and remain invariably, with all possible regard, your very humble and devoted,

Alessando (*sic*) Cagliostro.

Trente, the 16th February, 1789."

But Pierre Vigil's hope was really to reconcile the founder of the Egyptian Rite with the Catholic Church. Diverse hints encouraged him in the effort. Since Serafina had prostrated herself at San Mareo in Rovereto, the Count himself seemed to be on the verge of repentance.

Alone with Father Gianbattista Ghezzi, the vicar of Santa Maddalena, Cagliostro questioned him endlessly about the teachings of the Catholic Church, of which he seemed to be very ignorant. He showed great surprise when he was told that Freemasonry was not a divine creation, as he had imagined, but the work of the devil. The theologian gave an account of all the steps taken by the clergy to stamp out this plague. In 1789, Giuseppe Firrao, a Cardinal of the Holy Roman Church, had prohibited Catholics from belonging to Masonic societies under pain of death without absolution, and confiscation of goods. Every landlord who allowed a masonic gathering to be held in his house was liable to have it demolished. From the throne of Saint Peter, two pontiffs had successively condemned the sons of Hiram : Clement XII, in 1738, by the bull *In Eminenti*, and Benedict XIV, in 1751, by the bull *Providas Romanorum Pontificum.*

All this was a revelation to Cagliostro. He prolonged these meetings in the sacristy of Santa Maddalena. Finally, with sighs and tears, he put into Father Ghezzi's hands a complete abjuration of all his errors.

What a triumph it was for the guide who had led him, step by step, up to this solemn act ! And what a satisfaction for the Prince-Bishop who had encouraged their conversations ! But the critics refused to be silenced. They alleged that, on returning home, Cagliostro had told his wife, with cynical delight :

"Ah! I have utterly bamboozled the priest!"

In their view, the penitent had not mended his ways, not truly washed his heart in the blood of the Lamb. He corresponded in the same style and on the same subjects as before with all his disciples. If he discontinued the practice of his masonic ritual, it was only to keep up appearances. Secretly, he conferred with every Freemason who passed through the town, and had even ordered two screens for the use of the "pupils." So said merciless critics, but when injustice became as flagrant as this, Pierre Vigil, in annoyance, imposed silence on them.

The assurance of the prelate's support gave confidence even to Cagliostro. The Grand Cophte enthusiastically recurred to the project of union which had so attracted the Archbishop of Bourges and the Cardinal de Rohan. His Egyptian Rite, he declared, which was very different from profane Freemasonry, sought to supplant the High and the Strict Observances, as the first was given over to absurdly trivial practices, and the second was bitterly hostile to kings and priests. Let the Holy See but deign to recognise his Order, and confer the investiture on him, and the Grand Cophte would immediately become the foremost champion of Catholicism.

The Prince-Bishop thought it his duty to help the repentant sinner, and make his ways smooth. Assuredly, all roads lead to Rome; nevertheless, as the traveller was to pass by Bologna, the Prince-Bishop spared himself no pains. On the 7th March, 1789, he asked of his old classmate, the Cardinal Archetti, legate of Bologna, a safe conduct for the Count de Cagliostro. How indignant he was, when, instead of the favourable reply he expected, he was told that the newspapers of Bologna had published his appeal with deprecatory comments!

Pierre Vigil at once turned to Rome. His diplomatic agent at the Holy See, Filipo Orengo, was instructed to explain the position to the Cardinal Secretary of State, Boncompagni Ludovisi. Orengo conveyed to his Eminence a letter written by the Prince-Bishop himself, in which he zealously pleaded the cause of his protégés. He appealed first of all on behalf of the Countess de Cagliostro, who was a Roman by birth. This poor woman, virtuous, prudent and God-fearing, was torn between her desire to return to her native town, to her old father, and the fear that should the Papal authorities forbid him access to the territories of the Church, in spite of the many proofs he had given of contrition, her husband, with his violent temper, might relapse into his old disorderly ways. The eternal enemies of the faith, who were enraged by his abjuration, exerted themselves more than ever to divert him from the right path. Should the Church reject a soul which had wandered so far and yet was turning back to her?

The Cardinal Secretary of State's reply was as follows:

" *Illustrissimo e Pregiatissimo Signore.*

There being no charge against the seigneur Cagliostro in the papal state, he has no need of the safe conduct for which he has applied through your honourable mediation. I said as much to seigneur Orengo, when he brought me your letter. Taking this opportunity to confirm to you the assurance of my devotion, and always full of the most distinguished consideration, I take the liberty to kiss your hands.

Ignazio Boncompagni Ludovisi.

Rome, 4th April, 1789."

Without making any commitments for the future, this letter seemed, at any rate, to offer guarantees for what had passed. Not an integral and explicit amnesty surely, but a sort of safe conduct. And if the Count de Cagliostro feared that he might be confronted with Giuseppe Balsamo, he might be relieved to know that the Papal ministers had nothing against him, and that he could enter the Papal States as freely as any other traveller.

Another letter from Rome completely reassured Cagliostro. Serafina showed him on the 25th April, 1789, a letter she had received saying that no charges had been framed against Cagliostro in the Roman Courts. None of the earlier accusations were to be revived. The Cardinal Orsini, who might possibly have complained of the misuse that had been made of his name at Loretto, was dead. And who was putting this suggestion before Cagliostro? The man who had formerly denounced his son-in-law Balsamo to the Papal authorities, the father of Lorenza or Serafina—the copper-founder Feliciani.

Besides, an ever-present, ever-active influence, stronger than reason or memory, led Cagliostro irresistibly towards danger. The Countess did not like Trente. No doubt, the town was situated on the banks of a river, and the Alps formed a magnificent amphitheatre round it. Its dignified grey buildings looked picturesque with the lively, heraldic paintings on their walls. But the *tramontane* had blown all winter. Many mulberry trees had been destroyed. The Adige was frozen. Such severe cold had not been known for twenty-four years. Finally, the numerous *vicoli*, the narrow and vaulted passages which led from one street to the other, recalled to Serafina the vicolo delle Cripte, of happy memory, where her parents lived.

Since their return to Italy, in fact, she was thinking of nothing but her native town. Everywhere else she was uneasy and discontented. She demonstrated to her husband that he would get nowhere if he did not receive the Papal authorisation. If he missed this last chance, their fate would be to die somewhere in obscurity, worn out, disappointed, miserable, and in disgrace. Tears and sobs would overcome her and cut short her words. . . . At the same time, she secretly spoke to some of Pierre Vigil Thun's courtiers, who were friends of Cagliostro. Upon their advice, Cagliostro made up his mind. He would risk all in a final gamble. He began to collect letters of introduction to eminent personages in Rome.

Where else could he seek refuge ? He had no choice. The governments of Europe had shown him so little consideration that, if Rome too rejected him, he could take shelter nowhere but with the heretics or the Turks. True, Switzerland remained open, and Gertrude Sarasin affectionately pleaded for his return. She had sent New Year greetings from the " White House " on the 23rd December.

Jacques Sarasin, too, after long and painful hesitation, had sent the Grand Cophte a letter upon which he had been meditating for months, and of which the opening phrases had occurred to him at Riehen, during a visit to the Chinese kiosk :

" Well beloved father and venerated Master.

My heart bleeds to see myself so sorely misunderstood. Self-interest has never been my weakness, and never will be. Ah ! if only it had been, how much less would I have suffered on several occasions ! But ceaseless suffering seems to be my lot on earth.

Without the smallest fear, I can swear before the tribunal of God —*il Grande Iddio*—that my motives have always been loyal and sincere, and that if I have sinned latterly, it has never been with deliberate intent.

What can I add to this which will not be futile ? It is open to you, should you wish it, to read my inmost thoughts. Far from fearing that inspection, I invite it with all my heart.

Meanwhile, I try faithfully to follow the pure and spiritual doctrine by which I should be guided, not without hope that one day providence would accord me the privilege of a reconciliation with you.

I prostrate myself, with my dear wife, and all our brethren, at your feet. In commending myself once again to your kindness and fatherly solicitude, I remain, with veneration and love beyond question,

Your very humble son and servant,

Jacques Sarasin."

But the Grand Cophte had unpleasant recollections of the quarrels at Bienne. He was not at all anxious to go to Riehen and undertake the regeneration of the Sarasin couple. Receiving no reply from him, Jacques and Gertrude instructed one of their Bergamo agents, M. Hans Caspar Steiner, to call on him at Trente.

The Count welcomed the emissary graciously. Only, as the Master was then recollecting himself in view of the impending abjuration of his errors, M. Steiner, surprised at finding him alone, wrote to the " White House " that their benefactor was living incognito at Trente.

To Pierre Vigil Thun's surprise, a letter arrived soon after from the Emperor Joseph II, harshly upbraiding him for having given shelter to, and in a manner adopted, one of the most dangerous agitators in the whole of Europe. He must get rid of him. . . .

But the Prince-Bishop did not wish to abandon his friend, his protégé, his acolyte, before providing him with letters of recommendation to the Cardinals Boncompagni, Zelada, Colonna and Albani in Rome. In exchange, he was given a superb crystal cruet stand, worth at least fifty sequins and originally intended, so Cagliostro said, for George III. All the supporters and disciples of the Master were invited before his departure to a great feast, and magnificently entertained. But when he set out once more, on the 17th May, 1789, these extravagances had somewhat impaired his fortune. At Vicenza, he had to pawn a diamond ; he received more than seven thousand lire for it.

. . . .

On the way to Rome, Cagliostro was chiefly concerned about the attitude which the French Ambassador might adopt towards him. The persecutions he had endured in London, the perpetual surveillance of which he knew he was the victim, the measures of expulsion taken against him by the different governments in their anxiety to please the King of France, justified but too well his lively apprehensions.

True, the Cardinal de Bernis by himself could make Rome too hot for Cagliostro. His Eminence had all the necessary influence. Accredited for nearly forty years to the Holy See, he enjoyed a prestige superior to that of every other diplomat. Whatever might be the storms in France—and already the noise of the first thunder-claps had rolled across the mountains—nothing in Rome could shake the personal position of the Ambassador, as he himself wrote proudly to his chief, M. de Montmorin :

" A steadfast policy, free accessibility, amiability in intercourse, and firmness and dignity where necessary, prevent me from being reduced to an inferior rôle even in times of trouble and anarchy. I am always the second person in Rome."

But His Eminence gave so much attention to the news from Versailles and from Paris that he seemed uninterested in Cagliostro's arrival. Of what significance could it be for the King's cause, in such a grave emergency, that this adventurer had arrived on the 27th May, 1789, at the *Scalinata*, a popular hotel in the place d'Espagne, efficiently managed by one Pietro Mora ? But the other heads of embassies did not share this indifference. The Venetian Ambassador hastened to inform the Council of Ten about it, adding that Cagliostro's first visitors had come away disillusioned :

" Those who have seen him are surprised that he should have been able to cut such a figure in Paris and engross so much European attention. With unprepossessing features and an entire absence of charm or learning, there is nothing about him to justify his brilliant reputation."

In fact, the Roman nobility seemed but mildly interested.

The Princess Lambertini welcomed him warmly, and even invited him occasionally to dinner, but it was only because her illness disposed her favourably towards Cagliostro. Having heard this Æsculapius extolled highly, she put considerable faith in his pills and powders. Only the Marquis and the Marquise Vivaldi went into ecstasies over him with an ardour similar to that of certain French noblemen. Daily they saw him, or exchanged friendly notes. One day, when the Marquise Vivaldi happened to want a chambermaid, Serafina gladly let her have her own.

But generally speaking, the mystagogue's only friends in Rome were the noblemen who belonged to the Masonic Order. The Marquis Vivaldi was one of them. In the studio, where the young French painter Augustine Louis Belle secretly held meetings of the Lodge, *les Amis Sinceres*, the Marquis used to meet his friends, the Princes de Teora, de San Severo and de San Demetrio Pignatelli, as well as foreigners of rank. But in what esteem could these disciples hold Cagliostro, a rebel whom the majority of Freemasons looked upon as an apostate ? But *les Amis Sinceres*, harassed by the police, had not of late been in close touch with the Lodges in France and England.

On the other hand, why did the Master, who had so bitterly slandered ordinary Freemasons, deign to return to them at Rome, at the very moment when he needed the favour of ecclesiastical authorities to obtain recognition of his Rite ? Since his conversations with Father Ghezzi, he could not plead ignorance of the terrible penalties imposed by Cardinal Firrao's edict and the bulls of Clement XII and Benedict XIV. Should he not rather try to gain the confidence and goodwill of the cardinals to whom he had been so warmly recommended by the Prince-Bishop of Trente ?

At the *Scalinata*, the Grand Cophte made the acquaintance of a dignitary of the Order to which he was bound by the fondest ties, the memory of the Grand Master Pinto and the Chevalier d'Aquino. De Loras, though he wore the cross of Malta, was really a Freemason. Active, resourceful, brilliantly intelligent, but without discretion, and ruled by an insatiable ambition, he was moving heaven and earth to secure the post of ambassador of the Maltese Order in Rome. As he had very powerful supporters, it was thought that his success was probable. But all his efforts were thwarted by the Pontiff's personal bias. Pius VI was firmly opposed to his appointment. The Cardinal de Bernis liked the man and often invited him to dinner. Nevertheless, seeing that nothing could prevail against the Pope's opposition, he was careful not to commit himself to support his claims beyond a certain point. What could be the reason for the Pope's attitude ? Did he disapprove of the candidate's

Masonic connections? Whatever it may be, the Cardinal de Bernis informed M. de Montmorin that the Pope would never give way.

But the proud candidate, unable to reflect calmly and admit his shortcomings, cast about for some explanation of his disgrace. He told himself that his rival, the Prince Camille de Rohan, had the advantage of a great name. It was therefore necessary to get him out of the running. And he considered it a bright idea to secure his withdrawal by bringing pressure to bear on his uncle the Cardinal de Rohan. No sooner had the Grand Cophte arrived in Rome than he was overwhelmed with attention and flattery, and de Loras, with expressions of the most fervent devotion, begged to be admitted into the Egyptian Rite.

Cagliostro still had followers in the Order of Malta, including Commander de Maisonneuve and the lawyer Brest. But de Loras was to introduce to him a proselyte of quite a different type.

Father François Joseph, a Capuchin monk of the convent of the Marais in Paris, had been known, before he took orders, as Hyacinthe Antoine Roulier. He was a native of Saint Maurice, in Switzerland. He had got on very well in France, where he taught philosophy and theology with distinction, and was considered to be an excellent preacher by his superiors. Six years before, he had been promised the bishopric of Sion, in the Valais, or rather, a bishopric *in partibus*. As the promise still remained unredeemed, he had come to Rome towards the end of 1788 in the hope of obtaining its fulfilment. He had met with nothing but rebuffs. His enemies had poisoned the Holy Father's mind against him. Embittered, but resolved to obtain, if only by intrigue, the mitre of which he considered himself so worthy, he began to consort with the Freemasons. Could not Cagliostro, who had such extensive and mysteriously varied connections, and special influence on the Cardinal de Rohan, be of use to him? From the time the Grand Cophte had been imprisoned in the Bastille, Father Joseph had taken an interest in this extraordinary man. Having then tried to discover his origin and his destiny by means of the cabala, he had, after more than thirty hours of research, found this prophetic formula:

"*Cognosces cum Romae!* You will know him in Rome!"

And now in 1789, at the age of thirty-three, the monk was seeing the prediction fulfilled.

Their interests and tastes being similar, the new recruit greatly pleased Cagliostro. And as he required, wherever he was, a secretary to look after his correspondence and manage his affairs, he gladly accepted the monk's offer to act in that capacity. From the moment Father Joseph took up these duties the Grand Cophte's activities recovered all their former scope and vitality. As the weeks and the months passed without ever the police trying to meddle with him, his prudence was gradually relaxed. His language became bolder. He contemplated the formation of an Egyptian Lodge, and possibly even a women's branch, as in Paris and at the Hague. But in whose house were the meetings to be held? Cagliostro was genuinely fond of the Marquise Vivaldi, but that lady could not keep a silent tongue in her head. So he said to her with a sigh:

" *Che peccato che non siate segreta!* What a pity you are not discreet! You might be our goddess!"

Had he then trusted his other great admirer? One day, meeting Commander de Maisonneuve, the Marquise Vivaldi asked him in a whisper if the women's Lodge had been able to meet at the Princess Lambertini's. In an equally confidential tone, she was told that a sufficient number of applications had not yet been received, as the entrance fee was fifty scudi, a sum which alarmed many would-be candidates, Roman women not possessing too much money.

All the same, Cagliostro was too afraid of the Holy Office to venture to attend, on the anniversary of the nativity of Saint John the Baptist, the solemn gathering of *les Amis Sinceres*. In spite of the insistence of the monk and de Loras, he firmly declined to associate himself with their Masonic celebrations. It was as a great and exceptional favour that he accepted the invitation, four months later, to dine with the Marquis Vivaldi, and eighteen French initiates, at a club in the country.

No doubt, within a small coterie, the Grand Cophte was accorded the same veneration as at Strasbourg and Paris. But these tributes had no cash value. Though the Romans were curious about him personally, they would not pay money to hear him. In consequence, financial difficulties. A few more jewels had to go the same way as the diamond pawned in Vicenza. For reasons of economy, the Count was obliged, in August, to move regretfully out of the *Scalinata*, and leave his good friends Pietro and Francesca Mora, and their two sons. His position was such that he had no alternative but to migrate to the *casa* Conti, adjoining the place Farnese.

His new landlords, petty tradesmen with a narrow outlook, had no doubt but that the Count was doing them an honour by choosing to live with them. The first thing he did was to remove the holy images which adorned the bedroom walls. And Signor Conti, who was a churchwarden of San Girolamo della Carita, was horrified at this, and confided his indignation to his wife and daughter. What was more serious, he told all about it to the Feliciani, who lived almost next door. For if the Count had left the place d'Espagne from motives of economy, the Countess had chosen the place Farnese in order to be nearer to her family.

Nothing is known definitely of the relations which existed at the time between the Grand Cophte and Serafina's family. But if Giuseppe Balsamo had found them unbearable, twenty years before, the Count de Cagliostro was not likely to adapt himself to them after his brilliant career in courts and country houses. Giuseppe and Pasqua Feliciani were exactly what they had always been. Their special devotion to the holy Madonna del Carmine absorbed them more and more. Age had not only rendered them stupid but emphasised their ugliness. And it may be that they hated the Count de Cagliostro more bitterly even than Jacques Balsamo, for they knew who were responsible for the fact that their beloved Francesco had spent three years in a Spanish jail and returned home in broken health. If this were not a premeditated and cold-blooded vendetta, if it were necessary to seek an excuse for treachery, one might, no doubt, ascribe to the instigation of the parents the crime that was about to be committed. But for too long had the Countess been giving proofs of her capacity for mischief.

Now that she was in Rome, and under Papal jurisdiction, her demeanour changed almost instantly. The contrition she had shown at Basle and Rocaille, the blind submission of Aix-en-Savoie, of Rovereto and Trente, gave place to defiance. There had been terrible rows at the *Scalinata*. Enrichetta Rey, a servant in the inn, subsequently affirmed under oath that the Countess had asked her to smear the steps of the main staircase freely with soap. Though not fifty yet, the Count was very fat. He was agile and supple too, no doubt, but his corpulence inevitably incommoded him. A false step, a slip, and the magician would drop headlong into Hell, straight like a stone, and Serafina, shedding just enough tears to allay suspicion, would find herself free at last.

At the *casa* Conti, she ostentatiously resumed the petty observances of the Feliciani, the thousand small superstitions of the lower classes in Rome. It was necessary to irritate Cagliostro, provoke rash words from him, blasphemous words, in the presence of people who could be relied upon subsequently to bear witness against him. She urged not only her new chambermaid Francesca Mazzoni, but the hairdresser Gaetano Bossi also to take good note of the abuse flung at her one day by Cagliostro. Adjoining their bedroom was a private chapel, and according to the terms of their lease, the connecting door was always to be kept shut. That door was open, and Cagliostro angrily addressed his wife :

" What ! You have again gone in there to pray ? "

He had banged the door to, and violently scolded her in French. His severity might easily be represented as irreligion.

At the hours when Cagliostro usually returned home, the Countess would pretend to hide away, with a sigh, the religious books which, like the illiterate woman she was, she could only read word by word.

She alleged that her husband had forbidden her to read them.

At length, on the 26th September, 1789, the Holy Office was informed that the Countess of Cagliostro asked to make certain confessions indispensable to the peace of her conscience. The rule of the sacred tribunal being to avoid haste, often dangerous in such cases, it was not until the 11th November that the priest of Santa

Caterina della Ruota, dom Giuseppe Tosi, was ordered to take down Serafina's deposition.

To discharge this duty, he had to do without notaries, and carefully chose a suitable time and place, for the plaintiff had made it clear that if her husband came to know of it, there might be terrible consequences.

All these precautions were in vain. A good friend of the Master, Giuseppe Ferretti, got wind of the conspiracy, and gave the alarm. From then on, the treacherous woman was virtually kept a prisoner. Her movements were spied upon, her actions controlled. As an additional precaution, Cagliostro charged Father Joseph, whom he believed to be a devoted and incorruptible friend, to watch personally over his wife, and the monk agreed.

And in the meantime, convinced that the fresh revolt had been provoked by Serafina's misgivings about the future, and her fear of relapsing into utter penury, Cagliostro taxed his wits to find some way of making money.

He thought he would recruit disciples. Most of the Masonic lodges, in fact, were supported by fees and subscriptions. And the fifty scudi which Cagliostro demanded for a certificate of membership was not a negligible amount.

At two o'clock one Sunday morning, Cagliostro came into his bedroom with the architect Carlo Antonini and the lawyer Matteo Berardi. Both of them fell on their knees, put up their right hands and solemnly swore not to divulge anything they might see or hear. Urged by necessity, or an unconquerable passion for propaganda, the Master boldly invited his disciples to his room and explained to them the aims and organization of his Rite. Among these privileged persons were de Loras, the Marquis Vivaldi, a great Russian nobleman, the artist Belle and Father Joseph, the monk in whom the Master had absolute confidence. It is also said that the hierophant condescended to lend, as a special favour, the French manuscript of the Ritual of Egyptian Masonry, to the Princess Lambertini.

But the watchfulness of the Holy See prevented any effective preaching. No doubt, events in France were following the course predicted by the Grand Cophte. The States General was sitting at Versailles. There were no more *lettres de cachet*. It would not be long before the Bastille, taken by assault by the Parisian crowds, was turned into a public promenade. The Count's and the Countess's jailor, the Marquis de Launay, had been killed by the mob. These astonishing events fully justified Cagliostro. But of what use was his clairvoyance in Rome? It was not there, in the Eternal City, where the first shock of the French revolution had provoked grief and anger, that he could have exploited the extraordinary insight he had shown.

The Pope was watching with horror the spectacle presented by the eldest daughter of the Church. A fierce storm was ravaging that fair garden of lilies. Not only did he feel genuine sympathy for the royal family, but Pius VI was deeply alarmed about his own personal interests. Bad news came from Avignon. There was talk in the States-General, which had been converted into the National Assembly, of suppressing the annates. Where was it all leading? What would be the position of the priests and the monks under the new régime?

In September 1789, public prayers were prescribed at Rome for the Church attacked by innumerable enemies. And yet, in the midst of these calamities, petty private intrigues continued to preoccupy the sovereign pontiff. When finally, after long tergiversations, the Grand Master of Malta, Emmanuel-Jean-Marie-des-Neiges de Rohan, proposed to appoint the Prince Camille de Rohan as ambassador, it was the Pope himself who communicated that news, not without malice, to Cardinal de Bernis. The latter immediately forwarded it to Versailles with the following comment:

"Since this is so, it would be useless for M. de Loras to try and enlist the support of all the European governments in his favour. But he will remain, for a while, in Rome, to watch developments and try to get round Prince Camille."

Disconcerted by the turn his affairs had taken, M. de Loras persuaded the Master to intervene. Not content with making vigorous representations to the Cardinal de Rohan's diplomatic agent in Rome, the Abbé Roccanti, Cagliostro wrote direct to His Serene Highness, enjoining him to support de Loras's candidature. His instructions, written in a curt and peremptory style, permitted of no evasion. Even after four years of separation, the Grand Cophte had sufficient confidence in the power he exercised over his spiritual children to dictate to them like a father:

"Be assured that the interest of your family and the happiness of Prince Camille himself are bound up with the execution of the explicit and formal order we are giving you to use all your power and influence in this cause. Compel Prince Camille therefore to do all that is necessary to secure the appointment in his place of our son de Loras."

This astonishing letter was written by Father Joseph. It was also he who drafted an application on behalf of the Count, requesting the States General to revoke the unjust decrees by which he had been driven out of France.

"With the admiration and love that he felt for the French nation, and respect for its legislators and august representatives, Alexander de Caglistro ventured," thus wrote Father Joseph, "to submit to the Assembly in Paris, which was striving to restore their liberty to the French people and its original splendour to the first kingdom in the world, that he desired to be enabled to return and pass the rest of his days in a country whose glory and welfare had always been dear to his heart."

Cagliostro and the monk told Serafina that they were even thinking of returning to Paris, not indeed to inflame the agitation which prevailed there, but to mediate and re-establish harmony between the king and the nation.

Conflicting rumours about the Master's plans were being circulated at the time in Switzerland. Some anticipated his triumphant re-entry in France; others suggested that he was going to Naples. But they were all sincerely glad that he was leaving Rome, for, Lutherans and Calvinists as they were, they were all alarmed at the dangers to which the hierophant was exposed in that den of popery. When the news of his arrival in Rome first came, Sigismund Wildermett wrote to Gertrude Sarasin:

"What do you think, Madame, of the Count's staying in Rome? I cannot reconcile myself to the idea. I fear that something evil may occur."

The disciples also went into ecstasies over the prophetic insight of the Master in foretelling all that had come to pass in France.

If the National Assembly, of which the Cardinal de Rohan was a member, would but authorise his return, Cagliostro felt certain that active interest and sympathy would be shown for him in Paris. Serafina soon realised the danger of leaving Rome once more. The plot she had been laboriously weaving for two years would be ruined, and God alone knew when she might be able to pick up its thread again. She entreated her family to increase their pressure on the Holy Office.

Two new charges were accordingly added to the Count's indictment on the 27th November, 1789; one, brought forward by Carlo Antoni, was accompanied with details of the ritual with which he had been welcomed into the Egyptian Lodge, and the other was that of Giuseppe Feliciani.

This was not enough for Serafina. She wished to make an accomplice of the monk who had been told off to watch her. To free herself from Cagliostro, she employed all the tricks she had formerly learnt from Giuseppe Balsamo. The same tactics which had had such success with the Quaker in London were to lead to identical results here.

After she had laid her trap and felt sure of catching her prey, the Countess one day invited Father Joseph into her room. In modest but unmistakable language, she indicated to him that she had for a long time been reading his thoughts, and that she was no longer able to prevent herself from sharing his ardent desire. She was ready to follow him to the ends of the earth if he would but promise to keep and protect her. The poor fellow, fifty years old, impressionable, credulous, romantic, his heart aflame, swore to everything she asked.

Immediately Serafina broke the conversation and rejoined some people who were waiting for her in an adjoining room. It was not until the 6th December that she yielded to the entreaties of her victim. Having received a small gift of eighteen scudi, she kept another assignation and delighted him with her most loving caresses.

On the 23rd November, the monk's vigilance having been relaxed, a kindly neighbour went to fetch the priest of Santa Caterina della Ruota. Afraid to go up into the apartment, Dom Giuseppe Tosi hid himself in a small inner courtyard, and the plaintiff, standing at the window, made her deposition to him. But the Grand Cophte returning unexpectedly, they had to separate in haste, and the truncated deposition was submitted, such as it was, to the Holy Office on the 15th December.

For some weeks, the mystagogue had been living in acute anxiety. Though he did not in any way suspect the monk, he felt he was being spied upon, pursued. The earth was opening under his feet. Giuseppe Ferretti persistently repeated his warnings. He urged him to fly. What the Seven Celestial Angels said was obscure but disquieting.

One day, at St. Peter's, he tried to approach Father Custi, Cardinal Albani's Confessor. It may be that he hoped to disarm the suspicions of the Holy Office by a general and solemn confession. But there were unexpected difficulties, and he returned home disappointed with his failure.

Greatly alarmed though he was, it did not, strangely enough, occur to Cagliostro to burn his incriminating papers. He still kept, at the bottom of a drawer, his *Rituel de la Maçonnerie Egyptienne*, some cabalistic instruments, badges and emblematic ribbons, aprons, gloves, and all sorts of miscellaneous paraphernalia. Was he relying on the informal safe conduct which the Secretary of State had assured him in a letter to the Prince-Bishop of Trente? What madness! Since October, the Cardinal Boncompagni's office had been occupied by the Cardinal de Zelada, and who could tell whether the new Minister considered himself bound by the vague and ambiguous declaration of his predecessor! Common sense dictated that the thaumaturge should take to his heels.

Beneath their outward indifference and inertia, the ecclesiastical authorities were actively pursuing their enquiries. In a letter to the Secretary, dated the 3rd December, Pius VI committed the enquiry to the Supreme Tribunal of the Holy Office to which the Governor of Rome was to send all articles and documents found in the cause of the investigation. On the 16th December, the assessor submitted to the Sovereign Pontiff a summary of the charges, and begged that orders should be issued to simplify the procedure and arrest that pestilential fellow who was spreading noxious influences by his preaching. But Pius VI let Christmas pass without taking any action.

On the morning of Sunday, the 27th December, 1789, after Mass, the Holy Father went in person to the Cardinal Secretary of State's office. There, presided over by him, an important meeting was held, at which were present, besides Cardinals Antonelli, the Prefect of Propaganda, Pallotta, the Prefect of Council, and Campanelli, the *pro-dataire*. The affair was being dealt with as of high political significance. At the end of the deliberations, an order was sent to Monsignor Rinuccini, the Governor of Rome, to arrest Cagliostro and the monk Father Joseph immediately; to put Lorenza Serafina in a convent, and to make a careful search of the painter Augustin Louis Belle's lodgings.

These instructions were carried out by the evening of that very day.

The public were informed of it by a newspaper, the *Chracas*, on the 2nd January, 1790:

"Last Sunday evening, the Signor Giuseppe Balsamo, a man of wide and singular renown, who has travelled through Europe under the name of the Count Alexander de Cagliostro, was arrested, under official orders, by a company of grenadiers belonging to the Rossi regiment, and taken to the Château Saint Ange. His wife, who was also arrested, has been confined, by the Pope's orders, in the monastery of Santa Appollonia. After a strict search, the house has been sealed, as well as the documents found there."

Thus, the question which had perplexed men so different as Theveneau de Moranda, Clementino Vannetti and Goethe, presented no difficulty at all to the Holy Office. Without even taking the trouble to give its reasons, it coolly proclaimed to the world that it considered Giuseppe Balsamo and the Count de Cagliostro to be identical.

. . . .

Throughout the next fortnight, the whole of Europe, neglecting the French Revolution, seemed only to be interested in the extraordinary trial which had just begun in Rome. None of the diplomats accredited to the Holy See failed to report to their Governments about it. Cardinal de Bernis himself, knowing how much interest the Court of France took in the Grand Cophte's adventures, hastened to send the following detailed dispatch to M. de Montmorin on the 30th December:

"Three days ago the Count Cagliostro and his wife were arrested and taken, the one to the Château St. Ange and the other to a convent. The charlatan, who is more celebrated than he deserves to be, was permitted to enter Rome, last spring, at the keen solicitation of the Archbishop (*sic*) of Trente. Little is being said about his activities here. But it is alleged that he has been holding secret Masonic meetings, which are proscribed by a bull of Benedict XIV, and that, at these meetings, he sought to introduce, by means of superstitious ceremonies, the ideas of the German and Dutch sect of Illuminists. A monk, whose claim to a bishopric *in partibus* was supported by influential people, has also been arrested and sent to the Franciscan convent on the Capitol."

In this letter, the Cardinal did not mention the monk's name. M. de Montmorin came to know of it a little later through the following petition :

" Monseigneur,

I approach you with confidence, on behalf of a respectable family, to appeal to you to extend your powerful protection to Father Francis Joseph of Saint Maurice, a capucin of the convent of the Marais, in Paris. This monk, whose merits are not disputed, went to Rome a year ago, in the hope of obtaining a bishopric *in partibus* which was promised him by the Holy Father more than six years ago. He had already fulfilled all the conditions required of him, particularly that concerning his patrimony, and he was about to secure the appointment, when some jealous persons, poisoning the mind of His Holiness, not only destroyed this hope, but have caused him to be arrested and imprisoned without being told on what grounds, and though he has not done anything to incur this disgrace. The petitioner requests, Monseigneur, that you should secure the freedom of her relative. She does not doubt that it will be granted if your Highness should be pleased to demand it through the French Ambassador."

As Father Joseph was not of French nationality, M. de Montmorin contented himself with scribbling on the margin : " Cannot interfere in this affair. It seems that Father Joseph has been arrested for breaking Papal laws against Freemasonry."

The Cardinal de Bernis fully agreed with him :

" It would be very imprudent of me to interfere directly or indirectly in the affairs of Cagliostro and his confidant, Father Joseph."

But though he did not intervene, he kept his minister fully informed. It is evident from his dispatches, that the curia was firmly resolved not to enter a mysterious labyrinth in the vain search for the key to a fallacious enigma.

When first Cagliostro's relations with *les Amis Sinceres* became known, the authorities were panic-stricken. The manifold activities of the Freemasons, their correspondence with the blood suckers of Paris, some threats which Father Joseph had let fall in an unguarded moment, all this aroused the suspicion that the Count might have come to Rome for the purpose of organising a revolution on the French model. These cardinals and bishops knew next to nothing of Cagliostro's disputes with other Freemasons, his life or his teachings, and only saw in him the occult chief of a vast army of secret agitators. For a long time, his judges obstinately identified his Egyptian Rite with the Illuminists of Bavaria, and treated him as if he were a conspirator as dangerous as Weishaupt himself. They imagined they had captured a firebrand and a heresiarch. While punishing the sacrilege which had dared to violate the solemn interdictions of Clement XII and Benedict XIV, they intended to show to the factious that a revolution would be much more difficult in Rome than in Paris; and that Pius VI was not going to follow the weak example of Louis XVI.

The correspondence of de Bernis gives a clear idea of the prevailing state of opinion:

"The Tribunal of the Holy Office is still making inquiries with a view to discovering if Cagliostro was not the head of this sect of Illuminists who are beginning to disquiet the authorities here. It is said that a document has been found among Cagliostro's papers, announcing that Pius VI would be the last Pope and that the Church would be deprived of her territories."

The last Pope! . . . The abolition of the temporal possessions of the Church! The cardinals were not only scandalised, they were horrified. Cagliostro said he had sent an appeal to the principal Masonic centres abroad on the eve of his imprisonment. Would not his followers—of whom there were estimated to be five thousand in Rome—get out of hand and set fire to the Château Saint Ange in order to release their Grand Cophte? An unusual excitement prevailed in the outlying regions: in December there had been a mutiny in Valletri and Siniganglia. The Cardinal Chiaramonte reported to the Pope that an uprising was to be expected in the Marches. So great was the alarm felt in Rome that it was resolved to suppress the illuminations customary at Carnival time, for fear that the conspirators might take advantage of the disorder and tumult attendant on these rejoicings to push forward their own schemes.

As certain documents implicating de Loras were found in Cagliostro's house as well as Father Joseph's, de Loras called on the Cardinal de Bernis to explain his position. The Ambassador advised him to exculpate himself before the Cardinal Secretary of State. But what excuses could he make? After all, he could not pretend that he did not know that Freemasonry had been solemnly proscribed by two popes of the highest authority.

Other Frenchmen were compromised in this affair, and the Ambassador deplored the excitement which prevailed among the young boarders of the *Académie de France*:

"The director of our *Académie de France*, who is a prudent and enlightened man, has much difficulty in preventing his young pupils, the king's scholars, of whom some are Freemasons, from neglecting the study of the arts to read everything they can get hold of, and yielding to that spirit of independence and irreligion which is finding its way into this city."

In conclusion, the Cardinal informed M. de Montmorin of the awkward predicament in which Louis Belle and some other young French artists had placed themselves:

"The young artist Belle, who is very talented and, as they assure me, of excellent character, has allowed Masonic meetings to be held in his studio. He refused to break his vows and reveal the secrets of this curious organisation to the Holy Office, and has preferred to return to his father, who is one of the directors of the Gobelin factory."

How did the papal authorities manage to intimidate this artist? Perhaps M. Belle, for all his pride, had the heart of a Brutus. Was he afraid that he might be prevented from returning to France? that all his possessions found in his lodgings might be confiscated? The commissioners prevailed over his stubbornness, and there exists proof, unhappily, that M. Belle, accused as he himself was, had consented to turn witness for the prosecution. Until the end, Cardinal de Bernis did not know of this change in his attitude. Believing that the Holy Office had spared the young man out of regard for himself, the French Ambassador flattered himself by writing:

"I have taken steps to see that the young artist who left for Paris should be prudent and silent . . . and I may congratulate myself that it was out of consideration for me that he was allowed to go away. It was known that I was interested in him."

M. de Montmorin's replies to the Cardinal were written in a disinterested style, as though he considered this affair to be quite trivial. But the very number of his letters on the subject belied this pretence, and his Excellency was evidently anxious to show that he had never shared the extraordinary blindness of his predecessor, the Count de Vergennes:

"At any other time, the escapade of this 'Cagliostro' would have caused a commotion here, for he has still his supporters, owing to my predecessor's failure to publish all the information which he had collected about the activity of this Sicilian, who has made a number of dupes in different countries, and always by the same means."

In a letter of the 9th February, 1790, he referred again, and at greater length, to Cagliostro and the inexplicable kindness shown towards this swindler by the Count de Vergennes:

"The only gift he has is of putting forward two or three ideas and letting his imaginative hearers interpret them as they chose, so that it might be said that each of those who listen to him forges his own irons, and waxes enthusiastic over chimeras which he has himself built up. Cagliostro, in turn, borrows from these different creations what he thinks would help him to make fresh converts. He has reaped an ample harvest in France. His teaching, if it might be called such, was not, at the time he arrived, nearly as wonderful as it was when he left. We know more about the details of the charlatan's life than the public, even though it read the *Courrier de l'Europe*, for we receive our own reports from Poland and Sicily, not to mention the Police of Paris. M. the Count de Vergennes did not wish to publish them while Cagliostro was in the Bastille, and as the man has now left France, I have not thought it necessary to expose him."

It followed naturally that M. de Montmorin was a greater minister than M. de Vergennes.

. . . .

It was in the same official style that the Abbé Roccatani and the Seigneur Filippo Crengo, the diplomatic agents in Rome of the Cardinal de Rohan and the Prince-Bishop of Trente respectively, wrote to their chiefs about Cagliostro. Signor Orengo furnished some curious details about the arrest. On seeing the police enter, Cagliostro, it would appear, fired a shot at his wife, who was the principal cause of his arrest, but happily the pistol was not loaded.

The Cardinal de Rohan, absorbed by the Revolution, and finding himself in very serious difficulties, did not breathe a word, although proof of his intimate relations with Cagliostro had been found in the Grand Cophte's possession.

As for Pierre Vigile Thun who, perhaps, aspired to the Cardinal's purple, he was laid low by the calamity. Since the pontifical authorities, instead of congratulating him on the apparent conversion of Cagliostro, had thrown the Count into prison and begun his trial, the Prince-Bishop could do nothing but bow humbly before the wisdom of his superiors. He admitted he had been deceived. And the people to whom he had recommended Cagliostro received apologetic letters from Trente.

Whatever might have been their alarm, their bewilderment or their grief, these high dignitaries of the Church, a Cardinal de Rohan, and a Prince-Bishop of Trente, at least had the means of keeping themselves thoroughly informed of what was going on in Rome.

But how confused and distracted must have been the innumerable disciples who had no connections with Rome. The letters which they exchanged among themselves only varied in the shades of consternation and grief they expressed. Those who knew the Grand Cophte least, who had only known him in his capacity as a healer, were profoundly affected. Mme de Charriere, melting with pity and tenderness, protested against the tone in which certain journals referred to the prisoner, and extolled him without, however, concealing her dislike for Serafina :

" I was always much impressed by Cagliostro. He is not a wicked man. He may be deceiving himself, but he does no harm to anyone, and merely occupies himself in a striking and remarkable manner. He is impressionable and often performs good actions. As for his wife, for good reasons, I have the worst opinion of her. The late M. de Luternau has told me enough about her to cause me to despise her utterly."

Followed the terrible anecdote of the letter which Serafina had torn and burnt at Strasbourg. Then, after a few lamentations, this characteristically feminine hope :

" I always say—poor Cagliostro ! I wish that, as his only punishment, he may be compelled to give up the secret of his White and Yellow Pills. How much relief I got from them the other day when I had a terrible headache ! "

How much more poignant was the grief among those who honoured Cagliostro not only as a physician of genius, but as a spiritual father !

Instead of appealing to the *Sagesse Triomphante* at Lyons, the Mother Lodge, these orphans in mourning turned for guidance to him who was still in their eyes the Master's favourite disciple, and who had always served him faithfully and with unshakable devotion. As steadfast now as when the Count and the Countess had languished in the Bastille, Jacques Sarasin exhorted them to keep calm. A secret but confident voice assured him that the Grand Cophte had deliberately chosen prison as the most favourable spot for his spiritual development. The sword hanging over that revered head did not, therefore, alarm him excessively. Whether the sentence was imprisonment for life, or even a sentence of death, the only thing that mattered to him was the allegorical significance of the trial. By his harsh captivity, by the insults he suffered, by the torture he endured, in all these ways the victim was preparing himself for a glorious resurrection, after the example of God himself, who had suffered on the Cross. The transfiguration for which inferior souls like Jacques Sarasin or the Cardinal de Rohan had to shut themselves up secretly in the kiosk at Riehen, Cagliostro attained in the Château Saint Ange, at the very heart of Christendom. . . . At the " White House," the instructions were to await developments without fear or grief.

It was therefore in vain that a French adventurer who called himself the Count d'Estillac asked for an appointment with Jacques Sarasin to report to him a conversation with Cagliostro that, he alleged, he had been enabled to have by his personal connections with Cardinal de Zelada and the keeper of the Château Saint Ange. A plan of escape had been prepared. D'Estillac offered to put it before the wealthy Swiss merchant. But M. Sarasin brusquely rejected these advances in which he only discerned an acute desire to extort money from him.

" I am much obliged to you, Sir," he wrote, " for the details which you give me about my unfortunate friend, and I could even desire that they were more ample, if that were possible. I have always believed that there, as everywhere else, he has been the victim of his own peculiar methods. I even know (unless I am utterly mistaken) that he will come out of it as he came out of the Spanish Inquisition and the Portuguese Inquisition, out of the Bastille and twice out of the prisons of London. I think it would do more harm than good for me to interfere. As for arguments, one does not put them before the Pope ; power I have none to oppose to that which acts directly or indirectly (certainly against his own interests) ; money I have not to throw away, for I am, on the contrary, obliged to economise . . . and as for journeys, mine are all over, except the last. I scarcely see therefore how my friendship, however devoted it may be, could be of use to him."

And the self-styled d'Estillac having had the impudence to press his request, M. Sarasin silenced him with a still more emphatic refusal :

" If it were necessary to take but one step, or expend but one sou, I should not bestir myself, for I have learned to my cost that I shall only be engaging in a solemn futility. . . . The interest I take in this man is not a worldly interest. I am convinced that he will always be unhappy here, because he wishes to be and ought to be so."

The members of the Egyptian Rite, who thirsted for news of the Grand Cophte, passed to each other the following report published by the *Moniteur Universel* on the 6th February, 1780 :

" There has been a very violent hurricane here ; it has shaken and even damaged some buildings. A wooden staircase in the neighbourhood of the Château Saint Ange was brought down with a loud noise. Darkness adding to the terror, the warders grew anxious and sounded the alarm. It is said that those who hurried up to the château heard M. Cagliostro shout several times, like a man who had been expecting help and thought that they were coming to release him : ' Here I am ! here I am ! ' It is not true, however, that this incident has led to a doubling of the guard at the château, or that it has increased the apprehensions of the Vatican."

A person like Clementino Vannetti could not rest content with such accounts. He tried to obtain from Rome, through his academic correspondents and the numerous admirers he had in the highest circles, authentic information about the imprisonment and trial of the personage whom he was studying with a historian's penetrating sagacity. Next to the members of the Curia and the judges who were trying Cagliostro, Vannetti wished to be the one most thoroughly informed of all that was happening at the Château Saint Ange. In fact, he *was*.

One of the things which surprised observers most was the astonishing speed with which the investigators had been able, from the very beginning, to obtain the confessions which the prisoner had steadfastly refused to make since the exposures published by the *Courrier de l'Europe*. At the Château St. Ange, Cagliostro did not take long to own that he was Giuseppe Balsamo, the artist born in Palermo.

It might have been feared that he would, out of despair, take an attitude of defiant taciturnity. The promptness and good grace with which he answered every question was therefore a very agreeable surprise to the commissioners charged with his examination. They were the lawyer Paradisi and the Abbé Domenico Cavazzi, with the

Abbé Giuseppe Lelli acting as notary. These three submitted a report of their preliminary investigations to the Holy Office.

The Tribunal, which was presided over by Cardinal de Zelanda, the Secretary of State, consisted of Cardinals Antonelli, Pallotta, and Campanelli, the Governor of Rome, and the *inditore santissimo*, Reverelli. And Monsignor Barberi, by a very unusual arrangement, served as secretary.

Pius VI did not conceal the exceptionally keen interest he took in this case. He himself directed its progress. He demanded to know the smallest details and, when necessary, did not hesitate, in virtue of his sovereign authority, to modify the judicial formalities.

To complete the deposition which had been interrupted at the *casa* Conti, the priest of Santa Caterina della Ruota went to the Convent of Santa Apollonia, in the Transtevere, where Serafina Lorenza was confined. On the 13th and the 15th, the police carried out fresh searches of Cagliostro's house, as well as the monk's. Two counsellors of the Holy Office, brother Tommaso Vicenzo Pani and brother Francesco Contarini, undertook to summarise the Grand Cophte's teaching as it was given in the *Rituel de la Maçonnerie Egyptienne*. A leading physcian, De Micheli, assisted by three others, and a surgeon and a pharmacist, were analysing the contents of the bottles and flasks found in Cagliostro's house, in the hope that the examinations of these different liquids might explain the visions of the "pupils" and the "pigeons." While these expert theological and chemical investigations were proceeding, the foreign representatives of the Holy Office began to make enquiries wherever Cagliostro had passed, and specially in Palermo and Naples. Nothing was neglected. The Cardinal de Zelada did not even overlook the diamond pawned at Vicenza; the bishop of this city was begged to redeem it for 7273 lire.

Meanwhile, Cagliostro wrote letter upon letter to the Cardinal to call off the trial. What was he being accused of? What crime had he committed to deserve such severities? "I cannot suppose," he ceaselessly repeated, "that I am being kept in irons because of a manuscript entitled *Rituel de la Maçonnerie Egyptienne*, for I am not its author. It is the work of a certain George Cofton, rendered into French by one Rey de Morande." The Cardinal de Zelada, annoyed, ordered that all paper and pens should be removed from this too prolific correspondent. Still Cagliostro devised ways of writing to him.

Finally, all the formalities were over, and the investigators had in hand all the necessary facts. The proceedings began on the 4th May, 1790, and continued, without too many interruptions, up to the 12th November. While the monk had to appear only seven times between the 10th and the 23rd June, Cagliostro had to endure forty-three exhausting sessions.

The difficulty now was not so much to make him talk as to extract from him clear and relevant answers. Beg as his interlocutors might that he should confine himself to the essentials, it seemed scarcely possible to arrest that vehement and deafening torrent of words. To recover the thread of the story, he had usually to be led back, like a child, and gently steered through the maze of incidents and adventures.

The enormous amount of material that had been collected since Serafina lodged her complaint, the Holy Office divided under three main heads of accusation :

1. Those relating to Freemasonry.
2. Heretical propositions in matters of faith.
3. Offences against the common law.

Cagliostro did not deny having belonged to the Masonic order ; but he emphasised the need he had felt to withdraw from it. His own organisation, the Egyptian Rite, had but slight connections with the High and the Strict Observances. He had really intended that his Order should become, in the hands of its members, a formidable engine of war against heresy. The Cardinal de Rohan and the Archbishop of Bourges, in France, had so far recognised it that they had encouraged him to solicit the approbation of the Holy Father, and put this weapon in the service of religion and the Church. Moreover, the Grand Cophte admitted that he had had doubts and scruples about the employment of " pupils " and " pigeons."

As if to give point to his offers to associate Freemasonry with the Church, he entered in great detail into the organisation and the resources of the Freemasons. In 1780, on his way from Warsaw to Strasbourg, he had stopped at Frankfurt. The heads of the Illuminists of this town, Friedrich Hermann and Anselm Robert, after many demonstrations of friendship, had taken him to a house in the country where their secret archives were kept in a cellar. Among other documents of importance, Cagliostro had noticed a pledge, written with human blood and conceived in dreadful terms. Twelve Grand Masters of the Templars had solemnly vowed to pull down all despotic monarchs. The Bourbons were to be attacked first ; but soon after would come the turn of Italy, and more particularly of Rome.

The Freemasons, Cagliostro also said, had at least seven thousand lodges in Europe and America. They held enormous sums in the banks of Amsterdam, of Rotterdam, of London, Genoa and Venice, thanks to the annual contributions of some 180,000 Masons. This formidable and invisible power lacked nothing. It had its emissaries at all the courts. It maintained a fleet of vessels, ready to embark the armies which, landing at Terracine, were to seize Rome. An attempt was made to bribe Cagliostro with an offer of six hundred pounds in cash. Nevertheless, he had run away from them in horror. And when the Holy Office accused him of having allowed his disciples to worship him like a God, he exclaimed :

"If I had enjoyed worship and homage so much, would I not have stayed among the Freemasons and the Protestants, instead of coming to Rome?"

Moreover, in Rome he had refrained from attending the meetings of the Lodge *les Amis Sinceres*. He had never tried to make converts to his Egyptian Rite. The only two witnesses who accused him of it, Carlo Antoni and Berardi, contradicted each other, and it had been necessary to bring them face to face to reconcile their statements.

But had he not proposed to found a Women's Lodge in Rome? He denied it. And the Princess Lambertini, when questioned, confirmed his denial.

Cagliostro was also accused by numerous witnesses of having uttered blasphemies, and maintained heretical, erroneous and scandalous propositions against Our Lord, the Virgin, the saints, the Sacraments, and the Catholic religion in general.

When he was asked at the *casa* Conti, in the presence of the Feliciani family, if he truly believed Jesus to be the Son of God, he had replied with an affected carelessness:

"If he is, I venerate him; if not, I worship God."

Then again, on another occasion:

"Look here, when a man dies by the hand of the hangman, his family disclaim him and curse him for his ignoble death. Why then do you worship Jesus, who was executed by authority of the law?"

But one should have seen the anger with which Cagliostro now denied all these monstrous allegations. "Only enemies implacably bent on my ruin," he said, "could ascribe such infamous words to me." In fact, most of these charges were made by the Feliciani, and unhappily, also, by the Countess, who was still confined at Santa-Apollonia.

Serafina's maid, Francesca Mazzoni, and the owners of the *casa* Conti, accused Cagliostro of having frequently scoffed at the Madonna. In November or December, had he not made fun of the litanies chanted in her honour? Cagliostro's answer was that he had only laughed at the little boys who repeated the words inaccurately and out of tune. Far from having neglected or despised the Holy Virgin, he had had a special devotion for her since childhood. In prison, he had asked for a book of prayer specially dedicated to the Mother of the Redeemer, and had made himself a rosary of cherry stones. Nor, again, had he ever taken the liberty to disparage the Saints in filthy language. And when he was asked why, in that case, at the *casa* Conti, when moving into his new lodgings, he had insisted on the removal of the holy images, the accused replied that it was only out of reverence. To associate sacred personages with the commonplace incidents of daily life, to make them witnesses of all that passed in the intimacy of the conjugal chamber, had always seemed to him the height of indecency. And alluding to his wife's erotic paroxysms, he explained, not without shame, why it was that he had caused the *Ecce Homo* hung above their bed to be removed. But he had always held the saints in pious veneration, especially Saint John, the favourite disciple of Christ who was also the patron of the Egyptian Rite. That was why all the Egyptian Lodges celebrated the feast of the apostle and kept his image in their "master's room," above a bust of Cagliostro.

Did he not, besides, abstain from all worship, from all acts of piety? The maid Francesca Mazzoni had never seen him make the sign of the Cross. He seemed to hate Catholicism. On the 19th November, 1789, four witnesses had heard him express satisfaction at the complete suppression of the clergy in France and predict a similar development in Rome, before the end of the year. His brother-in-law, Francesco Feliciani, affirmed that during their travels in France and Spain, in 1775, he and his sister had had to tell their beads surreptitiously, for fear of provoking the terrible wrath of their tyrant. Had he not, even recently, praised an impious work, *Le Compére Mathieu*, which had been found in Belle's lodgings? . . . Cagliostro challenged all this, and proclaimed the rectitude and soundness of his beliefs. When in Catholic countries, he used to attend divine service frequently. Not a day did he fail to say his prayers, particularly the *Ave Maria*. Was it not the custom to recite the Psalms of David in the Egyptian Lodges? But Serafina pitilessly silenced these protests by telling how, in their travels through Europe, he had, in externals, invariably conformed to the religion of the country where he happened to be staying, and how he admitted everybody into his Rite without distinction of religion. Did not such indifference denote utter atheism?

Besides lubricities of word and act, he was charged with holding to false principles *in re vanerea*, in matters of sex. Had he not been teaching his wife, from the day they were married, that adultery, committed with the full consent of the husband for reasons of expediency, and impelled by no feelings of love, was not in the least reprehensible?

Under the rubric "offences against the common law," the Counsellors had included all the crimes imputed to Giuseppe Balsamo, thefts, forgeries, frauds and magical operations for various purposes, such as conjuring shades, discovering hidden treasure, and restoring youth or provoking eroticism. The recollection of these offences did not much affect the prisoner. He only opposed a vigorous denial to the charge brought forward by the jeweller Vincenzo Morano, of Palermo, that Cagliostro had robbed him of between sixty and a hundred ounces of gold.

In spite of its courage, Cagliostro's defence was not nearly as skilful as it had been at the Bastille. At the Château Saint Ange, he had to deal with a much stronger party. His incoherent volubility did not cut any ice with the counsellors of the Holy Office. They let the torrent sweep by. Then, very politely but firmly, they would bring him to the original point and confront him with his own assertions. For example, when he claimed that his conscience was at peace ever since the Egyptian Rite had received the approval of the Archbishop of Bourges and the Cardinal de Rohan, it was objected to him that he himself had confessed to having felt some qualms about using the " pupils " and " pigeons." He became very agitated, and replied hastily :

" I can't understand your quibbles. Alas ! I hardly understand myself. . . . I deplore my unfortunate position, and as for religion, I flounder in a morass of errors. . . ."

If pressed to say something about the powers he claimed to have received from God for the evocations, he would appear excited and uncomfortable.

" I have never collaborated with the devil in my researches," he would declare. " I have never resorted to any superstitious practices. I am a Roman Catholic, and if you don't believe in the beatific vision, all right, but I, I believe in it absolutely."

He was at length, after considerable pressure, induced to expound his doctrine. He maintained that the supernatural powers were closely connected with the beatific vision which Jesus, before the consummation of his sacrifice on the Cross, had offered to men : *Ego claritatem quam dedisti mihi dedi eis.* (I have given them the light that you gave me.) And sinner though he was, Cagliostro felt that he received this gift through an inward impulse or inspiration.

But he could not touch on theological problems without immediately betraying his monstrous ignorance. For all his pretensions to the most profound theological and sacred knowledge, he was ignorant of the elements of the catechism, and his replies disclosed a mind which had always dwelt remote from the Catholic Church.

In fact, the man whom the Inquisition was holding under lock and key at the Château Saint Ange was no more than the shadow of him who had in Paris recently awaited, with well-founded confidence, the decree of Parlement. Serafina's treachery had dealt him a mortal blow. This villainy was so inconceivable to him that, while he was being examined, he would constantly refer to her for confirmation. And when, subsequently, he would be told that she repudiated him and made fresh charges, he would exclaim sadly that the agents of the Queen of France had bribed his poor dear wife. Immediately after, he would express the most touching affection for her, and beg, as a favour, to be allowed to have her companionship in prison. The request was invariably turned down. Not only was Serafina not in the least anxious to return to him, but it was feared that he might regain his ascendancy over her, and dictate what she should say to the inquisitors. Locked up in the Château Saint Ange, the Grand Cophte was thus never again to see the Grand Mistress, a recluse in the Convent of Santa Apollonia.

. . . .

For forty-three sessions, Cagliostro coped single-handed with his judges. About the middle of November 1790, when his examination was over, the Count Gaetano Bernardini, the lawyer ordinarily assigned to the prisoners of the Holy Inquisition, was instructed to defend him. Later, Cagliostro's wish that the poor people's lawyer, Monsignor Carlo Luigi Constantini, should be appointed to collaborate with Count Bernardini, was graciously granted by the Holy Father. Complete liberty was accorded to the defending counsel to visit the prisoner.

When they entered his cell on the 24th November, 1790, the Grand Cophte begged his lawyers to have his bed changed, as it was swarming with vermin. Then he asked to be allowed to have his warm clothes, for it was cold in the cell, and a pair of trousers to replace the tattered ones he was wearing. His diet was wretched. He was given, every other day, a small flask of Orvieto. For dinner, he had a dish of ill-cooked macaroni, and a shockingly spiced meat stew, brought from a neighbouring restaurant. For supper, nothing at all. Cagliostro also begged to have permission to go occasionally into the next room, as he had done before the examinations commenced, and smoke, for he suffered very much by being deprived of his pipe. He hoped that they would not refuse to send him, either, a confessor, and some good books.

Count Bernardini and Monsignor Constantini passed on these requests, one by one, and particularly the last two, as they had themselves noted how badly Cagliostro was in need of Christian instruction. They thought that, by dissipating his crass ignorance and insinuating oneself into his heart in a true spirit of love, there might be a chance of effecting a genuine conversion.

Having pored over the *Defense du Pontificat romain et de l'Eglise catholique*, written by Father Niccola Maria Pallavicini, Cagliostro confessed that the scales had dropped from his eyes. Overcome with remorse and shame, he declared he was prepared to make a solemn recantation, in the hope of saving his soul. Then, still preoccupied with Serafina, he concluded :

" I agree to submit to the most severe punishment, or rather, I fervently desire it, so as to atone for the wrongs I have done to so many persons, and above all, to my wife, the involuntary accomplice in my errors, for it was on my advice that she became a member of the Egyptian Rite."

Thereupon, religious comforts were administered to him by brother Francesco Antonio Contarini, the Confessor to the Holy Office. The Grand Cophte threw himself at his feet, cursed the blindness in which he had lived for so long, and made such demonstrations of mournful repentance that he was about to faint, and brother Francesco had to console and soothe him. Finally, on the 15th December, 1790, Cagliostro sent to the Holy Father an abjuration written in the most abject vocabulary of contrition, and signed, "Giuseppe Balsamo, repentant sinner."

This statement did not in any way modify either the attitude of the jailers or of the judges. The proceedings followed their course. Determined to discharge their task in a spirit of complete independence and with all possible care, his lawyers studied voluminous files of documents. To those who urged them to give it up, Monsignor Constantini replied proudly :

"For my part, I shall remain firm as a rock. Thoroughly or not at all, I say. I have taken an oath, and even if I had not, I should discharge the duty that has devolved upon me as it ought to be discharged." If the Grand Cophte and Father Joseph could be saved at all, they would surely have been saved by these excellent lawyers.

Scornfully passing over the offences against the common law imputed to Giuseppe Balsamo, the defence emphasised the fact that none of these acts was committed in Rome. The Sicilian was not legally under the jurisdiction of the Papal Court, and that was why the Cardinal Boncompagni had been able to write in all sincerity to the Prince-Bishop of Trente, that the Count de Cagliostro had no need at all of a safe conduct for his journey to Rome.

The question of Freemasonry was then taken up, and the defence endeavoured to set it in its proper perspective. This secret society, they said, was nothing like the hydra which the Popes Clement XII and Benedict XIV had thought it their duty to suppress with their fulminations. The mysterious veil with which it pretended to cover itself had now been torn open. There remained nothing of its sulphurous halo. And vigorously tackling the question of the Egyptian Rite, M. Constantini firmly refused to regard Cagliostro as a heresiarch. With the rest of Europe, he saw nothing in him but a charlatan. Cagliostro had only imagined that he could give Freemasonry a more exotic, more striking form, one, above all, more lucrative to him personally. Besides, as there was no proof of his having obstinately clung to error, Cagliostro could not be considered to be a real heresiarch.

Thereupon, the lawyer proceeded to shatter the evidence for the prosecution. As against the spiteful charges of the Conti family, he set the warm friendship for Cagliostro shown by the manager of the *Scalinata*, Pietro Mora, and his family. The Countess's treachery was dealt with in some scathing phrases. If her husband had been a pimp in his relations with her, why had she not, on the 11th February, 1773, while a prisoner in Saint Pelagius, informed the French magistrates about it ? Why had she made the retraction at Bienne ? Nor did Monsignor Constantini spare the Feliciani couple, ever ready to slander their son-in-law. As for Francesco Feliciani, the lawyer recalled his scandalous friendship with the Baron de Santa Venera, and the three years in jail which this "honest citizen of Cadiz" had to spend in Spain!

The speech for the prosecution, on the contrary, was a dull and tiresome performance. It had to be delivered by Giovanni Domenico Libert, as Monsignor Barberi was serving as secretary. He declared that there were no extenuating circumstances in the case. He demanded nothing less than the death penalty for the Grand Cophte. With a cruel erudition, he cited barbarous medieval laws to justify his contention that no pity should be shown to the culprit, and that even his repentance must not be taken seriously:

"The most eminent among the authorities who have dealt with matters relevant to this case," recalled Giovanni Domenico Libert, "have strongly warned us to be on guard against such conversions and penitences; and instead of taking them on trust, to multiply severe and salutary tests before conceding the smallest hope of mercy."

After the prosecution had upheld these rigorous opinions, counsel for defence, according to custom, took the floor again, and gave a reply as able and cogent as the opening speech had been.

The General Assembly of the Holy Office, meeting on the 21st March, 1791, put the matter to the vote. But as the right of passing judgment belonged to the Pope, they met once more in the Vatican on the 7th April, when the Sovereign Pontiff was also present. And the sentence was what it might have been expected. . . .

Giuseppe Balsamo, native of Palermo, and known as the Count Alexander de Cagliostro, was charged with and convicted of several crimes. He had incurred the censures and penalties laid down against heretics proper, and the teachers, masters and sectaries of superstitious magic; penalties established not only by the apostolical laws of Clement XII and Benedict XIV, but by decree of the Council of State, against those who rendered themselves culpable of Freemasonry in Rome or in no matter what place under the pontifical jurisdiction. Out of mercy, the punishment which would deliver the culprit to the secular arm, that is to say, the executioner, was commuted to perpetual imprisonment. Balsamo, after a solemn abjuration, should be kept closely in the fortress of San Leo, without any hope of grace, *absque gratia spe*. . . .

For Father Joseph, ten years of imprisonment seemed an adequate penalty. As for Lorenza Balsamo, née Feliciani, she was allowed, in reward of her treachery, to end her days in the tranquillity of the Convent of Santa Apollonia, where the pontifical government consented to give her a small subvention.

On the 16th April, 1791, Cagliostro left for San Leo in a carriage surrounded by a mounted escort under the command of Sergeant Franceso Grilloni.

And, on the 3rd May, public notices were posted up in Rome, announcing that all articles belonging to Cagliostro's sect, and particularly the manuscript entitled *Rituel de la Maçonnerie Egyptienne*, were to be burnt by the public executioner at the place de la Minerva. The holocaust took place the next morning. For three-quarters of an hour, the citizens of Rome enjoyed it as though it were a festival. As each object was thrown into the fire, Masonic charters and diplomas and badges, they clapped their hands and shouted in glee.

XII

A PRISON IN THE SKY

IN those unsettled times, Alexander de Cagliostro was such a valuable hostage to the Holy See that the Cardinal de Zelada impatiently awaited news of the progress of his journey to San Leo. He was anxious to know that the prisoner had arrived safe and sound at Pesaro, which was the last stop on the way to the fortress.

Sergeant Grilloni was certainly no greenhorn. His superiors had the highest opinion of his loyalty, courage and intelligence. But the roads in the duchy of Urbino were said to be execrable. Who could tell whether Cagliostro's fanatical followers might not lay an ambush and try to release their beloved Master by force?

On reaching Pesaro, Grilloni had orders to deliver two letters from the Secretary of State to Cardinal Doria, the legate of Urbino. One of these informed his Eminence of the mission entrusted to the sergeant; the other was a copy of the instructions addressed to Count Sempronio Semproni, the Governor of San Leo.

As Cagliostro and his escort had left Rome on the 16th April, Cardinal de Zelada calculated that they would reach Pesaro by the 20th. Wishing to provide for the spiritual needs which were supreme in the eyes of the Church, he himself wrote to Monsignor Terzi, the Bishop of Montefeltro, in whose diocese the fortress lay, requesting him to delegate a virtuous, sound and prudent priest to offer religious consolations to the prisoner, and particularly the sacramental confession for which Balsamo had applied, and which his departure from Rome had prevented him from obtaining.

Cardinal de Zelada's calculations were right. The victim of the Inquisition reached Pesaro on the 20th April. And, two days later, Cardinal Doria was able to send his report to the Secretary of State.

The better to comprehend the Holy Father's desires, he had started by studying the letter destined for the Governor of San Leo. It ran as follows:

" Giuseppe Balsamo, known as the Count de Cagliostro, shall be taken as quietly as possible into the fortress and confined there for the rest of his natural life, under a strict guard and without hope of grace. By express orders of our Lord, I am writing to you personally for two reasons; first, in order that the man may be locked up the moment he arrives under escort, without waiting for permission from the military officer ; secondly, because His Holiness intends to hold you formally responsible for the safety of the prisoner, who should not be allowed to speak to any one or have in his possession, under any pretext, any writing materials. As for the rest, that is to say, as for his food and clothes, he is to be treated like any other prisoner. If you should consider this discipline too severe for him, let me know what alternative you suggest, for His Holiness desires that the prisoner should not be treated harshly."

As Count Semproni was then on leave at Urbino, his native town, his duties had devolved on his lieutenant, Pietro Gandini. It was to this young officer that Cardinal Doria wrote, instructing him to receive the prisoner. He ordered him to lodge Cagliostro provisionally in the dungeon *Tesoro*, while the *Pozzetto* was being got ready. To carry out the necessary repairs, the Cardinal sent a master mason who had formerly done some work in the fortress. The prisoner was not to be allowed to attend Mass until further orders. He should be treated kindly and assured of proper food.

In his report to the Secretary of State, Cardinal Doria gave his reasons for preferring the *Pozzetto*. This dungeon, which was the safest and best equipped in the fortress, was situated just above the porta del Maschio, under which the guards kept watch day and night. Three of its walls were isolated ; the fourth was one with the dungeon ; and the single small window of this cell, furnished with a triple row of bars and a grating, was on a level with the terrace where the sentries were stationed. They would therefore be able to watch every movement, every word of the captive ; they could overhear his slightest whisper.

. . . .

On assuming his office as ruler of the province, Cardinal Doria had not failed to pay a visit to San Leo, as it lay in his jurisdiction. But so terrible were his memories of that journey that he hoped never to have to repeat it.

What a warning for Cagliostro was that melancholy climb ! Turning their backs on the Adriatic, his escort led him into the hinterland by a rugged path clinging to the slopes of the Apennines. The short twilight fading, they rumbled on in silence, deafened and bruised by the jolt and clatter of the wheels. Some lights were visible about one o'clock in the morning. The carriage road stopped at Verucchio, twelve miles from Rimini. From there, up to San Leo, there were nothing but winding and precarious paths, safer for goats than for men, paths which endlessly mounted in crazy spirals over a fearful wilderness of wood and rock. Torrential rains and the melting of the snows had combined to flood the *Marecchia* ; fields, vineyards and orchards were all as a lake. Cagliostro's party had to leave the carriage and take shelter in a dilapidated inn, where, on the morrow, at eight o'clock, horses were brought round to them. Surrounded by Grilloni and four old soldiers armed with muskets, the Grand Cophte began painfully to ascend the rugged track which went winding above the gorge where the *Marecchia*, receding further and further, roared with torrential violence.

A desolate landscape opened before the travellers. Everything conspired to strike fear in the beholder. All the diverse elements of nature seemed to have united in the creation of this hideous scene. To the hills, and the chasms and the precipices, to the ravines cleft by torrent and glacier, they gave, as by design, a menacing, fantastic air. Larch trees replaced the oak ; and soon, all vegetation ceased. Not a bush, not a flower, not a plant, nothing but rocks and boulders everywhere. And the nearer they came to the summit, the more fearsome the prospect became, the more dismal this vast necropolis of slate and basalt.

Several times during the ascent, Cagliostro expressed his surprise that the towers of San Leo had not yet come within sight. By way of answer, his warders pointed to the left, where clouds veiled the tortuous mountain ranges of the republic of Saint Marin. They said that the peak they were ascending was similarly hidden by fog, and that the castle would be visible after a certain turning. The mist did not lift until noon. Then, unexpectedly, the summit was bared to view.

All at once, the condemned man was overwhelmed with self-pity. Never, not even in his nightmares, his deliriums, the gloomy reveries into which he would be plunged by reading the *Apocalypse*, had he imagined desolation so heartrending.

San Leo could not have been anything less than fearsome ; but San Leo was, in fact, awe-inspiring. The Apennines, in some frenzied travail, had thrown out an abortion. To all their other horrors, the cataclysms of the primal ages had here added a peculiar deformity. Like the teeth of a shark, like the horn of a rhinoceros, it was monstrous and incredible. An enormous excrescence had been thrust out from the depths of the earth, an excrescence of which the lumps and convolutions were an insult to the mind, a torture to the eye. Such ugliness had a haunting, diabolical character. Yet, hideous as the escarpment was, perched on it there were some white buildings, a church, an entire village.

But not at the highest point. Above this amazing rock there rose another, still more extraordinary. Rock upon rock, peak upon peak, cliff upon cliff, the dungeon of San Leo loomed above the hovels. One had to heave oneself up, through a narrow gate, on to the topmost projection. And as it stood there, poised vertically over an abyss, in a solitude and at a height equally dizzying, the fortress seemed to have no connection at all with the earth. It was inaccessible. The sky surrounded it on every side.

The inmates of San Leo had, in fact, little to do with life. They went there but to await death. And, as it was put in the Latin of the Holy Office, *absque gratia spe*, without hope of grace. . . .

. . . .

Exhausted by fear and fatigue, Cagliostro had convulsions the very evening of that fatal Thursday, the 21st April, 1791. Several soldiers together found it difficult to hold him. The attack was long and alarming. The physician at the fortress, who was summoned immediately, found him suffering from violent spasms, aggravated by acute hypogastric pain. The night was spent in agony unassuaged by opiates. On the third day, a high fever supervened, and it was found necessary to bleed the patient repeatedly.

As some blood was being drawn from him, Cagliostro earnestly envied the happy fate of Seneca. He told the sentries that if he had, like them, a pistol or a bayonet, he would immediately put an end to his torture. But his mind was still shaken and agitated in a delirium, and his thoughts, as he uttered these very un-Christian sentiments, formed, according to some of those present, a sort of eddy, a "mass of electric matter." Cagliostro showed extreme anxiety for his salvation, and it was not without interest that the Bishop of Montefeltro heard that he had asked for a confessor. Moved by these signs of piety, Monsignor Terzi hastened to inform Cardinal Doria of them, as though to reproach him delicately for having deprived the poor fellow of the benefits of the Holy Mass. And the legate of Urbino sent him this answer immediately :

"I feel obliged to warn you that the prisoner is an impious man, without religion, and capable of every iniquity. Whenever you think it suitable, I shall appraise the castellan that he may permit him to say his prayers in the chapel, but only in the absence of the other prisoners."

This was the beginning of an antagonism between the temporal and spiritual authorities which was to continue, courteously, but uninterruptedly. "This poor fallen soul could perhaps be reclaimed by kindness," the Bishop of Montefeltro would sigh.

"Not at all ! Let us be on our guard against such dangerous illusions !" would reply Cardinal Doria.

Cagliostro was thereafter admitted into the Chapel at the hours when it was deserted. The same picket escorted him on each occasion so as to give him the impression that the soldiers had been detailed especially to look after him, and that the fortress had a powerful and well-disciplined garrison.

Lieutenant Gandini allowed himself no reflection on Cardinal Doria's instructions. On the contrary, he argued that the *Tesoro* was in many respects superior to the *Pozzetto*, and that the prisoner should be confined there. From the *Pozzetto*, the Grand Cophte would be able to see the village, and observe the movements of its inhabitants ; to watch and to hear ; perhaps even to engage in conversation with the sentries upon whose loyalty, after all, the authorities could not absolutely rely. But nothing of the sort was possible at the *Tesoro*. No dungeon could be more inaccessible. Here was perfect safety : even if he had the courage to shout, the occupant of this cell would never be heard. The window, which had four rows of iron bars, would resist all violence. There was no view at all to be had from this formidable height. On rare, clear days, one might discern the cloud-capped tops of Mont Carpegna. At other times, only a vast blue misty wilderness stretched before the eyes. The *Tesoro* was thus that unique, incomparable thing : a prison in the sky.

Gandini had, therefore, taken it upon himself to send the master mason back to Pesaro, without allowing him to start the repair work. But, in his letter to the Cardinal, he professed the utmost respect for him, and swore that the instructions of the legate would always be dearer to him than his life. At the bottom of the *Tesoro*, the prisoner might take as many shapes as Proteus, and rival the witchcraft of Circe, but no sorcery would be of avail. Except the five soldiers, who had orders to visit him, collectively, every morning and evening and, in an emergency, the doctor or the priest, no living soul would thereafter set eyes on this ci-devant Count de Cagliostro.

Cardinal Doria wrote to Rome that the *Tesoro*, which was a fearful dungeon, exceptionally foul and barbarous, of the time of the Malatestas, did not seem to him to conform to the directions of His Holiness.

He was told, in reply, that the interests of justice should not be incompatible with mercy. If, therefore, this prison in the sky was so dreadful, it would be necessary to proceed with the repairs to the *Pozzetto*.

About this time, Count Semproni, returning to San Leo, resumed his office as Governor. He quickly realized that he had to deal with a man of a very trying temper. Cagliostro refused butcher's meat, and insisted on having chicken and pigeon. Every morning he must have a cup of chocolate ; at mid-day, three hot dishes, besides soup and fruit ; and in the evening, a soup with dish and fruit. Three loaves of bread and four litres of red wine a day. The cost of his table and bed linen, the barber, the washing, tobacco, etc., amounted to a very high figure. Of the eight scudi a month allowed him by the papal government, scarcely ten were left at the end of the year for the clothes, of which he was badly in need. He had only four shirts, a few pairs of socks, and drawers, and a thin overcoat which, in the winter, always severe in San Leo, gave no protection against the cold.

This information did not please Rome. Pius VI wrote to Count Semproni saying that he wished the prisoner to be treated kindly, not sumptuously ; it was his need that should be considered, not his greed or his caprice. As for clothes, no useless purchases were to be made. Let the castellan make some arrangement with Monsignor Ruffo, the treasurer general, who had in his charge the clothes and linen of the prisoner.

Count Semproni also reported that the prisoner, who was a past master of every trick, intending to arouse the pity and relax the discipline of the guards, was complaining of paralysis in the legs. It was quite untrue. Through a chink in the wall, the soldiers could see him walking about without much difficulty in his cell.

Count Semproni also communicated these discreditable reports to the Bishop of Montefeltro. But this prelate, who judged things with his heart rather than his head, and was always ready to forgive, deluded himself into thinking that it was enough to dispense spiritual aids to Cagliostro to bring him to a sincere repentance. On the 18th May, 1791, Canon Tardioli, father confessor of the chapel of Penna, arrived at the dungeon to hear the confessions of the prisoner. Semproni hastened to inform the Cardinal Doria of it:

"It began to-day in the chapel. Three soldiers stood guard at the door, because the reverend canon, revolted by the stench in the cell, had begged my permission to confess him in chapel, and above all because, as it is a question of a long general confession, it had to be adjourned and resumed several times. The prisoner Balsamo continues to simulate paralysis. He causes himself to be carried by two soldiers to the chapel. Not wishing to offend him now, I say nothing. But after the confession is over, and he has received communion, I shall not fail to bring him to his senses, and make him use his legs, without the help of others."

A triumphant letter of the Bishop of Montefeltro soon announced to the Cardinal de Zelada that the heresiarch of San Leo, after a confession lasting six days, had given many decisive proofs of repentance, as far as the human mind could judge. He had celebrated Easter in the chapel, all alone, in accordance with the Cardinal Doria's orders. Cardinal de Zelada must have been in a bad humour indeed, not to rejoice at such an edifying account. He wrote to Monsignor Terzi, on the 11th June, 1791:

"Of extreme comfort was your very welcome letter of the 28th instant, informing me that you have obtained from Giuseppe Balsamo signs of repentance and contrition. If, as you tell me, by external indications they are sincere, may they, by God's grace, prove equally lasting."

But His Eminence used quite a different style when it became known in Rome, through secret sources, that some persons in Rimini, belonging to the nobility, were claiming to have seen Cagliostro at San Leo, and even to have spoken with him for nearly half an hour. The Pope ordered an immediate enquiry, and in his anger prescribed the most severe penalties against the offenders.

The reprimands aimed at him from both Pesaro and Rome, finally drove the poor Semproni to distraction. Having no private means, he clung tenaciously to his post. The fear of destitution altered his character and made him ill-natured and savage. He began to hate the prisoner who was causing him such anxieties. In July and August, 1791, at the news that two or three Frenchmen were ambushed in the neighbourhood with the object of rescuing Balsamo in a balloon, he completely lost his head, and wrote pitiful letters to his superiors, complaining :

" I do not know how to defend a fortress against winged horses and a flying army ! . . ."

The aerial attack not occurring, Cagliostro, on the morning of Sunday, the 11th September, after Mass, was moved from the *Tesoro* to the *Pozzetto*. The furniture in his new quarters comprised a bed, a chair, a big plank attached to the wall, and a table.

It was discovered at the time of this transfer that the Grand Cophte had secretly improvised a pen from a blade of straw, and had written down his predictions with it in a small pocket diary given him by the adjutant Grilloni. These different articles were seized and despatched to Cardinal Doria.

Count Semproni soon began to have anxieties of a different sort. He states that his prisoner, whose ruinous appetite he had lately been cursing, was now starving himself. It was first on two days a week that the ascetic fasted on bread and water. Semproni attributed this not so much to the piety, true or false, of which Cagliostro made a great display, as to his concern about his health. Always tending to obesity, the Grand Cophte was now suffering from high blood pressure and indigestion, and was apparently afraid of an attack of apoplexy. Early in October, he took to a more severe diet and had nothing but bread and wine. Though he was offered the sweets of which he was fond, roasted capons and Naples macaroni, cooked in fresh butter and sprinkled with parmesan, he would not be tempted : he gave them away to his warders. Anxiously, the castellan consulted Cardinal Doria :

" I do not know what to think of this obstinate fasting. He wants to keep it up until All Saints' Day. Is it a masonic fast ? He used to be big and very fleshy, but has, naturally, grown thin."

Notwithstanding the weakness due to this régime, and his practice of devotions, Cagliostro's temper remained refractory. He objected to the routine inspection the guards had to make twice a day, very early in the morning, and about eleven in the night. These intrusions exasperated him. The corporal of the guard, having once, on the Governor's orders, instructed a jailer to lock him up, Cagliostro became furious at seeing him enter. Brandishing an intimate and familiar piece of pottery, he threatened to throw it at the jailer, who retreated in face of this comic attack. But he was soon deprived of the dangerous utensil.

Meanwhile, he was continuing to fast resolutely. Semproni, in his perplexity, wondered if it was a plan of suicide ; he informed the Bishop of Montefeltro about his suspicions. On the 18th October, 1791, Cagliostro agreed to confess to the Dominican Father Bussi, an itinerant preacher then in the neighbourhood.

In the end, the monk induced him to change his diet. When Cagliostro was asked why he imposed such strict abstinence on himself, he said it was because he could not bear the Corporal-Adjutant Marini. The castellan only shrugged his shoulders. "So much the worse for Balsamo," he said : "as for myself, I am determined not to change either the personnel or the discipline of the fortress."

One day towards the end of October, there occurred a dramatic incident. Cagliostro had finished his confession, and Father Bussi was about to give him absolution, when, unexpectedly, the penitent cried out :

"Hold on, Father ! Stop ! I don't want it, it is useless. . . . I believe neither in the Holy Father, nor in the Bishop, nor in you ; I proclaim myself a schismatic, and I call upon the Sacred College of Cardinals. . . ."

He began to insult the Sovereign Pontiff in the most dreadful way.

Running up at once to the *Pozzetto*, the castellan heard his blasphemies.

And, with an air of triumph, Cagliostro handed him a piece of paper on which he had managed, God knows how, to put his obscenities in writing, a piece of paper which the dominican, trembling with anger, was himself to convey to Monsignor Terzi. "I cannot understand how he got this bit of paper and how he was able to make use of it in this way," wrote Semproni bitterly to Cardinal Doria on the 1st November.

This terrible scandal had deplorable consequences for Cagliostro. Annoyed, the Cardinal de Zelada took the castellan to task. How could the prisoner have lifted up a wooden plank from his bed and wrenched off an enormous iron bolt ? He could not understand it at all. On the 9th November, 1791, Cardinal de Zelada wrote this significant note to the Bishop of Montefeltro :

"The prisoner Balsamo's audacity is truly distressing, and what you tell me in your communication of the 31st October, corroborated by Father Preacher Bussi's letter, fully shows the depravity of his character. Nevertheless, continue to give him spiritual help so as to promote, if it be still possible, a sincere repentance. It may not be useless, either, to give him to understand that, if he should persist in these abominable errors of speech and conduct, he will be risking the most severe corporal punishment."

Three days later the Secretary of State sent Cardinal Doria still more explicit instructions :

"Explain this well to the castellan of San Leo : he is not to fail, whenever the prisoner allows himself to indulge in such rashness of speech and conduct, to apply the penalties including corporal punishment, which those who do not behave properly, deserve."

But by his own confession, Semproni was unable to cope with the terrible cunning of his prisoner. On the 13th November, Cagliostro was again moved to the *Tesoro*, while the woodwork of his bed in the *Pozzetto* was being repaired. But first, the clothes he was wearing were taken away from him, and he was given a suit every inch of which had been carefully examined by the jailers :

"And lo ! about eleven at night, when the routine inspection was conducted, it was found that the walls of his cell were covered with drawings executed in some reddish colour. Such is his malice and ingenuity."

Cagliostro now ceased pretending that his legs were paralysed. To keep himself occupied in the cell, he incessantly painted inscriptions and diagrams on the walls.

But Cardinal Doria, wearied by the continual nagging of the Vatican officials, instructed the Count Semproni to take the opportunity of the repairs which were being made in the *Pozzetto*, to instal heavy iron chains and rings, the sight of which might perhaps lead the culprit to salutary reflections. And if this did not prove effective, they would have to apply the supreme remedy, the bastinado ; but carefully.

In a letter of the 17th December, he repeated the caution : "*ma con discretezza.*"

It was thus, on the 13th December, when the Grand Cophte was rejoicing at leaving the *Tesoro*, where he had suffered cruelly from the damp and the cold, that he was filled with horror and dismay to find in the *Pozzetto*, conspicuously displayed, a sinister mass of ironwork, the purpose of which was eagerly explained to him. The castellan, indeed, did not desire to resort to them, save in the last extremity. Notwithstanding this assurance, Cagliostro could not repress a tremor at the sight of the hideous apparatus. And it was in the profoundest dejection that he passed the last days of that calamitous year, 1791.

. . . .

What did he know of the external world during this period ? Did he surmise that the last few months had been disastrous to his dearest disciples ? In the midst of his mental torments, never had he been heard to complain of their desertion ; never had he accused them of ingratitude. One would have said that a mysterious influence kept him informed of their difficulties.

Between the Cardinal de Rohan, who was a victim of royal despotism, and the French Revolution, there was at first complete accord. In the States General, all those who hated the Court, looked upon him with a kindly eye. But it was not long before their fundamental incompatibility showed itself. When this grand seigneur and prince of the Church, Louis de Rohan-Guemenée, realised that the policy of his new friends was nothing less than the abolition of age-old feudal and ecclesiastical privileges, he deserted the seditious mobs and retired to his estate beyond the Rhine, where he believed he would be perfectly safe from French demagogy. But no revenue was now forthcoming from his benefices, and his beloved Cagliostro was no longer by his side to convert mercury into gold and cover him with pearls and diamonds. Faced with destitution, he thought that perhaps their common friend, Jacques Sarasin, his brother in the Egyptian Rite, would not refuse to make him some advances.

The Cardinal would doubtless have abstained from opening negotiations if he had known of the catastrophe which had broken upon the " White House." Gertrude Sarasin, whose health declined steadily when she was no longer able to consult her wonderful æsculapius, had died on the 26th January, 1791, after a slow agony. Jacques Sarasin was but the shadow of his former self. If he still endured the burden of life, it was but out of love for the numerous children with which his well-beloved Gertrude had presented him. In his thoughts he inhabitated an ideal world, where the hope of an eternal reunion kept perpetually alive the memory of her whom he had lost. Having withdrawn himself from the vanity of human enterprise, from the triviality of human discussions, he was as little interested in the Cardinal de Rohan's financial difficulties as in the self-styled Count d'Estillac's plans of escape for Cagliostro. All the same, he considered that brother Louis-Rene-Edouard de Rohan's appeal deserved, if not money, a salutary reproof. And it may be that, in the depths of his distress, the fervent Calvinist found some exquisite pleasure in coolly rebuking a Cardinal of the Holy Church. It was thus that he addressed to him, on the 5th February, this severe exhortation :

" Vanity of vanities, Monseigneur, all is vanity. Rank, title, birth, the goods of this world, health, prosperity, pleasure, ambition, human glory, all is nothing but emptiness and misery.

The fear of God, the blood of Christ, and the help of the Holy Spirit, these are the only permanent goods in this world, and no other.

You, Monseigneur, have lost by the inscrutable decrees of providence, everything that one can ever fear to lose in this world, and the finger of God is visibly on you, as on the whole of France. Perhaps He wishes to prepare you for other dignities, other delights and a nobler fatherland.

I, for my part, I have physically lost everything I held most dear in this world, my better half, she in whom and by whom I lived, without whom I would have had during twenty-one years, neither pleasure, nor pain, nor comfort, the mother of my eight children, my wife.

The Eternal Being has recalled her soul to him, and now, at this moment, she is praying for me and for you, Monseigneur, and for all our other brethren and sisters, that our eyes may be opened, and that we may be more worthy than we have been, to see the light. For, let us not disguise it, we are sinners all, from the greatest to the most humble, and we have all unworthily mingled the sacred with the profane. It is not to stir up your compassion that I inform you, Monseigneur, of this sad event. It is sad only for me. As for her, blessed are they whom the Lord hath taken. They rest from their labours, and their work followeth after them.

As regards the loan of which your Highness has written to me, I know of no one here with funds to invest. I wish, indeed, that someone would offer to buy my house, which has become too big for me, since I can no longer share it with her who was its principal ornament.

A thousand pardons, Monseigneur, if this letter is too frank, too fraternal : I cannot write in any other style.

I end by commending myself to the prayers of your Eminence, and by assuring you of my very humble respects.

Sarasin the Younger."

The Cardinal was apoplectic with rage. Never, even during these revolutionary times, had he received a letter so familiar and so didactic in tone. He felt himself obliged, all the same, to send a short note to Basle to express what the master of the " White House " called his compassion, that is to say, condolences.

. . . .

If the Grand Cophte observed a patient and sorrowful silence with regard to his disciples, he was, nevertheless, in the curse of this terrible year, 1792, to astonish his jailers constantly by the speed and precision with which he seemed to be aware of the smallest details of the French Revolution.

However, he who knew so well what was happening at a distance, was nearly always ignorant of events within the fortress. About the middle of February 1792, he became possessed with the idea that the principal officials of the Egyptian Rite, about five or six in number, were also incarcerated at San Leo. Likewise, he believed that Serafina was there, and his jailers had to listen to his strange and pathetic entreaties. He adjured them to treat the Countess kindly. Then, afraid that they might be cruel, he begged them to inflict no matter what punishment on him rather than hurt that innocent creature, his beloved wife.

His fasts and mortifications alternated with sudden fits of anger or arrogance. Some days, he would not be content to reject his food : he would foul it abominably so that no one else might have it. For himself, he would retain nothing but a jug of water and the wine. And if the jailers happened to give him by chance a napkin slightly coarser than usual, he would fly into a terrible fury. The Cardinal de Zelada urged the authorities of San Leo once again, at the Pope's special request, to employ " such of the corporal punishments as have been already suggested, and which seem to be the most effective means of recalling him to his duty."

The searches and inspections becoming more and more exacting, Cagliostro cried out one day that they would kill him with their pesterings. Then, glancing round his filthy cell, he murmured :

" I do not believe that God would punish sinners so ruthlessly in Hell. . . ."

As Holy Week drew near, he seemed ashamed of the trouble he had given. He humbly asked again to see the Father Confessor of Penna, Canon Tardioli, who appeared to have a soothing influence on him. The request was gladly accorded and, after being shut in for a couple of hours with the Canon, his devilish temper abated.

Count Semproni and Lieutenant Gandini then had a spell of relative calm. Though they were not sure of its continuance, they reported a sensible improvement in Cagliostro's conduct. Since his last interview with Canon Tardioli, he was quiet, gentle, resigned and submissive. When he was observed unawares, through the secret chink, he was never caught doing anything reprehensible. On the contrary, he would be seen praying. Often, in the midst of his meagre meal, he would raise his hands and eyes to heaven, like one offering thanks or invoking God's mercy. He spent the time decorating the walls of his dungeon, thinking, it may be, of the frescoes which Joseph Balsamo had executed once upon a time for Sir Edward Hales at Canterbury. For paint, he scraped the daubs made by one of his predecessors in the *Pozzetto*. Moreover, he dealt only with subjects taken from the Gospel, *cose pie, sacre e religiose*. Once, he drew a picture of himself holding a crucifix in the left hand, and ardently beating his chest with his right. Or he would draw St. Mary-Madelein, in the hope that she, who had been a sinner, would intercede in his favour. . . .

So utterly ashamed was he of his past life that he would not even permit the soldiers to call him " monsieur the Count." The only name by which he wished to be known was " Giuseppe the sinner." He deserved no other, he said, knowing himself to have been, in God's sight, the basest and most impious of men. Knowing that the jailer-drummer was the father of a large family, he would give away to him a portion of his meals, and commend himself to the prayers of his family.

The summer passed without any incident. And in the autumn, Canon Tardioli found him still holding so firmly to his piety, that he did not hesitate to give him communion. When the castellan Semproni asked him in astonishment if he believed Cagliostro to be truly worthy of it, the Canon replied in a mysterious voice :

"*Deus tantum est scrutator cordium.* God alone can enter the recesses of the heart. . . ."

But just as it happened about the same date a year ago, no sooner had Cagliostro received the sacrament than he relapsed into his eccentricities. On the 19th October, 1792, as the corporal-drummer, accompanied by the watch, paid him the usual eleven o'clock visit at night, Cagliostro accused them of having spent too much money on some purchases for him. Then, getting heated, he called them thieves. The altercation woke up the whole fortress, as Count Semproni relates :

"Fearing that he was going to be beaten, or perhaps merely to stage one of his customary farces, he lifted himself up by the bars of the window, and, with the whole power of his lungs, began to scream for help ; the noise he made was so great that all the soldiers who were off duty came running up, and were able to assure themselves with their own eyes that no one had so much as touched him. I was myself about to go down to the dungeon to apply the remedies which he needs all too badly, and which he tries to provoke by every imaginable means."

In consequence of this episode, orders were given that if he repeated the offence, Cagliostro should be administered a correction which, without doing him permanent injury, would yet abate his insolence somewhat. Cagliostro had threatened to wake up the whole village with his cries, and excite their sympathy. The Governor was therefore inclined to remove him again to the *Tesoro*, to that prison in the open sky where his screams would attract no attention. All the more, indeed, because, at the *Pozzetto*, the prisoner was able to overhear the sentries stationed in the *Place d'Armes*, which was perhaps the means by which he got his marvellously exact information about the French Revolution.

As they now had to deal with an incorrigible madman, the officers ceased to feel any scruples. Once, on the 28th October, Cagliostro, daring to raise his voice, the corporal-adjutant gave him such a blow that the victim was stunned for a long while. And his features expressed such an unspeakable amazement at the adjutant's audacity, that that officer, the execrable Angelo Marini, the evil spirit of the Governor, told him, in a menacing voice, that he would be beaten flat as a pancake if he showed any impertinence.

This threat was not without effect. Cagliostro withdrew into himself, went about with a humble air, and renewed all the mortifications he used to practise, depriving himself besides of tobacco and wine.

After Louis XVI's execution, he sent an offer, couched in enigmatic terms, to reveal to the supreme Pontiff some facts of extreme importance, adding that they would make for the greater glory of God and his Holy Church, and the benefit of the whole world, in the present and the future, as well as the cessation of the calamitous ills of that century.

Count Semproni was not interested in these dubious revelations. But the prisoner continued to importune him. Finally, on the 22nd March, he was able to open out his soul at leisure to the priest who had come to San Leo for Lent. The Grand Cophte declared that God had disclosed to him in a series of visions what his mission on earth was henceforth to be. It was to go about preaching in opposition to the principles which he had been wicked enough to propagate and, if necessary, face martyrdom so as to enlighten by his own example the bigoted enemies of the faith. The priest advised him to be careful, for such visions might be, after all, only figments of the imagination, phantoms.

Cagliostro emphatically asserted that to him they were as real and true as the Gospel, or the existence of God. The priest very severely warned him thereupon that he was blaspheming. Cagliostro wished to continue the discussion. But his interlocutor, wearied and scandalised by the indecent verbiage, turned his back on him and went away, to the Grand Cophte's great chagrin.

The indifference with which his imaginary predictions were received deprived " Giuseppe the sinner " of the little prestige that he still enjoyed among the gaolers. When, on the 30th July, 1793, annoyed by the usual morning inspection, Cagliostro rudely asked the officer what he wanted, the answer was simply :

" Carrying out orders, that is all ! "

Cagliostro was so exasperated that he began to abuse the soldier violently, and the adjutant-corporal had an impulse to box him on the ear. Suddenly, however, unable to control his rage, Cagliostro threw himself on the man whom he hated as one can only hate in prison ; he lifted him up, and was about to dash him to the ground, when the whole squad fell upon him. Then, as by some invisible signal, the methods sanctioned so long since by the Cardinals de Zelada and Doria, were instinctively put into action. The soldiers freely used their swords and canes, and the Master, soundly beaten, ran back into his cell, bewildered, aghast, and letting out fearful yells that must have reached the far end of the village. Like everyone else, Count Semproni must have heard them. Considering that the treatment was well merited, he did not fail to inform the Cardinal legate about it, adding that, on the next occasion, they would certainly use the infallible remedy if, indeed, they did not decide to put the culprit in chains. Such was the first official bastinado administered to Cagliostro, more than two years after his arrival at San Leo.

But nothing could subdue his intractable spirit. Notwithstanding the humiliations and the ill-treatment to which he was subjected, he derived an inexhaustible strength from his visions. He whom they called the Grand Architect of the Universe, or the Great God —*il grande Iddio*—consoled him for the stupidity and barbarity of men. At the beginning of the year 1794, he insisted so solemnly that he wished to divulge some secret concerning the life of the Holy Father that Count Semproni, though he cursed the whole business, could not but go down to the *Pozzetto*.

He could not in the least understand the prophet's vaticinations. He therefore asked Cagliostro to write down whatever it was that he wished to communicate to the Holy Father. Very willingly, Cagliostro commenced to write under the eyes of the perplexed jailers a lucubration of which the preamble recalled the language of the diplomas granted to members of his Rite :

> " We, Alexander I, Grand Master and Founder of the Egyptian Order, by the grace of God, direct those whom it may concern and those who have faith in the divine word . . ."

But suddenly, at this point, the thread of this thought was broken and the oracle stopped short. What he wrote further were but disconnected words, fervent but foolish prayers, and silly puns in Latin and Italian on the castellan's name :

Sempronius semper fuit
Sempronius
Vita di
Sempr.

Was he making fun of the Governor ? No, the Grand Cophte seemed really to have become incapable of following a train of thought. Invocations to Mary, the Queen of Heaven, and allusions to the hour of death, were jumbled quaintly with the names of the Seven Celestial Angels and the incantation : *Helion, Melion, Tretagrammaton.* This pitiful confusion only announced the torments of a mind upon which the darkness of imbecility was gathering close. . . . Semproni triumphantly forwarded the incoherent statement to Cardinal Doria on the 4th January, 1794, adding :

" Your Eminence can easily judge by this with what funds of ignorance Balsamo is endowed. . . ."

Snubbed and ridiculed as he was, the prophet kept quiet. But, a year later, he begged the castellan to come to see him for a conversation of the utmost importance. And Semproni having gone to the *Pozzetto*, the magician told him, after many absurd words, that he alone knew of a terrible plot being laid in the Vatican against the life of Pius VI. The castellan replied that, in default of a supernatural illumination, a prisoner excluded for four years from all intercourse with mankind had no means of knowing such a secret. But Cagliostro vigorously maintained that he was kept fully informed about everything. Certain enemies of the Holy Father, he said, had about two months ago, introduced into the pontifical palace a handsome young girl dressed in male clothes. With the liberty she enjoyed of going into the most private apartments, she was resolved to kill the supreme Pontiff by dagger or with poison. Some Cardinals were also involved in this plot. However ridiculous this story seemed to him, Semproni felt it his duty to communicate it, on the 21st April, 1795, to the Cardinal de Zelada, who replied disdainfully that such nonsense did not deserve attention.

In fact, the Grand Cophte was suspected more and more of having lost his reason. Canon Tardioli, who had formerly had so much influence on him, had been extremely dissatisfied on his last visit. He had refused to confess him, saying that he was mad, utterly mad.

That, apparently, was also the opinion of the physician in the fortress. Called to the *Pozzetto*, he refused to give the prisoner the medicines for which he clamoured, and merely shrugged his shoulders. Did he think it was a typical case of madness? Or was he giving up the fight against that secret disease, inveterate and complex, of which Carlo Sacchi boasted that he had once cured his master Cagliostro in Spain? Was it rather the plague which, in its last stage, was provoking these sudden alternations of mystical delirium and fury, this fantastic ferment of the imagination? The doctor would not express a definite opinion.

And there is no document in the archives of San Leo between the lines of which one might read the doctor's real conviction.

For another two years, 1794 and 1795, Cagliostro's wretched existence continued. He hardly ever stopped drawing and painting on the walls. But he no longer gave any sign of repentance. As even the priests had ceased to believe in his contrition, he openly revolted against the Church, constituted himself its critic and reformer, praised his visions highly, and interspersed his talk with monstrous sophisms about the mystery of the Holy Trinity. He evidently took a satanic delight in the role of heresiarch.

He did not even spare the holy person of the Supreme Father. Sometimes, running to his window, he would fling himself against the grating and give piercing shrieks, which would alarm the whole village. Neither the threat that he would be chained up, nor the actual penalty could prevent these paroxysms. He was so turbulent, so impetuous by nature, that even the bastinado did not make him see reason.

A man who was used to the pleasures and amenities of high life, to the company of the great, to the passionate adoration of his followers, could he for long bear this fate, this rigorous discipline? Yet, to the general astonishment, Cagliostro survived.

He had always been afraid of a sudden attack of apoplexy. On the 23rd August, 1795, he was attacked by paralysis of the left side. At first, there was some feeble hope of reconciling him to God, and everything was done to that end; but too late; it was no longer possible to save him. On the 26th August, as his jailers went their habitual round, they found him unconscious on the floor: a second attack had laid him low. While the doctor was endeavouring to reanimate the miserable corpse which was already no more than a husk, the chief priest offered the services of his ministry. But it was in vain that he looked for some sign of repentance. The Grand Cophte remained mute. Thus, impenitent, he expired about four o'clock in the afternoon.

The chief priest drew up the certificate of death. In exquisite Latin, he declared that the prisoner, born under the sign of misfortune, had lived an unfortunate life and died the most unfortunate of deaths. *Nascitur infelix, vixit infelicior, obiit infelicissime.* . . .

And as the hardened heretic had shown himself incapable of making a sincere repentance, the Bishop of Montefeltro himself, so indulgent towards the sinner, did not venture to grant to Giuseppe Balsamo, known as the Count de Cagliostro, the honours of Christian burial. No religious pomp attended that ceremony. No consecrated earth received the Grand Cophte's remains. Some soldiers dug a grave for him, at the highest point of the escarpment, at the point where the enormous rock of San Leo leans precipitously to the west. It was there that they buried him, far from men, under the open sky.

. . . .

Two or three months before, the scholar who had undertaken to write the Count's biography had gone to his last sleep. Chevalier Clementino Vannetti had died of pleurisy in his native town on the 13th March, 1795. Rovereto was in mourning. The *Accademia degli Agiati*, deprived of its permanent secretary, had suspended its meetings. Italian literature lost a devoted servant, a charming poet, a scholar of singular merit. Ippolito Pindemonte and the Abbé Pederzani exchanged long disconsolate letters.

And all the immense material which Vannetti had accumulated in six years of research for the vast work of which his *Liber memorialis* was but the brief prelude, was to remain useless, like the ruins of some superb palace left bare and incomplete for want of perseverance and resource.

But, as a matter of fact, even before his death, the Chevalier had renounced the project. In the spring of 1791, some weeks after Cagliostro's conviction, the Holy See had published a *Life of Giuseppe Balsamo*, based on authentic documents. This anonymous work is commonly ascribed to Monsignor Barberi, who had acted as secretary to the trial court. Although its title was scarcely sensational, this work went into a number of editions, and was immediately translated into several languages. Everybody wished to read it. Goethe considered it one of the most interesting books he had read. But as the Church had taken this opportunity to deliver an open attack against Freemasonry, replies were not wanting. In the midst of the tumult of the Revolution, controversy about Cagliostro grew to alarming proportions. The quarrel became so heated that Vannetti, who was of a mild and conciliatory temper, not wishing to be entangled in it, took up again with regret and disappointment his *Life of Cicero.*

After his death, his mother, Donna Bianca-Laura, bent with age, worn out by grief, but still passionately devoted to literature, wished that posterity should have a record of her beloved son's life. She wished that his best friends should write his biography. Every day, she had the Abbé Antonio Cesari come to her, and in her sonorous, virile, energetic voice, described at length to him the marvellous infancy and youth of her dear Clementino. And the Abbé, fired with interest in the work, declared that, if he ventured to write the life, while others would have been more worthy of doing so, it was only in obedience to the fond but pressing insistence of that incomparable lady, Clementino's mother.

The news of Cagliostro's death spread slowly through Europe. Numerous voices were then raised to accuse the Pope of having caused the death of his prisoner, after mercilessly ill-treating him. Others imagined that the Count de Cagliostro, having with heroic courage survived the terrible test imposed on him by his occult superiors, had been carried off in a chariot of fire. Such was the destiny of the disciples of Elijah. Cagliostro's stupid jailers had only buried a dummy.

One does not know with what feelings Jacques Sarasin heard of the death, actual or symbolical, of his master. He never said anything about it. More and more, he withdrew into himself, inconsolable at the loss of Gertrude, and yet filled with an intoxicating hope. Though he continued to live, as his duty to God, he was preparing himself earnestly for his impending transfiguration. When he went to Riehen, the sight of the Chinese kiosk troubled him not in the least. What did he care for physical regeneration now that his adorable wife was no longer alive? As for spiritual regeneration, Jacques Sarasin was not unaware how much a virtuous soul might learn from grief; he knew the sacred potency of sighs, of sobs, of tears. Meanwhile, his numerous progeny were growing up around him. His daughters married and left the "White House" one after the other. Felix, the old "pupil," intelligent, diligent, punctual, took up his father's business. And Lavater, when he made enquiries about the young man, could not prevent himself from asking:

"Does Felix long for the beautiful visions he used to have? Does he still have them?"

Jacques Sarasin did not reply to these indiscreet questions. Faithful to the cult of memory, he abjured nothing of what he had once loved and admired. He considered it sacreligious that Goethe should have put on the stage at Weimar a comedy entitled "The Grand Cophte." Alas! since the death of his wife, Jacques Sarasin could not ask anyone to share his grief and annoyance with him. Alone he wandered by the streams of Babylon, weeping at the memory of Sion. But he had glimpsed, by an unhoped-for grace, the celestial

Jerusalem ; and rather than repudiate the divine vision, he would that his tongue clove to his palate. With infinite gratitude, he blessed the Grand Architect of the Universe, he extolled his power, and was happy and proud to have been able to contemplate here below at least one of the lives of the Count de Cagliostro.